PRAISE FOR

# THEY JUST SEEM A LITTLE WEIRD

*Variety*'s "Best Music Books of 2020"

*The Globe and Mail*'s "Fifteen Music Books
That Struck a Chord in 2020"

*Best Classic Bands*' "Best Music Books of the Year"

"What's better than a terrific rock biography? Four terrific rock biographies packed into one, with nothing lost in the headbanging whiplash of going back and forth between a quartet of individually and collectively fascinating bands. For anyone who lived through the ascent of flamboyant guitar music in the 1970s...there could scarcely be a more entertaining read than *They Just Seem a Little Weird*. There's a deep level of reporting by Brod that results in one amusing or trenchant detail after another, as he brings the funny and, more importantly, brings the fondness." —*Variety*

"8 out of 10. Wildly entertaining. With a wonderful mix of anecdote and analysis...Brod depicts these groups in all the color they deserve." —*Classic Rock*

"Four stars! Brod's love of the music will send readers digging deep into the back catalogues, but he also acknowledges the absurdity and fuck-ups with knowing humor." —*MOJO*

"A fascinating journey....A never-ending treasure trove of jaw-dropping revelations and anecdotes. Brod possesses a droll sense of humor, and there are many laugh-out-loud moments peppered throughout this wonderfully engaging book. Highly recommended." —*Rock Candy*

"A fun, compassionate history of arena rock's finest hour—and the less-fine hours that followed." —*Kirkus Reviews*

"Rollicking....Fans—and anyone interested in true tales of rock and rock excess—will love this." —*Library Journal*

"A glittering backstage history of the 'party every day' people." —*The Globe and Mail*

"Absolutely required reading for any fan of rock music." —glammetal.com

"Remarkably enjoyable...exhaustive. A wildly entertaining book about four of the most influential hard-rock bands to come out of the 1970s." —*New Noise* magazine

"Enthralling...expertly researched and crafted." —*Hudson Valley 360*

"You'll be constantly entertained and enlightened by his backstage stories and newly unearthed connections. The book rock and rolls and parties all night, on every page."

—David Browne, author of *Fire and Rain: The Beatles, Simon & Garfunkel, James Taylor, CSNY, and the Lost Story of 1970*

"Doug Brod's detail-rich book exemplifies the same transfixing qualities of the bands he profiles: the over-the-top hysteria of KISS, the creative tension of Aerosmith, the charming accessibility of Cheap Trick, and the competency of Starz."

—Chuck Klosterman, author of *Fargo Rock City*

# THEY JUST SEEM A LITTLE

## How KISS, Cheap Trick, Aerosmith, and Starz Remade Rock and Roll

# DOUG BROD

BOOKS

**NEW YORK**

Hachette Books
Hachette Book Group
1290 Avenue of the Americas
New York, NY 10104
HachetteBooks.com
Twitter.com/HachetteBooks
Instagram.com/HachetteBooks

First Trade Paperback Edition: June 2022
First Hardcover Edition: December 2020

Published by Hachette Books, an imprint of Perseus Books, LLC, a subsidiary of Hachette Book Group, Inc. The Hachette Books name and logo is a trademark of the Hachette Book Group.

The Hachette Speakers Bureau provides a wide range of authors for speaking events.

To find out more, go to www.hachettespeakersbureau.com or call (866) 376-6591.

The publisher is not responsible for websites (or their content) that are not owned by the publisher.

Print book interior design by Jeff Williams.

Library of Congress Cataloging-in-Publication Data
Names: Brod, Doug, author.
Title: They just seem a little weird: how Kiss, Cheap Trick, Aerosmith, and Starz remade rock and roll / Doug Brod.
Description: [First.] | New York: Hachette Books, 2020. | Includes bibliographical references and index.
Identifiers: LCCN 2020023644 | ISBN 9780306845192 (hardcover) | ISBN 9780306845215 (ebook)
Subjects: LCSH: Rock music—1971–1980—History and criticism. | Rock music—1981–1990—History and criticism. | Kiss (Musical group) | Cheap Trick (Musical group) | Aerosmith (Musical group) | Starz (Musical group)
Classification: LCC ML3534 .B73 2020 | DDC 782.42166092/2 [B]—dc23
LC record available at https://lccn.loc.gov/2020023644

ISBNs: 978-0-306-84519-2 (hardcover), 978-0-306-84521-5 (ebook), 978-0-306-84522-2 (trade paperback)

Printed in the United States of America

LSC-C

Printing 1, 2022

For my parents, Helen and Michael,
who may have asked me to turn it down,
but never told me to shut it off.

And for Rachel and Sasha. For everything.

# CONTENTS

# CONTENTS

# INTRODUCTION

IN EARLY APRIL 1978, when Gene Simmons entered the Manor, a recording studio in the English countryside, his band KISS were, according to a Gallup poll, the most popular rock group in America. In the five years since forming in New York City, the outrageously greasepainted and costumed quartet had grown into a merchandising juggernaut, the likes of which the music business had never seen. Between 1977 and 1979, sales of KISS dolls, makeup kits, posters, lunch boxes, and other tchotchkes would eventually top an estimated $100 million internationally ($353 million in 2020 dollars). Their outlandish live act, combined with the novelty of their appearance, birthed one of the most successful gimmicks in the history of entertainment. For young people, especially boys coming of age and discovering music for themselves, they offered an image as powerful as Elvis's swiveling hips, the Beatles' long hair, and Mick Jagger's turkey strut.

Eager to take his charges to even greater commercial heights, KISS's manager, Bill Aucoin, sought to turn them into superheroes, and in 1977 did just that when Marvel published a comic book printed partially, and ickily, in the musicians' own blood. At Aucoin's urging, the band, who were taking a year-long break from touring, agreed to make their first movie, the NBC telefilm *KISS Meets the Phantom of the Park*, originally pitched as a combination of *A Hard Day's Night* (which starred the Beatles, whom Simmons and co-frontman Paul Stanley idolized) and *Star Wars* (a surprise blockbuster in 1977). The musicians would essentially play their fantastical alter egos in a science-fiction romp about a crazed inventor who wreaks vengeance on the amusement park that fired him, by creating evil android versions of the Demon (bassist-singer Simmons), the Starchild (guitarist-singer Stanley), the Catman (drummer Peter Criss), and the Spaceman (lead guitarist Ace Frehley).

Overseen by cartoon studio Hanna-Barbera and directed by Gordon Hessler, a veteran of pulpy thrillers, the production was by all accounts a miserable experience. "Nobody in the band had the slightest clue about acting. None of us read the script," Stanley later wrote. "When we started filming, it didn't take an expert . . . to know we were in deep shit and there was no getting out of it."

Simmons recalled that Hessler would typically film a scene and then ask the band members how things went. "What did we know?" Simmons wrote. "They basically shot around us because we were the stars."

Before he formed the alt-rock band Everclear, a sixteen-year-old Art Alexakis was tripping on acid when he and a friend entered the parking lot at the Magic Mountain theme park in Valencia, California, to be part of the audience for the movie's concert sequences. There, he discovered the difference between a film shoot and a rock show, and all the tedium that entailed. "They would stop in the middle of songs," he remembers. "Paul Stanley would shriek, '*Oh yeahhh!*' and then, 'Wait a minute—okay, kids, let's try that again.' And then he'd go right back into character."

Making the movie, predictably, exacerbated tensions among the band members that had been brewing for months—with clean-living Simmons and Stanley on one side and, on the other, Frehley and Criss, whose nonstop off-set debauchery was taking its toll. "We had broads in our trailer, six, seven broads at a time," Criss wrote. "We were just animals."

Tour manager Fritz Postlethwaite was responsible for making sure the band members arrived on set in the early morning and shuttling them home after a night of partying. He'd sleep for an hour or two before starting all over again. "They were not getting along," he says, "and trying to act as the peacemaker was draining." While celebrating both the last day of shooting and Postlethwaite's birthday, he and Criss took a ride in the drummer's leased Porsche. Doing ninety on Sepulveda Boulevard, Postlethwaite hit two telephone poles, a mailbox, and two cars before plowing into a post, which set the car ablaze. Thrown through the windshield and onto the pavement, Criss injured his ribs and fingers and sustained a concussion, while Postlethwaite, who was pinned inside the vehicle, suffered serious burns.

If making the movie wasn't embarrassment enough (in Frehley's case, after a bitter argument with the filmmakers, the monosyllabic guitarist stormed off the set, leaving his very obvious—and black—stuntman to stand in for him during close-ups), an early preview screening compounded the misery.

"People openly laughed," Stanley wrote. "It was humiliating." Animosity among the band members hardly abated when newspaper ads for the movie—which ultimately resembled a kooky, live-action version of Hanna-Barbera's *Scooby-Doo, Where Are You!*—featured Simmons's Demon character dwarfing the others. "The rest of the band was incensed," Simmons wrote. The movie debuted on NBC on October 28, 1978, and would eventually play in theaters elsewhere around the globe. "To be honest, I thought it was a natural step in the devolution of KISS," wrote Frehley, who at that point had one silver platform boot out the door. Simmons and Stanley, who bad-mouthed *KISS Meets the Phantom of the Park* for years until they released the European edit, titled *KISS in Attack of the Phantoms*, as part of an authorized DVD collection, teamed up with the actual Scooby-Doo in 2015 for a far less mortifying feature-length animated movie.

. . . .

AN OFTEN-REPEATED PIECE OF KISS mythology goes something like this: Around the time production on *KISS Meets the Phantom of the Park* commenced in May 1978, in an effort to keep the peace—and their chief earners intact—Aucoin and Neil Bogart, the head of Casablanca, their record label, had a brainstorm. *Let's get each member to record his own solo album*, they decided. *Even better: Let's release all four on the same day in September 1978, not long before the movie airs*. Aucoin and Bogart were always thinking big, *bigger*, BIGGEST, so why wouldn't they try a stunt no group had ever attempted?

"The band was really fractured then," Stanley says, "and people weren't speaking to each other. It was pretty awful." Frehley's announcement that he wanted to leave and go solo instigated the project, Stanley says. "Bill said, 'Stay in the band,'" he recalls. "'You can have your cake and eat it too. Everybody should do solo albums.'" All four musicians would have an opportunity to remain in the public eye and share the spotlight equally, which would not have been the case if only one were to release an album.

The fact, contrary to the legend, is that in the August 4, 1977, issue of the rock magazine *Circus*, Stanley and Simmons themselves revealed that each member would be recording his own solo album for release the following spring. So the records had to have been under discussion a year before production on the movie began. "They were talking about doing solo albums way before they became a reality," says former Aucoin production coordinator

Stephanie Tudor. "It wasn't that they had this strong desire at that time to do it, but they knew at one point they would. But whenever you do something like that, it always looks like the band is breaking up. So that was also a reason why it was put off."

"This was a way to make them happy," recalls Chris Lendt, then the liaison between KISS and their business managers, the New York firm Glickman/Marks, "and at the same time serve the greater good of KISS. It would give each person a chance to present themselves to their fans with their own music." The project was an attempt, Criss wrote, "to reinforce the idea that we were four larger-than-life superstars."

According to Carol Ross, who ran the Press Office, Aucoin's publicity arm, "Bill was the type of person who would take chances when people would say, 'You're crazy. Don't do it.' But he felt the guys deserved that individual attention."

They also had something to prove to their peers. "One of the things that KISS have always had is this attitude that they're looked down upon, which they are, by other musicians," says Eric Troyer, who contributed piano and vocals to Simmons's album and later did sessions with Peter Criss and Aerosmith, among many others. "So they had a bit of an inferiority complex about their playing and songwriting. The solo albums were an opportunity for them to show they could broaden their chops and try to get people to say, 'Wow, they can do *this* too!'"

Frehley, for one, loved the idea. "We could all pursue our musical interests . . . and give fans a virtual buffet table of choices from the guys in KISS," the guitarist wrote. "These solo packages," Stanley told *Circus*, "give us the opportunity to indulge."

And indulge they did. As Stanley, Criss, and Frehley dutifully cranked out records that displayed their influences, played to their strengths, and highlighted their weaknesses, Simmons, with his well-established ambition and arrogance in overdrive, began assembling what he called "the greatest show on earth"—with the goal of creating a work of art that would challenge the public's perception of him as a bed-hopping rock-and-roll animal. "When you see somebody who's confident and sure of himself and doesn't just talk the talk but walks the walk, 'Who the fuck does he think he is?' is usually the comment," he says. "But that's a very profound question: *Who do you think you are?* 'He thinks he's all that.' That's correct! Any champion of any walk of life must have an inflated sense of himself and have high expectations. Otherwise, you don't perform."

To test himself, Simmons would forego playing bass and instead pick up the guitar, an instrument with which he had far less aptitude. He tapped Sean Delaney, who had been at various times KISS's tour manager, creative consultant, and choreographer, to coproduce, and then drew up a wish list of celebrities to help bring his immense vision to aural life—"people you respected and people you hated," Simmons later admitted. "The notion of the record was to piss off KISS fans and push it in their faces to say that you're one dimensional and I don't wanna be."

At first glance, his proposed roll call seemed unprecedented, if not downright unrealistic: Paul McCartney and John Lennon (reunited!), David Bowie, Jerry Lee Lewis, middle-of-the-road pop siblings Donny and Marie Osmond, among many others. While those luminaries failed to materialize due to scheduling conflicts (as Simmons has claimed) or flat-out refusals (as others close to the recording suggest), he did manage to amass an eclectic array of talent that would almost certainly confound the KISS faithful: brassy "I Am Woman" singer Helen Reddy, Steely Dan and Doobie Brothers guitarist Jeff "Skunk" Baxter, feminist folkie (and Simmons neighbor) Janis Ian, disco goddess (and labelmate) Donna Summer, and, when the Fab Two declined, a couple of ringers from Broadway's *Beatlemania*: Joe Pecorino (Lennon) and Mitch Weissman (McCartney).

Also in the mix: pop superstar Cher, with whom the Israel-born, New York City–raised Simmons had recently started living in Malibu, California. "By that point, I was totally seduced by power, fame, and wealth, and women especially," he has said, admitting that the album "was probably the reflection of a completely disjointed guy who was just doing everything." Some of the songs had been written years earlier but were deemed not quite right for KISS; others were based on various discarded bits. One was a remake of a KISS song released just two years prior. But the more recent compositions left his paramour unmoved. "I excitedly played Cher the new songs I had been working on," he wrote, "but usually a blank look came over her face. She never really understood our music." Cher and Chastity, her nine-year-old daughter with Sonny Bono, would end up making an appearance on "Living in Sin," whose title dripped with irony since Simmons has claimed that around that time he was also seeing background vocalist Katey Sagal, who would later gain fame for portraying va-va-voomish housewife Peg Bundy on the TV sitcom *Married . . . with Children*.

Simmons recorded the album's basic tracks in around four weeks at the Manor, in the quaint village of Shipton-on-Cherwell, sixty-five miles northwest of London. The studio, then owned by Virgin Records magnate Richard Branson, was built in a sprawling sixteenth-century mansion, and its lush surroundings provided a comfortable living and work space for Simmons, Cher, her two kids, technicians, bodyguards, as well as the seasoned session pros—bassist Neil Jason, drummer Allan Schwartzberg, guitarist Elliott Randall, pianist Richard Gerstein (aka Richard T. Bear)—Simmons flew in from New York to form the core band. "We were all together in one place," Jason says, "so it fostered a much more creative, fast-working environment."

For the purposes of recording, Simmons and Delaney stationed the musicians in different parts of the house—the guitars and amps in one bedroom, Schwartzberg and his drums confined to the snooker room—with everyone communicating via mics and headphones. No rehearsals, no demos—and they worked out their parts on their own. "You'd get a lead sheet with the chords," the drummer says, "and you'd scratch out your chart."

While he enjoyed the overall experience, Schwartzberg did find himself on the receiving end of Simmons's infamous imperiousness. "We're all in the house," he remembers. "We've been playing for days and days, and he'd say, 'Drums, maybe the first bar you could come in with just bass drum.' And, 'Bass, just . . .' At one point we stopped him and said, 'Gene, everybody here has a name.'" Sufficiently chastened, Simmons acquiesced to calling them by their names, but Schwartzberg suspects he would have preferred to continue his less personal approach.

Gerstein remembers Simmons, whom he met through Delaney, as a micromanager who pushed people hard. "He was loud—he was an Israeli," Gerstein says. "You had to come to the table and provide something or you weren't around long." Nearly two weeks into the session, with cabin fever setting in, he approached Simmons: "Man, you've got a girlfriend here. We've all been here for like ten days—I'm sick of Rosie Palm and her five sisters." Gerstein's remark made him laugh, and the next day, after Simmons and Cher took off for a while, the keyboardist was shocked when a limousine pulled up in front of the Manor and out strode a bevy of attractive young women. "I knew what the tone of the evening was going to be when this one girl got out and she had on a Stiff Records T-shirt," he says. "You remember their motto: 'If It Ain't Stiff, It Ain't Worth a Fuck.'"

Returning to the states for overdubs, Simmons recorded many of his special guests at Hollywood's Cherokee Studios and Manhattan's Blue Rock Studio. Standing out among this diverse roster were three accomplished lead guitarists, all of them friends of Simmons's and members of bands with whom KISS shared stages and would be linked, by fans or by fate, for decades to come: Joe Perry of Aerosmith, Rick Nielsen of Cheap Trick, and Richie Ranno of Starz. And back in 1978, those three groups faced critical career junctures of their own.

Aerosmith were in free fall. Their smash albums, 1975's *Toys in the Attic* and 1976's *Rocks*, both produced by Jack Douglas, made them superstars, but their crippling drug habits (Perry and lead singer Steven Tyler had become known as "the Toxic Twins"), not to mention a punishing tour schedule, were taking their toll. The band's latest record, *Draw the Line*, released in December 1977, was widely considered a creative misstep and commercial disappointment, and July 1978 saw the premiere of a rotten movie of their own, the star-spackled debacle *Sgt. Pepper's Lonely Hearts Club Band*.

Perry was in Los Angeles when Simmons invited him over one night to hear some tracks that he thought the guitarist might want to play on. "We were buddies," Perry has said. "Us and KISS, we kind of came up side by side." On arriving at Cher's house at around 9 p.m., he was surprised to find the couple in bed in their pajamas: "I had changed out of my pajamas to come over." (Around this time he also helped Simmons out on a demo called "Mongoloid Man," which never got finished, although a few bits ended up in subsequent songs.)

It was at his recording session for the Simmons album where Perry, who can be heard on "Radioactive," has claimed he finally met and befriended the Cheap Trick guitarist, whom he had long admired. "I was sitting making use of the glass top of the pinball machine"—presumably, euphemistically, snorting cocaine—"and Rick Nielsen walked in," Perry said. "I see this goofy-looking guy and it's hard to miss him. He's got Cheap Trick written on his fucking eyelids." (Nielsen, however, insists he and Perry became acquainted well before this session.) Mitch Weissman recalls playing ping-pong with Nielsen during downtime, using the guitarist's plectrums in place of balls.

Nielsen's group were on the ascendant. Simmons, an early champion, went so far as to take Cheap Trick on the road the previous summer. At the end of April 1978, Cheap Trick would be heading to Japan to play what would become for them a very consequential string of dates. In May they'd be releasing their third studio album, *Heaven Tonight*, featuring their first, if minor, radio hit, "Surrender," with lyrics that famously name-check Simmons's band ("Got my KISS records out") and offer a description of parents that became the title of this book.

"I was just asked to come in and add my two cents. I was honored to get asked," says Nielsen, who played a predictably frantic and fantastic solo on

"See You in Your Dreams," a remake of a track off of KISS's fifth studio LP, *Rock and Roll Over*, and the Simmons album's rowdiest rocker. Cleverly, the first seven notes of Nielsen's solo evoke "When You Wish upon a Star," foreshadowing the album's closing track, an achingly sentimental cover of that same chestnut from Walt Disney's *Pinocchio*. "He hired me because he wanted me to play like I play," Nielsen says, explaining his MO. "I'm not a studio guy, and I'm not what they already have, so I play with what I bring." Simmons was particularly pleased with the guitarist's contribution, jokingly saying in a promotional interview, "The guy sounds like Page, the best Page you ever heard: page nine, page ten."

To show his appreciation, Simmons sent Nielsen a set of the four solo albums, which the guitarist never opened and kept in storage. On a 2013 episode of the junk-shop TV series *American Pickers*, he sold them for $200 to collector Frank Fritz. "I said, 'Gene probably won't like this, but here you go,'" Nielsen says. "Frank was such a fan. I think I'd have to go out and buy a record player anyhow."

Starz, the second band Aucoin signed to his management company, opened many times for Aerosmith, played a show with KISS in 1976, and scored a minor hit in May 1977 with the Jack Douglas–produced "Cherry Baby," which peaked at No. 33 on the *Billboard* singles chart. But they too were in a downward spiral, owing to Capitol Records' neglect (or so some members say) and a violent outburst at a promo film shoot.

Richie Ranno says his participation on Simmons's album came to him in a premonition. It was 1975 and KISS were determined but struggling, not yet the arena-filling monsters that the *Alive!* double LP would create when it took off later that year. Starz were in Detroit, rehearsing with Sean Delaney, who early on had a big hand in their creative decisions as well. "I had this weird dream that Gene made a solo album," Ranno told Delaney one morning, "and the only thing on the cover was his face. And I played on it." Three years later, while writing songs for Starz's *Coliseum Rock*, Ranno got word of the four albums and was bummed that he hadn't been asked to play on Simmons's. A few weeks before he was to head to Toronto to track what would turn out to be his band's final album, he got a call from Delaney; apparently Simmons didn't love either of the solos that Joe Perry and "Skunk" Baxter had added to "Tunnel of Love." Simmons initially requested Nils Lofgren, who was then enjoying a successful solo career after a fruitful association with Neil Young, as a replacement, but Delaney recommended Ranno.

"I said, 'Sean, you remember my dream, right?'" Ranno recalls. "And he said, 'Yes, I do!' So I went in. I'm the only guitar player on that song—not Perry and not Baxter—but they never changed the credits, which list all three of us." Perry, for his part, didn't dispute Ranno's claim. "When I listened to the track," he said, "I had trouble discerning whether I even played on it."

In a promotional interview for the album, Simmons said Ranno's solo came about when the guitarist "just happened by one day and said, 'What does that sound like?' I said, 'I don't know, give it a try.'" For their troubles, Nielsen and Ranno got their names misspelled "Neilson" and "Ritchie" on the back cover of the original pressing, where Simmons also thanks Steven Tyler and Doobie, presumably Ranno's bandmate Joe X. Dubé, who played on demos for the KISS bassist. (Keeping things all in the Aucoin family, Ranno bandmate Brendan Harkin contributed guitar to Peter Criss's solo album.)

. . . .

TO MAINTAIN CONTINUITY WITH the brand, the cover of each solo album featured the band logo on a portrait of the musician painted by Italian artist Eraldo Carugati, and the package included a poster that interlocked with inserts from the other three. "The game plan was, we've got to have some kind of hook, to make sure that anybody who buys Gene's album because they like his character will want the other three," says Gail Rodgers, Aucoin's publicity and promotion coordinator at the time. "It all worked on paper, but it didn't work in reality."

Stanley initially wasn't sure about this approach. "I was a bit shocked," he says. "But it was a way to unify something that was fractured, to give it a cohesive look and identity, as opposed to just putting the members' names on it." The idea to release the albums with similar covers came from Aucoin. "I was not thinking in those terms when we did them," Stanley says. "But he was right. It shored up the dam, and the dam held for a while."

Michele Slater, Delaney's production assistant, was in charge of locating, booking, and scheduling the guests for Simmons's album. She remembers the excitement in the Aucoin office being palpable. "We were absolutely convinced that these albums were going to explode," she says.

In a fit of commercial hubris or cocaine-fueled delusion—perhaps both—on September 18, 1978, Casablanca Records delivered more than 5.3 million KISS solo albums to stores, buttressed by a promotional budget of some $2.5 million. Label executives were shocked when nearly half came back unwanted and unsold. "KISS succumbed to their own hype," Rodgers says. "Bill succumbed to his own hype, thinking that everything will always go up, and that nobody will stop buying records. Believing that the demand would be 10x, they released 20x, and then of course they had to eat 15x, because the word got out that there's one cut on Ace's, two cuts on Paul's, nothing on Gene's, and maybe a half a cut on Peter's that can get radio play. You ended up with a gazillion returns. That never bodes well—for the record store, for the label, or for the artist, because someone's got to tell him, 'We just got two hundred thousand units returned.' Who wants to say that to an artist? Especially to guys who had been steadily selling millions of albums."

Chris Lendt, KISS's former tour business manager, says, "You sort of set yourself up for disappointment, because it's implausible to believe that every KISS fan is going to go out and buy four separate records."

For Stanley, the albums "turned out to be a Band-Aid on a gushing wound. Ultimately, the Band-Aid flew off, but it calmed things for a while. There was no love lost between band members during that period."

Though Frehley was the only one to score a hit single, a chugging version of Russ Ballard's Big Apple anthem "New York Groove"—a 1975 European smash for the British glam band Hello—Simmons's album, which rose to a modest No. 22, charted the highest. As an idiosyncratic document of Simmons's dual obsessions with women and the macabre, the album is a downright bizarre hodgepodge and hardly the best, or even most consistent, of the solo efforts—that would be Stanley's—but it at least affirms the courage of the artist's twisted convictions. He immediately sets the tone with a prelude that could easily soundtrack a Satanic mass in a grade-Z horror movie, and follows it with the catchy boogie pop of "Radioactive," which despite its allusion to "the Devil's daughter" and a guitar solo by one of the Toxic Twins, is otherwise safe as ultra-pasteurized milk. The heavier, surprisingly funky "Burning Up with Fever" features a strong gospel-style assist from Donna Summer, while other tracks reveal Simmons's uncanny Beatles mimicry and penchant for predatory balladry cloaked in pretty melodies. "Tunnel of Love," perhaps the most quintessentially *Gene* song of the collection, is an unabashed ode to an unidentified vulva, which includes a couplet ("You wanted my disease / You'll have to do as I please") that provocatively suggests an attempt to woo a potential lover with the promise of an STD. Simmons has said he needed to record the symphonically schmaltzy "When You Wish upon a Star" "to pay back Jiminy Cricket because my dreams at that point had come true," which could be the sincerest thing he's ever uttered. Near the end of the track, his voice cracks from crying.

The bassist Neil Jason, who admits he wasn't much of a KISS fan when he took the gig, nevertheless admires Simmons for making the artistic leap. "Everybody can second-guess him and say, 'You should have just done a KISS record as the God of Thunder and you would've been a fucking genius,'" he says. "But that was pretty much what he did every day of his life." *Beatlemania's* Mitch Weissman has a similar take. "What was cool was, everything about the album was Gene and not just the persona you saw in KISS," he says. "But that may have thrown fans."

The performer and producer Butch Walker, who as a kid in rural Georgia worshipped KISS, hears all over the album a twisted simulacrum of the Beatles. "It's like some weird heavy metal *Sgt. Pepper's* or *The White Album*," he says. "You would think Gene's the one in the band who was on drugs."

· · · ·

**DESPITE ITS INITIAL COMMERCIAL** failure and artistic miscalculation ("I'd give it one star," Simmons himself has opined), the album became the first and only recording to feature members of four bands that would remake rock and roll.

Four distinctly American bands that drew from some of the same primary sources—Chuck Berry, the Beatles, British blues rock—but devised vastly different sounds.

Four bands that represented a paradigm shift: from the earnest, mustachioed, puka-shelled strains of the chart-topping Crosby, Stills, Nash & Young; Doobie Brothers; and Eagles to a flashy, hook-filled, often disreputable, *teen-targeted* hard rock.

Four bands that flamboyantly strutted into the dazed and confused early '70s, reveling in revved-up, exhilarating anthems and—inspired by U.K. bands like Slade, the Move, the Who, T. Rex, and Mott the Hoople—boasting a theatricality rarely seen before on the U.S. concert stage.

Four bands that rose, fell, and (sometimes) soared again, both together and separately, often sharing stages, producers, engineers, managers, agents, roadies, and fans—and that were still collaborating decades later.

Four bands that, between them, occupied seven spots on a *Circus* magazine Top 20 readers' poll in January 1979.

Four bands that went on to collectively sell an estimated quarter of a billion albums worldwide.

Four bands that were still touring more than forty years after their initial successes.

Four bands—three of them now enshrined in the Rock and Roll Hall of Fame—that inspired multiple generations of musicians, in particular laying the foundation for two of rock's most popular, yet diametrically opposed, genres: the hair metal of Bon Jovi, Poison, Skid Row, and Mötley Crüe in the '80s and the grunge of Nirvana, Pearl Jam, Alice in Chains, Soundgarden, and the Melvins in the '90s.

Four bands that showcased a new kind of rock star: preening, clowning, sometimes spitting blood (and fire!). Not content to just stand there and play, they brought the celebration to the crowd, encouraging fans to dream on, surrender, sing it shout it tell the world about it, and party *EH-VUH-REE* day.

## CHAPTER I

# STRUTTER

**"WHAT THE FUCK WAS THAT?"**

Standing on the sidewalk in front of 10 East Twenty-Third Street in Manhattan in November 1972, Tom Werman felt his boss's words sting in the crisp fall air. Don Ellis, Epic Records' vice president of artists and repertoire, wasn't angry. He simply didn't understand. Werman, a young representative in the A&R department, had just walked out of a shabby loft with Ellis, where they'd taken in a performance by a rock-and-roll trio that included two guys Werman had previously scouted for the label.

With faces smeared white with makeup and framed by long, bushy manes, the band members were quite a sight: the hulking singer-bassist decked out in a sailor's uniform with his hair tinted silver; the pretty-boy singer-guitarist in red-suspendered dungarees, with a scarf and beret; the drummer in a dark, spangly shirt, with a shiny tie around his bare neck. They resembled nothing so much as hippie mimes, not exactly an original concept since a New York group called the Hello People already sported similar gear. For this special occasion, the band converted their rehearsal space into a makeshift theater and ran through a few new compositions, including "Strutter," "Deuce," and "Firehouse." Each incorporated a coarsely effective guitar riff anchored by lyrics concerning a woman who, by turns, will only make you cry, should throw some sex her hardworking man's way, and is like bad weather but still sets your soul on fire. As the final song reached its climax, the guitarist grabbed a metal bucket and chucked the contents directly at the assembled guests, all of whom ducked, thinking they were about to get soaked with water. They ended up picking silver confetti out of their hair.

Werman, who thought the songs were anthemic and well played, was bowled over by the performance, while Ellis, whose taste ran more toward the more traditional bluesy rock of Steve Miller and Boz Skaggs, left completely nonplussed. As he was fairly new to Epic, Werman lacked the confidence to try to persuade his boss otherwise and was loath to risk getting labeled as difficult. "All A&R men are basically chickenshits," he says. "They're scared to put themselves on the line, for fear that they'll lose their jobs." (Ellis would also pass on Lynyrd Skynyrd and Rush, two other bands Werman brought to him.)

Werman had met bassist Gene Klein and guitarist Stan Eisen some months earlier in their previous incarnation as a quintet and was impressed with their ambition. Klein, born Chaim Witz in Haifa in 1949, had emigrated to New York at age eight with his Holocaust survivor mother and, after learning English by reading comic books and watching television, went on to a variety of jobs after college, including editorial assistant at *Vogue* magazine, deli counter clerk, typist, and public school teacher. Eisen, nearly three years his junior, was a native New Yorker self-conscious about his deformed right ear, and drove a cab.

An engineer named Ron Johnsen had given Werman an in-progress tape of the band, then called Wicked Lester, that he was recording in fits and starts, the result of Klein and Eisen working on "spec" time, whenever paying clients had left Electric Lady Studios in Greenwich Village, which Jimi Hendrix had opened just two years earlier. Intrigued, Werman decided to sit in on a bunch of sessions and liked what he heard: urban, vaguely funky, vaguely psychedelic rock, not dissimilar to that of Three Dog Night, Spirit, and Rare Earth, all of whom had been enjoying varying degrees of success. The music featured de rigueur flutes, horns, keyboards, and percussion, and he was particularly fond of the group's harmonies and pop sensibility. But as an industry newbie, he was slightly unprepared for the extramusical activities to which he'd soon bear witness.

One night at the studio, Klein left to get a hot dog and didn't return, prompting Werman to go look for him. Walking into another of the building's studios, which was dark and seemingly empty, he heard noise coming from an enclosed glass drum booth. Peeking in, he found Klein and Eisen on the floor, having their way with a female admirer. "I turned around and left," he says. "That was one of my first experiences seeing typical rock-star behavior." In his memoir *Kiss and Make-Up*, the bassist managed to make the scene even more unseemly, recalling the woman, whom he had just picked up, "servicing the entire band at once!"

Despite a general lack of enthusiasm, Epic decided to buy the masters, for "probably thirty-five or fifty thousand dollars," Werman recalls. The price was right, he guesses, because the acquisition came on the heels of a similar deal the label had cut with an Illinois band called REO Speedwagon. Werman was pleased with the finished album, which had taken nearly a year to record. Originals like "She" (written when Klein was in a band called Bullfrog Bheer during college) and "Love Her All I Can" were busy and overstuffed but did have commercial appeal, and covers of Barry Mann and Gerry Goffin's "Sweet Ophelia" and the Hollies' "I Wanna Shout" (retitled "We Want to Shout It Out Loud") revealed real pop smarts. But by the time Epic was thinking of releasing it, Klein and Eisen—who soon changed their names to Gene Simmons and Paul Stanley—had dissolved the band, unhappy with the direction the music had taken. "I'm embarrassed by that album," said Simmons, who aspired to create a group with a more specific sound and image, like that of the Who or the Rolling Stones. "It was as good as a Looking Glass LP but that's about it." Stanley called it "a Frankenstein monster that evolved in the studio."

With no band to promote it, the album was shelved.

Forty-six years later, Werman revises his appraisal of the finished product. "It was a namby-pamby record, sugar sweet," he says. "A couple of good songs, but generally not hard hitting."

"Other than being present at a few of the sessions, Tom Werman had virtually nothing to do with Wicked Lester," Stanley says. "Frankly, I would rather blame it on him, but that's not the truth."

Peter Criss (né Criscuola) had been playing with Stanley and Simmons for only a couple of months before the Epic showcase. The pair found the Brooklyn native after answering an ad the drummer had placed in the August 31, 1972, issue of *Rolling Stone*, looking for a group doing "soft & hard music." Criss also had a connection to Johnsen, who'd engineered the sole album by his garage-psych band Chelsea the year before. After his first audition for the revamped Wicked Lester at Electric Lady flopped—he couldn't get a feel for the borrowed drums—Criss offered his handclaps to a song Johnsen happened to be recording that day with singer Lyn Christopher, for whom Simmons and Stanley had contributed backing vocals. Her eponymous 1973 collection of smooth pop on Paramount Records would be the last album anyone would suspect to be the first album to feature three musicians who'd soon transform into one of the most beloved, despised, extravagant, important, ridiculous, popular, and influential bands of the '70s.

• • • •

**IN THE THREE MONTHS** after their Epic rejection, Wicked Lester supplemented their sound with the addition of lead guitarist Paul "Ace" Frehley, a Bronx-born space cadet with a loose style that perfectly complemented Stanley's spirited but choppy rhythm approach. Binky Philips, a musician friend of Stanley's from high school who would later collaborate with the band, saw Frehley at one of the guitarist's early tryouts and liked his technique. "He didn't have a large palette of ideas with his left hand," he says. "He seemed to know only about four or five licks, but he had the attack and the tone.

"As far as Peter and Ace go, I think Paul and Gene were getting desperate," Philips continues. "They were both older than me. The fact that Peter wasn't a fantastic drummer was something they would put up with, because here was a guy willing to paint his face blue if that's what they called for, which is what they did call for. I have no memory of either Gene or Paul ever saying, 'Our fucking drummer, man. This fucking guy is good.' It was just, 'This guy'll do.' Years on the road turned him into a drummer, but he wasn't that good early on. He had a clunky feel and he didn't swing, although he wound up swinging."

Stanley did say Criss's drum solos sounded like "someone banging pots and pans on New Year's Eve," but it all worked in the context of the band. "Would it have been better with another drummer? No."

When the name Wicked Lester had lost its appeal, they came up with a new one. Fuck, suggested by Simmons, lost out to Stanley's more demure KISS (inspired by an earlier Criss band called Lips), and thanks to Frehley and Stanley's design capabilities, they had a striking logo notable for its two final letters resembling quasi–lightning bolts (or, as some would insist, the symbol for the Nazis' SS paramilitary organization). Armed with a focus and determination that would put most other bands to shame, they were off.

But they didn't count on the utter shamelessness of the New York Dolls—scrungy, teased-out reprobates in thrift-shop fishnets, stiletto stilts, and clumpy eyeliner—who basked in the sounds of '60s girl groups and vintage rhythm and blues. Fronted by an impossibly skinny junior Jagger named David Johansen, who found his Richardsian foil in the heroin sheik Johnny Thunders, the Dolls set out to out-stone the Stones, kicking up chaos like a punky Pig-Pen gleefully engulfed in his own private haboob. The Dolls innately knew that pure rock and roll was 50 percent visual and if they could keep their guitars in tune, which they couldn't, so much the better. But really, who cared when they looked like this?

"They were the crazy version of the greatest rock band in the world in 1972," says Bob "Nitebob" Czaykowski, one of the Dolls' early sound engineers. "If you wanted to be successful, you patterned yourself after the Stones." Paul Stanley remembers thinking of them as "the Stones on acid. It was almost a bizarre extreme personification of the Stones."

The Dolls essentially made the Mercer Arts Center, a performance space in Greenwich Village, their home base, playing a gleefully shambolic Tuesday-night residency beginning in June 1972. Binky Philips, after hearing they were "incredible" from one friend and "the worst" from another, had to check them out for himself the following Tuesday. "I think Gene and Paul saw them within four weeks," he says.

"The Dolls," says Philips, "had the same effect on Paul and Gene as they did on virtually every band in New York, which was, *Oh my God, they suck! Oh my God, how can we be them?*" In fact, in KISS's first publicity still, from 1973, the four men pose not in what would evolve into their signature makeup, but in copycat rouged-up quasi-drag, a bunch of streetwalking cheaters with mugs full of Avon. "They looked completely ridiculous," says Philips. "But to their credit, they realized that none of them were skinny little guys with big noses like Johnny Thunders or completely strange stick figures like David Johansen."

Simmons has said of the first time he and Stanley laid eyes and ears on the Dolls, "When they started playing, we turned to each other and said: 'We'll kill 'em.' . . . Songs were all right—'Personality Crisis'—but they could not play guitars. Horrific." As if that were an obstacle. As Ira Robbins, who chronicled the New York scene, among others, in his magazine *Trouser Press*, observes, "The Dolls were extremely limited by their refusal to be acceptable." Simmons and Stanley, on the other hand, were clearly willing to do whatever it took.

"I thought their music was very, very simple," Dolls guitarist Sylvain Sylvain has said of KISS. "The reason why I think they made it and we didn't is because it was an easier pill for America to fuckin' swallow."

• • • •

ON JANUARY 30, 1973, Stevie Wonder's fierce and funky "Superstition" was the biggest single in America; the all-star aquatic disaster *The Poseidon Adventure* ruled the movie box office; two of President Richard Nixon's henchmen, G. Gordon Liddy and James McCord, were found guilty of conspiracy, burglary, and other crimes as the Watergate scandal deepened; and KISS played their first gig—to a virtually empty room—at a dive called Coventry. Located just minutes from Manhattan in the working-class neighborhood of Sunnyside, Queens, Coventry was an outer-borough outpost for the Dolls and other bands—such as Harlots of 42nd Street, the Brats, and Queen Elizabeth—that rose in their glittery wake. KISS's set list was a mix of Wicked Lester songs and newer ones like "Deuce" and "Watchin' You." It wasn't until the next night that they wore their prototypical makeup. Sher Bach, a backup singer and dancer in Ruby and the Rednecks whose husband fronted the Harlots, remembers seeing KISS experimenting with cosmetics. "We were going, 'What the fuck?'" she says. "And it's still a bone of contention with my ex-husband that they got as big as they did. He's very bitter about their success, because he thought his band was more professional and better musicians. And I said, 'KISS put on a better show, babe. You may be a better singer than Paul Stanley, but . . .'"

Despite his appreciation of such dazzling showmen as Alice Cooper, T. Rex's Marc Bolan, and David Bowie, Ira Robbins was skeptical of KISS. "I guess the dividing line for me was the arrogance," he says. "The glam bands knew they were taking the piss. You were meant to understand it as a kind of theater. KISS rolled it all up as 'We're the monsters, we're the toughest guys, we're the biggest stars.' There's no acknowledgment that this is silly. There's no self-awareness, other than just sheer boasting."

That was all because KISS took what they did deadly seriously. Stanley considered the other New York bands to be the soundtrack to a fashion show, more concerned with being seen and making the scene at Max's Kansas City, the artsy hipster boîte that embraced the Dolls but shunned KISS. "We were rehearsing literally seven days a week," he said, "so we had no kinship. We had nothing in common with them. We weren't cool."

In March, thanks to Ron Johnsen's contacts, KISS recorded a demo with engineer Eddie Kramer, who helped build Electric Lady Studios and had worked with Led Zeppelin, Humble Pie, and Jimi Hendrix. That all five of the songs—"Deuce," "Cold Gin," "Strutter," "Watchin' You," and "Black Diamond"—would still be live staples nearly a half century later is testament to KISS's knack for matching indelible riffs with such universal themes as booze, cockteasing, and prostitution.

After schlepping their gear from their rehearsal space on East Twenty-Third Street to Coventry in Queens and a Long Island club called the Daisy, in May the band finally secured a gig in Manhattan, at a loft party organized by the Brats. A month later, some of the KISS members went to Madison Square Garden to see Alice Cooper's Billion Dollar Babies show and left gob-smacked by the shock rocker's elaborate staging, which incorporated such Grand Guignol sights as a guillotine, a boa constrictor, and the top-hatted frontman mutilating baby dolls. It was loud, heavy rock with a touch of caba-ret and tunes for miles. When they returned to their loft, Peter Criss recalled the epiphany that shook them: "We played and said, 'Wait a minute, what if there was four Alice Coopers?'"

On Friday, July 13, the Brats and KISS put on their own show at a ball-room in the Hotel Diplomat, a dump in the skeevy heart of Times Square. The Dolls, who by then included Criss's childhood friend Jerry Nolan on drums, had begun playing there the previous year, when bands that were get-ting no love from club owners discovered all they needed to set up a gig was a few hundred dollars and a permit from the city to hold a public dance. If you charged $3 at the door, you didn't need a whole lot of attendees to start making money.

Stanley had invited Binky Philips's band, the Planets, to open. KISS, who went on second, finally began dressing the part of monstrous rock stars: Simmons in a black T-shirt emblazoned with the KISS logo, shiny black pants, a white grease mask corrupted by an exaggerated widow's peak and black-blotched eyes that formed an infernal Rorschach, his topknot resem-bling a steel-wool mushroom cloud; Stanley, with a big black star covering his right eye, in studded jeans with a black motorcycle jacket over a tight black tee; Criss in a dark tank top, his face a tamer version of Simmons's, softened further by the addition of whiskers; and Frehley in a satiny black blouse decorated with a metallic eagle-like creature (which his mom helped make), glittering stars enshrouding his eyes, as though he were some kind of interstellar panda.

"It was one of those ballrooms where the stage was on the long wall, as opposed to the narrow wall," says Philips. "The makeup wasn't very well done—nothing like the way they wound up looking, nowhere near as crisp, defined, and simplified, so that it would read two hundred feet out." Philips wanted to hate them, on one hand strictly from a competitive point of view, and on the other because he thought, *How could you want to get yourself trapped into something like that?* But, he recalls thinking, *I've got to admit, these fucking songs are good.* "When they did 'Strutter' and 'Deuce' and 'Firehouse,'" he says, "I remembered them very vividly from the rehearsals. Most of the audience left after KISS, and I don't know if that was because most of the audience was there for KISS or because after KISS you didn't need to see anything else."

It was at the next Diplomat gig, on August 10, where KISS's career would be made. Simmons, a fan of the TV show *Flipside*, a terrific half hour that served up studio sessions by the likes of Edgar Winter, the Raspberries, and John Lennon and Yoko Ono, had been sending its producer-director, Bill Aucoin, press kits, including fake reviews, urging him to come see the show. Aucoin attended the gig, was awed by the band's ingenuity, and set up a meeting, where he told them that if he could get them a record deal in thirty days, they should hire him as manager. Aucoin, a dapper, fastidious Massachusetts native with solid industry connections, made good on his promise. In September he hooked the band up with Casablanca, a brand-new label bankrolled by Warner Bros. and run by Neil Bogart, a former executive at Buddah Records who had built much of his reputation on hits by faceless bubblegum-pop acts manufactured in the studio. KISS were both a continuation and the antithesis of this concept, as they came to him well developed and full of face, but they were still, fundamentally, a big sticky wad of Bazooka. (They even inspired the top bubblegum producers Jerry Kasenetz and Jeff Katz, who had worked with Bogart at Buddah, to create FURR, a knockoff whose sole bait-and-switch album, from 1977, features a cover painting that crudely approximates the look of KISS and music that sounds like the ungodly union of Grand Funk Railroad and the Partridge Family.)

By mid-October, KISS had a contract with Aucoin for representation. By mid-November, they were in Manhattan's Bell Sound Studios, recording their first album with producers Kenny Kerner and Richie Wise, who had scored some hits with Gladys Knight and the Pips and Stories and some misses with the heavy New York rock band Dust, of which Wise was also a member along with future Ramones drummer Marc Bell. Bogart was so welcoming of KISS, he even released a Kerner/Wise–produced single by Tomorrow Morning, essentially the renamed remnants of an earlier Frehley band called Molimo, who offered a filthy-footed East Coast take on the Mamas & the Papas with a twist—that being, they were five years too late.

By December, KISS's self-titled debut was finished and the band headlined Coventry for the last time, replete with full makeup and costumes, finally playing in front of a large, enthusiastic crowd.

## CHAPTER 2

# DREAM ON

"LADIES AND GENTLEMEN, *thank you very much. Right now, we wanna do a little instrumental thing for you, Joe Perry and Brad Whitford on guitars extraordinaire. We call it 'We Don't Wanna Fuck You, We Just Wanna Eat Your Sandwiches.'"*

So shouteth Steven Tyler in his rat-a-tat scat patois from the cramped stage at Max's Kansas City, the dark scenester hangout near Manhattan's Union Square. In a crowd that routinely attracted the likes of Iggy Pop, Lou Reed, and sundry Warhol Superstars, the uptown Columbia Records president Clive Davis and Atlantic Records' Jerry Greenberg and Ahmet Ertegun merged with the downtown obliterati to witness five hungry Boston gypsy longhairs blaring blues-besotted rave-ups with reckless wit and a sloppy, grubby grace.

In Davis's telling, the veteran music executive stumbled upon Tyler's group purely by accident. He happened to be at Max's on the evening of August 5, 1972, to see, and possibly sign, a different band. But when Aerosmith hit the stage and blazed through their set, he beheld a star in the making. "I had no idea who they were when they came on," he says. "Steven Tyler was mesmerizing and charismatic right from the get-go." There was no doubt in Davis's mind that he needed to have this band on his label, but Tyler's uncanny resemblance to one of the world's most famous rock stars triggered him. *Wow,* he thought, *this guy looks like an American Mick Jagger.* "Of course, he was to become no version of anybody else," Davis says.

Steve Leber has a different recollection of the evening: Davis, along with Greenberg and Ertegun—an Atlantic vice president and the label's cofounder/president, respectively—came to Max's as invited guests, there to witness a showcase performance of a new band with whom Leber and his partner, David Krebs, were working. Ertegun didn't bite—he already had one Mick Jagger attached to his label, namely Mick Jagger—but he told Leber he'd do him a favor. "This band sucks," he said, "but if you stand here and talk to me long enough, Clive will sign the group for a lot of money."

Davis did end up securing Aerosmith for $125,000—technically a production deal with Leber-Krebs—"clearly an indication that there was competitive interest in them," Davis says, "because that was a substantial amount of money." He was also taking something of a risk since Columbia, whose established rock acts—Santana; Chicago; Blood, Sweat & Tears—leaned toward the jazzier side, had little experience with heavy, noisy guitars. In fact, almost exactly a year before he closed the deal, Davis signed Looking Glass, pop softies who would later transform into the frequent Aerosmith opening act Starz.

It was around the time of the Max's showcase when Aerosmith bassist Tom Hamilton and tour manager Bob "Kelly" Kelleher first encountered a member of KISS, before KISS even existed. Aerosmith were staying at the Ramada Inn on Eighth Avenue in Manhattan, feeling on top of the world. "We had a big party and a girl we knew brought a friend," Hamilton has said, "this guy with a high crackly voice and an easy laugh. When he said something funny, his voice would go up in a high register." That guy was Ace Frehley and, like everyone else at the party, he got bombed. "Ace, in his snakeskin boots and his bad complexion, had passed out on the bed in Tom's room," Kelleher says. "I had to go in and wake him up. 'C'mon, Ace, gotta go. Party's over.'"

If their resemblance to the Stones seemed obvious, Aerosmith had ties to the New York Dolls that were even more direct. Not only did Leber and Krebs manage both bands, but as a teen, Tyler, who grew up Steven Tallarico in Yonkers, a suburb north of New York City, attended Quintano's School for Young Professionals in Manhattan, where three of the Dolls—Johnny Thunders (né Genzale), Sylvain Sylvain (né Mizrahi), and original drummer Billy Murcia (dead at twenty-one on November 6, 1972), who were all a few years younger—met. As a student at the small private alternative high school for the dramatically and musically inclined—where much of the student body spent their days getting fucked up and fucking off—Tyler had his first experience in a recording studio, contributing backing vocals to a few songs for the Left Banke, the baroque pop group of "Walk Away Renée" fame, which featured one of his classmates, Steve Martin Caro.

Tyler also sang and played drums in the Strangeurs, who opened gigs for the Byrds, the Lovin' Spoonful, and the Beach Boys, the last of which led to interest from Date Records, a subsidiary of CBS. The label issued a sunny, Zombies-esque single by the band, renamed Chain Reaction, in 1966. Chain Reaction released another 45, an even brighter bit of British Invasion–indebted pop, on Verve before breaking up.

Tyler formed Aerosmith in 1970 after meeting guitarist Joe Perry and bassist Tom Hamilton in Sunapee, New Hampshire, where Tyler's family had a vacation lodge. He gave up drumming to devote his energies to being the center of attention, entrusting the stool to old Yonkers friend Joey Kramer and another guitar to Ray Tabano, a leather-goods store owner and childhood buddy of Tyler's. The following year Brad Whitford took over for Tabano, who, it turned out, was better suited to be their merch guy and later designed the band's original logo, a circled A with wings. Now living together—and living it up—in an apartment at 1325 Commonwealth Avenue in Boston, Aerosmith signed a management deal with a well-connected promoter named Frank Connelly, who after taking them as far as he thought he could, essentially sold the band to Leber-Krebs. "He knew he needed somebody in New York," says Leber, "but Frank is the one who really believed in the band and kept them together at the very beginning of their career."

"We used to call them Leper and Crabs," says major East Coast concert promoter Ron Delsener, who adopted a devious voice to add, "'And you will make a lot of money. Come with us and cash in.' Aerosmith fell for that line. And they locked them up forever."

Not long after signing with Leber-Krebs, Joe Perry, like KISS, saw the Dolls at the Mercer Arts Center. "I thought they were the best band in the world," he has said, "although it took me a couple of minutes to get my ears adjusted to the fact that they were out of tune most of the time." The rest of Aerosmith, he said, hated them. (Steven Tyler eventually married, then divorced, Cyrinda Foxe, who left her husband, David Johansen, for him.)

Columbia released Aerosmith's self-titled debut with no fanfare on January 5, 1973, the same day the label put out an album by another new signing, Bruce Springsteen's *Greetings from Asbury Park, N.J.* Aerosmith's landed with barely a thud.

With the exception of Tyler, the band members had little experience in a recording studio and their tentativeness seeped through the grooves. Nor were the songs particularly well served by Adrian Barber, whose wan, arid production extracted much of the juice from such potentially raucous material as "Mama Kin" and "Somebody." Joey Kramer, in particular, sounds as if he's slapping wooden spoons against ten-pound bags of rice. Only "Dream On," written by Tyler as a teenager a few years before the band started, manages to shine through the murk.

"Because it doesn't sell," Leber says, "Clive doesn't pick up the option [to release future albums], so David and I panicked. I go to Clive, 'Do me a favor, put out a single.' In those days, album rock is what sold and they had sold 30,000 copies." The label relented and released "Dream On," which went to No. 59. "That's what put Aerosmith on the map. They then sold 300,000 albums, and Clive recognized how important they were, and he picked up the option."

For Krebs, the key was to build Aerosmith's fan base on the backs of groups in modest decline—Mott the Hoople, Argent, Slade, Suzi Quatro—"bands whose audience we could cop," the manager said in 1976. "Even if we didn't blow them off the stage every time, we could at least count on some to buy an Aerosmith album."

"They were out for blood, especially as an opening act," says "Nitebob" Czaykowski, who mixed their live sound after having worked with the Dolls. "When you see a lot of bands, especially in a combat situation, you begin to think, *Aerosmith are working a lot harder than the Dolls, because they want it more and they know how to get it.* They were listening to more people around them."

As Aerosmith became more successful and Leber-Krebs began to beef up its roster, the managers took a different tack when it came to booking opening bands. "We had a simple theory that worked," Krebs says. "If you went to see Aerosmith, that's not the only group that you'd like that was similar. That's why we thought we could break Ted Nugent off of Aerosmith, and we could break AC/DC off of Aerosmith and Nugent, and we could break the Scorpions. And the list goes on."

. . . .

JACK DOUGLAS, A FLINTY, street-smart Bronx native, had been, in an earlier life, a bassist for blond-pompadoured white-soul sensation Wayne Cochran. He later played with Privilege—fuzzy, organ-drenched psychrockers formed from the ashes of Soul Survivors (one-hit wonders responsible for 1967's "Expressway to Your Heart") and signed to T-Neck, a label founded by the Isley Brothers. After the Isleys tarted up the band's 1969 debut album with horns and soulful-sister harmonies, to Douglas's dissatisfaction, he offered to remix it and enjoyed the process so much that he decided to focus his career behind a board, not in front of an amp. An audio engineering course led to a job, as a janitor, at a new Manhattan studio called the Record Plant, where he worked on John Lennon's *Imagine* and, later, engineered the New York Dolls' debut for producer Todd Rundgren. "Todd hated the band," Douglas has said. "They were hot, and they were doing something no one else was doing—proving that you could be a band that didn't know how to play their instruments but still have a sound."

"It was very chaotic in the studio," recalls Bebe Buell, Rundgren's then girlfriend. "Johnny Thunders was already an incredibly unusual and gifted guitarist. Both he and Sylvain had worked out how to complement each other perfectly."

Douglas has claimed his role on that record effectively amounted to that of an uncredited coproducer. "Todd didn't come in a whole lot," he has said, "but we managed to get the record done."

According to Joe Perry, Columbia insisted that Bob Ezrin, flush from his success with Alice Cooper, produce Aerosmith's second album. Ezrin didn't feel the band were quite there yet, but thought it'd be a great project for Douglas, with whom he worked on the 1973 Cooper albums *Billion Dollar Babies* and *Muscle of Love* and who had been made a member of Nimbus 9, Ezrin and Jack Richardson's production group. Douglas had had a busy 1973, also teaming up with engineer Jay Messina for the debut album by the New England band BUX, which featured singer Ralph Morman, who six years later would become the first frontman for the Joe Perry Project. BUX were signed to Frank Connelly, Aerosmith's original manager, and broke up soon after completing the LP, which Capitol released in 1976 to piggyback off bassist Mickie Jones and guitarist Punky Meadows's latest endeavor, Angel. A sort of divine anti-KISS, Angel were discovered by Gene Simmons and signed to Casablanca and blessed with an ingenious logo that read the same upside down. One of Douglas's former bandmates in Privilege, guitarist-singer Eddie Leonetti, would go on to a producing career of his own, working with Angel, as well as the Leber-Krebs bands Artful Dodger and Rex.

Perry recalled Ezrin showing up "three or four times, but only to make suggestions." Douglas, who shared producer credit with Ray Colcord—the Columbia A&R executive instrumental in their signing, who was there to watch the clock—connected with the band through their mutual love of the Yardbirds. In Douglas, they saw a peer, not a suit, and someone who could keep up with them. "He wasn't like one of those record-label jerks," Perry said. "Instead, he was someone you could laugh with."

"He knew how to get the best out of the band," says Steve Leber, "and he put up with a lot of their shit. If they were doing coke, he was doing coke—whatever he had to do to get the music made."

On *Get Your Wings*, the fruit of this first collaboration, Aerosmith proved themselves to be contenders. In particular, Tyler, who admitted to altering his vocals on the debut so he'd sound like a bluesman, finally found his true voice—that of a wired and wiry slangy satyr. On the opener "Same Old Song and Dance," amid the martial beat, braying sax solo, and tangled guitar interplay, that new language introduced to the world the words "moidah" and "hoidy goidy." On the snakily seductive pimps-and-hookers tableau "Lord of the Thighs," whose intro beat would later mutate into "Walk This Way," the band demonstrated their mastery of slinky, draggy-bellbottomed hard rock. The subsequent tour found Aerosmith playing with two bands with whom they would forever be associated—as Tyler put it, "KISS at the beginning of their career, and the Dolls at the end of theirs."

Brad Elvis, a drummer who would go on to play with the Elvis Brothers (who shared management with Cheap Trick) and later the Romantics, was in a Peoria, Illinois–based cover band called the Jetz in 1974 when he bought *Get Your Wings* and urged his bandmates to learn "Train Kept A Rollin'" and "Pandora's Box" to complement the "Bowie and all the other crap we were doing," he says. When Aerosmith came to play Illinois State University in nearby Normal on July 25, 1974, the Jetz positioned themselves right in front of the stage, close to Tyler's scarves-draped mic stand and Perry's pedal board. The guitarist strutted around in mirrored aviator shades and beat-up Beatle boots, Elvis recalls, "like he had had them for years and slept in them and puked on them."

After the show, the Jetz were hanging outside the venue, where they spotted Tyler. "Hey, what a good show," Elvis recalls saying. "Tyler's voice was kind of blown out. It's raspy anyway, but he probably sang better than he could talk. He said, 'What's your band name? The Jetz? That's cool.' We said, 'Yeah, we do some of your songs.' '*What*—you play some of our songs? What songs do you do? *Wow!* Hey, you guys, come here. These guys play some of our songs.' He was super-excited. And the rest of the band came over. '*What*—you play our songs?'

"We were probably the first band anywhere to play Aerosmith songs," Elvis continues. "They were wide-eyed. They were just like youngsters."

## CHAPTER 3

# HOTTER THAN HELL

IF KISS WERE A KIND of ghoulish Eliza Doolittle, the uncouth commoner with loads of potential, then Sean Delaney could be considered their Henry Higgins. Delaney was an intense singer-songwriter from Arizona, by way of Utah and New Jersey, who had played with the 101st Airborne Division Band and knocked around New York City in various groups of little consequence and even less renown. He was also Bill Aucoin's live-in lover and the person charged with developing KISS's decidedly primitive act. He would put the lugs through their paces in a dank, rat-infested cellar at 257 Church Street in lower Manhattan, a space that doubled as the aptly named Basement, an Off-Off-Broadway theater managed by Zecca Esquibel, a young Brazil-born, Washington, D.C.–raised musician then known as Joe.

As a gay man taking advantage of the robust New York scene of the early '70s, Esquibel frequented Ty's, a West Village saloon presided over by bartender and playwright Doric Wilson. One day, Wilson announced there was someone Esquibel just had to meet. "You're so much like this other guy," Wilson told him. "Either you'll hate each other instantly or you'll become inseparable."

The bartender's second instinct was correct. Esquibel and Sean Delaney became infamous conjoined twins, drinking and drugging with abandon, two aggressively prankish spirits up for seemingly anything. "We would walk into the bar," Esquibel recalls, "and people would go, 'Batten down the hatches.'" It wasn't unusual for the buddies to stroll down Christopher Street to the pier across the West Side Highway to get side-by-side blow jobs while tripping on acid. If there was anything new and wild going down, these two just had to experience it, but the opening of the Anvil, a gay BDSM sex club in Chelsea, tested their mettle. "There was a floor show with a lot of blood," Esquibel recalls. "One of us looked at the other and said, 'Well, I guess we did it.' And the other one said, 'Yeah, I think we did.'" They turned around and split, having finally recognized their limit.

In 1973, Wilson shared with the pair his idea to create the first openly gay theater company in the U.S. The Other Side of Silence (TOSOS) would be a haven for new writers to freely explore the homosexual experience while controlling the presentation of their work. Delaney wasn't unfamiliar with the theater scene; he'd been acting in experimental plays since the late '60s and claimed he worked briefly as an assistant to playwrights Tennessee Williams and James Leo Herlihy.

He found a subterranean loft in the Tribeca neighborhood in September for the purposes of band rehearsals, plays, and parties—and as a living space for Esquibel. They built a stage and installed a hot water heater. On nights when KISS didn't practice, TOSOS held planning meetings and put together *Lovers*, a groundbreaking musical revue Esquibel describes as "a refutation of *Boys in the Band*. It was the first to show gay men as having normal healthy lives and not being self-loathing." He played one half of a leather couple, a role he landed when Delaney, who was initially cast in the part, got too busy with KISS. (David Fernandez, who played Esquibel's partner, would later shorten his surname to Andez and figure prominently in another of Delaney's musical endeavors.)

Bill Aucoin's background in television meant that KISS always had access to video equipment, which the band used to their advantage, shooting, then reviewing rehearsals to determine what was and wasn't working. "Initially we resisted," Simmons wrote. "But it was eye-opening. We actually saw ourselves and thought, *Wow. We look cool.*"

According to Binky Philips, who hung around the band a lot in the early days, Delaney had a very heavy hand in their development. "A lot of shit that's just pure, traditional KISS started with Sean," he says. "I remember Paul being derisive about the choreography. A lot of the stuff Sean rammed down their throats, they're very glad he did now. I don't think anyone in that band wanted to go as far as Sean did: They wanted to put on the makeup and be a rock band." Delaney took them to S&M shops to buy studded collars and chains, helped refine their stage moves, and made each member amplify his character. If Paul's scalp started to itch while he played, then *goddammit* he was going to run his fingers through his mane and shake it out like a rock god. If Simmons was going to call himself the Demon, then he'd better lift his knees and stomp around the stage like one. "You can hit a guitar string so your hand only goes a foot and a half in the air, and no one sees it," Delaney said, "or you can throw your entire arm straight up into the air, making a grand gesture. I taught them how to make grand gestures." He also taught the three guitarists to line up and sway in unison, a move since replicated by countless bands.

"Sean saw the big picture," says Carol Kaye, a former publicist at the Press Office, Aucoin's PR shop. "He was able to transform a little performance into a grandiose one."

Throughout his time with the band, Esquibel got the full measure of their personalities. "Gene was very gregarious and a delight to be around," he says. "Paul was a little full of himself; he wears the star on his eye for a reason. Peter deferred to them a lot, and Ace was on Jupiter. I could never have a full conversation with him." When the band left after a few months, so too did half of Esquibel's income. Eventually, *Lovers*, the Basement's literal underground sensation, became an Off-Broadway success without him. When money was tight, he would work as a messenger for Aucoin. He would later go on to play keyboards for New York City punk diva Cherry Vanilla, acing an audition arranged for him by Delaney, as well as for the early-'80s new-wave pop duo Get Wet, who were signed by Joyce Bogart to Boardwalk Records, her and Neil's post-Casablanca label.

. . . .

FOR A HEAVY ROCK RECORD released in February 1974—one month before Aerosmith's *Get Your Wings* and Grand Funk Railroad's *Shinin' On*—*KISS* is a bone-dry, oddly stripped-down affair, closer to boogie than to metal. Modest sonics notwithstanding, the songs are tough and rhythmic, with memorable riffs, solos, and choruses—not to mention lyrics that set a pretty (ugly) low bar. In one song Simmons tries to pressure his lady into trying anal sex and succeeds. (Unnaturally, this one, titled "Nothin' to Lose," was chosen as the first single.) Another track, which suggests that imbibing cold gin will enhance intimacy, has the added bonus of being written by a drunk and sung by someone who claims to have never touched alcohol. Simmons and Stanley trade vocals on "Let Me Know," an amiable reworking of Wicked Lester's "Sunday Driver." Even the garage-band-style cover of '50s teen idol Bobby Rydell's "Kissin' Time," recorded at Neil Bogart's insistence as a single and tacked on to a July repressing of the album, feels perfectly of a piece, despite its blatantly hucksterish origin. And as if to show how funny KISS could be (all right, maybe not funny ha-ha, but funny peculiar), they named a sinuously grooved (all right, kind of porny) jazz-funk instrumental "Love Theme from KISS," even though it was obviously written as a soundtrack to fucking. The presumably unintended punch line: it clocks in at 2:24, the shortest song on the LP.

Finally, with an album under their studded belts, the band set their sights beyond New York, venturing to Canada, Los Angeles (for a lavish coming-out party thrown by Casablanca at the Century Plaza Hotel), and other cities, opening for such incongruous acts as the proggy Argent and Renaissance and the bluesy Rory Gallagher and Savoy Brown, as well as more congruous ones, like the New York Dolls and Aerosmith.

Not only did KISS perform as if they were the headliner when they were merely a support act, but they also traveled with a production to match their colossal sense of self, an idea that wasn't exactly embraced by their contemporaries, who'd constantly push back on some of the band's extraordinary demands. This, coupled with the common practice of headliners limiting the support acts' volume and/or stage space, often led to confrontations between road crews. "It was a struggle," says early KISS sound engineer Jay "Hot Sam" Barth, who later did a number of tours with Cheap Trick. "It was like, 'You're gonna put all that shit in front of our shit? You want bombs and fire? We don't have any bombs and fire.' You had to fight for what you got a lot of times."

When KISS opened for Dutch rockers Golden Earring in New Jersey in 1974, Sean Delaney had heard a rumor that the headliner's crew intended to unplug KISS while they played. "The Delaneys are Irish and we had a mean-ass father who taught us well, so we were waiting for them," says Sean's brother Leon Delaney, who roadied for KISS in the early years. "We were punching and kicking the shit out of them, and Gene, onstage, looked around the amps and saw the fight. Needless to say, they weren't unplugged."

On Saturday, March 23, 1974, KISS supported Argent and Redbone at New York's Academy of Music on Fourteenth Street. When the next evening's show with Argent in Washington, D.C., got canceled, KISS managed to secure a slot opening for Aerosmith, whose Get Your Wings had just been released, at the Painter's Mill Music Fair in Owings Mills, Maryland, a 2,500-capacity theater in the round, twenty miles northwest of Baltimore.

Joe Perry, who has alternately, and mistakenly, placed this gig at either a dinner theater or a parking lot in Marion, Ohio—where KISS have never played—saw KISS's set and was stunned by the audience's response. "People went nuts because it's impossible not to when some guy is breathing fire," he recalled. "It wasn't about the music at all." After Aerosmith finished their set and left the stage to modest applause, the guitarist became enraged. "We're busting our asses trying to write great songs and play them right," he fumed. Was his band now going to have to dress up like clowns to get a reaction? He was also envious of the fact that, despite having a pair of fuckups in their ranks, as a group KISS appeared to be able to hold things together. "They'd have their pyro and smoke and then we'd come out," Perry said, "five drunk guys arguing between songs about what to play next."

Tom Hamilton, likewise, wasn't keen on having to follow that spectacle. "It felt like we were going out with our pants down," the bassist has said. "The impact of what KISS was doing was undeniable, even though I felt it was kind of corny. We had a rivalry from then on."

Whatever animosity may have been shooting off of Aerosmith was not felt by KISS. "I thought their vibe live was terrific, and they wore their influences well," Paul Stanley says. "It was very comfortable for them. They were much better than their first album." Stanley did, however, see the other contenders for America's hard-rock throne as competition. "That's the nature of the beast," he says. "It doesn't make necessarily for uncomfortable rivalry, but you ultimately are rooting for your team. We tried to be friends with every band because we were fans of a lot of the bands. But we drew the line when we went up the steps to the stage. That's when we were there to kick ass and knock everyone else out. That was not personal. That was about guardianship of the mantle." And KISS had foot soldiers ready to die, figuratively or otherwise, defending the band's honor.

On this tour, KISS brought with them a drum riser comprised of a platform and a motorized forklift-like contraption framed by seven-foot-high, half-inch-thick steel, which, when it worked, and it sometimes didn't, lifted Peter Criss some six feet above the stage. But no way was Aerosmith's tour manager, Bob "Kelly" Kelleher, going to allow KISS to use it and show up the headliner. And no way was KISS tour manager Sean Delaney going to take no for an answer. "I got into several shoving matches with Aerosmith's guys over being told that we couldn't use Peter's riser," Delaney said. "They wanted him to set up on the floor, which we never did."

"We had a fight" is how Kelleher characterizes the altercation in Maryland. "We had a knock-down, drag-out brawl." And from his perspective, the fight was hardly fair. The KISS crew, he says, were "a bunch of New York goons with black T-shirts, leather wristbands, and knives, though

I'm not sure knives were actually pulled." According to Kelleher, Delaney ("a gravel-voiced, abrasive New York asshole") cold-cocked Aerosmith crew member Nick Spiegel, setting off the melee: "It was like, 'Okay. We'll deal with this.'" Perry shared Kelleher's estimation of KISS's road crew. "They had a cutthroat scene going," he said of the band. "They were good people surrounded by shit."

Peter "Moose" Oreckinto, the KISS roadie in charge of operating the drum riser, doesn't recall ever having to shut it down. "It'd shut itself down," he says of the temperamental device. "We didn't know what was going to break on that thing, and we didn't have the parts—bearings, pulleys, any of that junk—that thing needed."

Reflecting on the period years later, Brad Whitford admitted that he felt KISS had an unfair advantage, but also that "they were playing my favorite kind of music, which is guitar hard rock, really simple. It was a really powerful show."

"KISS was in the same place as us," Perry has said. "I always looked at it as us having a friendly competition." Tyler, however, did not agree with this perspective. From that show on, the Aerosmith frontman saw KISS as nothing less than an existential threat. "I remember when we went out with KISS in '76 or something," Tyler later said, off by a couple of years, "one of our roadies got into a knife fight with their guys. So, I hated them ever since."

When Casablanca executive Larry Harris worked his industry contacts to land KISS on the bill of a promotional concert for Detroit radio station WABX two weeks later, again opening for Aerosmith, tensions between the crews had hardly abated. The city, home to a proudly, defiantly blue-collar scene—rich with homegrown heroes like Mitch Ryder and the Detroit Wheels, the MC5, the Stooges, Bob Seger, Ted Nugent, and Grand Funk Railroad from nearby Flint—was for greenhorns like KISS and Aerosmith crucial Midwest ground they needed to conquer.

One story goes that Harris wanted to persuade deejay Mark Parenteau, a Boston buddy of Aerosmith's, to start playing KISS on the station. Parenteau had seen the band perform at the Casablanca launch party in L.A. and walked away knocked out by the show but disliking the music. Harris told him the label would pay the production cost for a KISS radio concert and WABX could book the other bands. If the audience responded favorably to KISS, he stipulated, Parenteau had to agree to put their debut album in heavy rotation.

The April 7 concert, which also featured the Mojo Boogie Band from neighboring Ann Arbor and Michael Fennelly, formerly of two underrated bands that sounded nothing alike—the Millennium and Crabby Appleton—was supposed to close out the sixth annual WABX Kite-In and Balloon Fly, a daylong event to benefit the cleanup of Belle Isle, an island park located between Detroit and Windsor, Ontario. Rain and temperatures in the low forties put a damper on the afternoon's outdoor activities, but not the concert, which was held later that evening at the Michigan Palace, five miles to the west. Aerosmith were familiar with the grand former movie theater, having opened for the New York Dolls' Detroit debut there seven months earlier.

WABX, 99.5 on the FM dial, was, in 1974, one of the most influential freeform radio stations in America. Freeform, by design a sort of anti-format, relied on the personality and taste of deejays as opposed to the commercial considerations of a program director. It was a haven for adventurous disc jockeys who, if the mood struck them, could segue from the Rolling Stones into Benny Goodman into the Last Poets into Tim Buckley into Ken Nordine word jazz. "We survived on the premise that we would play what we wanted when we wanted," former deejay Ken Calvert says, "and we would base it on nothing other than the integrity of the artist, the air staff, and the content."

"We were *the* guys in town," says Dan Carlisle, one of the station's founding deejays, "so for us to sponsor a show for you, it put you on the map with people who bought records." For the headliner, it was a different story. "Aerosmith were repaying favors," he says. "At one time playing Aerosmith wasn't making us any friends. And we did for at least a year or two before they broke nationally."

The night before the show, Kelleher was called into a meeting with some of the WABX jocks. Walking in with two crew members, he was surprised to find ten people, including Larry Harris, waiting for him. He immediately thought, *I'm being ambushed.* Harris made it clear he wanted KISS to have access to whatever lights and sound they required. Kelleher agreed to the request, but the next day at the theater, he dropped a metaphoric sandbag, prohibiting KISS's crew from using Aerosmith's upstage, or rear, lighting. "They bitched and moaned," he says. "But we put our backdrop on the rear lighting truss and raised it like the American flag during the first song. It was our special effect."

His move incensed the Casablanca executive. "If you don't work this out," Harris told Kelleher, "you'll never get another record played in the country." Kelleher called David Krebs from the lobby to communicate the threat. "What should I do?" he asked the band's comanager. Having gotten the response he expected, Kelleher relayed the message to Harris: "Larry, with all due respect, David Krebs says, 'Go fuck yourself.'"

Being part of a road crew in the '70s typically involved all manner of strategic brinksmanship. "When Aerosmith opened for Mott the Hoople, they didn't get backlighting either," Kelleher says. "It's part of the game." To achieve his goals, he applied skills he learned playing hockey in Boston: "You don't slash back at the opponent when he hits you. You wait till you get him in the corner, when the referee's not looking, and you drop him. That was my logic. 'You can use the lights: There's some on the left, there's some on the right. That's it.'"

In his recollection, KISS crew member Oreckinto says the big issue involved the amount of space Aerosmith were allotting KISS on the stage. "Aerosmith wouldn't move their amp line back so we could set up, so buck knives came out," he says. "Not that we would ever hurt anybody."

Paul Stanley was proud of how his loyal crew protected KISS's territory but places the knife fight in Maryland. "It's not uncommon, to this day and certainly back then, for the headliner to handicap or sabotage the other acts," he says. "I've always believed that if you need to tie someone's hand behind their back to beat them in the ring, then you should be in the gym more." Stanley remembers Aerosmith's amps being moved so far downstage in Maryland, KISS were left with virtually no room to perform, "except to basically walk like crabs sideways." The band and their roadies weren't going to stand for it since there was more room to be had. "So, when push came to shove, push came to shove," says Stanley. "I certainly don't condone it, but when things escalated a bit, our crew made it clear that Aerosmith's gear was going to be moved back to make way for us to have a fair and fighting chance."

"KISS wanted to dominate the stage," says Steve Leber. "It was much easier to work with AC/DC, who also blew Aerosmith off the stage. KISS was a show, Aerosmith wasn't. It was something new and different. We should have said, 'If you want to open for Aerosmith, we want half the management.' We should have made Bill Aucoin give us a piece."

Michael Fennelly, who was promoting his debut solo album, Lane Changer, recalls that he also fell victim to a band's technical demands at Michigan Palace, but they weren't Aerosmith's. That afternoon, he and his group found themselves sitting in the auditorium waiting to do their soundcheck. And then waiting some more. And then some more. It was a soundcheck they never got to do because of KISS. "We watched their rehearsal and they weren't in all their regalia," he says. "They were just guys running through some songs. We were surprised at how terrible they were, that they were playing out of tune." After KISS were done, their difficulties extended to a piece of malfunctioning gear, which their roadies attempted to repair right in the center of the stage. "Not carrying it off and working on it," says Fennelly. "They just set it in front of the drum kit. We thought that was pretty fucking rude."

While all of this drama played out backstage and onstage, outside had the makings of a disaster movie. Steve Glantz, who routinely booked rock acts at the Michigan Palace, was the nominal promoter of the show, but since it was a station-sponsored affair, the WABX staff had been drafted to coordinate the event on the ground. "We were perhaps the worst people in the world to run a concert, because we don't like alienating people," Dan Carlisle says. "We may ask you to not do something, and if you continue to do it, what are we going to do about it?"

The trouble began when dozens of kids who had come early to take refuge from the lousy weather pushed forcefully against one of the theater's glass doors, smashing it. The organizers opened up another entrance to alleviate the strain and prevent injuries, and in the process allowed some three hundred kids to rush the venue. "A bunch of them were sitting in the fucking theater while the rehearsals were going on," Carlisle says. "Right away, we weren't in control of the situation."

The role of de facto stage manager fell to this station veteran. "I would say to the two hundred people that were wandering backstage, 'Please don't go back there. We're trying to set this thing up,'" he says. "It was a free-for-all. We were lucky nobody was killed." As for Larry Harris and Mark Parenteau's purported deal, "that's bullshit," Carlisle says. "We were already playing KISS. Harris wanted the band to be seen, and this was a good way to achieve that."

KISS's and Aerosmith's sets, which were simulcast on the station, and now can be heard on the internet and via bootlegs, reveal two young bands just hitting their strides yet fully in command of their craft. Tyler oozes sexy menace with his feral yowling, at one point telling the crowd, "If you keep touching me, I'm gonna shock off your balls." Donald Handy was a sixteen-year-old high school student when he dropped acid before attending the concert. "Near the end," he says, "someone announced that the next song would be their last, to which I shouted something like, 'No, it's not!' I then felt everyone turn around and stare at me, along with the band members. They did come back out for one more encore."

While this would be the last time the two bands played together for nearly thirty years, sound mixer "Nitebob" Czaykowski recalls KISS members attending an Aerosmith show in the '70s as observers. "KISS were playing two nights before," he says. "I'm sure they wanted to see them because when you're on tour, you don't see the other guys' show. They were like runners in a race, and KISS were a little behind until their fourth record."

KISS returned to Michigan Palace a week after they played with Aerosmith, to open two sold-out shows headlined by Blue Öyster Cult. And while KISS would release two records, *Hotter Than Hell* and *Dressed to Kill*, within a year, in the battle between the rock behemoths, Aerosmith ultimately prevailed when their third album, 1975's *Toys in the Attic*, spawned the Top 10 hit "Walk This Way" and eventually sold eight million copies. But the bat-winged freaks remained close behind, nipping at their Cuban heels. Soon, Detroit would be theirs.

. . . .

**BEFORE SHE BECAME THE** bassist for the Runaways, Jackie Fox attended the taping of KISS's performance on NBC's *Midnight Special* in Los Angeles in 1975. She barged into their dressing room and introduced herself since she wanted to be in a band so badly and had no idea how to go about starting one. "Because," she says, "that was something girls did not do." She discovered KISS and instantly became a fan when a school friend showed her the cover of their debut album. After taking the record home and giving it a listen, she had an epiphany: *I can play this!* That to her was a big part of KISS's appeal. "As a teenage musician without a whole lot of training, they made me want to get up and rock," she says. "But they also made me think that I could do that. Then I saw them, and they're still the most dynamic live act I've ever seen."

For Fox the crudeness of their words never mattered. "The songs were nonsensical. 'Get up and get your grandma outta here.' What the fuck does that mean?" she says. "You weren't listening to the lyrics, you were just listening to the rhythm. You were getting into Paul and Gene doing that back-and-forth rocking thing. You were watching somebody walk around in gigantic heels. It's hard to believe now, but there was something dark and menacing about them that was really cool. I never really thought about gender.

"It wasn't like the Rolling Stones," she continues. "You listened to the Stones, you thought about gender. You heard 'Under My Thumb'— 'the squirmin' dog who's just had her day'—*that* made you feel icky."

Back then, when they'd go to L.A., Simmons and Stanley would hit the Starwood, a club where bands played live on one side while a discotheque pumped out rock on the other. "They used to come in all the time, no makeup," Fox says. "But you knew it was them, because they were wearing KISS jackets. It was, *I don't want to be recognized, but I do want to be recognized.*"

One night, she and a friend approached Stanley, who was standing at the edge of the dance floor watching others move. Led Zeppelin's "Trampled Under Foot" boomed from the speakers and the girls asked him to come down and dance. "He looked at us and said, 'I want to dance with you, but not to this,'" Fox says. "Then we went, 'Okay,' and started dancing. It wasn't something that you would think of as a great dance song, but still . . ."

She can even pinpoint the time frame: it was spring 1975, because that same night at the Starwood, influential radio deejay and scenester Rodney Bingenheimer came up to her and asked if she played an instrument. When she said yes, he introduced her to Kim Fowley, a producer who was putting together a rock band made up of teen girls. When she went to audition to play lead guitar with drummer Sandy West and guitarist Joan Jett, the only song all three knew was KISS's "Strutter." They failed to click, but when Fox returned to try out on bass, she got the gig. Each of the five girls in the band adopted the persona of their idols: if Jett modeled herself on Suzi Quatro and Cherie Currie on David Bowie, then Fox was Gene Simmons.

## CHAPTER 4

# ROCK THIS TOWN

FIFTH GRADER JEFF GROB began playing drums—actually a single, solitary blue-and-silver-lacquer Slingerland snare—in his elementary school's marching band in Orange, New Jersey. It wasn't until his family moved to Chicago that he took it upon himself to MacGyver his first full kit with the addition of a thirteen-inch cymbal, a bunch of empty packing boxes, a set of bongos, and some wood, leather, and string. Sensing his son's passion, but still not convinced of his dedication, Grob's father rented him a three-piece set of white pearl Ludwigs. When the contract was up three months later, not only had Grob earned enough money to buy them, he also purchased a floor tom.

From the start, Grob idolized Gene Krupa, whose dexterous and wildly inventive playing was matched only by his showmanship. When he was thirteen, Grob had his dad take him to Chicago's London House jazz club to see the drummer's trio. "Krupa looked like he just rolled out of bed," Grob says. "I'm sitting right in front, and I'm just staring at him." After the set, his dad approached Krupa to ask if he'd swing by their table. A few minutes later, the drummer appeared holding a cocktail and sat down. "I introduce myself and tell him I'm a huge fan," Grob says. "He says, 'You play the drums?' I go, 'Oh yeah!' He says, 'Let me give you a tip.' And I'm thinking, *Here it comes, man! He's gonna give me the key!* He says, 'Whatever you do, stay in school. Get that high school diploma.' I said, 'Yeah?' thinking, *What else you got?*"

In 1965, the high school sophomore moved to Janesville, Wisconsin, and within two weeks joined a working band. Called the Denims, they were booked by Ken Adamany, a local agent who had played keyboards in a group with Steve Miller and Boz Scaggs. Adamany's stable included more than eighty combos sporting names like the Van-Tels, the Esquires, the Canterbury Tayles, and Peter Risch & the Chevrons ("featuring the world's smallest drummer," boasted one of his brochures). Another of his bands, the Rockford, Illinois–based Boll Weevils, featured a guitarist named Tom Peterson, who in 1967 would join a band called the Grim Reapers with guitarist-keyboardist Rick Nielsen. Grob was fifteen, playing five sets of rock and R&B covers every night—forty-five minutes on, fifteen off, 9 p.m. to 1 a.m.—for drunks in crummy beer bars, a far cry from the VFW halls and high school gyms he fed to his father.

After the family moved back to Jersey in Grob's senior year, his psychology teacher, a recent graduate of Rutgers University, mentioned that he knew of a band looking for a drummer. Interested, Grob threw his gear into his dad's Cadillac and drove down to New Brunswick, to a tenement next door to a whorehouse, dragged his kit up five flights, met a guitarist and bassist, and ended up jamming like Cream for two hours.

· · · ·

LOOKING GLASS WERE A BUNCH of college kids covering Hendrix, the Stones, and the Rascals at frat parties and school dances when bassist Pieter Sweval decided to leave and form Tracks with Grob, guitarist Marc Tauber, and singer–harmonica player Skip Roberts. The rest of Looking Glass preferred making real money playing Top 40 covers in local lounges. In the summer of 1969, the year after Grob graduated high school, Tracks played clubs on the Jersey Shore nearly every week, sometimes on bills with Child, which featured a hot-shit frontman named Bruce Springsteen. It wasn't long before Looking Glass guitarist Elliot Lurie and keyboardist Larry Gonsky tired of the grind and hooked up with Sweval and Grob, who was now attending college.

Once Sweval, Gonsky, and Lurie graduated and felt they had become popular enough locally that they should shoot for a record deal, they rented an old stone farmhouse on more than eighty acres in the woods of Glen Gardner, New Jersey, near the Pennsylvania border. Splitting the $220 monthly rent, the three stayed in upstairs bedrooms and wrote and practiced in the downstairs living room. Inspired by shaggy coed collectives like Delaney & Bonnie and Joe Cocker's *Mad Dogs & Englishmen* crew, they even toyed with putting a couple of female vocalists up front. "We must have auditioned fifty chicks," Grob says. "Some of them were good. Some of them were so horrible. But then we realized: all chicks are nuts!"

It was decided instead that Lurie and Sweval would split lead vocals, much the way they did in the band's earlier incarnation. "It served us well as a cover band because it gave us more range," says Lurie. "There were certain things that were very suitable for Pieter and things that were more suitable for me." They had begun calling themselves Home Brew until Gonsky suggested they revert to the already established Looking Glass so they could get more work. On the weekends, sometimes even during the week, whenever the gigs would come, they'd load up Grob's van, drive to a venue, then return to cut demos in the dining room and enjoy the creative solitude. It was a charmed existence, to be sure, a hippie idyll of bucolic and urban balance.

This woodshedding went on for nearly a year before the band met Mike Gershman, a press agent who had worked with the Doors and Jefferson Airplane and was looking to move into management. Using his connections, Gershman got them a slot supporting Ten Years After and Edgar Winter's White Trash at Gaelic Park in the Bronx on August 6, 1971, a show swarming with representatives from CBS Records, the headliners' corporate bosses. After Looking Glass's set, the band were asked if they'd mind setting up a gig so that Clive Davis, president of CBS's Columbia label, could check them out. The following week they were opening in Greenwich Village for Buddy Guy and Junior Wells, whose pure, unruly blues seemed an unlikely fit for these four skinny freaks. "Anyway," says Grob, "we play, Clive comes backstage—I'm schvitzing all over his Guccis—and he says, 'I like you guys. I wanna sign you.'"

Davis, who placed them on Epic, his label for baby bands, sent Looking Glass to Memphis to cut four songs—including "Brandy (You're a Fine Girl)," a Lurie tune that he loved—with Steve Cropper, who had played guitar for funky-soul instrumentalists and Stax house band Booker T. and the MG's in the '60s. But the resulting recordings were deemed not quite right. "Too much of a Memphis groove," Grob figures. A session with Sandy Linzer yielded better results, until the old-school pop producer decided to add some sweetening to "Brandy" on his own. Grob recalls entering Olmstead Studios in Midtown Manhattan for the playback: "We sit on the couch, he hits PLAY, and all of a sudden you hear the sounds of the sea—*whoosh*—and seagulls—*caw-caw-caw*—and then the track starts. We're going, 'What the fuck is that?' '*It's a hit, it's a hit!*' We're going, 'We don't *think* so.'"

However schlocky the embellishment, the band were happy with their performance, so they took the sixteen-track recording over to another studio, Regent Sound on Fifty-Seventh Street, and with the help of engineer

Bob Liftin stripped it down and built up "Brandy" the way they had always envisioned. They ended up recording three more Lurie tunes and four by Sweval. After completing the album with Liftin, they were particularly enamored of Lurie's "Don't It Make You Feel Good," with its boogie-woogie piano, playful horns, and shouty female backing vocals best capturing the coveted Delaney & Bonnie vibe. They insisted Epic release it as the first single—because, Sweval said, "it made us dance in the studio"—and were disappointed when it immediately stiffed. But when a Washington, D.C., deejay began playing "Brandy," a song the band were already sick of, their fortunes changed. Soon, the track, a luscious soft-rock tribute to a foxy bartender, became inescapable and the band's first and only No. 1 hit.

A second Looking Glass album, *Subway Serenade*, was released shortly after Columbia fired Davis in May 1973. The executive had been implicated in a payola scandal and accused of misappropriating nearly $94,000 in company funds to pay for, among other things, his son's lavish bar mitzvah. (Though he was not charged with any crime at the time, Davis pleaded guilty three years later to evading taxes from 1972.)

Looking Glass worked hard to push the albums, headlining clubs and opening for bigger acts like Steely Dan, Jeff Beck, and, strangely enough, Alice Cooper. "At that time, he had the show where he cut off his head with a guillotine," says Lurie, "and the people who came to see him do that were not in the mood for 'Brandy.'"

It was while they were wrapping up *Subway Serenade*—which delivered another Top 40 hit, Lurie's "Jimmy Loves Mary-Anne"—that the singer dropped a bomb. He convened a band meeting in Central Park, not far from his apartment on Manhattan's Upper West Side. "'It appears that the public is gravitating more towards the stuff that I write and sing,'" Grob—who was by then calling himself Joe X. Dubé, in tribute to a champion weight lifter—remembers him saying. "'I think what we ought to do is call ourselves Elliot Lurie and Looking Glass, or I might have to go solo.' And me, Pieter, and Larry looked at each other and went, 'Good luck! Let us know if we can help!'"

Lurie contends that clearly what the audience and label expected from the group was the sound of "Brandy" and "Jimmy Loves Mary-Anne," which meant *his* lead vocals and a more polished pop direction. Having two singers—Sweval a tenor and Lurie a baritone—may have been an asset for a cover band, but once they started recording, a certain schizophrenia came to the fore with Sweval's laid-back, countrified songs chafing against Lurie's own soulful, atmospheric tracks. "We were at least two sounds in one—maybe more," Lurie says. "There was no way that I or Pieter could see his style becoming what Looking Glass was at that point. So that was what caused the breakup."

It made a lot of sense to Gonsky. "Elliot was a lot slicker and probably a lot more commercially savvy than we were," he says. "We just wanted to be artists, and he was smarter." To ease the transition, the group decided to add to their ranks. Brendan Harkin was a folkie from Westchester County, New York, who had spent a few years at the turn of the '70s working for Elektra Records in L.A., transcribing songs by artists like the Doors and Jackson Browne so that they could then be copyrighted. Upon returning to New York, he started Papa Nebo, a terminally mellow jazz-folk septet that eventually morphed into Free Beer, whose appearance in club listings should have all but guaranteed packed houses. After spotting an ad for a band seeking a guitarist, Harkin (who went by the alternate spelling "Brenden" for much of his early career) nailed his audition with Looking Glass and made his first appearance as a member on daytime TV's *The Mike Douglas Show* in November 1973.

Lurie soon saw the writing on the wall and there was a mirrored ball spinning in front of it. After splitting from Looking Glass, but still signed to Epic, he released a self-produced "Brandy"-like single in 1974, followed by an eponymous solo album, whose opening track, "Disco (Where You Gonna Go)," could be seen as a self-explanatory concession to the zeitgeist. Bedecked with sumptuous strings, oh-so-tasteful piano and horn interludes, and of-the-moment wakka-wakka guitars, it proved an appropriately plush vehicle for Lurie's louche Qiana croon. Its failure to chart, however, led to his quick exit from the label.

Undeterred by the loss of Lurie, and faced with bookings that needed to be honored, the remaining Looking Glass members placed an ad in the alternative newspaper the *Village Voice* for a singer-guitarist. Among the applicants was a Southern boy eager to enter the New York scene.

• • • •

MICHAEL LEE SMITH WAS born in Birmingham, Alabama, to an advertising executive father and a psychologist/opera singer stay-at-home mom on October 9, 1951. His father moved the family (which would ultimately include three other boys) to Jacksonville, Florida, then to Chicago when he was promoted to the home office. "That was a life-changing experience for me," Smith says, "because I was a beach kid." He grew up fishing and catching crabs in lagoons but soon discovered snow, basements, and model railroading.

"My whole world turned upside down because I didn't know what any of that stuff was."

In elementary school he realized he had a voice like Frankie Valli's. "I'd sing 'Sherry' at school and the girls would be swooning," he says. "That was my first taste of that kind of appreciation." It wasn't long before the family returned to the South, settling in Greenville, South Carolina. "In later years I asked my father, 'Why did we have to move there of all places?' Then he killed me when he said, 'Well, son, I had two choices: Hawthorne, California, or Greenville.' I'm like, 'Dad, Hawthorne is the home of the Beach Boys. We could have had a woodie and surfed.'"

From Greenville, it was on to Atlanta for Smith's senior year, at North Fulton High School, where he became instantly infamous after performing at a pep rally "Thank You John," Willie Tee's provocative 1965 New Orleans soul single, sung from the perspective of a pimp who soothes his hooker girlfriend as he threatens her abusive client "They were going crazy," Smith recalls of his fellow students. *"How can this guy be singing this song in high school?"*

The appearance led to his joining his first band, and through a mutual acquaintance, doing his first studio session, with local legend Joe South— winner of two Grammys in 1969 for "Games People Play" and writer of such hits as Deep Purple's "Hush" and Lynn Anderson's "Rose Garden"—who taught him everything about mic technique. After a bit of college, Smith arrived in Manhattan in 1972. With $400 and an itch to perform, he enrolled in the Lee Strasberg Theatre Institute, working as a waiter and cab driver to supplement the odd Off-Broadway gig. He met his future wife, Lynda Lee Lawley (aka Linda Lawley), when she was performing on Broadway in *Hair*. "This was a great thing," he says, "because I got to see her naked before I even took her on a date." Lawley, an accomplished singer, had been a member of the psychedelic pop group Eternity's Children, best known for the minor 1968 hit "Mrs. Bluebird," and sang backup on the Lyn Christopher album that also featured Gene Simmons, Paul Stanley, and Peter Criss. Not long after they hooked up, Lawley, working on sessions at Electric Lady, invited Smith over to meet this band there that she described as "insane—you'll just laugh when you see them."

"They're these Jewish guys," she told him, "but they're weird."

"That's how I met Chaim and Stanley—that's how I was introduced to them," Smith says. "I sat in and watched the session. They were guys with a dream and they were driven. They were unique—totally of themselves. They were coming from a completely different place."

Smith had heard from a couple of friends who'd failed to nail the audition that Looking Glass were seeking a frontman. He knew "Brandy," sure, but wasn't exactly a fan. He remembers walking home at night from a temp gig as a telephone solicitor, listening to his little transistor radio, and whenever the song came on, changing the station. "I was like, 'Oh my God, fuck this shit. I can't stand this crap,'" he says. It just wasn't rock and roll enough for this avowed Anglophile, who counted David Bowie, Spooky Tooth, and the Who among his favorites. "It's ironic that I wound up singing in that band," he says. "But it was a great thing. Once I hooked up with them, I was no longer starving."

It was coming on winter 1973 and beginning to get cold, and he had moved up north without proper clothing. While doing a show at the New York Shakespeare Festival, he spotted a swank ultrasuede overcoat lying unclaimed at the theater's lost and found. "Every day I passed it and I finally asked the girl there, 'I see that coat is always here. What's the deal?' 'It's been here like a month, so if it's not claimed in another three or four days, I'll give it to you.'" He finally got a winter coat, but the only shoes he had were clogs. "Nothing to keep my feet warm. And that's what I wore to audition for Looking Glass."

He needn't have worried about his appearance. "He was fucking phenomenal," Dubé says. Harkin, too, was excited by the singer, whose full lips offsetting a chipped-tooth grin gave him the look of a dinged pinup. "I thought, *Man, this guy is like Elvis Presley*," he says. "*We gotta get him in the band.*"

With Smith on board, the group—still signed to Epic and rechristened Lookinglass to distinguish it from the previous incarnation—issued the single "Highway to Hollywood," written by Gonsky, produced by Harkin, and mixed with Phil Ramone. By turns jaunty and sultry, it bears more than a brassy resemblance to Blood, Sweat & Tears and Chicago. Coincidentally, the record appeared with Elliot Lurie's first solo effort, "Your Love Song," in *Billboard*'s Top Single Picks column for July 13, 1974. While Lurie's track hit the Easy Listening Top 40, theirs went nowhere.

But they kept on playing. "We'd leave New York City on a Tuesday or Wednesday morning and usually go to the Midwest or the South," Smith says. "And then it was just bang, bang, bang!" They would play a state fair, then a car show, then a nightclub, then a dinner theater—gig after gig after gig, until they were on a plane Monday morning, flying back home. Their road manager would walk up and down the aisle, handing the guys airsickness bags stuffed with cash.

As far as Smith could tell, audiences never questioned his singing "Brandy." To relieve the tedium of having to perform the hit over and over, Dubé and Smith bought an ape mask they spotted in a shop window. That evening, after Smith left the stage as the band started vamping the opening chords of "Brandy," Sweval stepped up to the mic to announce a special guest. The crowd cheered as a disguised Smith sauntered out holding a drink, cigarette jammed between the rubber lips. "They just wanted to hear the song," Smith says. "They didn't care that the singer was wearing a gorilla mask."

Dubé, however, recalled the club owner being none too pleased. "He had had several complaints from the patrons and he himself had witnessed history as well from the bar," the drummer recounted in an unpublished essay. "He walked on up to Michael Lee and spit right into his unmasked face, 'If I'd wanted jokes, I woulda hired a damn comedian, boy!'"

After a few more months as Lookinglass, the guys collectively thought, *You can't pay us enough to keep doing this.* "We had really moved on to much heavier stuff," says Dubé. With new managers Alan Miller and Peter Glick in tow, the group, now called Fallen Angels, were scouted by Bob Feiden, the A&R director of Arista Records, which Clive Davis, on the rebound after his firing from Columbia, had just founded after taking over, restructuring, and renaming Bell Records. They became one of the label's first signings.

In the November 23, 1974, issues of the industry magazines *Billboard* and *Cash Box*, Arista ran a four-page advertisement announcing its formation and initial roster. Bell holdovers such as Barry Manilow and Suzi Quatro shared a spread with newbies like the Outlaws and the Brecker Brothers. Nowhere to be found: Fallen Angels, who in just a few weeks would be heading to Toronto's Soundstage studio to record an album with producer Jack Richardson, who counted the Guess Who and Alice Cooper among his successes and created the heavy-hitting Nimbus 9 production group.

Arista creative director Bob Heimall recalls visiting the band in the studio with photographer Benno Friedman to shoot the album cover and promotional stills. Since he was the label representative, Heimall felt obliged to treat the group to a nice dinner but didn't anticipate their extravagant tastes. "One band member ordered an eight-hundred-dollar bottle of wine," Heimall says. "I got nervous and said, 'Wow, that's a lot of money.' But I figured, 'It's a corporate card, they're the artists. I'll pretend I'm in A&R or promotion.'" The tab ended up running almost $1,000 ($5,200 in 2020 dollars).

Friedman's photos captured a shaggy band clad in leather and patchwork denim still lacking a cohesive style. Dubé ditched the turban he sported on the *Subway Serenade* cover but kept the Snidely Whiplash mustache. Smith, whose short brown curls framed soulful-puppy eyes, and the only member to be clean-shaven, was clearly positioned as the heartthrob.

Like the two Looking Glass LPs, the Fallen Angels album suffers from an imbalance engendered by two lead vocalists with clashing musical styles, but what a fascinating mishmash it is. Smith in particular sparkles on "The Kid Gets Hot," "Tear It Down," and the nearly seven-minute "Ulysses," on which the band proffer the kind of barrelhouse crocodile rock and epic balladry that Elton John was taking to the top of the charts. "Ride It to the End of the Line" provides a chugging workout for Gonsky's Deep Purplish organ and Harkin's caustic guitar before resolving in a memorable bossa nova piano riff.

Smith supplies lovely harmonies as Sweval takes the lead on "Wasn't Really There at All," a lilting country-rock tune reminiscent of the Eagles. Things take a turn for the deep with "Elouisa," Sweval's other showcase (written with Gonsky). Over a whining guitar and soaring strings, the bassist-singer confesses to the titular woman, "I gotta get it straight to you about the kind of life I lead. . . . But if I want to be a man, it's up to me to be just what I am." What comes off as ambiguous on record was inspired by a profound real-life event. "It's about the time that Pete came out to me," says his sister Kristina Sweval Peters, whose middle name, Louise, he tweaked for the title. As for the opportune time he chose to reveal his true self: "He was teaching me how to shoot craps on the bathroom floor."

The otherwise fairly innocuous—anodyne, even—content is rudely interrupted by the genuinely startling "Madison Avenue Hitler," which opens with newsreel audio of Adolf Hitler speechifying, adds the percussive clomping of goose-stepping Nazis and a scary chorus of *seig heils*, before settling into a smoky cocktail-jazz groove and offering up lyrics like "Make sure you feed the war machine" and "I'd like to pick your carcass clean." "I had written a song in the '70s predicting the Watergate scandal," says Gonsky. "But the band wanted to morph it into something more rock-and-roll violent, so Pieter rewrote some of the words and it became that."

With a full-page ad in *Cash Box* in March, Arista announced Fallen Angels' first single, a cover of "Just Like Romeo and Juliet," a doo-woppy hit for the Reflections that eleven years earlier had reached No. 6. But apparently the label was unaware that concurrently Kama Sutra Records was releasing a new version of the same song by Sha Na Na, a gang of glib fake greasers. While the Fallen Angels rendition bubbled under at No. 106 in

May 1975, Sha Na Na's peaked at No. 55—no big deal, but it nevertheless became the long-running '50s-nostalgia act's most successful single. When Fallen Angels' follow-up 45, "The Kid Gets Hot," failed to chart at all, Arista shelved the completed album and severed its relationship with the group. Some of the band members believe that Clive Davis, a Jew, had been so offended by "Madison Avenue Hitler," which was cowritten by someone also of the faith, that he refused to release the LP. "I guess he didn't listen to the words, which were about Richard Nixon," says Harkin.

When asked about the band forty-four years later, Davis says, "I honestly have no recall of them," explaining that since the group were unknown and at that point dependent on hit singles, it's no surprise the label decided to withhold the album. The speculation that "Madison Avenue Hitler" played a part in that decision is unfounded, he adds, insisting that he fully supported freedom of expression for all the artists on his roster, which would come to include Patti Smith (who would soon be singing about a "Rock N Roll Nigger") and Lou Reed (who had already been singing about junkies and head-giving transsexuals). There was precedent for the band's suspicion, however. Early in his career as a young lawyer at Columbia, Davis had to tell Bob Dylan that the label, fearing a libel suit, wouldn't let him include on *The Freewheelin' Bob Dylan* the satirical "Talkin' John Birch Society Blues," in which the singer likened John Birchers to Fascists.

Still, the fact that the Fallen Angels album went unreleased surprised Arista's Bob Heimall, who during his career designed classic albums for the Stooges, the Doors, and Carly Simon. "That was very rare," he says. "That might have happened maybe three or four times in twenty years of my doing covers."

Though the record remains officially unavailable, back then Harkin was instrumental in getting a few of the songs heard by an audience that would likely not be paying much attention to them. Living in Manhattan, he had become friendly with a guy who worked in the burgeoning porn industry and needed some music for a film. "I said, 'We made this record that never went anyplace. Maybe you could put some of it in there and give us some money,'" Harkin recalls. He managed to smuggle three songs—"The Kid Gets Hot," "Tear It Down," and "Rock This Town" (the B side of Lookinglass's "Highway to Hollywood")—onto the soundtrack of 1976's X-rated *The Divine Obsession*, directed by Lloyd Kaufman, who would go on to Z-movie infamy as cofounder of Troma Entertainment, home of the Toxic Avenger.

# CHAPTER 5

# SO GOOD TO SEE YOU

**HUNTZ HALL LIKED HIS MARIJUANA.**

And on the twenty-eighth of October in 1948, the same year he appeared as the dimwitted, putty-mugged Sach in four movies starring the Bowery Boys, the comic actor was arrested for possession, becoming one of the first Hollywood stars to be so charged. Though he was acquitted, the ensuing notoriety quite possibly endeared him to an unlikely group of allies, the Beatles, who included him in the collage on the cover of *Sgt. Pepper's Lonely Hearts Club Band* (top right, two in from Bob Dylan).

Nearly two months after the bust, on December 22, Richard Alan Nielsen, a man who would rock Sach's bug-eyed and ball-capped look all the way to the Rock and Roll Hall of Fame, was born in Elmhurst, Illinois, a western suburb of Chicago, the only child of Ralph and Marilyn Nielsen, opera singers of some renown who also performed church music. Ralph, a tenor, was also a choral director whose Temple Time Choir sang regularly on the radio. In 1956, the family moved eighty miles northwest to Rockford, a city known for its furniture manufacturing, as the birthplace of the Sock Monkey, and for its large population of fellow Swedes, who had begun migrating there one hundred years earlier. In Rockford, his parents bought a music store, rechristening it the Ralph Nielsen Music House.

"My dad graduated college at sixteen," the younger Nielsen says. "But he wanted to be a singer. And a good Christian. So, in other words, we were broke all the time. I always tell people, 'I'm a musician. I'm supposed to be poor.' It didn't work out that way."

Nielsen didn't have much interest in the liturgical sounds favored by his folks, who became very influential in the local music community. He did, however, enjoy traveling the country to watch them perform. Instruments being always within arm's reach, at age eight he began playing drums. At thirteen he picked up the guitar, out of necessity, he says, after discovering he had perfect pitch, the uncommon ability to identify or reproduce a musical tone without any reference. "We were doing cover songs, so whatever you're playing is close, but it's not right," he says of one early combo. "I had to keep getting off the drums to make my two cents known that this is wrong." After figuring out a problem, he'd show his bandmates what to do, until he tired of teaching them. By 1962, he and his band, the Phaetons, were practicing their twangy surf rock in his family's Spring Creek Road garage.

Nielsen knew from an early age that he wanted to be an entertainer and displayed his talents at school as a class clown. Despite being a first chair in junior high, he was tossed out, barred from entering any music programs for the rest of his public school years, after telling the band director he was a drunken fool who "didn't know how to take the gift of music and do anything to inspire these people to something great.

"I was a seventh-grade kid with a big mouth who told the truth to people in authority that they didn't want to hear," Nielsen continues. "But I was correct." And his parents were horrified.

Owing to various personnel changes, the Phaetons had by 1965 evolved into the Grim Reapers, whose lineup would remain fluid throughout their existence. Eventually they would count among their ranks a bassist named Tom Peterson, who joined the band with guitarist Craig Myers and singer Joe Sundberg. Drummer Chip Greenman had also played with Peterson and Myers in a group called Toast and Jam. Despite his role as bandleader, in this new Grim Reapers lineup Nielsen played organ and rhythm guitar, leaving most of the guitars to the preternaturally gifted Myers.

Ken Adamany was booking bands out of Wisconsin when Nielsen approached him in March 1967 hyping his group. Adamany had dozens of area bands on his roster but saw in the lanky, enterprising teenager something different. He agreed to take on the Grim Reapers, who had been playing gyms, armories, skating rinks, even a Jewish temple, and got them gigs in, among other places, the Factory, his nightclub in a remodeled warehouse at 315 West Gorham Street in Madison. The Grim Reapers practically became the venue's house band, supporting major acts like Wilson Pickett, and were scheduled to open two shows for Otis Redding on Sunday, December 10, 1967. The Grim Reapers' name took on an ironic twist when the soul star, four members of his backing band, the Bar-Kays, and two others were killed en route to the show after their twin-engine Beechcraft plane crashed into icy Lake Monona just a mile away. Despite the tragedy, the Grim Reapers ended up playing one set and Adamany was able to quickly secure the Milwaukee soul act Lee Brown and the Cheaters to complete the show. "The Madison Police Department asked that we stay open that night, fearing the worst," Adamany says. "I had it announced over the radio and outside, where ticket holders were waiting to get in, that the doors would stay open and the performances would be free." Nielsen, recalling the night's audience with some understatement years later, said, "Not everybody was in a great mood."

In 1968, Nielsen and Peterson took a two-week vacation in London to take in some shopping and check out the scene, going to gigs by the Gun, Barclay James Harvest, Jethro Tull, and Family, among others. Upon their return, the Grim Reapers became one of the first bands in the States to add to their arsenal a mellotron—an electronic keyboard favored by the Moody Blues and the Beatles that essentially sampled recorded tape to replicate the sound of orchestras—which Nielsen had shipped over. That same year the Grim Reapers issued a 45 on Adamany's Smack label, a cover of "Hound Dog," the Elvis Presley hit, which begins straightforwardly enough before abruptly switching thirty-six seconds in to a snarling soul update. But it was no innovative arrangement. Nielsen admits that his band essentially copied the version released earlier that year by British psych-poppers Plastic Penny. "But ours didn't sound one-tenth as good," he says. Backed with "Cruisin' for Burgers," a competent, if more generic, blues-rock original, the single sparked the interest of Epic Records, whose representatives caught the band at the Kinetic Playground in Chicago, where the Grim Reapers were opening for British singer Terry Reid, and soon offered a deal.

Epic stipulated that the band, most of whom were still teenagers, needed to change their name, which the label considered too dark. "One suggestion was Thunderclap," Adamany says, "but the band didn't like it." Two others were Man's Nuts and the Fleetwood Turks. They settled on Fuse. Epic rereleased the "Hound Dog" single before putting out their eponymous debut album, produced by Jackie Mills, who had little feel for rock (he'd soon work with such teeny-poppers as Bobby Sherman and the Brady Bunch). The result was nothing-special, psych-inflected Britblooze with a splash of Cream and a hint of Status Quo. Its only distinguishing marks: Nielsen's scorching Hammond organ and otherworldly mellotron and Joe Sundberg's throaty howl, which, although fairly anonymous, defiantly belied his seventeen years. Upon its release in January 1970, the record stiffed. According to Adamany, Mills had convinced the band they didn't need a manager, so they fired him and had two sets of parents take over. Epic, frustrated with the change, stopped working the first album and did not pick up the option for a second. Fuse re-signed with Adamany shortly thereafter.

Speaking to *Trouser Press*'s Ira Robbins in 1977, Nielsen and Petersson (who by then had added an *s* to his surname) had nothing good to say about Fuse. Calling Sundberg "a junior Tom Jones," the bassist summed up the album with one word: "Horrendous." "It's neat that it was out," offered Nielsen, "because it's something to talk about. It's better than saying, 'Gee, I never did anything.' But it stinks."

Fifty-one years after making the record, Nielsen is much less withering. "If it would have done well, maybe I would have thought differently," he says. "But it never really got as far as I wanted to get."

• • • •

**BRAD CARLSON (WHO'D LATER** become known as Bun E. Carlos) was thirteen when his mother bought him a drum kit from Ralph Nielsen's store. Setting them up in his basement where his family also had a jukebox, he'd turn up the volume and play along to the collection of singles.

One day, his older sister Jan came home from school and announced, "This kid's throwing rocks at me."

"My mom said, 'I'll go talk to his dad. He has a music store on Seventh Street,'" Carlos recalls. "So I knew Rick from then on. We all went through junior high school and high school together."

Seeing the Beatles on *The Ed Sullivan Show* in 1964 made a huge impact on him, as well as many of his peers, leading in 1965 to an explosion of bands. All across the country, in towns very much like Rockford, most of them had a garage or basement in which to practice, the kind of real estate not available to many big-city kids. But the preponderance of musicians certainly didn't mean they were all worth hearing. "I knew guys who had drum sets they'd play backwards," Carlos says. "They'd be playing into the snare on the one and three." His own band, the Paegans, put out a single in 1967, a cover of the Beatles' "Good Day Sunshine," backed with a version of Them's "I Can Only Give You Everything," on Rampro, a label owned by Adamany. It received some local airplay, which was a very big deal for a bunch of teenagers.

The Paegans even competed in a few battles of the bands against Nielsen's Grim Reapers.

Carlos ended up playing in the last couple of Fuse lineups, which along with Nielsen and Peterson featured at various times Robert "Stewkey" Antoni and Thom Mooney, late of Todd Rundgren's band the Nazz. Carlos sums up those personnel-packed years thusly: "In the spring of '71, Stewkey and Mooney came to Rockford and replaced Chip and Joe. A few months later Peterson and Mooney left to go to L.A. Rick switched over to bass, Craig was on guitar, Stewkey sang, and I joined on drums. In September the band split up. Then in '72, Rick joined Stewkey in Philly to prepare for a possible Stewkey album. Then Tom joined them that summer. I was working as a roofer for my dad and trying to stay out of the army. I went to Philly with Rick's brother-in-law. That's when I joined [Rick and Tom in] Sick Man of Europe, which lasted from fall of '72 to spring of '73. Then we moved from Philly back to Rockford because Rick's wife was pregnant. Tom, Rick, and Ken decided Stewkey was not quite the right singer, so they fired him. Of course, Stewkey had given up his apartment in Philly to come here. So Stewkey decided to leave and Tom said, 'I hate it here too.' He went with Stewkey. Rick and I had gigs booked for, like, three weeks, so I knew some singers, called Robin Zander, but he had a gig up at the Dells [a resort area in southern Wisconsin] for another couple summers, so I called Xeno [aka Randy Hogan], his buddy, who he used to sing with. I'd been in bands with both of them. 'Yeah,' he said, 'I'll do it.' And Rick knew this bass player, Stu Erickson. We practiced for a week and the guy's wife wouldn't let him play, so we knew another guy, Sluggo—Rick Szeluga. He joined the band and we started playing in June '73. In November '73, we switched bass players. Tom came back. Xeno was a real good singer, but he sang through all the solos, too much Robert Plant or Steve Marriott. In September '74, he left to join Straight Up, a Minneapolis band. I got ahold of Robin, who was going to join a country band in Colorado, and I said, 'This is a good band. We want to go somewhere and do something.' After Fuse disbanded, Rick had started writing stuff like 'So Good to See You' and 'Mandocello'"—songs that would appear on Cheap Trick albums. (Szeluga, along with former Fuse drummer Chip Greenman and guitarist Rick Pemberton—all of them members of short-lived Rockford power-poppers the Names—would appear as a fictional, KISS-style shock-rock group called the Clowns in the low-budget 1980 slasher flick *Terror on Tour*.)

"Our whole thing was musical super glue," Zander has said of the band's beginnings. "We connected, musically, after three days of rehearsal in

1974. . . . We played all covers at that time, and maybe one or two original songs. But literally we knew at that time, all of us knew, that we were the best rock band around."

Cary Baker was a student at Northern Illinois University in DeKalb in the mid-'70s when a roommate hipped him to a new group "that's like the Move, the Kinks, and the Who all in one . . . from Rockford!" "I said, 'That's bullshit. Nobody's from Rockford,'" remembers Baker, then an aspiring journalist who would briefly do publicity work for Cheap Trick in the late '90s. He made a point of seeing them when they returned to DeKalb at a bar called the Uprising. "Oh my God, he was understating it," Baker says. "It changed my life. Three sets, probably a five-dollar cover, that logo, the original four members, those songs. They were going places, and they comported themselves like they were from the very start."

# ROCK AND ROLL ALL NITE

**BEGINNING IN AUGUST 1974,** KISS recorded two more albums in quick succession. *Hotter Than Hell*, made in L.A., where Kenny Kerner and Richie Wise had moved, was a difficult birth for a number of reasons. First, the band's stockpile of songs had run low, so they needed to write quickly on the road, supplementing the new batch with leftovers from their early days. Additionally, the band members, all born-and-bred New Yorkers, felt out of sorts in the sunny, palm-treed environs, though that didn't stop them from indulging in the attendant decadent lifestyle, even on a salary of just $85 per week. For the four of them, that meant getting laid, but for Frehley and Criss it also meant getting hammered, which only served to highlight the personality differences that began to generate tension within the group. One night, Frehley damaged his kisser in a drunken car wreck, which led to a compromised photo shoot, resulting in pictures of his half-made-up face in profile.

Perhaps worst of all, the producers failed to capture the sound they wanted. "It was overly compressed and overdriven," said Wise, lamenting the record's brittleness. Still, some potent songs emerge from the buzzy haze, including the proto–groove metal "Watchin' You," the fizzy power-pop "Comin' Home," the supremely nasty rifferama "Parasite," and the brusque come-on title track. Even soft-headed throwaways like "Mainline," Sladean boogie-pomp enlivened by an astringent Catman roar, and the Chuck Berry gimme "Let Me Go, Rock 'n' Roll" end up dazzling. Of the heavier songs, at first blush you would think "Goin' Blind," a majestic Simmons dirge with a stinging Frehley solo, is, considering the source, extolling the pleasures of masturbation. But, in fact, it details a nonagenarian's age-inappropriate lust for a teenage girl and the onset of his age-appropriate sightlessness.

*Dressed to Kill*, recorded just six months later back in New York, benefited from better production, by the band themselves, though Bogart, who acted as cheerleader, also received credit. Owing to a dearth of record-ready material—with the exception of the delicate-to-deadly "Rock Bottom," side 1 feels particularly anemic—KISS once again dipped into the Wicked Lester library for smart redos of "She," now without flute and horns but with way more shredding, and "Love Her All I Can," which apes the Who by way of the Nazz.

Though neither album made much of a dent upon initial release, KISS's reputation was growing. And the band toured on . . .

. . . .

*"YOU WANTED THE BEST and you got it, the hottest band in the land . . . KISS!"*

With that bold announcement to a frenetic crowd, road manager J.R. Smalling uttered the first words on what would arguably become the greatest live (or at least kinda live) rock-and-roll album of all time.

When the smoke coughed up by the fog machine and the pyro cleared, KISS were a bona fide concert sensation, but Casablanca was clearly in trouble. Neil Bogart split from Warner Bros. in September 1974 to go independent, but he was still spending money as if it belonged to someone else. He had also made a massive miscalculation by releasing, in November, a two-LP collection of bits from Johnny Carson's *Tonight Show*, expecting that a chunk of the host's fourteen-million-strong audience would want a purely audio iteration of his televisual bits. It didn't.

Bogart also wasn't paying Aucoin and the band agreed-upon royalties, leaving the manager to entertain offers from other labels, including Atlantic. It didn't help that Aucoin's partner, Joyce Biawitz, and Bogart had coupled up, adding a conflict of interest to the already tempestuous mix. Biawitz eventually quit Aucoin to work at Casablanca, and in May 1975 the band re-upped with the label.

Despite KISS's records not selling all that well, Bogart kept pressure on the band to keep churning out albums at a furious pace in order to provide the company with cash flow. Aucoin decided to do a live album next because it was cheaper to record and would showcase the band out in the wild, where they did their best work. He hastily arranged a tour, financing it with

$300,000 in credit card debt when Casablanca held up their payments, and hired Eddie Kramer to record the band at shows in four cities: Detroit; Cleveland; Davenport, Iowa; and Wildwood, New Jersey. When Kramer played the tapes, with all the mistakes and deficiencies clearly audible, he had the band do some extensive sweetening, not an unusual practice, inside Electric Lady. Still, *Alive!* stands as the essential—or at least quintessential—you-are-there document of '70s hard rock, a double album that presents the band as they were meant to be heard, amid explosions and screams, an idea not lost on the guys creating the music. "Somehow," Simmons observed, "taking the audience away from our songs makes it a lot more clinical or colder."

Radio agreed. "Rock and Roll All Nite," as electrifying a dirtbag cri de coeur as has ever been written, peaked at No. 12, while *Alive!* itself made it to the Top 10, going gold (that is, shipping 500,000 copies) within three months and eventually selling more than nine million copies, becoming KISS's biggest album. *Alive!* also offers the first professionally recorded evidence of Stanley's between-song kaffeeklatsching with the crowd, a predilection that would reach its zenith with the infamous bootleg collection *People, Let Me Get This Off My Chest*, which hilariously strings together more than an hour's worth of his inane spiels. The album's hint of spuriousness extended to *Alive!*'s cover photo, which was staged at Michigan Palace, where the band rehearsed. But questions of authenticity became moot for a band that desperately needed to bring their concert experience to their fans' homes and cars. And *Alive!* was an album that would go on to inspire some of the most important purveyors of heavy music.

"I first heard 'Rock and Roll All Nite' on the car radio and was blown away," says Anthrax guitarist Scott Ian of the album's first and only single. "The deejay never back-announced it, so I had no idea who was singing it. I was singing along by the end. I saw them on television not long after that: *Here's KISS with their hit single 'Rock and Roll All Nite'!* The skies parted, the sea parted, and a lightning bolt hit me. That was it. I was hooked."

As a kid in Canada, Sebastian Bach, who would join Skid Row in 1987, was a fan of Marvel Comics before he got into KISS, and didn't even know what the band looked like when he bought a 1975 compilation album called *Convoy: 20 of Today's Hits* that featured "Rock & Roll All Night" [sic], a song that he immediately fell for. "But this was one of those fake K-tel-style records that didn't even list the names of the bands," he says, unaware that the song was actually a cover by something called the C.B. Radio Music Ensemble. When a friend showed him pictures of KISS, with Simmons vomiting blood,

Bach was thoroughly disgusted. "I said to my friend, 'How could you listen to that?' Then one day after school my buddy dropped the needle and it was 'Rock and Roll All Nite.' I was like, 'You've got to be fucking kidding me! These are the guys?'" Bach would soon be buying KISS records sound unheard. "I don't judge them: *Oh, they've got to top that last record.* I look at it, like, *This person is going to be dead one day, and I want as much art from them as they can possibly give me.*"

When Kim Thayil first heard "Rock and Roll All Nite" on the radio in Chicago, he had no idea what KISS looked like either. It sounded to him like Bachman-Turner Overdrive, the anthemic Canadians whose "Takin' Care of Business" and "You Ain't Seen Nothing Yet" ruled rock radio in 1974. But when the deejay announced the band, he thought there had to be some mistake. KISS? That name had to belong to an R&B band or some girl group, right?

He grew even more confused when he found a copy of *Alive!* at a local shop and glared at the cover. He was expecting to see some open-collared beardos along the lines of the Average White Band. Who and what were these creatures? They didn't look at all like any rock band he'd ever encountered, except maybe Alice Cooper. He flipped the cover over and investigated the song titles. "'Strutter,' the word, looked cool," he says, "though I wasn't sure what it referenced." Then he noticed a song about booze: "Cold Gin." He thought they must be oriented toward more adult themes, which appealed to this suburban fifteen-year-old like the sweetest forbidden fruit. But then he saw "Parasite" and "Hotter Than Hell," titles more in line with the glam-and-horror bent of Fin Costello's jacket photo. He needed to hear more.

After a few weeks of skipping school lunch, he had saved up enough money to do just that. He walked into the record store in the Park Forest Plaza shopping center and buttonholed a clerk named Tom Zutaut, whom he knew from high school. "If I liked 'Rock and Roll All Nite,' which I do, will I like these other songs?" Thayil asked. "The titles look like they might be rocking."

"Yeah, it's pretty consistent," Zutaut responded. That was good enough for Thayil. (Zutaut would later put his perceptive ear to extraordinary use as an A&R executive, signing Mötley Crüe and Guns N' Roses to major-label deals.) "This was an important question because if you liked a song you heard on the radio, it might have been the only good thing on that album," Thayil explains. "You'd have an album built around the Top 40 hit, maybe two Top 40 hits, and then everything else was filler."

But that wasn't the case with *Alive!* and KISS immediately became his favorite band. "They were the heaviest thing in my or my friends' record collections," he says. "It was going beyond the Beatles or Elton John or Bachman-Turner Overdrive." To catch up on the KISS studio albums he had missed, Thayil signed up for the Columbia Record & Tape Club, a mail-order service that offered discounted introductory packages—say, eleven records or tapes for a penny, provided you agreed to buy as few as eight more selections at regular prices in the coming three years. "I was able to take a risk on bands I had read about or heard of on FM radio. I also got *Toys in the Attic*, Ted Nugent, Jethro Tull—and some crappy records I ended up selling to a used record store to get money for cigarettes or gas."

Thayil, who in 1984 would start Soundgarden in Seattle with Chris Cornell and Hiro Yamamoto, hadn't picked up a guitar yet, but was inspired by KISS's look, if not their musicianship, to do just that. "Paul Stanley was pretty cool," he says, "the guitar hanging there, strapped low." The difficult aspect of his fanaticism was trying to legitimize KISS to disbelieving friends, a rite of passage that has been endured by nearly every admirer of the band. Thayil recalls buying a KISS songbook and learning that "Nothin' to Lose" was in 7/4. He'd grab a buddy and say, "Seven-four, man! Check it out!" Some of his friends would concede that 7/4 was a difficult time signature to play. "But," Thayil avers, "nobody was having any of it. They thought it didn't compare to Zeppelin, and they were right. It took me a while to understand that. I don't think anyone appraised KISS as musicians in any regard. At best, they were underrated. I mean, they were playing their instruments while wearing high heels, with their legs spread and the guitars at the weird angle." Thayil and his band would later pay homage to KISS (sort of) with the jokey scream-fest "Sub Pop Rock City."

With the success of *Alive!*, Bill Aucoin moved his company to a tony office tower at 645 Madison Avenue, staffed up, and created a space—filled with mirrors, chrome, and flowers—that reflected his refined taste and the seriousness with which he took his business. A gilded palace where he could begin to build an empire.

CHAPTER 7

# NUMBERS

MANHATTAN'S WEST VILLAGE HAS long been the center of New York City's gay scene. The Stonewall Inn, at 53 Christopher Street, was the site of clashes between police and protesters that lasted for six days in 1969 and gave rise to the gay rights movement. In 1975, the Eagle, a popular leather-and-denim bar off the West Side Highway, just north of the neighborhood, would have seemed an unlikely venue to make a rock-and-roll connection. But it was either there (as Joe X. Dubé claims) or at a bathhouse (as Michael Lee Smith recalls) where Sean Delaney first met and befriended Pieter Sweval. The KISS collaborator fell hard for Sweval's band, Fallen Angels, and brought them to the attention of his lover, Bill Aucoin, who signed on to manage them.

Peter Glick was out, and Alan Miller took a job at Aucoin as their day-to-day handler, while Delaney, Aucoin's de facto head of A&R, became their guru, choreographer, and sometime songwriting partner. "When we started working with Sean," Brendan Harkin says, "we'd rehearse and write songs every day, all day long, for weeks and weeks on end."

Early into his tenure with the band, Delaney decided they needed to add a guitarist. "This isn't the Allman Brothers," he told them. "It's not working. It could work great with two guitar players and be a really heavy rock band." Harkin didn't know what to think because he'd never played in a band like the one Delaney was describing. "It wasn't my favorite kind of music," he admits. "But I had to roll with the punches. So I said, 'If that's what the deal is, that's what we've got to do.'"

The band hadn't anticipated how difficult it would be to find a guitarist with hard-rock chops in 1975 New York, and so they ended up auditioning dozens of musicians. Paul Stanley's friend Binky Philips, who had been gigging around the city for a few years with his band the Planets, was one of them. "Back then," Philips says, "all the guys in KISS called Bill Aucoin 'Gui'"—short for Guillaume, French for William. "So, Paul called me and said, 'Gui just found a new band and they've got everything but a lead guitarist. Gene and I really want you to audition for this. We really want you to make it.'" Philips knew going in that it would just be an exercise. He had no intention of leaving his own band, which had been building a reputation as one of the best on the scene. "I *was* the Planets," he says. "I wasn't the lead guitarist of the Planets. I was Pete Townshend, I was Jimmy Page—writing the stuff, doing most of the arranging. So I'd be quitting *myself*."

At the audition, in Sweval's Chinatown loft, Philips adapted pretty quickly. "I was there to play lead guitar," he says, "so I didn't really need to know every chord change exactly. Once they'd showed me the song, Sean would have us do it again, except then he'd say, 'Okay, when you do the solo, Binky, walk over to Brendan, and I want the two of you to aim your guitars straight up in the air and then turn to Michael Lee.' All of which we were doing—the guys in the band knew the drill. But I was like, 'Are you fucking kidding me with this shit?'

"I could see that the band was completely under Sean's sway, which was something that didn't appeal to me," Philips continues. "The moves that he was having us do—he wasn't replicating KISS, but I was supposed to throw my right leg out and then Brendan was supposed to throw his left leg out in front of mine, and then we were supposed to turn to each other. I actually loved all of the Paul Revere & the Raiders choreography, but by the early '70s, it was corny."

Still, the audition ended up going well for Philips, so well that an impassioned Delaney brought him off to the side and began the hard sell: *You gotta do this. Gene and Paul really want you to do this. They told me it was really important that you do this for them.* "But I'm hemming and hawing," Philips says. "When Sean sees that he's getting nowhere with me, he leans forward and goes, 'Look, you're not going to get anywhere with niggers.' My bass player was biracial and looked Latino. And our lead singer was black, black, black—as black as Sonny Liston."

Delaney made him so uncomfortable, Philips says, "I couldn't get out of there fast enough."

· · · ·

**LIKE SO MANY OF** his contemporaries, fourteen-year-old Richie Ranno tuned into *The Ed Sullivan Show* on Sunday, February 9, 1964, at home in Teaneck, New Jersey, and just like that he was gone. He had been playing the piano and clarinet for a while but had quickly gotten bored with what he saw as those instruments' limited potential. After noticing John Lennon's Rickenbacker and George Harrison's Gretsch, he thought, *That's what I have to play—that thing!* Already a proficient reader of music, Ranno needed only a few weeks to learn the fundamentals of guitar. "I was very lucky to get an accomplished jazz guitar teacher—an older guy, obviously—who didn't like rock and roll," he recalls. "But he said, 'When I teach you how to play, and you listen to everything I say, and do exactly the right thing, and really practice hard, you'll be able to play any kind of music.'" Ranno followed his rules until, finally, his instructor said, "I can't teach you anymore because you really want to play rock and roll." Three months later, Ranno was playing instrumentals as a member of a rock trio called the Mystics.

Then came Andy's Gang, who mostly performed Rascals, Vanilla Fudge, and Stones covers, their name alluding both to a popular '50s kids' TV show and to their keyboardist, one Andy Harris, whose father Van was a popular comedian at the resort hotels of the Catskill Mountains in upstate New York. One day during band rehearsal in the Harris basement, Van made a proposal: "You guys want to do some gigs up in the Catskills?" Soon the teens were playing every three-day weekend, plus Christmas and Easter, at such Borscht Belt staples as the Concord, Grossinger's, and Kutsher's. (Ace Frehley and Gene Simmons also played the Catskills early on.)

In 1968, Ranno spent the summer between junior and senior year of high school at the Tamarack Lodge, which had a small but beautiful theater where the Who, Vanilla Fudge, and the Box Tops played. Andy's Gang didn't share the stage with these bands—they played in the lobby before the opening act and then afterward—but on July 29 they did get to stand right in front and watch the Who, for free. "We only had to play an hour or so at the Tamarack for room and board and we split maybe fifty bucks for the week," Ranno says. Two or three nights a week, they'd also play nearby bungalow colonies, small vacation homes clustered in what were affectionately known as the Jewish Alps. "And we'd split another hundred dollars. It was a lot of money back then. You could fill your tank up for six bucks."

After Andy's Gang dissolved, Ranno's parents insisted he go to college, but he couldn't focus and lasted just a year and a half. By 1970, the Beatles were disintegrating, but the Rolling Stones, Led Zeppelin, the Who, and the Kinks were thriving at home and abroad. Also in the U.K.: dolled-up space case David Bowie was preparing to leave London for the Milky Way, while up north, Black Sabbath were on the verge of achieving total heaviosity. Back in the States, the action was scattered. The Midwest had the Stooges, MC5, and Grand Funk Railroad. Creedence Clearwater Revival, the Doors, the Grateful Dead, and Jefferson Airplane reigned on the West Coast. But in New York the only real racket was coming from Long Island's Mountain and Cactus. There certainly wasn't much going on in Manhattan.

Greenwich Village had a burgeoning folk scene, and national acts played the Fillmore East until it closed in 1971, but in a city that would soon birth one of popular music's most exciting and influential scenes, with its nucleus at a dive called CBGB, there was little homegrown hard rock to be had. Ranno just wanted to play Hendrix, Cream, and Zeppelin, which is how he found a gig at the Metropole Cafe, a jazz club turned go-go bar on Seventh Avenue, near Forty-Eighth Street, where Peter Criss had honed his chops before joining KISS. There, dancers in heels, thongs, and pasties gyrated to rock bands performing on a small stage behind the bar. "Left to right, it would be a semi-naked girl, guitar player, semi-naked girl, drummer, semi-naked girl, bass player, semi-naked girl," he recalls. Sets ran forty-five minutes, then another lineup appeared. You'd go to a back room and hang out before reemerging for another forty-five. Seven sets a night, six nights a week. Ranno had just turned twenty and had been doing this for a while.

One night a couple of guys came in, liked what they heard, and asked the guitarist to come out to Wisconsin, where a scene had developed around all the college towns. Regarding his options in New York as limited, Ranno decided, "Fuck it, how bad could it be?" and invited the pair over to jam at his house in Jersey. A week later they were on the road to Appleton, a hundred miles northeast of Madison. Ranno was pleasantly surprised to discover that they had spoken the truth: the place was lousy with students who wanted to get drunk to live rock and roll. After a few weeks, he ditched the pair and found a more compatible bass player and drummer and started Bungi (with a hard g), playing a mix of covers and originals. Eventually settling in Madison, the trio found some regional success with a psych-boogie take on the popular trucker anthem "Six Days on the Road." A squalling, biting Ranno solo highlights one of their B sides, the shuffling "Numbers," which, forty-five years later, would appear on a compilation album of heavy-rock obscurities called *Brown Acid—The Fourth Trip.*

Ranno exulted in playing stuff he cared about for receptive crowds five nights a week, supporting, on occasion, the likes of Bob Seger and Styx. In one weekend in 1970 Bungi were booked by Ken Adamany to open back-to-back gigs for REO Speedwagon and MC5 at Dewey's, a club in Madison. On September 20 of that year, they found themselves on a bill with recent Paramount Records signees Crowfoot at the University of Wisconsin–Oshkosh, along with Fuse, Rick Nielsen and Tom Petersson's early band. "We knocked the place out," Ranno says. "The place almost emptied when we were done, that's how big we went over. And Fuse didn't care, they weren't intimidated. They were great. That's how we became friends." (It was at a peace vigil in Oshkosh, to commemorate the May 1970 shootings at Kent State that left four students dead, where Ranno met a hulking six-foot-eight kid who called himself Jolly and brought him on as Bungi's roadie. Jolly would later become a part of Cheap Trick's crew and, after that, Gene Simmons's bodyguard.)

In a nod to the glam rock that was increasingly influencing their repertoire, Ranno took to wearing a skin-clinging silver bodysuit and a dark velvet ensemble that exposed his hirsute chest, and bassist-singer Jon Parrot began painting shapes around his eyes. "We were doing Slade and Bowie songs more than Queen," Ranno says, "because they were a little harder to cover."

By the summer of 1973, the members of Bungi felt confident enough to take their show east, but they didn't anticipate the disaster that awaited. "We booked the gigs, and we'd get to the place, and they wouldn't pay us," Ranno says. "We were eating out of people's gardens." He'd reached his breaking point by the time the tour ended, and instead of returning to Wisconsin, he asked to be dropped off at his folks' in Jersey.

Through a connection he made on the road, Ranno got the opportunity to join Stories, after guitarist Steve Love left to play with Jobriath, a hotly tipped American Bowie manqué. The New York–based Stories had recently hit No. 1 with "Brother Louie," a gritty, soulful take on a song that a few months earlier had been a U.K. smash for Hot Chocolate. Their third (and final) album, *Traveling Underground*, credited to Ian Lloyd & Stories, had already been recorded by the time Ranno signed on, so besides touring that one, Ranno recorded a single with them for producers Kenny Kerner and Richie Wise. Called "Another Love," it's a blatant but still effective "Brother Louie" soundalike that boldly, for 1974, substituted the earlier song's interracial relationship with a bisexual one.

· · · ·

**WHEN HE RECORDED HIS GUITARS,** Ranno always preferred to play outside the booth, near the soundboard, listening through speakers rather than headphones. One day during a break, Wise announced that he had recently produced a new band called KISS. As he held the album up, Ranno said, "What the hell is that?"

"What do you mean?"

"I don't understand," Ranno responded. "Is that a drawing?"

"No, it's their faces."

"How could it be their faces?"

"They're painted."

"That's amazing! What kind of music is it?"

"Hard rock."

That's all Ranno needed to hear. He was admittedly one-dimensional in his taste back then, so if something sounded remotely like Slade, Deep Purple, or Zeppelin, he was all in. With little cajoling, Wise gave Ranno his promo copy of the album, which wouldn't be released for a couple of weeks. After a few spins, Ranno offered Wise his take: "Oh my God! I love this."

Stories were doing some dates on the West Coast in August 1974 and, after driving down from San Francisco, ended up late one evening at a Ramada Inn on Sunset Boulevard in Los Angeles. Ranno recalls seeing an "Italian, Brooklyn type of girl" inside, a description that was confirmed when he heard her speak.

"Where you from—Brooklyn?" he asked her.

"Yeah!"

"What are you doing here?"

"I'm here with KISS!"

"You're here with KISS? Where are they?"

"They're in the pool."

"You're kidding!"

"No, I'm Lydia. I'm married to Peter Criss."

After checking in, Stories headed outside, where the four members of KISS, in town to record their second album, were lounging in and around the pool. They had just come from a photo shoot for the *Hotter Than Hell* cover and were still in their makeup and costumes. After some small talk, Stories headed to their rooms.

The next morning Ranno saw the KISS members again, this time without the face paint, and told them he was a big fan of their debut. "Of course, they loved that," he says, "because every musician hated them. I think they were all intimidated by KISS."

At Ranno's urging, KISS showed up at the Whisky a Go Go for a Stories gig. "I had a little amp backstage, and I knew their songs and could play them all," he says. "I started with 'Nothin' to Lose,' and then I was playing one after another, and they were all standing around me, and we were singing KISS songs together."

KISS invited Ranno and Stories drummer Bryan Madey and bassist Kenny Aaronson (who had played with Richie Wise in Dust) to the Village Recorder studios, where they told him that their manager was looking to take on another band, so maybe he should consider putting together his own hard-rock group. Ranno wasn't about to quit a band that was coasting on a number one record, but he did like the idea.

Rick Stuart worked security at Manhattan's Fillmore East and the Academy of Music and at Passaic, New Jersey's Capitol Theatre before he took a job traveling with Stories as their lighting director, drum roadie, and enforcer. "Working for Stories was like going down a big hill, because after 'Brother Louie,' they couldn't buy another hit," he says. "I started to feel like I was a paid audience." After the tour ended, he hooked up with Lou Reed and soon was hired by Bill Aucoin to become head of KISS's security.

When Ian Lloyd & Stories split in late 1974, Ranno stayed on a few months for Lloyd's solo project, until a fellow band member's indiscreet cocaine use drove the anti-drug guitarist out. He tried to get something else together, but the dearth of New York hard-rock players frustrated him. One day in September 1975, a roadie friend alerted Ranno to an ad in the *Village Voice* seeking a guitarist for a band under the aegis of Rock Steady, KISS's management. So Ranno called the number provided.

Sean Delaney answered. *"Are you the greatest guitar player who ever lived?"* he screamed through the receiver.

"I'm gonna say no," Ranno replied.

"Well, then, we don't need you. We've already got the greatest guitar player who ever lived."

Taken aback by this show of hubris, Ranno agreed with the maniac on the line: "You're right. You don't need me."

Just as Ranno was about to hang up, Delaney asked, "Well, how good *are* you?"

"Even though I'm not the greatest guitar player, and even though you already *have* the greatest guitar player, I'll come down anyway," he told him.

Ranno expected to walk into an unprofessional setup at the audition, so he didn't bother wearing his rock-star gear, which at that point included an Art Deco spacesuit-style top designed by Larry LeGaspi, reminiscent of the one Ace Frehley would soon start wearing. Instead, he showed up in street clothes and clogs. "This is gonna suck," he told his girlfriend on the drive over to the Chinatown loft. "I'm really not into this, but I gotta do it." His suspicions were confirmed when, upon their arrival, Delaney shouted, *"No girls allowed!"*

Ranno recalls her being shunted off, away from the action, as he was getting increasingly pissed. Entering the practice space, he remembers somebody offering, curtly, "There's the plug."

"No one from the band even looks in my direction," he says. "I plug in and hear, 'Ready? Okay. *One. Two!*' And I said, 'You should at least tell me the key.' I'm thinking, I really want to just put this guitar down and walk out." The guys began a decent rock tune, which he went along with for a minute and a half, before the band suddenly stopped to ask him his name and whom he had played with. Joe X. Dubé got up from behind his kit.

"Do you know how to write songs?" he asked.

"Absolutely!"

"Good, because we're working on this thing."

After Larry Gonsky proceeded to play a few bright, ascending chords on the keyboard, Ranno told the band they needed an intro, which he provided on the spot. (The song would later evolve into "[She's Just a] Fallen Angel," off the first Starz album.) When they asked if he wanted in, Ranno recalls, "I said yeah. And that was it."

The band's first gig with Ranno, and under Aucoin's auspices, was supporting the popular New York bar band the Good Rats at My Father's Place on Long Island. On another early date, their opening act was a young guy who stood silently and awkwardly onstage as the theme from the Mighty Mouse cartoon played on a nearby phonograph. He would wait for just the right moment before breaking through the boredom by lip-syncing the triumphant line, *"Here I come to save the day!"* On October 11, 1975, this comedian would bring his shtick to the first episode of *Saturday Night Live*, and Andy Kaufman would become a star virtually overnight.

A week earlier, on October 3, before an audience of nearly 3,000, Fallen Angels played their biggest gig yet, opening for Rock Steady stablemates

KISS at the Tower Theater, just outside of Philadelphia. It was an eventful night for the support act. "Right in the middle of the set, Larry's keyboards didn't work," Harkin says. "And that's the genesis of Sean going, 'We need to get rid of this guy.'" Michael Lee Smith remembers the audience, there to see KISS and only KISS, not buying the "imitation Steely Dan" that the Fallen Angels were selling. At the end of their set, the emcee gamely attempted to encourage an encore by announcing, "Let's give them a hand!" After being struck by a hail of boos, he sheepishly added, "C'mon, guys, they weren't *that* bad." "The crowd," says Smith, "wasn't having it."

Delaney, who had had issues with Gonsky for a while, devised a way to force him out without being seen as the villain. "Larry was a nice guy, and it wasn't my call," Ranno remembers. "So Sean, clever guy that he was, says after the gig, 'What do you think of the keyboard player—do you think he fits?' 'I don't know,' I say. He says, 'I want him out. How do you feel about that?' I say, 'I'm the new guy in the band—don't ask me.' And he goes, 'No, I need to know how you feel about it.' I say, 'Well, I don't think keyboard players belong in two-guitar hard-rock bands period.' So he says, 'You want him out.'

"He goes to the second newest guy to join: 'Michael, Richie and I really don't think Larry belongs in the band.' Michael says, 'Yeah, I see that too.' Then he goes to Brendan, the next newest guy: 'Me, Richie, and Michael want Larry out of the band.'

"Now he has to go to Dubé and Pieter—the guys who were in Looking Glass with Larry. And he says, 'We all want him out. He doesn't fit.' They reluctantly agree because they were good friends. But it was a move in the right direction."

Gonsky certainly didn't look the part. "Everybody else was a drop-dead good-looking, long-haired rock-star guy," says Harkin. "Larry was a little 'Afternoon Delight.' So we had a meeting, and he didn't take it well."

Jack Douglas has said he became involved with the band soon after they hooked up with Aucoin, when he got a call from Alan Miller. "When I first saw them, they had a keyboard player," the producer said in 1976. "I didn't say he had to go, but I think Bill did because there was an image he was looking for onstage and you can't make moves if you're sitting down."

By his own admission, Gonsky never fit in with the new structure: "It was all about the glitz and seven-inch platform shoes. And I was like, 'What about the music?'" He remembers Delaney at one point telling him to start spitting on old people at the supermarket so that he could get his name in the paper. Gonsky couldn't tell if he was kidding. "We didn't see eye to eye, so I left," he says. "It was musical. It wasn't personal."

. . . .

**DELANEY DECIDED THAT FALLEN** Angels didn't accurately reflect the harder approach the music was taking. And Starz was the name that was going to launch them into the galaxy. The band members were fairly indifferent to the suggestion, until they were presented with a nifty logo designed by Michael Doret, whose lettering graced the poster for the 1974 Sean Connery science-fiction film *Zardoz*, and whose striking mosaic-tile illustration appeared on the back cover of Looking Glass's *Subway Serenade*.

With Gonsky gone, the band retreated from the stage but continued to write and rehearse. And with his focus no longer on KISS, Delaney put his all into Starz, directing their look (dark, form-fitting spandex outfits with metallic accents and chunky platform boots) and their stage moves (Sweval and Harkin punching the air in tandem, swaying together with their backs to the audience), the band members (except for Dubé, who was stationed behind a massive double bass kit) constantly on the run. "Sean was a brilliant guy," says Ranno. "Lots of energy. Unfortunately, he got into doing way too much coke, to the point where he'd be up for four or five days, collapse, and go to the hospital. It was crazy energy, but it was positive." Most of the time.

When the band had a well-rehearsed set, Aucoin, riding high on the success of *Alive!*, sent them out on the road. With KISS as leverage, he eschewed building Starz a grassroots following via club gigs and instead used his clout to land them slots opening for established artists like ZZ Top and Peter Frampton, rare opportunities for an unsigned band. "Rather than slog away at the bottom of the circuit, we took a big jump," Smith, reflecting on the strategy, said in 1977. "It was a gamble, we could have fallen flat on our faces, but we didn't." Besides, he said, their whole act had been engineered to play big venues. "You've got to learn to *project*, project yourself right to the back of the arena, 2,000 feet away. . . . We simply wouldn't work anywhere else."

Aucoin shopped around a demo produced by Delaney and invited labels to see Starz on a bill with Roxy Music at the Calderone Concert Hall in Hempstead, Long Island, on March 8, 1976. Capitol bit. John Carter, the A&R executive who signed the group, had a stellar track record. Having shaped Steve Miller into a hitmaker for the label, he was currently orchestrating Bob Seger's breakout (and in the 1980s, he'd play a prominent role in Tina Turner's resurgence). Carter's boss, Rupert Perry, then Capitol's vice president of A&R, says that Aucoin made a very persuasive case for his second band: "He told us, 'This is my next project, and I want to make it as big and successful as KISS. Here's how I'm going to do it.'"

One of those ideas, apparently, was to not release a single before the album or before the band had a chance to make an impression in a live setting. "It could hurt their chances," Aucoin said in 1976, "because the image of Starz would be based solely on what that single was, which might not be the band at all. It might be just a small part of the band. So, you can't afford to narrow down what a fan thinks, until that fan actually sees the group."

Bruce Ravid, who served as Capitol's Midwest AOR promotion coordinator, saw Starz filling a conspicuous hole in the label's roster. "Capitol was the first label to form a department dedicated to promoting album-oriented rock," he says. "The Aucoin connection was a big plus. Aerosmith had broken, and probably a lot of us saw that Starz were right in that vein—a lot closer to Aerosmith, maybe, than to KISS. We didn't really have a band that was close to what was going on, so I thought it was a great fit."

Former Aucoin publicist Carol Ross recalls that Capitol initially wasn't gung ho about the band. "But having Jack Douglas produce was an important factor because of his name value," she says. "So Capitol figured if he was going to produce the band, then maybe there was something here that we should take another look at."

Ranno, who thought Aerosmith's debut album sounded as if it were recorded "in a submarine with a microphone above the water," had been blown away by Douglas's work on *Get Your Wings*. At an early meeting with Starz, the producer showed up at a soundcheck in Atlanta. For a moment, Ranno stopped doing his choreographed steps, which rankled Sean Delaney, who jumped onto the stage and flicked a lit cigarette right in the guitarist's face.

*"You should always be doing the moves!"* Delaney screamed.

"We're doing a soundcheck, asshole!"

Ranno says he could have killed him. "But I had the guitar on."

When they finally got down to preproduction for the debut album, Douglas, who was working nights with Starz and afternoons with Aerosmith on *Rocks*, found he had some tweaks to make. "They really were all good players. It was hiding in there," he said in 1976. "If you said, 'Play anything you want individually,' they'd sit down and play great things. The two guitar players are both good; they play off each other real well, but live they weren't doing it."

Douglas praised Harkin's melody lines and Ranno's forceful sound and harmonizing. "Brendan could never really make things sound too tough," he said, "but Richie could. He could also do a lot of screaming on the guitar. But before preproduction the wrong things were screaming." Douglas could achieve his goal of making them sound powerful with huge drums and guitars, but first he had to work with them on editing. "There was a lot of stuff that needed to come out," he said. "They would go into these extended solos that went nowhere. There were songs inside of songs and I kept pulling this stuff out, changing a little thing here and there."

Judging by the finished product, his adjustments did the trick.

## CHAPTER 8

# GREAT EXPECTATIONS

FOR A BAND MADE up of "four Alice Coopers," it was only a matter of time before they worked with the producer behind that shock rocker's classic albums. Bob Ezrin's 1971–1973 run with Cooper, from *Love It to Death* to *Killer* to *School's Out* to *Billion Dollar Babies*, by any measure constituted an artistic pinnacle. As a member of Nimbus 9, he was mentored by Jack Richardson (who produced the Fallen Angels debut) and counted among his own protégés Jack Douglas (for whom he executive-produced Aerosmith's *Get Your Wings*).

Ezrin has said his objective for *Destroyer* was to record for KISS a sort of aural comic book, while at the same time making them more palatable for radio. To do this, he had to get them to stop writing songs about fucking, make them seem vulnerable and romantic—and more accessible to girls. In short, he needed to expand their audience beyond their core of teen boys. He brought in Jay Messina, who was behind the board for Aerosmith's biggest albums, to engineer along with Corky Stasiak, an assistant on *Toys in the Attic*. Messina, like many others who found themselves in KISS's orbit, initially took the band at face value. "When I first saw them, I was laughing," he says. "It was a joke to me that they were wearing makeup."

To keep the band focused, Ezrin wore a whistle around his neck and generally acted both as a drill sergeant and a teacher, not taking any shit, but also endeavoring to bring out the best in everyone. Sometimes that meant bypassing Ace Frehley entirely, in favor of a guitar solo by Dick Wagner, a ringer Ezrin used for Lou Reed and Alice Cooper sessions and who had played on Aerosmith's *Get Your Wings*. Other times, it meant snapping at his charges. Ezrin, like Douglas, had enormous facility with editing—chopping, say, a good intro and chorus from one take and combining them with other pieces to make an even better take. At one point, Simmons decided to stop playing during a take, which set the producer off. "Bob got on the talkback," Messina says, "and he yelled at them, kind of tongue-in-cheek, scolding them like they're children: 'Don't you *ever* stop a take unless I tell you!' I remember Gene and Paul looking at each other like, *Wow, we're getting yelled at here.* And so that became the joke of the album. Anytime something would go wrong, somebody would yell, 'Don't you *ever!*'"

That didn't mean there wasn't any time for partying. Frehley has said he first tried cocaine after seeing Ezrin do it during the *Destroyer* sessions and asking Criss to score for him. Coke not only felt almost as good as sex, the guitarist wrote, it made him a better boozer: "It allowed me to drink longer and harder without passing out."

In March 1976, KISS unleashed *Destroyer*, their fourth studio album in two years, an ornate and extravagant collection chockablock with faintly creepy odes to rock-star excess ("Great Expectations," "Do You Love Me," "King of the Night Time World") and vivid expressions of innocuous rebellion aimed squarely at their zit-studded constituency ("Flaming Youth," "Detroit Rock City," "Shout It Out Loud"). Initially, the album angered many fans, its highfalutin filigrees—warbling courtesy of the Brooklyn Boys Choir, orchestrations featuring members of the New York Philharmonic, an adaptation of a Beethoven piano sonata, a calliope, and Christmas bells, *fercrissakes!*—marking a severe departure from the stunted bluntness of its predecessors. The band members themselves were initially dismayed by the results, fearing that Ezrin took them too far out of their comfort zone and made them sound less like KISS than they wanted. In Aucoin's eyes, the album wasn't a total success, owing to the band's efforts to appease Ezrin. "We might've done a little too much production," he said at the time, before adding, "The strong rock fans didn't relate to that. Now KISS's older audience has related to it, but that's not where we're really centered."

But perhaps the same experimentation that caused such distress would finally earn them kudos in the press that had so far eluded them. Though most rock critics never cared for KISS, maybe, just maybe, they'd come around for this one. In the *Village Voice*, the heretofore sympathetic Robert Christgau lamented Ezrin's addition of "bombast and melodrama," labeling *Destroyer* KISS's "least interesting record." *Rolling Stone*'s John Milward called it the band's "best album yet" but bemoaned what he considered to be "lackluster performances" and "trite" lyrics, writing that "KISS still lacks that flash of creative madness that could have made their music interesting, or at least listenable." Even in *Creem*, a usually supportive venue, Rick Johnson wrote that Ezrin "deprived them of much of their rusty coat-hanger appeal." (A few months later, in his *Circus* review of their next album, *Rock and Roll Over*, Lester Bangs would offer his take, calling *Destroyer* "one of Bob Ezrin's all-time masterpieces. . . . I liked it better than Aerosmith's *Rocks* even.")

The reception in the U.K. was predictably dismissive. "KISS are suffering from one overwhelming problem," wrote Max Bell in the *New Musical Express*, "their own success." Claiming that "KISS retread old territory," *Melody Maker*'s Harry Doherty nonetheless admitted "they do well by all the clichés."

Nevertheless, the record generated the band's first Top 10 hit, the Criss-sung, piano-and-strings-driven power ballad "Beth," originally the B side of the "Detroit Rock City" single and remarkably a track on which only one band member appears. The song ended up goosing the initially slow sales of *Destroyer*, which eventually became KISS's first platinum LP.

"After we did *Destroyer*," Paul Stanley says, "we all got cold feet and felt that perhaps we had lost the plot, which is ironic because more of the songs from *Destroyer* remain in the set than any other album." So for their next record, Aucoin reached out to the in-demand Jack Douglas, who had recently finished Starz's debut, to add the rawness Ezrin had removed and bring the band back down to the streets. "It was done unbeknownst to Bob Ezrin, which was not the way to do things," Stanley says, "if for no other reason than the two of them were close. It was not handled well."

Douglas told Ezrin he had been contacted by KISS "and that he would never even think about it if that would bother me," Ezrin has said. To Ezrin, Aucoin's actions amounted to a betrayal, and he was so stunned he told Douglas to take the gig. "I said, 'Fuck those guys!'" Ezrin has said. "I don't know what I had done to deserve that. I thought we made a really great record and it was going to be a big record for them."

For his part, Douglas has said, "I could have done KISS and made a lot of money, but that would have been unfair to Aerosmith because by 1977 KISS was their only competition, at least among American rock bands." For the rest of his and KISS's career, Douglas never worked with the band. Ezrin, however, would go on to produce two other KISS albums. "But I don't hold grudges, and [*Destroyer*] was wildly successful," he said in 2005. "That makes it hard for people to stay mad."

Though *Destroyer* saw an uncertain KISS taking a huge creative flier, *Rocks*, released two months later, unveiled a supremely confident Aerosmith at the peak of their powers. It's an unrelenting collection of colossal riffs and sneering choruses, all coated in Tyler's slinky, stinking word funk. "When I got *Rocks*, that was it," says Butch Walker. "I just remember hearing that record and thinking, 'Oh man, this is nuts!'" Among the many other musicians who shared that opinion were Kurt Cobain, Dave Grohl, Kim Thayil, James Hetfield, and Slash.

"It wasn't pristine and perfect, but it gelled together perfectly," the Guns N' Roses guitarist has said. "*Rocks* was also right up my alley because I was one of *those* kids. I was bad in school. I had long hair and wore jeans. . . . I was basically just a punk who didn't fit in anywhere."

• • • •

TO RECORD ROCK AND ROLL OVER, KISS handed the reins to Eddie Kramer. Released in November 1976, it indeed marked a return to the muscularity of their earlier albums. And if the first single, the gritty ballad "Hard Luck Woman," ended up sounding familiar to the guys in Starz, it's because, as Paul Stanley has admitted, Looking Glass's "Brandy" inspired the lyrics. While very happy with this album, Stanley nevertheless began to feel neglected by management, claiming that Bill Aucoin and Sean Delaney were devoting way too much energy to their newer acts—which, along with Starz, now included Piper. He was also angered by what he perceived to be Aucoin's cynical approach: "Give a band a look and logo and they would become as big as KISS. . . . There was more to us than a logo, platform boots, and makeup." Stanley felt that Aucoin's approach oversimplified what made KISS successful in the first place. "It turns it into something superficial," he says, "when in fact if it was that easy, there would be a menagerie of bands today dressed as giraffes and wearing rabbit ears—who knows?"

"I know that KISS didn't like that Bill was managing other people," says Rick Stuart, the band's former security chief. "But it wasn't something they beat to death. KISS didn't want to know about Starz, because Starz was a much better band—each individual player was a better player."

From the perspective of Sher Bach, who worked in promotion at Aucoin, "To put it bluntly, KISS was the baby and the other bands were all stepchildren. They were tax write-offs." The publicity materials she sent to the trade papers and magazines rarely focused on any band other than KISS.

In early 1977, Jackie Fox, nearing the end of her run in the Runaways, hoped to scoop up some of the mojo that powered KISS and Aerosmith, spending her last $600 to fly east to try to convince Jack Douglas to produce her band and Bill Aucoin to manage them. She spoke on the phone to Douglas, who agreed to executive-produce an album and suggested as producer his associate Eddie Leonetti, whom Fox says she loved "because his name always sounded like it was three people, two of whom were named Eddie." When she met with Aucoin, he told her he wanted to take them on, but it would cost him $50,000 to buy out their manager, Kim Fowley, who had helped out with songs on *Destroyer*, and then he'd have to sink another $50,000 into the band. "Get rid of Kim Fowley first and then I'll manage you," Aucoin said.

"So I brought that back to the band," Fox says. But at that point they were all just wasted and apathetic. "So that never happened."

# CHAPTER 9

# BOYS IN ACTION

RELEASED IN AUGUST 1976, the self-titled debut album by Starz seemingly had it all. Aerosmith's dick-swinging swagger. KISS's fist-pumping potency. And stirring pop hooks ported over from Looking Glass and Stories. Not that the band members told anyone about their earlier groups. "I explained to everybody that we're doing hard rock," Ranno says. "If you're doing hard rock and people know you were in Looking Glass or Stories, you're a bunch of phonies."

Well, how hard rock is it? So hard rock that the album opens on a squawking guitar solo, before Smith starts singing about Detroit girls ("the sweetest in the whole damn world—*yeah!*"), thus establishing the casual, often comical, sexism that would permeate much of the band's output. Oh, but those tunes! Like "(She's Just a) Fallen Angel," on which a gently strummed riff explodes after twenty seconds—*boom!*—into a candy-colored Fourth of July shower of sparks.

"Starz like to take a perverse view of the world whenever possible," Smith once told an interviewer. And he wasn't lying. The lyrical influence of Willie Tee's "Thank You John" is all over the album, with songs sung by a serial rapist ("not really a rapist—but he likes to go around trying young virgins, and gently initiating them into the niceties of sexual fulfillment," Smith helpfully clarified) as well as a guy who wants to terminate his beloved, who's on life support. Confidently walking Spinal Tap's fine line between stupid and clever, the latter song, "Pull the Plug," a sardonic, bluesy take on euthanasia ("It's been so long since your vital signs went / And you don't look the same in that oxygen tent"), caused a bit of commotion. Partly inspired by the plight of Karen Ann Quinlan, a comatose young woman whose parents successfully fought a legal battle to remove her ventilator, the song earned Starz a news item in *Rolling Stone*, in which Vin Scelsa, music director for leading New York rock station WNEW-FM tut-tutted, "The issue for me was taste, not religious or moral conviction. I felt it was a piece of shit, which was my impression of the band as a whole." Continuing this bathroom talk, the article also mentioned "Piss Party," a then-unreleased Starz toss-off that gloriously nicks riffs from KISS's "Firehouse" and Mountain's "Mississippi Queen" to provide backing for Smith's spoken-word rap recounting a urine-soaked soirée attended by— who else?—hot chicks.

Some of the other lyrics could be seen as funny if they weren't so nasty. From "Boys in Action": "When we come, it tastes just like a milkshake / Have a milkshake all night long." From "Monkey Business," a harrowing but high-energy addiction elegy inspired by the overdose death of a Smith friend: "Yeah, monkey got my brother / Kicked him in the mouth / His head went north / And his teeth went south."

"Capitol's culture at the time was blue-collar," says Ray Tusken, who served as the label's national AOR promotion manager. "It was guys from the Midwest who drove motorcycles." Capitol's rock artists, accordingly, tended toward unpretentious heartland music, what Tusken characterizes as "keeping-it-real-straight songs talking about real life." But by 1977 the label and its affiliates were developing new artists that would smash that model, including British art rockers Be-Bop Deluxe, Canadian prog-poppers Klaatu, and the retro garage soul of Mink DeVille. Which is where Starz should have fit in.

"On paper everything looked as though it should go gold," says former Capitol A&R executive Rupert Perry. "Great management, constant touring, good attitude, good-looking lead singer, great songs, great producer in Jack Douglas. In theory it should have worked."

But it didn't help that the band members often found themselves batting down accusations that they were little more than a KISS copy, a comparison that even the label pushed in its press release for the album. "The only way I would say that our music sounds like KISS, at all, is that Starz does play 'active' music and so does KISS," Smith said in 1978. Besides, he added, he wasn't particularly a fan of then-current loud rock, preferring instead "Supertramp and the more classical stuff. Usually, I don't like to hear rock and roll because I hear it in my head all day long. I write it. I go out and sing it. I just can't listen to it 24 hours a day!"

Asked if he ever felt humbled by KISS, Smith responded, "I might have if I was a KISS fan. I figure that the management wouldn't want us around if they didn't think we could do as well as them or better." On another occasion, Smith noted, "Sometimes we'll get people who say, 'You guys are the ones that are owned by KISS, right?' Owned by KISS? That's disgusting. How can people be so stupid! It's like we're an investment that KISS had made."

"Well, I think people just need someone to compare us to. . . . But I don't think we are that similar to KISS," Ranno told one interviewer before introducing the other obvious analog. "I think a lot of press will pick up our album and see Jack Douglas' name on it and say, 'They act like Aerosmith and KISS,' when we're really not."

Early on, even Douglas had to swat away naysayers. "Bill Aucoin, as far as I know, has nothing to do with what the band sounds like," he has said. "Sean Delaney was helping them out and he's an influence in terms of choreography and a certain amount of punch—that kind of KISS thing. . . . But they're not a KISS-like band and I don't think they ever want to be. They think differently visually."

But at least one KISS member wasn't buying it. Paul Stanley says that right away he saw Starz as a conscious attempt by management to re-create KISS's success. "Even down to, 'Let's give them singular colors. We'll give them black and yellow as opposed to KISS's black and silver, and we'll give them a logo,'" he says. "The songs, quite honestly, were so familiar to me that when I heard that first album, I could've played all of them." Although Stanley's suspicion may be earned, the complex guitar interplay in, say, "Now I Can" goes far beyond the Neanderthal thump of the first few KISS albums. Nor were KISS very interested at that time in such provocative, canny-when-they-wanna-be lyrics. KISS were smart guys writing dumb songs for smart people—dumb ones too. And they were brilliant at it.

Reviewers also noticed similarities between Starz and KISS and the country's other reigning hard-rock band. "With KISS and Aerosmith leading the race, Starz are one more example that America can indeed produce first-rate rock bands," *Cash Box* raved. *New Musical Express* described Starz as "you guessed it—Aerosmith meets KISS, only without the makeup and a soupçon more overdrive in the volume knob. They have a certain energy, too bad they forgot to connect it to their brain," before concluding, "Should be a pretty big band." In his *Circus* review, Lester Bangs devoted six paragraphs to KISS and Aerosmith before writing that "KISS is a product—in fact, the *best* product of the past half-decade—and so are Starz," adding, probably facetiously, considering the sardonic source, that *Starz* is a "great album, and it's not even on Casablanca." *Creem* later called Starz "a promising middleweight contender in the Aerosmooch sweepstakes."

To generate word of mouth for its recent signees, Capitol sponsored a series of free concerts (with ads breathlessly touting "the sensational new group that's burning up the airwaves from coast to coast") in such major markets as Los Angeles, Atlanta, Cleveland, St. Louis, and Detroit. "We were absolutely full-out trying to break them," says Rupert Perry. "A lot of time, money, energy, and commitment was spent on making that happen."

The plan included a television segment introducing the band on the *ABC Evening News*, an extraordinary promotional coup. Anchor Ted Koppel introduced the report, which included footage of the band in the studio with Douglas and Messina and onstage at Pittsburgh's Stanley Theatre on October 26, 1976. The story presented Starz as an example of how the music industry was breaking new artists. A pie-chart graphic revealed what all went into the $3 wholesale price for an album with a $6.98 list at retail, which, it was pointed out, was a $2 increase from five years earlier. That number accounted for the rising costs of polyvinyl chloride (for the LP)—a direct result of the 1973 oil crisis—and paper (for the packaging). Manufacturing, profit, and promotion each deducted 50 cents from that total, while the artist royalty subtracted 75 cents, as did the failure rate (assuming stores returned one in four albums). Ranno, interviewed in the piece, said it took $8,000 per week to keep the band on the road. Throughout much of their career in Starz, the musicians themselves earned $150 a week in salary and received a $10 per diem while on tour. They all had significant others who worked. "Everybody dumped a ton of dough into us. Every week, we were climbing deeper in the hole," Dubé says. "Capitol was always charging against future royalties, which was the piddly-shit rate that we signed. We'd never recoup [our advance]."

Starz were on tour with Bob Seger & the Silver Bullet Band in 1977 when a teenage Chip Z'Nuff caught them in Chicago. "It was jam-packed, sold out," recalls the musician, who would later cofound Enuff Z'Nuff. "The crowd really wanted to see Bob Seger, because at the time he had a foothold on radio. But Starz won everybody over. The band was terrific live." Years later Z'Nuff met Richie Ranno and told him how big an influence Starz were on his own band, which on its early albums dressed up Cheap Trick– and Starz-style pop rock in poodle-metal drag. "I even pillaged 'Pull the Plug' for a song on our first record called 'In the Groove,'" he says.

"Jack Douglas put everything he had into that band," Z'Nuff adds. "And if you really listen, their albums were produced like his Aerosmith records—the way the guitars have great separation, the vocals are always on top, a really strong mix. I thought they were gifted songwriters. They're just one of those bands that slipped through the cracks. At that time there was too much product, not enough demand."

Not all early gigs went as well as the one Z'Nuff attended. At Detroit's Masonic Auditorium on October 29, 1976, Starz opened for Manfred Mann's Earth Band before a crowd of 3,500. "We had an open date and were in the area, so they put us on the bill," Ranno says of the fill-in gig. "No one bought a ticket to see us." Ranno contends that Manfred Mann's fans were mostly older, more conservative, and likely Canadians from nearby Windsor, Ontario: "They didn't want any part of our rock." During "Boys in Action," when the song slowed down, Smith always ad-libbed some audience-baiting stage banter. "He would say, 'We were in St. Louis last night and those people really know how to rock. How about you people? *You know how to rock?*' And the crowd would go berserk," Ranno says. "He did this in Detroit, but the audience didn't respond. He said, 'You know what? They were right. You're a bunch of fucking assholes. This is the worst crowd of all time. You people suck!'"

At the end of their set, to the deafening roar of disapproval, Dubé kicked his bass drums off the stage, leaving his roadie to fetch them. "All five of us gave the audience double middle fingers," says Ranno, who recalls seeing a few Capitol executives at the show. "They were very upset with us."

• • • •

IN 1976, BOTH AEROSMITH and KISS graduated from indoor arenas, where they'd play for 20,000 fans, to the occasional stadium, on multi-band bills, before twice that amount or more. For Aerosmith, then promoting *Rocks*, that meant headline dates at such venues as the Pontiac Silverdome in Michigan, Seattle's Kingdome, and Anaheim's Angel Stadium.

And on July 10, at Comiskey Park, then home to the Chicago White Sox. The promoters, Windy City Productions, described the concert, dubbed Game #1 of the World Series of Rock, as "the first major attempt to bring outdoor concerts to Chicago." The city hadn't hosted a large open-air rock show in six years, following a riot at a free Sly and the Family Stone gig in Grant Park that was attended by an estimated 75,000. At that fiasco, the headliner never played, three people got shot, at least one hundred were hospitalized, and police made more than one hundred fifty arrests.

After opening sets by Jeff Beck (backed by the Jan Hammer Group), Rick Derringer, and Stu Daye (whose album, produced by Jack Douglas, featured guest vocals by Steven Tyler), Aerosmith played Comiskey to some 62,000 attendees in one-hundred-degree heat. Earlier, the concert had almost ended in tragedy. As Beck performed, huge clouds of black smoke wafted through the stadium—the result of errant cigarettes and firecrackers igniting a portion of the roof and upper grandstand—leading firefighters to evacuate 5,000 fans and turn their hoses on the overheated crowd. The show went on, despite heatstroke and drug overdoses sending dozens to the hospital. Afterward, a newspaper advertisement promoting July 31's Game #2—to be headlined by KISS, along with Uriah Heep, Ted Nugent, Bob Seger & the Silver Bullet Band, and Starz—thanked fans for their "excellent conduct" at the Aerosmith show. That second concert, however, never happened. The standard line had KISS canceling after the stadium wanted to impose a 6 p.m. curfew, which meant the band would have had to put on their pyro-heavy show in the daylight. It was more likely that the stadium and the city got spooked by the near-disaster three weeks earlier. (Game #3, featuring Yes, Peter Frampton, Lynyrd Skynyrd, Gary Wright, and Natural Gas, got relocated to a nearby racetrack.)

With July 31 now free, American Talent International (ATI), KISS's agency, quickly booked the 7,500-capacity Toledo Sports Arena with support from Starz, whose debut album was about to be released. Nine months after opening for KISS in Pennsylvania, the new iteration of Fallen Angels would be playing their first show with them.

Backstage after Starz's performance, right before KISS were set to go on, photographer Chip Dayton, who did some work for Aucoin, took pictures of the two bands together. He remembers showing Simmons one of the shots sometime later and was surprised by the bassist's response: "He looks down, and I'm expecting him to go, 'Wow, this is really good.' And he goes, 'I don't know why we took this photo.' Like, he didn't like the idea. I felt like saying, 'Well, you're managed by the same guy,' but I didn't. He didn't like Bill managing other bands—that's what it was."

• • • •

IT'S A QUESTION THAT has confounded, even haunted, Starz fans forever. The band had the same manager as KISS. Same booking agency. Similarly cocksure stage show. Songs that would have segued nicely into KISS's on the playlist of the imaginary APW-FM, "The Home of Hard Rock in a Perfect

World." Piper and New England, also on the Aucoin roster, opened multiple KISS shows. So why didn't Starz?

Drummer Joe X. Dubé thinks the reasons were obvious. "Suppose I've got a problem," he says, "and I say to my manager, 'Go yell at the other bands.' That doesn't work. And we were trying to maintain a separate identity, instead of being KISS Junior or Little KISS." For Dubé, that separate identity extended to his gear endorsement, a transaction still popular today, in which a company supplies a musician with free or discounted equipment in exchange for their promoting its products in ads and through personal appearances. When it came time to negotiate a deal for drums, Aucoin asked Dubé if he wanted to go with Pearl. "No, Peter Criss plays Pearl," Dubé remembers telling his manager. "I want something else."

"Well, there's this other company from Japan," Aucoin replied. "How about them?" He then arranged for Dubé to meet at a Japanese restaurant with the president of Tama, which had just started making inroads in the U.S. Five pots of sake later, they had an agreement.

"Bill thought that we were a powerful enough force to establish ourselves separately," Brendan Harkin says, "and that it would be better for everybody that we wouldn't be competition for KISS."

"I never felt that Starz and KISS were competing," says Carol Ross, who directed publicity for both bands at Aucoin. "The issue was that Starz were always in the shadow of KISS."

Richie Ranno says it was Sean Delaney who encouraged the separation. "We don't want to see a problem arise between good friends," Delaney told him. When, years later, fans would ask him why Starz never toured with KISS, Ranno always responded, "What would have been the difference between KISS and Aerosmith?"—with whom Starz played many shows. "They were the two biggest rock groups, and we fit in with either of them perfectly. So I don't think it was detrimental to not go out with KISS. But I'm sure they would have been a lot nicer to us than Aerosmith was."

Rick Stuart, who, later, briefly managed Starz and their short-lived early-'80s spin-off band Hellcats, thinks pairing the band with KISS seemed like a natural move and would have helped to break them. "When Starz went out," he says, "they went out with their drum riser and their [elaborate] set, and a lot of headliners wouldn't let them use it."

When it came to touring, it was understood that KISS would often take out bands managed by Leber-Krebs, including Ted Nugent and AC/DC— even Artful Dodger, a Jack Douglas–produced group whose benign power pop (upbeat, catchy melodic rock often marked by cheerful harmonies and undercurrents of despair) seemed as different from KISS as Captain & Tennille were from Captain Beefheart. "There was a system of trade between some management companies," Paul Stanley says. "Bill Aucoin and David Krebs would trade opening spots on their bigger bands." Which explains why Starz spent so much of their time on the road with Aerosmith and Nugent.

"In some cases, the headliner did not want your junior band playing on their shows," says Jeff Franklin, then head of ATI, KISS and Starz's booking agency. "That way, the manager didn't have a problem, because you always had egos involved."

That is, ultimately, what appears to have been the case with KISS and Starz. "It's a bit of a delicate question," Stanley says before pausing as if to find the right, diplomatic words. "We liked them as people, certainly, but I don't think any of us were enamored with them as a band. It was too cookie-cutter close to us. It was just too premeditated paint by numbers."

That's an opinion shared by Billy Squier, who fronted Piper, another of Aucoin's bands in the mid-'70s. "I think that [Aucoin was] trying to manufacture something that could ride on KISS's coattails," he has said. "It was something that didn't have any real authenticity to it." Rick Nielsen, whose group never played with Starz, has a similar take. "They were one of those bands trying to be somebody else," he says. "You have to be yourself. That's why I've said I could never dress up like Jimmy Page. If you've got to tell people that you're cool, then you're not."

Although they may have been disinclined to tour together, members of KISS and Starz did socialize and work with one another. In 1976, Bill Aucoin, Alan Miller, and Sean Delaney brought Simmons and Stanley along to a party thrown by Pieter Sweval and his partner, Steve Von Schreiber, in the pair's Chinatown loft. "Besides the band, they would invite some of their more colorful friends: Cannoli Ear, the Purple People, Norma Desmond, and the lovely and mysterious Miss Thing," Joe X. Dubé wrote in an unpublished essay. As the party rolled along, someone pulled out the ape mask Michael Lee Smith had worn to perform "Brandy." It became an immediate hit.

"Everyone started passing the Brandy Mask around," Dubé wrote, "and when Paul tried it on, I tossed my stupid little 110mm pocket camera to somebody and they snapped away. KISS, unmasked, with a mask on. Very weird. I had the pictures of Gene and Paul sans makeup for years but I was never tempted to ever sell or 'leak' them. Why should I? What would be the point of that? I had a great amount of respect for their thing and be it far from me to do something to screw it up, which at the time, would have been a very big deal."

One day that same year, Dubé ran into Simmons at the Aucoin offices and invited him to grab lunch. "We go down the elevator," the drummer says. "We're walking around the corner to a coffee shop to get tuna fish sandwiches. This kid sees me and goes, 'Oh my God! It's Joe Dubé from Starz!' We had just played the Palladium or something. 'You guys are fucking amazing!' And Gene's standing there. I say, 'You ought to see my friend's band play— they're good too!' And he looks at Gene and goes, 'Yeah. Okay. Fuckin' Starz is awesome.' And here's Gene seething. Stuff like that made him crazy."

In 1976 and 1977, when Criss was unavailable, Simmons and Stanley would ask Dubé to help record demos, paying him a session player's usual rate. "Just the two of us," the drummer says. "Either me and Gene or me and Paul. They would come in with fragments that they were working on, they'd book time, and we would just work shit out." One late night, naked, about to go to bed in Hoboken, New Jersey, he received a call from Simmons: "Dubé, come on over. I got time."

"I put on my pants, put on my shirt, kissed my wife goodbye," Dubé says, "got in my car, drove over to the city, parked, and we recorded till dawn. But it was fun because we were just making shit up on the spot, trying stuff out, singing two-part harmony."

Since they were demos, the songs were never intended for release, but two of his collaborations with Simmons—"I Know Who You Are," which morphed into the 1978 solo album's "Living in Sin," and "Eat Your Heart Out," which was later recorded by KISS for 2012's *Monster*—ended up on Simmons's massive CD box set, *The Vault*, in 2017. Dubé's work with Stanley, including a demo for *Love Gun*'s "I Stole Your Love," remains unavailable.

Michael Lee Smith, on the other hand, had little interaction with KISS, even though they shared management for years. But when he did run into the band members, in the office or at some function, just to fuck with them he called Simmons and Stanley by the names he'd learned when they were introduced at Electric Lady. "I'd go, 'Chaim, how are you?'" Smith says. "The very first thing out of his mouth was always, 'So, you making money? How much money do you have? You have a big house now?' It always was about money."

## CHAPTER 10

# ELO KIDDIES

IN WAUKESHA, WISCONSIN, A city eighteen miles west of Milwaukee, stands Sunset Bowl, a sports and entertainment complex offering two dozen lanes, dartboards, pool tables, shuffleboard, even a giant Jenga. Back in the '70s, a separate lounge—a long, narrow room, mostly taken up by a large bar—regularly hosted on its high stage such local bands as El Rey and the Night Beats, Ramrock, and Daebreak. Cheap Trick had played the venue a number of times before—it was, after all, only a ninety-minute drive from Rockford—and always attracted a rowdy crowd.

With his lean, unfussy, but resolutely powerful records, Jack Douglas was steadily building a reputation as one of the premier architects of the '70s hard-rock sound. When he walked into Sunset Bowl on Sunday night, March 14, 1976, he had some idea of what he was going to hear, but he wasn't prepared for the spectacle he was about to see. The previous month, Ken Adamany sent a note to the producer at the Copley Plaza hotel in Boston, where Douglas was staying while working on Aerosmith's *Rocks*, making arrangements to have him flown in for the show. Adamany, impressed by Douglas's efforts on Aerosmith's *Get Your Wings* and *Toys in the Attic*—as well as with the band's chart success—had been courting him for a while. "I thought, *Are these the best-sounding records I know?*" Adamany says. "So I started contacting him. It took a long time, but I did get through." He eventually sent Douglas multiple tapes of original material, both live and studio sessions.

The members of Cheap Trick also liked what they heard on the Aerosmith albums: "Up-to-date, good production" was Bun E. Carlos's assessment; "When I heard *Rocks*, it was, *Holy cow, that record sounded good!*" was Rick

Nielsen's. But at the time they weren't so sure about the band itself. "I knew of them," Nielsen says. "But back then it was, 'Aerosmith—isn't that the guy that looks like Mick Jagger singing, and the guitar player trying to be Keith Richards?' We had read that they were way more popular on the East Coast than they were in other places." Carlos remembers Tom Petersson going to see Aerosmith early on and calling them "a bad Rolling Stones," but he also says the bassist was prone to hyperbole. "So maybe they weren't that bad." But to the drummer's ears, "Dream On" was just another "Hairway to Steven"—in other words, the kind of overly dramatic bloat for which his own group had no time.

As Cheap Trick were about to start their set, the producer reached into his bag and pulled out a metronome.

"What are you doing?" asked Adamany, who hadn't seen one of those devices since his younger days playing classical piano.

"Believe me, I do this a lot," replied Douglas, who wanted to check that the drummer could keep time.

"You're not going to need that," Adamany assured him.

Halfway through the first song, Douglas stuffed the timepiece back in his bag.

It was a typically manic show for Cheap Trick: three sets comprised of many songs that would end up appearing on their first three albums. Also typical were the band's gross earnings for the evening: $562.

Douglas remembers the beginnings of his involvement with the band differently. In his version, he was visiting relatives in Waukesha, when his brother-in-law told him he just had to see this band playing the local bowling alley. Douglas has said that he was aware of Cheap Trick because of the reputation they had built in the Midwest, and the gig just confirmed their greatness. "I was knocked out. I couldn't believe how good they were," he said in a 2019 podcast. "It was more like a carnival act. It was so bawdy." Douglas was likely referring, at least in part, to the so-called Carnival Game, the portion of the show—often during the jammy middle of their cover of Manfred Mann's Earth Band's cover of Bob Dylan's raunchy "Please, Mrs. Henry"—when Nielsen would interact with the audience for an extended period.

Drummer Brad Elvis, who would eventually open for Cheap Trick as a member of three different bands, saw the group numerous times in their infancy and recalls the scenario: "Rick gets some girl up onstage and everybody is like, 'Woo-hoo!' It's the second or third set and everybody is drunk on beer, and he goes, 'I'm gonna guess your weight.' So he lies down on the floor with the mic and says, 'You gotta come over here and sit on me. No, no, no, you've got to sit on my face!' Of course, everyone in the place goes nuts trying to look—they're yelling and screaming. The band's still playing quietly in the background, keeping the excitement going. Then the girl squats over his face and sits on him. When she gets up to leave, Rick of course says, 'Pee-yew' or 'Oh my God'—all these dumb jokes." Sometimes for the big reveal, Nielsen would snigger and announce he had no idea how much she weighed.

Douglas has said that after the show he immediately called Tom Werman, head of talent acquisition at Epic Records, and urged him to see the band as soon as possible or he'd bring them to RCA, a competitor. Werman came out a few weeks later to a gig at the Catacombs, a club in Quincy, Illinois. "They were great and extremely loud," he remembers—so loud that he had to go and stand outside to appreciate the songs. "I couldn't actually hear the notes. They bent. There's a kind of Doppler effect that happens when music gets too loud—you can't hear the key. And that's what was happening to me." Nevertheless, he was particularly taken by Zander's vocals ("The best rock and roll voice I'd ever heard") and Carlos's drumming ("I loved all his rhythms and patterns").

When Cheap Trick sent the label a tape of four songs—"Southern Girls," "Come On, Come On," "Taxman, Mr. Thief," and "Fan Club" (recorded at Memphis's Ardent Studios in the fall of 1975)—they insisted they'd be self-sufficient and would gladly take to the road and work as hard as necessary to promote their debut album. "We're big boys and we know how to do this stuff," Carlos remembers saying. "We want a record deal. We don't want a big advance. We want tour support, because we're going to be out there losing our ass."

Adamany received a letter in early April from Douglas's lawyer, in which the producer agreed to work with the band. With a superstar producer now attached, things began to move quickly, until one unexpected development threatened to derail the entire enterprise. In early June, at the Char Bar in Jefferson, Wisconsin, the night before executives from Columbia Records were to fly in to see—and, possibly, sign—the band, Carlos fractured his arm after tripping over a cord. Adamany called New York and San Francisco and told them not to come out. To fill in for a while, the band enlisted Hank Ransome, a friend from Philadelphia who had Nazz connections and at one point played in Sick Man of Europe. "He wasn't quite up to snuff," Carlos says, but he was necessary. As his arm healed in its cast, Carlos played with just one hand, while Ransome bashed on another kit. "So," Carlos says, "we had a drummer and a half for a month and a half."

Columbia's loss became Epic's gain, as Werman now had more time to convince the rest of his team to check out the band. The Epic executives flew in to attend one of the first performances with the tandem drummers and were satisfied enough to offer a contract. "As a four-piece," Carlos stresses. "Hank was never part of the deal. Hearing Rick a few years ago, you would think he was." (Nielsen told *Rolling Stone* in 2015, "We were signed with two drummers. . . . We got signed as a five-piece band.")

"At the end of the thing with Hank," Carlos continues, "Rick and Tom were going, 'We think we should have two drummers. It's so cool onstage.' I said, 'This wasn't two drummers. This was a drummer and a half. Two drummers, it's like a tank. It doesn't move very fast and it's not very nimble. I'm not interested in being in a band if there's going to be two drummers.'" Carlos says he ended up getting fired for two shows while the band tried out Ransome by himself and later had Thom Mooney from the Nazz sit in. "Then they had me rejoin the band," he says. "It wasn't a real pleasant time in my life. These guys tried to throw me out of the band that me and Rick put together. But there you go."

Carlos also takes issue with Douglas's embellishment of his role in their origin story. In 2018, he finally approached the producer about it: "I said, 'Jack, you didn't discover us. We called you, bought you a plane ticket, and flew you to Waukesha. We sent a limo, we gave you the board tapes that night, and you sat there with your pen and paper, writing notes. You didn't just walk into a bar.' 'Well,' he says, 'my story sounds better.' So Jack's rewriting history now." (Tom Petersson articulated his own version of events in his speech at the group's 2016 induction into the Rock and Roll Hall of Fame: "One night in the middle of winter in Waukesha, Wisconsin, at the Sunset Bowling Alley, Sir Jack Douglas saw our group and agreed to produce our first album if we secured a record deal.")

Cheap Trick signed to Epic on August 1, 1976. After a few weeks of pre-production in Madison, Douglas and the group traveled to the Record Plant in Manhattan to track the album with engineer Jay Messina.

．．．．

IN ITS PLUSH '70S heyday, the Record Plant, at 321 West Forty-Fourth Street, between Eighth and Ninth Avenues, resembled nothing less than a hot nightclub—lots of fancy rugs and just the right mood lighting to distinguish it from other studios in the city, like A&R Recording, Phil Ramone's place. Messina, who was on staff at the Record Plant for fifteen years, remembers that since it was close to grungy Forty-Second Street, he didn't like spending too much time outside at three in the morning, which was often when he finished work.

Cheap Trick were scheduled to occupy Studio A from September 1–26. Messina wrapped up KISS's *Destroyer* with Bob Ezrin there in February, and he and Douglas also recorded Aerosmith's *Rocks* and Starz's debut at the Record Plant early that year. For an in-demand team like Douglas and Messina, whose 1976 output also included albums by hard rockers Moxy and Montrose and punk poet Patti Smith, working at this furious pace was hardly unusual. "It was either Jack or me in the control room sequencing the album we just finished," he says. "The other one of us was out in the studio setting up for the next album, not even taking a day off."

When it came to capturing Cheap Trick on tape, Douglas's goal was simple: "If someone buys the record and comes to see us, we've got to sound like the record," Carlos recalls of the producer's philosophy. "If someone comes to see us and then buys the record, the record has to sound like us. They have to be one." Among the many songs recorded (the album's liner notes say twenty-two, Messina recalls nineteen, Douglas nearly thirty, Carlos figures eighteen or nineteen, Nielsen reckons it was more like twenty-eight) were such road-tested favorites as "Daddy Should Have Stayed in High School," "Downed," "The Ballad of Richard Speck," "I Want You to Want Me," "Surrender," "Disco Paradise," and a heavy cover of British blues-rocker Terry Reid's "Speak Now or Forever Hold Your Peace."

On September 16, after basic tracks had been completed and before Zander would be adding his vocals, the band played a showcase at Max's Kansas City. The reasons for the gig were threefold. Adamany saw an opportunity to expose some of the album material to an audience of journalists and influencers in New York City, where the band had never played. It was also a chance for the folks at Epic to experience Cheap Trick live and—fingers crossed—become enthusiastic about the new signees. "We were based in New York and no one had really seen them," says Jim Charne, the band's first product manager at the label. "And you want people to see them because they're so visual." For the group, there was an overriding practical purpose. "The singer hadn't sung in a couple weeks," says Carlos, "so he'd go out and do a gig and scream and yell and get his voice back into shape."

Among the names on the guest list: Patti Smith and her guitarist Lenny Kaye, Jack Douglas and Jay Messina, Richie Ranno, Aerosmith and KISS recording engineer Corky Stasiak, scenester and punk singer Cherry Vanilla, Columbia Records executive Mark Spector, booking agents from International Creative Management (ICM), disco personality Monti Rock III (whom Nielsen had recently befriended), and Gene Simmons. The band played three blistering one-hour sets that night. At one point, Nielsen, in playful Chuck Berry mode, jumped on Simmons's table, prompting the KISS bassist to toss a $20 bill at him, as if tipping a stripper. "Without missing a beat," Simmons told a Minnesota radio show in 2017, as part of a panel interview featuring Nielsen, "he swoops up the twenty, smashes it to his forehead, which is full of sweat, and he continues playing. And I said, 'Wow, that's Jew royalty right there: a guy who carries money on his forehead.'"

This prompted Nielsen to chime in: "And then I took it off my forehead and chewed it. And ate Gene's money." Nielsen exaggerated eating the bill, which Simmons originally claimed was a hundred, because the Cheap Trick guitarist was trying to make an impression. "Give me my money back," Simmons comically pleaded all night long. Forty-four years later, Nielsen couldn't recall if he actually swallowed: "That's the one detail I can't remember."

Any fears Nielsen may have had about his ability to arouse Simmons were unwarranted. "Literally, I was smitten," Simmons said. "I mean, if I was gay, I would have mounted Rick Nielsen onstage in front of his children."

．．．．

CHEAP TRICK WERE SO confident about the quality of the ten songs (eight of them written by Nielsen) included on their self-titled debut that the LP, which hit stores the following February, had no B side. Instead, there was a side A and a side 1.

Side A opens with the frenzied "Hot Love"—no relation to the 1971 T. Rex song of the same name, though Nielsen probably knew and loved it. As guitars saw and burn around him, Zander, in the sweetly sung bridge, asks his intended why she won't let him inside her tonight, a plea that presages what would emerge as a vital Nielsen songwriting trope: his romanticizing of lasciviousness. Initially resembling a delirious booty call, the song becomes in his skillful hands a dig at the earnest chauvinism espoused by so many of his tight-trousered, party-rockin' peers. As if to put a fine point on the Douglas-Aerosmith connection—or perhaps to indulge his own mischievousness—during the fade-out, the guitarist can be heard shouting what sounds like "I'm Steven Tyler, glad to meet you!" into his instrument's pickup. "We used to make fun of everyone," Nielsen says by way of explanation. "Then we found out we weren't as hot as we thought we were."

"Speak Now or Forever Hold Your Peace" follows Terry Reid's 1969 original fairly closely until Zander lets loose with a larynx-frazzling final verse. "He's a Whore," with its punkishly curt and slashing riff and conspicuous quoting of the Beatles' "Any Time at All," turns promiscuity on its head, criticizing a gigolo who'll do *anything* for money —even go beyond fucking a client with green teeth and a clock-stopping face. As if to allow listeners to catch their collective breath, the gossamer ballad "Mandocello" (named for an antiquated eight-stringed instrument Nielsen plays on it) proves the band could do luscious, hazy art pop as well as, if not better than, Nielsen darlings Procol Harum.

"The Ballad of T.V. Violence (I'm Not the Only Boy)," a bluesy shuffle that devolves into an unhinged screamfest, was originally titled "The Ballad of Richard Speck," after the serial killer who murdered eight student nurses in Chicago in 1966. Nielsen was so concerned about the eclectic array of songs, at one point he asked Petersson if it would be wise to adopt pen names. "'Mandocello' was so different from 'The Ballad of Richard Speck,'" he explains. "One's sweet and the other one is real sicko-psycho." The bassist talked him out of it. However, fearing a lawsuit from the victims' families, Epic encouraged the band to retitle the latter track. "I'm not glorifying the guy," Nielsen says. "Twenty-five years later you hear he's got a boob job and there's a video of him snorting coke with his lover in prison. At least I changed the title to something I thought would be topical in the future." It's the type of defense he's found himself making more than a few times, since he often gets inspiration from tabloid trash like the *National Enquirer*. "Half the stuff is true; the other half is fake," he says. "Kind of like reality."

Side 1's opener, "ELO Kiddies"—whose title seems to reference both the band that the Move, a Nielsen favorite, turned into, as well as a bunch of cartoon Japanese cats—is a glittery anthem of youthful disaffection teetering toward rebellion. That it segues so naturally into "Daddy Should Have Stayed in High School" is probably the album's most insidious joke, as Zander sings from the perspective of a thirty-year-old man—clean of body but dirty of mind—who abducts and gags a teenager after having stalked her for five years. "I wasn't trying to be crazy, or noncommercial," Nielsen says of his songs' frequently unsavory themes. "What I wanted to write about usually wasn't what was being written about at the time."

On "Taxman, Mr. Thief," Nielsen reserves his scorn for the titular target ("He hates you, he loves money / And he'll steal your shit and think that it's funny"), who was also excoriated by the Beatles on *Revolver*. Zander even name-checks that band in the second verse and, with a vocal assist by Nielsen, calls out in the chorus the Fab Four's similarly greedy Mr. Heath. The album's weakest track, "Cry, Cry," is a slow-building blues jam that quotes "Heartbreak Hotel." "Oh, Candy," which closes out the side, could be the most winsome-sounding song ever written about suicide, a subject Nielsen would revisit several times.

The brilliance of *Cheap Trick* (and, for that matter, Cheap Trick) is its ability to sprint along the razor's edge between being loud as hell and not being moronic, recasting with wit, intelligence, and subversiveness what was standard operating procedure for a lot of hard rock in 1977. It helps that Nielsen writes songs specifically for Zander's voice, with narrative heft and the kind of dynamic and drama the singer can effortlessly deliver. Nielsen never lets his musicianship overtake the songs; he's a great guitar player who's perfectly secure not showing off his great guitar playing. He doesn't have to. He builds his performance around the riff, not around his ability to shred or improvise. Onstage, it's almost as if he pulls back. Even though he's aggressively flashy, hamming it up, tossing plectrums into the crowd as if he were dealing poker in fast-forward, he often appears to not be playing much at all. One chord, sustained, followed by a flurry of quick notes. *Repeat.* That's virtually all he needs to do to get his point across. "The way he plays is precision-optional," says guitarist Alex Kane, who opened for Cheap Trick while in a band called Holland (booked by Ken Adamany) and worked with Nielsen on an album by ditzy MTV scarecrow Jesse Camp. "He plays for the bigness of the sound rather than for perfection." By Nielsen's own admission, he's a songwriter first—one who plays guitar to make the song better, not to make himself look better. "I'm not a virtuoso," he says. "I never liked that kind of stuff anyhow."

For the cover, Epic hired Jim Houghton, who had shot Ted Nugent's *Free-for-All* for the label and would eventually create indelible imagery for AC/DC and Billy Joel. In the moody black-and-white photo that would introduce the nation, if not the world, to the band, the two dreamboats (one salt, the other pepper) are flanked by the shlubby, bespectacled drummer (ubiquitous cigarette dangling from under his scraggly mustache) and the gangly, pop-eyed guitarist (upturned ball cap concealing his balding pate, affixed to his noggin like some nudnick toupee), a yin-yang conceit the band would be more than happy to exploit throughout their career.

Eric Van Lustbader, a young writer in Epic's publicity department, got the assignment to compose a bio of the band that would appear on the record's inner sleeve. It began, "This band has no past. Literally"—and went on to wax colorfully about the musicians' fanciful ancestry and purported international adventures: Bun E. Carlos was, in Van Lustbader's telling, from Venezuela, his name was "short for Bunezuela," and his family was involved in the construction of the Panama Canal. For Nielsen, it was crucial that the write-up not peddle any Midwestern-bar-band-playing-five-sets-a-night-six-nights-a-week clichés and yet still manage to sound somewhat believable. "All those things had real references," he has said. "None of it was totally made up."

"I'm so naive. I swear, I thought Bun E. came from Venezuela," says Susan Blond, who headed up Epic's publicity department. "Maybe it was a joke even on us." Many gullible rock hacks also swallowed this prankish fabulism whole, and it won the band few new fans at home. "The people in Rockford didn't like it," Carlos says. "The word in town was, 'They must be ashamed of Rockford.' Well, there really wasn't anything in Rockford to brag about." The liner notes undoubtedly prepared Van Lustbader for a successful career in fiction—he went on to become the best-selling author of dozens of thrillers, including more than ten books in the Jason Bourne series.

Critical response to the album was, from the get-go, overwhelmingly positive. Ira Robbins, who would become the most prolific, and perhaps most impassioned, early chronicler of the band, had been turned on to them by his friend Bruce Harris, an A&R executive at Epic. Robbins recalls being treated to a listening session at ear-splitting volume in Harris's office. "I never heard of them before that," he says. "I was like, 'Oh my God, this is so fucking great!' Just everything about it." In his *Trouser Press* review, Robbins, while noting that Douglas's guiding hand gave the album a certain Aerosmith jump, called the band "sarcastic, smart, nasty, powerful, tight, casual, and destined for something great." Charles M. Young raved in *Rolling Stone*, "These guys play rock & roll like Vince Lombardi coached football: heavy emphasis on basics with a strain of demented violence to keep the opposition intimidated." In a generally favorable capsule review in the *Village Voice*, Robert Christgau, considered one of the most important and erudite rock critics, wrote that their sound "recalls the Aerosmith of *Rocks*. Nor am I shocked that they're not as powerful as the Aerosmith of *Rocks*, Jack Douglas or no Jack Douglas."

One of the few high-profile dissenters, *Circus*'s Ken Tucker remarked that the group "established no original style and little ingratiation beyond a certain smug sassiness," before bemoaning "their aggressively snide, winking misogyny and simple guitar riffs that escape being catchy."

The fact that Cheap Trick couldn't be so easily slotted didn't do them any favors. In the same year that saw the release of *Never Mind the Bollocks, Here's the Sex Pistols*, Elvis Costello's *My Aim Is True*, Television's *Marquee Moon*, and AC/DC's *Let There Be Rock*, it was hard to figure out what to make of these guys. Were they heavy metal? Nah, too poppy. Were they punk? Nah, too pretty. Were they hard rock? New wave? Maybe, perhaps, but they sure didn't look like either. These distinctions never troubled the band. "Right before we got signed," Carlos says, "someone from the label was like, 'They're not going to know if you're a rock band or a comedy band,' and we were like, 'They'll fucking figure it out when they put the record on, won't they?'"

Kim Thayil was one of those listeners who understood right away. "Aerosmith's *Rocks* and the first Cheap Trick album, they're siblings," he says. "The way they sound, they're both produced by Jack Douglas, and they both have primarily black-themed covers. The songs are like cousins. Those two records fit together."

Despite the praise and the band's live reputation, CBS's U.K. arm declined to release the album. "The problem, so it seemed," Adamany says, "was they thought since they had Aerosmith, they didn't need Cheap Trick." Carlos was told that the record sounded too "heavy." Jake Riviera, cofounder of Stiff Records, the British indie label that was making new waves with like-minded iconoclasts the Damned and Elvis Costello, stepped in and offered to put it out, but CBS refused. (The album finally surfaced there, on Epic, in May 1980, more than three years after its U.S. release.)

In support of the album, the band did scattered dates with Rush, Boston, Kansas, and the Runaways, before embarking on a brief run opening for the Kinks. Considering Cheap Trick's professed Anglophilia, the pairing could not have seemed more perfect, but in reality it was something else entirely. "The Kinks threw us off the tour because we wouldn't give them kickbacks halfway through," Carlos says. "Five hundred bucks a night! We were making, like, fifteen hundred dollars."

This predicament, compounded by a lack of radio play and a single, "Oh, Candy," that explicitly referenced hard-drug use and failed to chart, left the band scrambling to get heard. ICM, their booking agency, presented them with a few dates opening for British baroque-and-rollers Procol Harum, whose most recent stateside hit, "Conquistador," was already five years old. "One show in New Jersey and three in eastern Canada," Carlos harrumphs. "That's not an album tour."

. . . .

**DEPENDING ON WHOM YOU ASK**, it was either Bill Elson, an agent at ATI, which represented KISS, or Gene Simmons himself who hatched the idea to invite Cheap Trick to open the summer 1977 Love Gun arena tour. The wheels may have been greased even earlier by a giant of a man named Jolly. The six-foot-eight Jolly had been a roadie for Richie Ranno's Bungi, before joining Cheap Trick as their lighting designer and de facto road manager. Eventually he was hired away by KISS, "but for some reason it just wasn't working out," Adamany says. Jolly, who wore one of the first black T-shirts adorned with the Cheap Trick logo—the band name stacked six times in a smudged, Courier-like font, designed by fan and future screenwriter Christopher Crowe—did manage to talk up Cheap Trick to his bosses at every opportunity, and Adamany hoped that at some point a pairing could be arranged.

In what was a fairly uncommon deal at the time, Cheap Trick signed with ICM before they even had a record contract. Elson, whose ties to Adamany went back to the late '60s, knew from speaking with Bill Aucoin that Simmons and Stanley loved the band, so he raised his hand at a KISS meeting and asked, "Would you guys be interested in having Cheap Trick on your next tour?"

KISS had been on Cheap Trick's radar for a while. Nielsen wrote "Surrender," with its well-known mention of the band, in early 1976, and it was one of the songs that was recorded for, but didn't make, the debut album. When asked in 1998 why Nielsen included the KISS reference in the lyrics, Zander jokingly responded, "They were the lamest, most famous band we could think of." Nielsen, who has called KISS "the band that your parents love to hate," offered a more diplomatic explanation in 2016: "You know when you're growing up you need your parents, but you don't want to be associated with them because you're trying to have your own life. Then the worst thing your parents can do is try to emulate you. And here's something that's like, you got my KISS records out. Oh my god! New lows."

Cheap Trick had been on KISS's radar even longer. "I had seen photos beforehand of Sick Man of Europe," Paul Stanley says. "It was pretty out there and pretty cool. By the time Cheap Trick happened, not only was the music really fresh—Beatlesque, Roy Wood reminiscent—but the image of the band was so great."

"We were amazingly flattered," Gene Simmons has said of "Surrender." "First, it's a great tune, whether KISS is mentioned in it or not. But for anyone to give us the time of day, much less mention us in a song, is amazing."

It wasn't for lack of trying that Adamany had been unable to secure support slots with the New Yorkers. The closest he came was a February 1976 date at the Dane County Memorial Coliseum in Madison, but that gig (and part of the tour) went instead to Southern rockers Point Blank, who were also represented by ATI. In a 2018 email to Carlos, Adamany recalled that when he went to Simmons's hotel suite after the show, the bassist was accompanied by "a very attractive student from the Delta Gamma house just down the street."

One night while on the road with Cheap Trick, Adamany got a call from Elson. "I said, 'How good are you at making snap decisions? Do you want to go out on tour with KISS, and wouldn't you like to have ATI represent Cheap Trick?'" the agent remembers asking.

"I'll call you right back," the manager responded.

Adamany knew that making the leap could lead to a lawsuit, but this was the break his band needed. Nielsen, who was also in the room, overheard half of the conversation and asked, "What was that?"

"Tour with KISS."

"Yeah, that's a good idea," Nielsen said. "We should do it."

"It was not easy," Adamany recalls. "I had to extricate us from the ICM deal and we did have to pay something."

Nielsen, at the time, wasn't sure what to make of Simmons's band. "I wasn't a big KISS fan. I wasn't in the KISS Army," he says. "I was a fan of the fact they were doing great." Despite their initial indifference to the headliner, Cheap Trick saw the offer of $1,000 per show as an opportunity to play for big crowds in large venues in cities out west they had yet to hit. It was the means to a potentially lucrative end.

Simmons, Carlos says, also suggested that the band enter the studio and get their second record ready to go in order to capitalize on the upcoming exposure. Buzz was building for Cheap Trick in New York and Los Angeles, where they played a well-received string of dates at the Starwood in March 1977, in front of such tastemakers as KROQ deejay Rodney Bingenheimer, Kim Fowley, and members of the eccentric glam band Sparks. Cheap Trick may not have had an album that sold, but they got reams of good press. "We had bandwidth, mindwidth," Jim Charne says, which led him to demand of his bosses at Epic, "We can't wait a year for another record. We have to keep building this." Fortunately, the band had a huge inventory of songs from which to choose.

Due to the debut's lack of hits, Epic was not particularly high on bringing back Jack Douglas, who was busy with Aerosmith's *Draw the Line*. Douglas has said that he chose not to return and that he recommended Rick Derringer to take over for him.

Tom Werman, the A&R chief who signed them, decided to produce. The executive, who'd worked with Wicked Lester early in his career, had few production credits to his name, but he did manage to mold Leber-Krebs's talented knuckle-dragger Ted Nugent into a viable commercial entity. Unlike Douglas, who merely wanted to replicate the sound of the band live, company man Werman considered his first duty to be to the label, and that meant brightening the songs to get Cheap Trick on the radio. "If they wanted to make more records like the first one, they probably could've built up a nice following," Werman says. "But it takes a hit single to sell a shitload of albums."

The recording came together quickly since the band were set to embark on the KISS dates in July. They started out in Hollywood's Cherokee Studios for a week in May, when part of the building was under construction. This turned out to be not the only notable disruption. "We were in the middle of a take and Art Garfunkel walked through the room going to another studio and blew it," Carlos recalls. "He was like, 'Sorry, guys.' We were like, 'What the fuck's going on?'" After a few days, they decamped to a studio in Burbank and finished the album around three weeks later.

Before the start of the tour, Simmons gave the opening band advance cassettes of *Love Gun*. Carlos, who had liked *Alive!* and *Destroyer* and a few of the early singles, remembers playing the tape and thinking the production was about half as good as the last album's. "The songs weren't bad," he says, though he feels that at that point KISS had begun to cut corners, "just throwing product out there to support the tour, instead of touring to support the product." He attributes what he perceived as a dip in quality to the band's brutal schedule: "It's hard to write a song in a hotel room."

KISS devotees would disagree with his assessment. If nothing else, *Love Gun* is the purest distillation of the KISS essence: disreputable, joyous, and not a little funky. Side 2 even contains two songs—one each by Stanley and Simmons—glorifying their cocks. *Love Gun* might also be the best representation of the band in the studio. By eschewing the parched sonics of the first three albums, resisting the pomposity of *Destroyer*, and featuring two better songs (including Frehley's wonderfully chugging S&M plea "Shock Me" and the so-catchy-it's-criminal jailbait anthem "Christine Sixteen") than *Rock and Roll Over*, it strikes a perfect balance between the band's extremes.

What turned Carlos off most were KISS's onstage antics. "Here's a band, they shoot fire and bombs go off," he says. "We were anti that stuff. That's one of the reasons we were called Cheap Trick. We didn't have lasers and bombs and capes like Yes or ELP. KISS were an act. We weren't. We were a rock-and-roll band." One thing Carlos did admire about KISS was that they were never afraid of being upstaged. "KISS wanted the best band in the world on before them," he says. "KISS had supreme confidence in KISS. Other bands weren't like KISS, though."

Stanley acknowledges that that was KISS's intention from the start. "You can speak to pretty much any band who opened for us," he says. "The idea that we wouldn't give them every opportunity to blow the audience away just wasn't part of our MO. You get thrown into the lion's den, and if you make it out, you deserve it."

Cheap Trick would, all told, open more than two dozen shows on the Love Gun tour, which took the bands from Halifax, Nova Scotia, on July 8 to Regina, Saskatchewan, through Salt Lake City and the Pacific Northwest, and finally to Los Angeles, where they played three big shows, from August 26 to 28, at the Forum. To prepare for the tour, Cheap Trick splurged on a new thirty-eight-foot GMC truck for their gear. "That first year we had that truck," recalls stage manager and drum tech John "Muzzy" Muzzarelli, "we put one hundred twenty-eight thousand miles on it, just doing KISS." The band had done arenas before, opening for Queen and Ted Nugent, but this would be their first sustained effort to play them. And they could not wait.

The Cheap Trick guys, who already knew Simmons and Stanley, met the rest of KISS on day one of the tour. Since the first half of the trek went through Canada, where there was little access to hard drugs ("You couldn't even find weed up there," says Carlos, who liked to partake), the normally hard-partying Frehley and Criss were well-behaved. After watching every night from the side of the stage, Carlos eventually came around to the headliner's production, awed by the pure showbiz glitz of it all.

Nielsen, who appreciated what macabre performers like Alice Cooper and Screamin' Jay Hawkins had been doing with their boa constrictors and coffins, grew to respect KISS as well. "They were terrific," he says. "I understood the theatrics of it." He was more ambivalent about Simmons's songwriting. "Some of the songs are excellent," Nielsen says, "and some are just kids' songs. 'All right. What's the most offensive thing I can say?' He falls into his own trap a bit." In what could be interpreted as either a sly dig or the ultimate compliment, Nielsen, who was often playful with the press, told an interviewer shortly after the tour, "That's not really makeup they wear at all: It's tattooed right on their faces. It's amazing to me as a musician that they'd be into their act enough to do that. I mean, this baseball hat I'm wearing is not sewn to my head. It does come off every time I go for a transplant."

Nielsen was not above complaining, after the July 14 Ottawa show, that KISS used a limiter to suppress his band's loudness. "We were doing well on that tour," Nielsen said in 1988. "They gave us a very good break . . . but at the same time they really didn't have so much to worry about that they should stop us from doing anything. Their show should have been good enough that they don't have to lower our volume."

Barry Ackom, who roadied for Frehley and Stanley, believes that a piece of tape may have been put over the main volume, which allowed the slider to go up only a certain amount. "So naturally when KISS came on, it was going to be quite a bit louder," he says. "You don't want an opening band that is going to overshadow you in some way."

Given Nielsen's and Simmons's outsize personalities, it was only natural that the pair would click and spend time together on tour. "I'm a cartoon character too," Nielsen says. "I mean, who is Gene going to hang out with, the guy who does his merchandise? He can't just hang out. He doesn't do that. At least back then he didn't do that."

It wasn't long before Simmons, a notorious buttinsky, was doling out his unsolicited two cents to anyone within earshot. "Sit down with Gene and he'll start telling you how to run your band or what he liked and what he didn't like," says Carlos. "Every night it was, 'Why are you wearing that shirt? Get a newer shirt.' We would just sit there and go, 'Yeah, sure.' We always got a laugh out of these entertainment people. We weren't laughing *at* Gene, but we would take this stuff with a grain of salt."

Then there was that time Carlos wasn't laughing at all. The drummer, a passionate music collector—who as a fan would bring a tape machine to record Jimi Hendrix, Rolling Stones, and Cream gigs—showed up backstage at the Seattle Center Coliseum for the August 12 date toting a KISS bootleg LP he had just picked up. Simmons, fiercely protective of his band's intellectual property even back then, was less than pleased. "They didn't like that," Carlos says. "I got out of there real quick."

Not only did the tour afford Cheap Trick receptive crowds beyond their wildest imagination, critics started taking notice of their live chops. In a write-up of the Spokane, Washington, show, the *Spokesman-Review* called Cheap Trick "an up-and-thundering hard rock band. The group out-shocked KISS by their sheer understatement. . . . And they can play, with a sound fondly reminiscent of early Who."

"We were getting great reviews," Nielsen says, "and Gene would always say, 'Yeah, but we brought the people here.' We were an unknown, basically. Getting good reviews at a KISS show for the opening act—that's probably unheard of."

"Cheap Trick were a perfect match with the KISS audience," says former KISS tour manager Fritz Postlethwaite. "And they were fun to tour with. Hanging out with Tom Petersson in some Holiday Inn bar in the Dakotas was great."

It was when the tour hit the states that Carlos noticed the blemishes emerging from beneath the greasepaint. Frehley, frequently blotto on champagne, sometimes required a roadie to walk alongside him so he wouldn't trip and fall. On the second night of the Forum run, an emergency nearly led to Carlos sitting in the Catman's seat. After Cheap Trick's set, Simmons walked into their dressing room and told the drummer, "You might want to get some makeup on. You might need to play tonight. Peter's pretty fucked up." And if he needed to fill in, Carlos was ready. "I knew about half their stuff by then," he says, "so I could've stumbled through it."

Paul Stanley, more than forty years later, had no memory of this incident, though Lydia Criss remembers her husband's condition that night. "I don't think Peter was familiar with the drug he took," she says. "They got a doctor in to give him an injection, and eventually he straightened up. But it took about an hour." Carlos says that throughout KISS's set, a roadie had to sit behind Criss, his hands propping up the drummer to prevent him from falling backward.

Steven McDonald, bassist for Redd Kross and the Melvins, went to one of the Forum shows and had the occasion many years later to reminisce about the concert with Tom Petersson. "Tom said, 'We didn't want Peter to die or anything, but I was really disappointed when they woke him up and we didn't get to see Bun E. in Peter Criss drag playing with KISS,'" McDonald says.

It was also at the Forum shows, which KISS were recording for *Alive II*, where Eddie Kramer saw Cheap Trick and decided he wanted to produce them. "He always seemed interested in the band and he was knocked out by the song 'Fan Club,'" says Adamany. "I had him in to look at another group or two, and at those times he asked to hear tapes of Cheap Trick's demos and new songs." Despite the mutual admiration, the collaboration never materialized.

Carlos remembers Simmons telling Cheap Trick before the start of the tour, "They'll be firing shit at you. You'll be ducking stuff. Our fans hate all our opening acts. You guys are good, but they're gonna have you for lunch." Nielsen has said his band were warned, "Wait till you go on tour with them. The audience will kill you. They've murdered all these groups." Petersson heard they'd be dodging bottles and M-80s all night: "And we're all, 'Fuck! Well, all right!'"

But the exposure was worth any pain: the tour introduced the hardworking Midwest band to much of North America. "It's where a lot of the audience for *In Color* and *Heaven Tonight* first saw us," Carlos says. "You still hear about it today: 'You know, I was thirteen, I went to KISS and I came out a Cheap Trick fan.'"

Indeed, some of those teens would themselves become renowned musicians. Gilby Clarke, who would later play guitar with Guns N' Roses and Slash's Snakepit, moved to California from Cleveland, where he had already seen a KISS concert, in the summer of 1977 and caught the tour there. "*In Color* wasn't out yet, but Cheap Trick were playing songs from that record, which really resonated with me," he says. He had never been exposed to them and was stunned he could remember their songs after a single hearing. So he was surprised when he picked up their album at a record store the next day and didn't find "Southern Girls" and "Hello There" on it. He'd have to wait a few weeks until the second LP's release. "When I saw Cheap Trick, it really was like that light bulb went off," he says. "They had good, loud guitars, the drums were nasty, the singer had a golden, natural rasp, and the songs were melodic. It really was everything that I was trying to do as a musician."

For ten-year-old Steven McDonald, whose older brother Jeff brought him to the Forum, Cheap Trick's set was a revelation. Steven, who would later form Redd Kross with Jeff, had never heard them before and remembers being slightly confused by the way they presented themselves, particularly since Carlos looked just like his middle school principal. "When *Budokan* came out a few years later, when they broke through to the mainstream and were getting lots of radio airplay, I knew every song just from that one time seeing them," he says, "because their songs are just so strong and so good."

"We realized when we were out with KISS," Nielsen has said, "the songs that went over best were mostly direct and had the easiest thing to get across.

How do you expect someone who's never seen you or heard you before to know anything about your songs?"

. . . .

**ACCORDING TO JACK DOUGLAS,** it was he who was largely responsible for all of this activity. "I needed them to make that next step," he said of Cheap Trick in 2019, "so I wanted them to tour with Aerosmith. But you couldn't say [to Aerosmith], 'Listen, I have a band.' They were like, 'Really, Jack? You know you're not supposed to ask us, no matter whether you're our brother or not, you know.' So what I did was I booked them into Max's Kansas City and I invited Gene Simmons and Paul Stanley to the show. I just convinced them that they had to come see this band, and they came." In Douglas's recollection, Simmons told him after the gig, "I want this band to tour, to open for us. Jack, what do I do?"

"That was my plan, and it worked out perfectly," Douglas said. "They went out on tour with KISS, and Aerosmith came to me and said, 'What the fuck, man?' It was like, 'They're out with our *competitors*? I mean, come on, man. How come *we* didn't get them to tour?' And I said, 'Well, that could be arranged.' And that started a long, long relationship of those two bands touring together."

"That's all bullshit," counters Ken Adamany. "Jack is just great at making up all these stories. Bill Elson was instrumental in putting us together with both KISS and Aerosmith."

. . . .

**IN COLOR WAS RELEASED** in August 1977, just six months after the debut, as the KISS tour was coming to an end. It fared better than its predecessor but didn't make much of a dent on the *Billboard* albums chart, peaking at No. 73 in October. The band thought Nielsen's inordinately bouncy "I Want You to Want Me" (no relation to the same-named 1963 tune by British beat band the Shadows), which they also recorded for the first album, had the potential to be big. "It was a parody of a pop song," said Petersson. "Let's just do the most sickening pop song we can think of . . . as a joke."

"When we first played it live, Rick would say, 'We're going to do our hit single,'" Carlos remembers, and the song did indeed become a game changer for the band. But the version they cut with Werman for *In Color* took on a life of its own. And not a particularly healthy one.

For the rendition left off of the debut, Douglas put the emphasis on Zander's increasingly desperate vocals, Carlos's locomotive skiffle beat, and Nielsen's scrappy guitar, which practically acts as a background singer, before having it all collapse in a repetitive, anarchic heap. Werman, conversely, heard in the song a finger-snapping 1930s dancehall motif that he wanted to flesh out by adding, to the middle and end, an old-timey barroom piano, courtesy of session ace Jai Winding. (The producer also called in guitarist Jay Graydon to provide the intro lick and a quick rockabilly solo.) "As far as I remember, I had permission to do pretty much anything I wanted," Werman says, recalling that although the band did express their dissatisfaction with the piano, Nielsen shrugged and told him, "You're the producer."

Nielsen contends that Werman made the inclusion without the band's foreknowledge. "We always tell the guys that we work with, 'Don't ad-lib,'" he says, adding that after the band returned from touring, they were shocked to hear what Werman had done. "We came back and it was like, 'What?'"

Carlos recalls the scenario differently. "We knew what was coming," he says. "We just thought it was dopey." What sounded on the first album's sessions like a combination of the Who and the Yardbirds, the band lamented, became on *In Color* a more lightweight Freddie and the Dreamers or Gary Lewis and the Playboys. As the first single from the album, "I Want You to Want Me" failed to even chart.

Werman admits the album is "a little light" ("sounds like cardboard," says Carlos), but his arrangements did bring to the fore the band's innate pop sensibility, which was partially buried beneath the sturm und clang of the debut. If *Cheap Trick* is the noisy, messy beginnings of a band yowling and cooing their way out of Midwestern beer bars, *In Color* brightens their dark visions with concision and catchiness. "Big Eyes," with its echoes of the ominous early Fleetwood Mac single "The Green Manalishi (with the Two Prong Crown)," hints at the proggy British blues rock of which Nielsen was so fond. But the homonymic and homophilic pun in the chorus, which sounds—intentionally or otherwise—like "I keep falling for those big guys," suggests the songwriter could rarely keep a straight face. "Downed," the second of Cheap Trick's recordings to mention suicide, begins with a lovely stroll through Strawberry Fields before shifting into a crunching tribute to Nielsen's attempt to emigrate to Australia in his early twenties. Or maybe it's just about the deadening effects of quaaludes, a synthetic depressant that was all the rage in the '70s. "Clock Strikes Ten" sounds like the Move covering

Bill Haley and His Comets, a party anthem with nothing on its mind but getting money, getting going, and finally getting down. With Carlos's superb metronomic gallop setting the pace, "Southern Girls," the album's second (and, alas, doomed) single, finds Zander praising the young ladies who make it hard, oh so hard. "So Good to See You" and "Oh Caroline" serve to showcase Werman's deft touch with the material, as Zander's sweet and tart delivery doesn't quite mask the lyrics' undercurrents of anger and anguish.

Petersson, in particular, hated the result. "The label tried to make us radio-friendly and safe because our first record didn't do well, and it completely wrecked the way we sounded," he has said. "They said, 'We love you guys, if only you sounded like someone else, it would be great.' To me, that makes no fucking sense. The label thought we were too heavy and too weird." When asked in a 1978 interview which producer the band felt handled the group best, Petersson replied, "I'll put it to you this way and let you guess which is which: one guy was unbelievably great. One guy didn't know what the hell he was doing."

Even though Werman smoothed out Cheap Trick's presentation on *In Color*, Carlos recalls the label's U.K. arm once again taking issue with the material. "We get word that CBS England doesn't know if they're going to put it out," he says, "and we're like, 'Now what?' 'Well, they think it's too pop.' 'Wait a minute! Six months ago, the record was too heavy. Now this one's too pop? What the fuck do these limeys want?' We were the biggest fans of England and we couldn't give it away there." In the end, the record got released as scheduled and they still couldn't give it away there.

The cover photos once again put a fine point on the band's visual dichotomy—Zander and Petersson coolly straddling Harley-Davidsons on the front, Carlos and Nielsen awkwardly sitting astride wheelie bikes on the flip. Paul Stanley, for one, marveled at the setup. "It's not cartoonish in a demeaning way," he says, "but in a colorful way that gave them more breadth, more scope, and made them more than just a bunch of guys playing instruments."

Art Alexakis, leader of alternative rockers Everclear, was excited about attending the big New Year's Eve concert at Southern California's Long Beach Arena in 1977, headlined by humorless prog-boogie giants Kansas. The openers were a band he had heard about but had never actually heard. "I'd seen a poster of them and thought they looked a little goofy," he says. "On the way to the concert, my friend was playing the cassette of *In Color*, and I'm like, 'Who the fuck is this?' And I was just blown away when I saw them live. They were automatically my new favorite band. I thought Rick

Nielsen was going to kill himself because he was flicking picks up in the air and catching them in his mouth, spitting them out, playing the leads."

One thing about seeing them that night bugged Alexakis, however, and it illustrates just how different, exciting, and ingenious Cheap Trick were at the time, and in many ways still are. "They were this badass rock-and-roll band." he says. "Why were they playing with Kansas?"

• • • •

**WHILE THE U.S. TOOK ITS TIME,** Japan got on board early. Japanese music journalists took notice of the odd-looking quartet when they visited the States to cover Queen in 1977. Captivated, *Music Life*, one of Japan's biggest music magazines, invited Nielsen to contribute an article about opening for the flamboyant Brits, which led to Cheap Trick receiving fan mail from that country even before the debut album had been released. "They put a lot of emphasis on what a band looked like," Zander said of the Japanese. "And the more colorful a band looked, the more they liked them. I think that's why colorful bands like Cheap Trick and KISS were big in Japan."

Carlos recalls that even before they showed up to cover the KISS tour, Japanese journalists attended a gig at the Royal Oak Music Theatre, on March 5, 1977, and saw Cheap Trick open for the Runaways, which led to more glowing coverage in *Music Life* and *Ongaku Senka*, another major rock publication. Apparently, there was plenty to write about. "I was standing on the side of the stage during Cheap Trick's set," says Jackie Fox, bassist for the headliner. "Some of our fans were heckling Cheap Trick, and Rick jumped onto a monitor and—not missing a beat as he was strumming—started spitting Good & Plenties at a guy who was giving him shit. It was spectacular! Tom Petersson and I just looked at each other like, 'Oh my God, can you believe this?'"

In Japan, *In Color* produced two Top 10 hits, "Clock Strikes Ten" and "I Want You to Want Me." "It was inspiration," Rue Togo, editor in chief of *Music Life*, said of Cheap Trick. "Kiss and Queen and Aerosmith were most popular at the time. But they were too big; it was time for something new."

• • • •

**IF CHEAP TRICK'S DEBUT ALBUM** presented a scuffed, unpolished mission statement and *In Color* was the buffed and shined compromise, then *Heaven Tonight* found the more-than-happy medium. Despite their dissatisfaction with the production on *In Color*, they once again teamed with Tom

Werman, who this time brought a richness that had been missing from their records. "Werman fell into his role," says Carlos. "[Engineer] Gary Ladinsky was dialing it in. The stuff sounded good. It was the first Cheap Trick record that we all were pretty much satisfied with."

Arguably the band's finest album, *Heaven Tonight* carefully balances their tunefulness and dynamism without taming their recklessness, and contains one of the perfect first sides of '70s hard rock—jumping off with the whirling, controlled chaos of "Surrender" and crashing down on the devastating "Auf Wiedersehen" (suicide song number three). Side 2 is no slouch either: The narcotized title track, while owing much of its apocalyptic allure to Procol Harum's "Repent Walpurgis," plays as either another hymn to the effects of downers or a cautionary tale of same. True to its name, "Stiff Competition," save for its delicate bridge, riotously parodies cock rock—quite literally— while paying homage to both AC/DC (in the bludgeoning first riff) and the Ramones (in the sauntering second), and includes one of Nielsen's cleverest double entendres ("I looked hard in your eyes"). "How Are You," a jaunty piano-driven ditty very much in the vein of "I Want You to Want Me" (which it even quotes), closes the album on a fascinating note, given the discontent over *In Color*.

The album contains the first recorded use of Petersson's twelve-string bass, which gave him a huge, atypically heavy tone and had been added to their live arsenal to try "to get more sound out of a three piece and a vocalist," says Nielsen. Petersson designed it himself for Hamer, an Illinois-based company that also created custom instruments for the Cheap Trick guitarist, including five-neck models and the famous Uncle Dick, a double-neck (more like two-legged) guitar designed in Nielsen's cartoonish image.

To capitalize on *In Color*'s overseas success and promote the just-released *Heaven Tonight*, the band traveled to Japan for six shows, from April 25 to May 1, 1978. Despite a relentless touring schedule that had Cheap Trick playing almost three hundred dates a year, their first three albums failed to gain much traction in the U.S. and the band members found themselves a million dollars in debt.

Upon their arrival in Japan, pandemonium reigned. Thousands of fans greeted them at the airport, hoping to catch a glimpse of the newly minted pop idols. But the perils of superstardom soon made themselves known. The musicians couldn't leave their hotels to grab a bite or take in the sights, for fear that kids might inadvertently harm them—or themselves—in the process. Even so, Zander got stabbed in the back of his neck when an overzealous admirer tried to snip off some of his golden locks. And when the band needed to travel, they'd have to lie down on the car floor to avoid being spotted. "We couldn't even look out our hotel windows," Carlos says, "because fans might see curtains open, back into the street, and get hit by a car."

At least one Japanese music-industry executive seemed stunned by the extent of their success there. "As a producer in Japan, I was trying to sell them as a younger brother band of Aerosmith," said Norio Nonaka, of Epic/Sony's international division, "but I totally didn't expect them to be such hits."

The Japan gigs showcased a typically incendiary band righteously ablaze with the promise of a real breakthrough. Four of the shows were held at smaller halls, but for each of their two nights at Tokyo's Budokan arena, the band played to thousands of screaming fans. Cheap Trick had faced crowds of this size before, but only as an opening act; here, with no support band, all eyes and ears fixed on them. Nielsen, a jittery dervish bouncing around the stage in a cardigan, bow tie, and ever-present baseball cap, maniacally and mockingly attacked his guitar, while the dreamy Zander went from a whisper to a wail, an effortlessly cool Petersson created an orchestra with a mere twelve strings, and Carlos, both ferocious and subtle, pounded his kit with precision and polish. The sets culled songs from all three studio albums, plus three previously unreleased tracks, the rambunctious and teasing "Lookout," the grand trance-blues "Need Your Love," and a cover of John Lennon's cover of Fats Domino's "Ain't That a Shame." "I Want You to Want Me," which Cheap Trick had dropped from the setlist many months prior, became a last-minute addition when they had a slot to fill.

Their label liaison in Japan, a young man called Joe, was a big fan of the band and helped the tour run smoothly. "He was unbelievable," Adamany says. "If you left your hairbrush at the airport or you needed milk for your coffee, he'd knock on your door and within five minutes, it seemed, it would be there." It was only when the tour ended that the manager learned the runner, Hideo "Joe" Morita, had hid his notable pedigree the entire time. He was the son of Akio Morita, the cofounder of Sony.

If the trip served as a vindication, it also presented an opportunity for self-doubt to creep in. "Nobody knew that we'd get popular in Japan," says Nielsen. "They were the smartest people on earth, I thought. What's wrong with Iowa or the other places we played? Why don't they like us like this?" For Carlos, the potent effect of this localized acclaim began to wear off as soon as he boarded the flight home. "I'm sitting in row 43B, thinking, *We just did Budokan for ten thousand people and I'm riding in fucking economy*," he says. "At that time, we were more famous than our circumstances were." He proudly took a cassette tape of one of the shows home to his mother and told her, "Listen to this. You hear that band in the background? That's us. We're huge in Japan, but we're not huge anywhere else." That complaint, fortunately, would prove to be short-lived.

. . . .

"I HAD OFFERED AEROSMITH to make a live album of their concert at Budokan one year before, but was turned down," said former Epic/Sony executive Norio Nonaka. "So, we were desperate to have a chance to make a live album of Cheap Trick."

Sony had sent engineers to record the two shows at Budokan and one from Osaka's Kosei Nenkin Kaikan concert hall in order to create a live album for the Japanese market, but when the band heard the tapes, they realized they had a bit of additional work to do. Tom Werman, with whom they were recording their next studio album, *Dream Police*, even suggested they rent a theater to rerecord the shows. Instead, they teamed with Jack Douglas and Jay Messina to fix some glaring flaws. The biggest problem for Messina was the kick drum, which, he says, "sounded more like a cowbell." Having gotten to a place where they were satisfied, the band found other headaches on the horizon. Carlos says Sony at first screwed up the album's mastering— the postproduction process that balances the mix and creates uniformity of sound among all the tracks—and later exported to the States 50,000 copies of the uncorrected version.

Epic distributed a promotional EP, titled *From Tokyo to You*, to U.S. radio stations, featuring seven songs from an album that was never intended for release outside Japan. But when stations began playing the supercharged "I Want You to Want Me," positive listener response and ensuing demand led to imports of *Cheap Trick at Budokan* showing up in stores. "Our position was, we weren't going to stop the imports at all," says former Epic product manager Jim Charne. "We were going to encourage them."

Carlos was happy for the exposure but wary about the label's approach. "We would only get half a royalty because it was a foreign royalty," he says. "But CBS didn't give a fuck. The import was like twenty-five, thirty bucks. Then, imports of the Canadian pressing started showing up in the northern states. We finally had our lawyer call New York and go, 'You guys are fucking us. You're cutting our royalty rate and making twice as much money on the records.'"

Epic finally released a domestic version of *Budokan* in February 1979. In Great Britain, a full-page ad in the *NME* declared, "Yellow Fever hits U.K!" and touted the group's upcoming tour there as well as a limited-edition pressing of 10,000 copies (on "kamikaze yellow" vinyl). "Nip on down to the record shop," the ad indelicately implored, "and order your dose of yellow fever now!"

As KISS had done three and a half years before, Cheap Trick finally broke through to a mass audience on the back of a live album and a single with roaring sonics that put the rinky-dink studio version to shame. But it wasn't an album they particularly liked. "I think it's a pretty shitty record, really," Zander has said, "but it did real well, played to the strengths of the personality of the band and the songs [themselves]." Petersson agreed: "*Budokan* came out and sort of screwed us up. I don't think that's a very good album, really."

The band returned to Japan for twelve shows in 1979, a trip that journalist Daisann McLane would document for a cover story in *Rolling Stone*. In a release dated April 17, the band's publicist, Lois Marino, described the overseas madness. "We barely escaped from the hall doing the old 'KISS' style exit," she wrote of the March 19 Budokan gig. "The band finish their last encore, throw their instruments to the roadies and run like hell into the waiting cars." Near the end of her report, she added, "It seems no one else at this time even comes close to generating the sales and hysteria of Cheap Trick. (KISS, who were here last year, for some unknown reason are not returning this year. Otherwise, they are still probably our only competition.)"

In July, "I Want You to Want Me" reached No. 7 on the *Billboard* Hot 100, and its follow-up, "Ain't That a Shame," made it to No. 35, helping the live album eventually sell more than three million copies. "*Budokan* obviously recharged them commercially," Ira Robbins says. "But for a bunch of Midwest goobers who were hardworking musicians but had never dreamed of being the Beatles except maybe in their wildest fantasies, to suddenly be living that, I think they were completely bowled over. Not only did they have a wonderful time and feel like superstars there, but then in a weird, backhanded, sideways, unexpected way, that record became their key to American success."

"It was that perfect time," says Tracii Guns, who founded L.A. Guns. "I was probably in ninth grade and all my friends were into *Budokan*. They're a really powerful live band, so I just played that and didn't even buy *In Color* or the other records for about a year. Rick was a new wave guy before new wave even happened. You'd just look at the images and you knew how he was moving onstage without ever seeing him move. They represented the mid- to late

'70s in such a magical way: I was straight out of Elton John to Cheap Trick, like, 'Goodbye, yellow brick road! ELO kiddies!'"

As *Budokan* soared, *Dream Police*, which they feverishly recorded in thirty days ("That's from moving in to setting up and delivering the record, which was in those days unbelievable," says Werman), sat on the shelf for eight months.

"We're on a roll and we're ready to cut a new record," Carlos says. "*Dream Police* is already old news and it's not even out yet. That's when frustration sets in. The music gets out of sync with the band and the label. Suddenly the band's famous for what it did a year and a half ago, and things get screwed up."

When it was finally released, in September 1979, *Dream Police* found the band wholeheartedly embracing elaborate orchestrations and studio trick-ery. If the heavy-metal power pop of "Way of the World," "I'll Be with You Tonight," "Writing on the Wall," and the title track weren't enough to make this one of the most stunningly crafted albums of the '70s, the gorgeously layered call-and-response ballad "Voices" gives it that extra push. Nielsen's familiar themes of paranoia and distrust are keenly represented on the title track as well as the downright vicious "Gonna Raise Hell" and "The House Is Rockin' (With Domestic Problems)." And the studio version of the throb-bing, pleading "Need Your Love" (a highlight of *Budokan*) is positively mes-merizing. Considering how knowledgeable Nielsen was of the late-'60s Brit scene, it comes as something of a surprise that the album title doesn't ref-erence the Scottish band of the same name. Dream Police had three 1970 singles on Decca, shared bills with the Move, and featured a singer-guitarist, Hamish Stuart, who later played with Paul McCartney and Ringo Starr. Their stirring psych-soul, reminiscent of Nielsen's beloved Family, would seem to be right up the guitarist's dark alley. Nielsen claims to have never heard of them.

"The press gave us a little grief," Nielsen says of the record's reception. "It was like, 'Oh, this old album.' It's like, 'Gee, sorry we had some success.' So we were all prepared to go out and bang it again." And bang it they did. The Dream Police tour, at the band's commercial peak, took them to Madison Square Garden, where they headlined a New York City arena for the first and, it would turn out, only time.

## CHAPTER 11

# COMIN' HOME

BEFORE 1981, WHEN MTV began to codify the look and sound of multiple genres of rock and roll, and before the internet rendered the look and sound of multiple genres of rock and roll virtually irrelevant, culture spread at what seemed like a one-legged turtle's pace. Bands in the '70s relied on radio and television to spread the word, but broadcasting could only spread that word so far. Radio playlists, rigid as they were, and rare, very-late-night glimpses of bands actually performing (relievedly not lip-syncing) on shows such as *In Concert*, *Don Kirshner's Rock Concert*, and *The Midnight Special*, played huge roles in launching artists. Newspapers, when they cared, were useful for promoting tours and spurring record and ticket sales, but it fell to the rock press to fill in the blanks, burnishing the old myths while creating new ones. In the mid-'60s, Rick Nielsen had the weekly U.K. music tabloid *Melody Maker* airmailed to him (it usually arrived six to eight weeks late) because, he says, "There was no national rock magazine in the United States, and all my heroes were English." But how many kids ringing up groceries in Cincinnati could afford that luxury?

In the U.S., *Rolling Stone* and *Crawdaddy* took the music seriously but were fairly—some would say, unfairly—narrow in their tastes, holding their noses at anything that had the faintest whiff of pandering. The Beatles began as yeah-yeah-yeahing teen idols before dosing and seeing Lucy in the sky with diamonds. The early Stones may have bashed out the blues, but by the '70s they would dabble in funk, reggae, punk, and disco like a bunch of pub-booth ethnomusicologists. Both bands grew up, got more sophisticated, matured along with their audiences. On the other hand, it could be argued that KISS, Aerosmith, Cheap Trick, and Starz never did. And though *Rolling Stone* would be slightly more welcoming of Aerosmith and Cheap Trick, KISS and Starz never stood a chance, offending from day one these arbiters of good taste, who prized seriousness and authenticity above all else.

So it was up to *Circus, Creem, Hit Parader, Rock Scene*, and the like to pack their pages with the latest on these Unfab Four, not to mention the second-stringer likes of the Godz, Mahogany Rush, Angel, and Detective. *Circus* had the distinct advantage of coming out twice a month in the mid-'70s. Production considerations rendered the others, primarily monthlies, many weeks behind on the news, but that hardly mattered to the photo- and info-starved masses who craved rock and roll.

If the magazines had personalities, *Rolling Stone* was the high school teacher in the flowery Huk-A-Poo shirt and flared Wranglers who was rumored to have once shared doobage with his trig students. *Circus* was the class president, sometimes trying just a little too hard to be hip. And *Creem*? *Creem* was the snide but fun-to-be-around, politically savvy wake-and-baker who always aced his physics tests despite never studying. Initially based out of Detroit, the magazine, which published its first issue in 1969, a little more than a year after *Rolling Stone*, didn't start out commercially minded. Its goal was to get intimate with artists and to avoid the prevailing press-release blather. "Something would happen and then three months later you'd get a copy of *Hit Parader* or *Creem*," says former Aerosmith crew member "Nite-bob" Czaykowski. "You used to wait for *Creem* because it was like news from the front—instead of the instant news of today, when something bad happens and everybody knows."

Bebe Buell, scenester, singer, muse, and a former girlfriend of Steven Tyler's (and mother of his daughter Liv), appeared in the magazine so often she counted herself among *Creem*'s official mascots. "So how could I avoid *Creem?*" she says. "And we all looked at *Circus* and *Rock Scene*. It was part of our youth and our culture, the same way you would look at teen magazines when you were younger. But back then, you got your information off the street. Magazines were what came out after the event had happened, the vanity project where you read the articles and looked at all the cool pictures."

As the record label or band management's press departments helped secure features, request reviews, and plant gossip, KISS, Cheap Trick, Aerosmith, and Starz all participated in the coverage, some more willingly than the others. Robert Duncan, a former *Creem* editor, remembers going to Manhattan's Plaza Hotel to interview Steven Tyler and Joe Perry. "First of all," he says. "I was surprised by how tiny they were. I'm good friends with the guys in Blue Öyster Cult, so I know that there's lots of tiny rock stars. This must have been the height of their coke period. They were so incoherent. They were just assholes. Their PR agency was telling me, 'Well, you know, Aerosmith's on another level.' The level that I met at the Plaza Hotel was pretty low."

Duncan soon found out how easy it was for a rock hack to sell a story about KISS. "I consciously would write an article slagging them off one week in one publication," he says, "and then write for another publication, saying they were the greatest thing ever." In his quickie 1978 paperback bio of the band, Duncan ended up analyzing the members' handwriting when he ran out of things to say. "I took them as a platform on which to clown, to get laughs," he says. "I remember putting together issues where it didn't matter if you're pro or con, as long as you could have their name on the cover."

What distinguished Jaan Uhelszki, KISS's biggest booster at *Creem*, from her colleagues was the fact that she actually liked the band. "They were just irreverent and really dangerous and punk rockish before that term was there," says the writer, who in 1975 famously got face-painted by the band and contributed "I Dreamed I Was Onstage with KISS in My Maidenform Bra." To her, KISS symbolized the death of rock. "It was the mid-'70s, the end of that peace-love flower revolution that was so wonderful," she says. "And this was just something darker and primitive. It tapped into something unknowable. I had this funny feeling that they would be massive." Despite all the ink, within the offices KISS weren't necessarily seen as a "*Creem* band." "I really did force them down everybody's throat," Uhelszki says. "It was humiliating how hard I had to fight for them, like, 'I know that is a great idea. Please trust me. Just give me this one.'"

The magazine's voice was rarely more impious than in a regular feature called "*Creem*'s Profiles," a fake promotional page on which a band touted Boy Howdy!, the magazine's fake signature beer. Among the (fabricated) KISS questionnaire responses: "Home: Last House on the Left; Hobbies: Measuring the EKG's of the nubile young."

Among Starz's: "Hobbies: Trying to get their pictures on the front covers of their albums; Profile: . . . They're still as dumb as ever—thank god."

Among Cheap Trick's: "Profession: Ex-stock boys, pin setters, and teenage waitress pinchers; now professional pick-spitting poseurs."

For Aerosmith, the magazine couldn't resist a KISS comparison: "Last Accomplishment: Becoming the most popular heavy metal band in America without sticking their tongues out or incinerating their audience."

Lynn Goldsmith, who in the early '70s directed ABC's *In Concert* and comanaged Grand Funk Railroad, turned to photography in the mid-'70s, and her pictures of KISS, Cheap Trick, and Aerosmith enlivened many issues of *Creem*, *Circus*, and *Rolling Stone*. She always admired Cheap Trick's visual savvy, loving how Nielsen became the focal point despite not being the frontman, comparing Robin Zander and Tom Petersson to *Archie* comics' Betty and Veronica, and likening Carlos to "a strange nerd businessman." "It's almost as planned out as KISS deciding to be superhero characters," she says. "It's just that KISS were more obvious."

Goldsmith adored shooting KISS and appreciated that they came to their photo sessions with a clear sense of who they were. "Because they trusted me," she says, "they were willing to take it further and to do more." Which may account for her pictures of the Starchild eating vegetarian takeout and the Demon wearing dental braces, tonguing an album cover of paramour Diana Ross. She had done so many sessions with KISS, in fact, that they kept a set of costumes at her studio. "Unbeknownst to them—and Paul probably wouldn't have liked it—when people would come over, I told them I had KISS's clothes," she says. Laraine Newman from *Saturday Night Live* was shot wearing Stanley's boots and jacket, and Goldsmith herself played dress-up one Halloween.

A photo session with Cheap Trick in 1979 wonderfully played up the band's connection to their former tour mates. When he saw Stanley's outfit, Bun E. Carlos decided to roll up his baggy trousers to the knees and put on the black platform boots adorned with silver chains and wear the KISS frontman's bejeweled black jacket over his own Salvation Army dress shirt and skinny red tie. In the photos, Petersson, in all white, and Zander, in all black, prop him up to keep him from teetering. "Everybody always loved KISS clothing," Goldsmith says. "It was like, *These clothes are fabulous. Let's play.*" Everybody, it seemed, but Tommy Hilfiger. In 1993, while shooting portraits of the fashion designer, she pulled out Stanley's boots. "He picked up the phone and called Paul," she says. "Paul said, 'Lynn, you have my boots? Do you think you could send them back to me?' I said sure. So that was the end of photographing people in Paul's boots. But I took good care of them."

· · · ·

**"THE COLORFUL BANDS WITH** the quotable copy had their finger on the pulse. They got lots of ink," says Ira Robbins, whose *Trouser Press* evolved from its mid-'70s Anglophilic origins to focus on the burgeoning punk and new wave scenes. "It was no surprise that KISS were endlessly covered, even though they really didn't have anything to say. And then Cheap Trick did roughly the same thing. They became very colorful." In other words, both bands' often-entertaining line of bullshit made for entertaining stories.

"The *Trouser Press* consensus was that we were much more interested in the quality of the art, to put a really pretentious slogan on it," Robbins says. "We were not immune to colorful bands that had good patter, but we didn't start there. We were very slow to embrace that. Obviously, we ended up covering them all, Cheap Trick a lot more than KISS, but that wasn't because of their quotability or because they were two nerdy guys and two handsome guys. That was never a part of the story." In Robbins's view, the fact that Led Zeppelin very quickly became infamous for their bad behavior made it easy to write about them, so everyone did. The difference was, *Trouser Press* published a four-part series on Jimmy Page's session work. "We had a sense of connection to the music that to a large degree excepted the imagery," he says.

Robbins's Cheap Trick fanaticism led to his becoming so trusted a confidant that an Epic representative would frequently call to get them all together whenever the band came to town. One afternoon in the late '70s, he met Rick Nielsen, Tom Petersson, and their buddy Gene Simmons for lunch at one of Manhattan's few Japanese restaurants. The cuisine hadn't yet hit the city in a big way, so the editor saw the choice of venue as a way for the well-traveled musicians to jovially show off their knowledge of the foreign culture. Robbins had met Simmons, a longtime subscriber to the magazine, before, and throughout the meal the bassist played the part of a smarmy New Yorker, at one point referring to miso soup as "snot soup." One of the musicians told Robbins, who had never eaten Japanese before, to enhance the flavor of his food by adding some green mustard. "I put a tablespoon of wasabi on a piece of sushi and almost burned my hair off, and they're laughing," he says. "These are grown men having a good meal in a nice restaurant and they're winding up the journalist with wasabi and talking about snot soup. The idea of eating raw fish was already one of those 'I'm going to get through this, I'm not going to puke' moments."

Some journalists, like Michael Gross, enjoyed the glamour and decadence. "The reason you became a rock writer was because if you had no musical ability, it was a way to live that life," he says. It started with getting free records to review for your college paper. Then came the free concert tickets. And then the free food at press events. "Two years in," he says, "you realize that after the concert, you can go to the party. Then you go and think, 'Well, the band is going to get the four best-looking girls in the room, but there are twenty-five more girls here who are only incrementally less interesting.' You could ride around in limousines and sample all of the myriad indulgences that were available in that world."

As a senior at Vassar College, Gross arranged his classes so he only needed to be in upstate Poughkeepsie one day a week. He spent the rest of the week in Manhattan hustling for freelance work. Upon graduating in June 1974, he soon discovered that skin mags paid a lot more than rock rags did. Suddenly he was making $600 for an article instead of $60. After pitching a Led Zeppelin one-shot to Myron Fass, the notorious publisher of garish pulp magazines offered Gross a full-time position as editor in chief of *Rock*. Gross, cocking an eyebrow, pointed out that another publication already had the name. Fass told him not to worry, then insisted the logo be set, à la *Creem*, in a red toothpaste-out-of-the-tube typeface. Again, Gross was told not to worry. He doesn't know if *Creem* ever sued or sent a cease-and-desist letter, but Gross soon found himself editing a magazine called *Blast* instead. "Then Myron brought back *Rock*," he says. "So in alternate months, I would do a *Rock* and then a *Blast*, then a *Rock* and then a *Blast*." Fass's other music magazines included the evocatively titled *Acid Rock*, *Groupie Rock*, *Rock Mania*, *Punk Rock*, and *Super Rock*. In 1979, he published *Rock Spectacular Cheap Trick Special* with additional cover lines touting both Aerosmith and KISS (including GENE SAYS KISS IS BETTER).

Gross first encountered KISS on New Year's Eve 1973 at the Academy of Music in Manhattan—opening for Teenage Lust, Iggy Pop, and Blue Öyster Cult—the band's first big New York show. "I thought they were a load of shit musically, but the makeup was fun and the bat lizard blew fire," he says. "I didn't even stay in my seat for KISS. I recall watching from the back of the hall and thinking, 'It's Halloween! This is interesting!'" They would not be relevant to him at all until a few years later when he had to think about whom he was going to put on a cover.

In March 1977, Gross was one of the many journalists who accompanied KISS on their first tour of Japan. "Gene would take Polaroids of every girl, all of his conquests," he says. "And there was one who we shared on that trip. Gene actually gave me one of the Polaroids of her. It was made clear to me that Gene had droit du seigneur"—the right of the lord, or, in other words, first dibs—"I think it was probably made clear to everyone who was straight on that trip. One of the only memories I have of that interview is asking him why he took Polaroids. He said, 'It's so when I'm in the Old Rock

Stars Home in my wheelchair, I can take out my scrapbooks and laugh and laugh and laugh.'" (Simmons also granted Rick Nielsen an audience with his photos. "Have you seen a seventy-year-old man naked?" Nielsen says, before deadpanning, "You don't want to." The Cheap Trick guitarist playfully adds that he has also been privy to videos: "I recall, 'Come to Daddy, come to Daddy'—that's what he was saying in one of them.")

As for the other members, Gross, who would also be a consultant on the first KISS comic book, recalls Frehley being impossible to talk to, Criss seeming like a humble married guy, and Stanley playing the rock god, which led to residual benefits for the writer. "Even though he's much taller than I am, I had hair down to here and girls would chase me around thinking I was Paul," he says. "I would literally be backed into corners and forced to sign Paul Stanley autographs."

· · · ·

**"I DIDN'T EVEN LOOK** at *Rolling Stone*," says Gerald Rothberg, former publisher and editor in chief of *Circus*, which he founded as *Hullabaloo* in 1966, the first major U.S. magazine to treat rock stars, like the Doors, the Who, the Beatles, the Monkees, and the Rolling Stones—even a few bands lacking the definite article—as pop stars. An early home to rock writers such as Paul Nelson, Kurt Loder, Fred Schruers, and David Fricke, the magazine enjoyed its heyday in the mid-'70s, as hard rock helped goose sales toward one million copies per issue. "Obviously the writing staff looked at *Rolling Stone*, because they eventually wound up going there," Rothberg says, "but I was focused on what we had to do. We had to structure an editorial focus on the one hand, then push for circulation on the other hand, and get advertising on the third hand. That's the only way you'd survive."

It may sound like a suburban-parking-lot cliché now, but Rothberg had convenience stores like 7-Eleven to thank for the uptick. "You'd get the slushy drink and go over to the magazine rack," he says, "and fortunately, we were displayed prominently." One of *Circus*'s advantages was its glossy paper stock, which showed off concert photography better than the more newsprint-reliant periodicals. Rothberg looked to *Sports Illustrated* as a model, because of its sharply focused, well-lit pictures. Since photographers had no control over concert lighting, he insisted they use flash, which bands usually forbade. "One photographer told me, 'You've got to start paying us combat pay,'" he recalls. "It was funny, but it was also true, because kids would lunge at them, and photographers in those days had expensive equipment."

"At *Circus* there was a lot of attention paid to bands that were good-looking," says writer Wesley Strick. "Also, because the magazine was sometimes just appealing to a teenybopper base, they would put pretty people on their covers." Which helps to explain the discordant covers pairing Robert Plant with Linda Ronstadt and Debbie Harry.

While the editors and publishers denied any horse-trading or pay to play, Casablanca executive Larry Harris was vocal about participating in quid pro quo. He claimed that ad pages, which he paid for with thousands of free promotional albums, helped to buy KISS coverage in *Creem*. In fact, one *Creem KISS Special Edition* from 1977 featured not only Starz and Aerosmith cover lines, but also full-page ads for KISS and two other Casablanca artists, Parliament and Meco. Harris also admitted that the label was not shy about stuffing the ballot box for *Circus's* readers' poll, which helps to explain KISS's perpetual showings, and said the fact that he ran ads on the magazine's back cover for a long period of time "gave *Circus* the incentive to cover KISS as much as possible."

Before becoming a Hollywood screenwriter and producer, Strick was a prolific New York City rock journalist toiling for the likes of *Circus*, *Creem*, and *Rolling Stone*. For the first, he would write so many stories and reviews that his editor assigned him pseudonyms. "There was a certain formula to *Circus* features that you learned to follow pretty quickly," Strick says. "You were mostly conveying excitement with maybe a tiny undercurrent of snark. But you could never afford to let that go too far because it just wasn't that sort of magazine." Many of his pieces were about KISS, a beat he stumbled on when Gene Simmons took a liking to him during an interview one evening around the release of *Alive!* They had been chatting on the phone when Simmons suddenly interjected, "Where are you?"

"I'm on Seventy-Eighth Street and Lexington," Strick responded.

"Jump on the bus and come over, and we'll do this in person. It'll be more fun."

When Strick arrived at Simmons's Upper West Side apartment, he too had to share in the rock star's triumphs. "He had books piled up, very carefully arranged by country," he says, adding that every page contained numerous photos of naked young women Simmons had brought back to his hotel rooms on the road. All of them relaxed on his bed exactly the same way, with their legs spread, exposing themselves. "I was like, 'Whoa!' And he stood there just wanting me to admire all of his conquests, which was weird. But that's how we forged our friendship, I guess, in his mind."

From then on, whenever there was a KISS feature to be written for *Circus*, Simmons would request that Strick get the gig. But like others who wrote about the group at the time—Michael Gross and Robert Duncan, to name two—Strick was dubious and hardly a fan, not to mention ten years older than those he perceived to be in the band's target audience. "I always thought KISS pandered," he says. "They were almost like the Donald Trump of '70s rock. There was just something shameless about them." But he played along, thrilled for all the work, happy to record for posterity every Stanley boast ("The best thing about being so successful is we haven't sold out") and every casually sexist and/or racist Simmons comment ("Japanese women were slanted in our favor").

Strick was far more fascinated with Starz, about whom he also wrote for *Circus*. "They were a relief from the bombast of KISS," he says. "They were aiming for something clever. There was some pop craft to Starz's songwriting that appealed to my ear." He also admired their lyrical preoccupations, particularly those on *Violation*, the band's stab at a concept album. "Hidden behind the pop artifice was something darker and stranger—the social commentary and the sense of dread about modernity—which I thought might lead them to some kind of lasting success." The fact that lyricist Michael Lee Smith was a Southern boy made things even more interesting. "You weren't expecting that sort of cultural commentary from him," Strick says.

In June 1976, for a short *Circus* profile promoting Starz's debut album, Strick traveled with the band and their manager, Bill Aucoin, to Massachusetts's Cape Cod Coliseum for a gig with ZZ Top and Blue Öyster Cult. On returning to his hotel room after the show, Strick answered a knock on his door. It was Aucoin. "He walked in and immediately put a hand down my jeans and said, 'Do you want to go for a walk on the beach?'" Strick says. "I said, 'No,' and froze up like people do in those situations. He didn't take it any further. He just pulled his hand out and left. It's funny, I didn't really think of it as sexual assault per se, until the #MeToo movement." The incident didn't make it into the story, although acknowledgment of the band's libidinous manner did: "Starz sweats sex. . . . Starz celebrate the Primal Throb."

Despite his earlier praise about their way around a tune ("'Cherry Baby' . . . *sounds like a classic*"), in a review of 1978's *Attention Shoppers!*, Strick killed them with unkindness: most bands wouldn't mind having a song (in this case, "Hold On to the Night") compared favorably to Big Star, but before getting there, he calls Starz "a band without any convincing *raison d'être* apart from success . . . a self-styled Instant Group still looking for Gratification."

"I don't remember the record well," Strick admits, adding that by then he had entered a phase in his reviewing career where he tended to dismiss much of what he heard. "It's more fun to write a pan than a rave. But I took stock at some point and realized that the last twenty or thirty reviews I'd written were pans, and it struck me that maybe this had run its course. That was part of the reason I stopped the rock writing."

• • • •

FOR JONATHAN DANIEL, WHO played bass and wrote songs for Candy and Electric Angels—two major-label glam-metal strivers that emerged in the '80s—and later found success as a manager of Fall Out Boy, Panic! At the Disco, and Green Day, all it took was one magazine's promotional effort to introduce him to KISS and Aerosmith and set him on a career path. "*Creem* had an offer where if you subscribed you got either *Destroyer* or *Rocks*," he recalls. "So that, for me, is the link between those two records, because I got *Destroyer* and my friend got *Rocks*. Then we taped each other's records." Which led to his discovery of Starz. "I bought *Starz* because it had the Rock Steady logo on it. And then Cheap Trick opened for KISS. So they're all super-connected."

Other artists echo the significant role *Creem* and *Circus* played in shaping their musical tastes. "That's how I learned about these bands and their tours," says Everclear's Art Alexakis. "I cut out the pictures and put them up on the wall. I saw ads for Starz and they looked cool and I saw that they had some sort of connection to Aerosmith."

Says Gilby Clarke, "The only information we got back in those days was from *Creem* and *Hit Parader* and stuff like that, so I was definitely being fed whatever they were selling."

"You saw KISS or Alice Cooper on the cover of *Circus*, and these were the bands that we were exposed to," says Gary Cherone, lead vocalist of Extreme. "We were suburban white kids, and what we were exposed to was rock and roll."

Growing up in a Chicago suburb, Soundgarden's Kim Thayil didn't have money to spend on magazines, so he would go to the library and pore over issues of *Creem*, which not only satisfied his fanboy urge to see KISS both onstage and among mere mortals, but also put the music in context and apprised him of such associated bands as Angel, the Godz, Piper, and Starz. "*Creem* would talk about KISS being from this hard-rock tradition that was started by the Stooges and the MC5, two of my favorite bands," he says, "and how they embraced this unusual style established by the New York Dolls. I wasn't acquainted with any of those bands. By 1975, they had broken up and their records were out of print." KISS became for Thayil the foundational band that connected him with heavy metal, hard rock, and FM radio. Eventually they would lead him to punk and change his life.

When Danny Goldberg wrote for *Circus* in the early '70s, he saw rock magazines as vital, but not nearly as much as radio airplay and concert bills were. "I say that with some regret as a former journalist and public-relations person, but it's just the reality," he admits. "The press was important for the imaging, the photos and quotes, and the cultural dimension to it. But Cheap Trick certainly wouldn't have been Cheap Trick without having hits. And booking agencies would put packages together and get these bands in front of big audiences. *They* were much more important power brokers."

## CHAPTER 12

# GET IT UP

**IF THE BOOKERS, AS** Danny Goldberg suggests, were the ultimate power brokers of '70s hard rock, Premier Talent Agency's Frank Barsalona and American Talent International's Jeff Franklin were vying to be Robert Moses. There were other agencies representing bands back then—like ICM, which handled Aerosmith, Fleetwood Mac, Heart, Kansas, and Styx—but Barsalona and Franklin had market share. In addition to booking KISS and Cheap Trick in 1979 (and Starz until 1978), ATI worked with AC/DC, Bob Seger, Rod Stewart, Blue Öyster Cult, ZZ Top, and Neil Young, to name just a few.

Barsalona founded Premier in 1964 as the first agency to concentrate solely on rock and roll. In his view, the bands, the promoters, and the record companies needed to work in concert to achieve one goal: to build artists' careers. And his innovations were legion. He treated the music as a serious art form, not as some disposable kiddie fad, transforming the multi-artist revues popularized by impresarios like Murray the K—where acts simply flogged a few of their hits before making way for the next product on a rock-and-roll conveyor belt—and gave headliners the opportunity to play full sets. Realizing there was a market for live rock beyond the occasional promotional appearance, he created monthslong tour cycles, providing bands with another potentially huge source of income beyond record sales. In the '60s, he brought the Rolling Stones, the Beatles, the Who, the Yardbirds, and Led Zeppelin over for their first U.S. tours. By 1979, he was representing Black Sabbath, Boston, Peter Frampton, Lynyrd Skynyrd, Santana, Bruce Springsteen, the Who, and Yes, among many others.

In the late '60s, local promoters in cities across America began adopting the booking policy Bill Graham established for the Fillmore West. People attended shows in that era partly because of who was on the bill and partly because of the venue's status as a gathering place. Barsalona collected promoters all over the country—Howard Stein in New York, Don Law in Boston, Larry Magid in Philadelphia, Mike and Jules Belkin in Cleveland, Alex Cooley in Atlanta—to create a dedicated network of venues where he'd place his acts. These promoters encouraged customer loyalty by improving the quality of the presentation, paying more attention to lights, sound, staging, and savvy billing, pairing developing acts with sympatico artists to grow fan bases while satisfying the already devoted. "Frank made this alliance with the main guys," former agent Bill Elson says, "which basically was, 'You have to have a ballroom, and if you help me break new talent, they are yours in that market forever.'" Not only did this foster allegiances, but for talent buyers it also avoided regional bidding wars. Barsalona hired Elson to find new promoters in the Midwest, an area that had been largely ignored by Premier.

John Scher, who promoted concerts in the New York area and ran the Capitol Theatre, a major midsize venue in New Jersey, considered himself a beneficiary of Premier's largesse. "If they thought you really did the best job on every level, you got anointed," he says. "It was almost like Major League Baseball—you got a franchise."

With this structure in place, a band could open out to eventually conquer the country. Even those that never became national names could create fan bases in particular regions, due to the connections and branding of the local promoters.

Elson, who represented Cheap Trick for eleven years, worked for Barsalona from 1970 to 1977, when Jeff Franklin lured him away. "What I learned from Frank was truly invaluable," he says. "But there was nowhere to go. He was a poor Italian guy from Staten Island who wouldn't buy an extra paper clip if he didn't have to."

It was—and still is—a booking agent's job to negotiate gigs with local promoters. The geographic area often was specified by the artist manager or record company, with the goal of enhancing the band's presence there. With superstar acts, the goal was to produce revenue. In 1977, Aerosmith and KISS were not so much looking to increase awareness as they were just wanting to make money, satisfying a demand for their appearance. At that time Cheap Trick were still developing. Their success was mostly concentrated in the

Midwest—Illinois and Wisconsin, in particular—so any concerts they played outside the area would have been to promote an album and get better known.

As an arena headliner in 1977, a band like KISS or Aerosmith could command a guarantee of $25,000 versus 85 percent of the net receipts. So if a ticket cost $10, in a sold-out 15,000-seater, gross receipts would total $150,000. After deducting the promoter's expenses, say, $70,000, there was $80,000 left to divvy up, which would leave the band members with around 85 percent of $80,000, or $68,000.

Most openers, according to Elson, didn't earn more than $1,000 a night. "And that was the case for like fifteen years," he says. "In some cases, it was five hundred dollars or seven hundred fifty dollars." John Scher recalls paying some opening bands as much as $3,000, which was approximately how much Starz would eventually make per show.

Early in KISS's touring career, Jeff Franklin—a close friend of Neil Bogart's who helped launch Casablanca—sometimes had to pay promoters to book them. "We had to literally force them," he says. "They didn't want to play them because it was too expensive, too risky. The first two tours didn't really work. Major headliners didn't want them as an opening act. It was not easy to book KISS. KISS was a real fucking job."

Some promoters also had to be convinced KISS were worth the trouble. Ron Delsener recalls being approached in the Beverly Hills Hotel by Casablanca's Larry Harris, who told the New York–based promoter he just had to book this band. "I said, 'Hey, man, it's not my shit. I don't play that,'" Delsener says. "I like Bob Dylan, Phil Ochs. I'm into meaningful lyrics." He finally relented and booked two shows for March 21, 1975, at Manhattan's Beacon Theatre, which quickly sold out (and earned KISS a positive review in the *New York Times*, of all places) and prompted Delsener to tell Harris, "Man, I'm in! Hello! I'm a believer."

• • • •

IN THE '70S, IT was not unusual for a record to take hold regionally before breaking out nationwide. Before "Lady" became a No. 6 hit for Styx in 1975, it received radio play in 1973 in the band's native Chicago, a few other places in the Midwest, and in Utah.

Styx were one of the few acts to be booked on bills with KISS, Cheap Trick, Aerosmith, and Starz—a distinction also shared by Rush, Ted Nugent, Bob Seger, ZZ Top, and Blue Öyster Cult. When Styx weren't opening for more established bands, they would be able to do, say, one night in Wisconsin, and then drive on to headline another show in South Dakota.

It was there, on June 10, 1974, where they were scheduled to play the Central States Fairgrounds in Rapid City, with KISS, an opening band that was unknown to Styx lead singer Dennis DeYoung. A torrential downpour forced the cancellation of the outdoor gig, and DeYoung found himself in a hotel bar, chatting with Gene Simmons and Paul Stanley. "They obviously didn't have any makeup on, so I didn't even know they wore makeup," he says. "Of course, right after that, they went on to become *KISS* and we continued to be the bridesmaid."

When DeYoung finally got to share a stage with them, in November 1975, his band would be opening. "In those days, there wasn't a great deal of camaraderie and backslapping and *good for you!*" DeYoung says of the reversal. "Everybody was in competition. It was dog-eat-dog. You're duking it out, album after album, tour after tour. This is the arrogant side of any performer: When the tables turn, you know what you think? *Fucking right, I earned it!*" That night, floored by the number of kids he saw in copycat makeup, DeYoung understood KISS's appeal. "And I thought, *Geez, these guys are loud*," he says. "It was interesting to watch what they were doing. It was more like the circus than any of the other bands we played with."

Just a few months earlier, Styx had headlined a festival at Fairmont Speedway in southern Minnesota, where a fledgling Cheap Trick were among the openers. "I didn't know who the hell they were," says DeYoung, who always watched the support acts. "They weren't in full regalia at this point. I don't think Rick had completely discovered the value of [the checkerboard pattern]. At that time Rick Nielsen was less like Rick Nielsen and more like the Midwestern Pete Townshend. He was jumping around and I thought the band was interesting."

DeYoung recalls the first time he encountered Starz on tour. Styx had just pulled into the venue's parking lot when he spied the support band's beautiful bus. "They were all dressed to the nines—money was being spent," he says. "We thought, 'Who are these guys?'

"I think Bill Aucoin was trying to make another KISS, but KISS was so unique that Starz was not going to be that thing," he continues. "No disrespect to them. I've watched them. They were a competent band. They went out there and did that rock-star thing. It was a little too much style over substance."

When Styx played with Aerosmith in 1977, DeYoung saw a different kind of circus, one that seemed nearly as colorful as KISS's but a lot more dangerous. "I'm pretty sure they didn't like each other much," he says, "and they were certainly not in charge of their faculties." At the Spectrum in Philadelphia, on October 9, DeYoung was behind the stage when an M-80 thrown at the band exploded, searing Steven Tyler's cornea and maiming Joe Perry's hand. The injuries forced Aerosmith off the road for a month but gave Tyler and Perry the opportunity to head back to the Record Plant to finish *Draw the Line*.

Perry later dubbed that album, Aerosmith's fifth—recorded in a miasma of coke, heroin, downers, and guns in a former New York convent—"the beginning of the end." Jack Douglas admitted that as the band grew apathetic about the project, so did he. "For five days a week, they would all drive up in their Ferraris and stay in this amazing mansion with three cooks twenty-four hours a day," says Sam Ginsberg, an assistant engineer on the album, who also worked with Cheap Trick and Starz. "Steven would wake me up at three a.m.—'C'mon, Sam, I wanna hear something'—so I'd mix something for him. But it was a really good idea for that band to go there, because, at that point, it was hard to get them to show up anywhere all together." Despite, or perhaps because of, the anarchy, they managed to eke out one stone classic—the fiery title track—and two near-misses, the swampy "Get It Up" and the epic "Kings and Queens." (And though the album shipped one million copies, it wouldn't be certified double platinum until 1996.) Subsequent inconsistent and drug-drenched gigs served as an unfortunate lead-up to Perry's euphemistic finale. Art Alexakis took in the show at the Los Angeles Forum in November 1977. "They weren't the same band I had seen two years earlier," he says. "Just too sloppy. They looked great, but they were going through the motions at that point."

"A lot of the time we really sucked," Perry admitted. "But we'd stopped giving a shit."

## CHAPTER 13

# COLISEUM ROCK

**CAPITOL RELEASED THE SECOND** Starz album, *Violation*, produced once again by Jack Douglas, in May 1977. The band originally intended for it to be a concept album set in a postwar dystopian future where rock and roll has been outlawed until the hero discovers a scratchy old copy of Aerosmith's "Walk This Way" in a thrift store and the music begins to flourish once more. But that was before Capitol and Aucoin decided to reorder the songs so that the strongest ones led on side 1, thus muddling the narrative.

Even in this altered state, *Violation* remains one of the great underheard albums of the era, with a surfeit of tunes that would make many bands envious. The opening track, "Cherry Baby," blends a furiously melodic guitar riff with a chorus hookier than a detention hall full of truants, before charging into a clap-along not unlike the one that enlivens Neil Diamond's "Cherry, Cherry." And if the graceful intro to "Sing It, Shout It" sounds like the perfect backing to a scrolling community calendar on a local TV station's public affairs program, that's because it was used as such—in Toronto, at least. That song in particular is a superb showcase for Michael Lee Smith's imaginative way with words and mastery of inner rhyming ("Her lips are all I need to survive / So she blitzes me with kisses just to keep me alive"). Continuing Smith's fascination with repellent characters and twisted wordplay, one song is sung by a rapist serial killer and another by a guy who gets jerked off in a movie theater while watching a Western ("The redskins were shootin' at the wagon train / That's when me and the cavalry came").

In addition to the Aerosmith allusion on "Rock Six Times," on the title track the band subtly invoke KISS during the barking chorus response "No, that's a violation!" "I used to sing like Gene Simmons just for fun," Ranno recalls. "So Michael wrote that section and said, 'I'd like Gene to do it, but why don't you just do your impression?'"

That year found Starz supporting Aerosmith on the Rocks tour (which began in 1976). Steven Tyler and Joe Perry were deep into their various addictions, irritating the members of Starz, whose primary intoxicant of choice was beer. "Brad and Tom and Joey were very friendly with us," Ranno says of the attempts at backstage camaraderie. "The other two were in their own world."

Joe X. Dubé recalls once leaning on a road case after the band had been touring with Aerosmith for a while: "Tyler walks up to me and says, 'You know, you guys are okay, but I'm not so sure about that lead singer.' And I said, 'What's the matter, his lips are too big?' And he just looked at me, spun on his heel, and walked away. I don't think he said anything to me after that ever again." And while he had many pleasant breakfasts with Tom Hamilton and Brad Whitford, Dubé says, "Joey Kramer couldn't pick me out of a lineup if there were only two people and one of them was him. I never spoke to him."

As for the Starz frontman, he kept to himself—in a matter of speaking. "I didn't really interact with any of them," Smith says. "When we got done with our sets, everybody else would hang out, but I was already back at the hotel with a girl, preferably more than one." The singer had a system whereby he would arrange for his roadie to receive four extra room keys. Then, during the show, Smith would point out which girls in the crowd deserved one. "Half the time," Smith says, "they'd be waiting in the room by the time we got back." Smith says he and his wife had an agreement: *You don't ever bring anything home and you don't ever do anything if we're available to each other.* "I'd go on the road six weeks at a time or longer," he recalls. "She'd go all over Europe or to Japan with Petula Clark for a long, long time. What are you going to do? Things are going to happen. It's unrealistic [to think otherwise]."

Brendan Harkin recalls seeing Aerosmith watching his band, in essence checking out the competition. "And we scared the shit out of them," he says. "We'd do a good show every night. And to their credit, they never kicked us off the tour because we were too good. But I think they screwed around with our sound. They would limit our volume."

On August 29, 1976, Starz played an outdoor radio station concert in Buffalo, New York, with Roger McGuinn and Talas. For their next gig, opening for Aerosmith across the country at Seattle's Kingdome on September 3, the band took their bus west for three days, stopping only for food and fuel. "I would go to bed," Dubé says, "wake up, peek out the curtains, and say, 'Ah, Madison!'"

Upon their arrival in Washington, the promoter had a surprise waiting. He had added another act to the lineup and told Starz that if they wanted to play, they needed to start at 7:30, in order to abide by a union-imposed curfew. "We go, 'What the fuck?'" says Dubé, adding that the band begrudgingly went on in front of 10,000 in a venue that could hold more than 60,000. "It looks like nobody's there. We do our hot half hour, as we liked to call it—we had our set time down to twenty-nine and a half minutes, because all Aerosmith would give us was thirty before they'd pull the plug. So eight o'clock rolls around. By then it was dark, so they turn on the stage lights. The place starts looking like a real concert, and the emcee comes out and says, 'Ladies and gentleman, that was Starz. And now, the juggler!' And this guy comes out on a unicycle, juggling balls. I turn to Brendan and say, 'We just traveled twenty-six hundred miles to open for a fucking juggler, who has got better lights. Is this what it's come to?'"

In April 1977, Starz's tour manager, Arnie Silver, succeeded in finagling for the band what they thought would be a better spot on a lineup at Bill Graham's Winterland in San Francisco, where they were sharing the stage with headliner Bob Seger & the Silver Bullet Band and newcomers Tom Petty and the Heartbreakers. No matter that "Breakdown," Petty's first single from his debut album, had made some ripples and the follow-up, "American Girl," had just been released, Silver told the promoter Starz would not go on before him.

"Well, Tom Petty opened and the place went nuts," he says. "Then we had to go on, and the crowd was lukewarm." After the show, when Silver approached Graham to get paid, the legendarily hotheaded impresario laid into him: "I've been promoting these fucking concerts for years, and I'm telling you I know how to set it up. You fucking guys think because you're with KISS you can run the world." Silver got his money, but not before Graham told him to get his skinny ass out of there. "We couldn't follow Tom Petty," Silver says. "A lot of people left after him."

When Starz opened for the J. Geils Band in Providence, Rhode Island, on New Year's Eve in 1978, Steven Tyler met up with the band backstage and finally acknowledged the shout-out in "Rock Six Times." "He thought that was really cool," Ranno says. "We were shocked that he came back and hung out with us and was acting like a friend for the first time." But Aerosmith's indifference toward the band resurfaced twenty years later, when, in the authorized oral history *Walk This Way*, Starz were dismissed as "an English knock-off of KISS."

The connection between Starz and Aerosmith extended beyond their sharing Jack Douglas and concert stages, and into their romantic lives. At a Runaways gig in Baltimore, bassist Jackie Fox recalls seeing her bandmate Joan Jett hitting on a girl who looked like Stevie Nicks. "Joan was saying, 'Oh, I really like your scarf,'" Fox says. "I kid you not: women don't have any better lines than men do."

"Thank you," the girl told Jett. "Steven Tyler gave it to me."

"I remember internally rolling my eyes and wandering off because I'd seen this situation before and it wasn't of interest to me," Fox says. "The next day, Joan was just gushing about her." That's when Fox first heard about Valeri Kendall, who dated both Steven Tyler and Michael Lee Smith: "She was in love with Michael Lee Smith while we were friends. She ended up moving out here [to L.A.] and marrying Alex Van Halen."

Fox finally met Tyler at an Aerosmith concert in the late '90s: "After he did the whole new BFF thing he does with everybody, 'cause he's really amazing that way, I asked him if 'Sweet Emotion' was about her"—as Kendall had claimed. "He said, 'No, that song existed before Valeri ever came on the scene.' But then he leaned over and said, 'She's the kind of girl I would've written that song for,' and then whispered, 'What ever happened to her?' Then he got whisked away by his handlers, and I was left to wonder what the hell that meant. She was enough of a thing that he remembered her twenty years later and still thought of her as this hot young thing."

Kendall did, however, inspire Smith to write a song about her: "So Young, So Bad" on Starz's fourth album, *Coliseum Rock*. "To this day," he says, "I love Valeri Kendall."

• • • •

AS A KID ON Long Island in the '70s, Steve West, cofounder of New York rockers Danger Danger, would pick up anything marked with the Rock Steady imprimatur, and after seeing Starz perform on *Don Kirshner's Rock Concert* in October 1976, he rushed out to buy their debut album; they immediately became one of his most cherished bands. "Their music was up there with everyone else's," the drummer says. "Starz is brilliant—the harmonies, the guitar. There's a lot of well-thought-out stuff going on. The way Dubé plays is bizarre, his beats and fills are weird, not straight-ahead, four-on-the-floor rock and roll." They motivated a young West to form a band called Violation, who played KISS, Starz, Aerosmith, and Cheap Trick songs in his suburban basement. Years later, he realized how much Starz influenced the lyrics he wrote for Danger Danger. "I got a lot of vibe subconsciously from them," he says. "There's a lot of sexual innuendo and double entendres in Michael's lyrics, more so than in Aerosmith, KISS, and Cheap Trick. Starz songs are a little wackier, but really good musically, way beyond KISS." Following in the tradition of "Surrender" and "Rock Six Times"—which shout out to others' records—"Cherry Cherry" off Danger Danger's 2000 album *The Return of the Great Gildersleeves* quotes both "Surrender" and "Cherry Baby." "I didn't realize until I got older that Rick Nielsen would take from the Beatles and the Move," he says. "You have artistic license to do that. So, whenever I get stuck with writer's block and the record has to be done, I'll just steal a Cheap Trick lyric."

Starz appealed not only to bands that liked to double their nouns, but also to musicians who liked to double their consonants. Mötley Crüe's Nikki Sixx told *Details* magazine in 1991 that the first Starz album changed his life. "Yeah, 1976 had Aerosmith, and yeah, it had KISS, but back then this was new, and only *I* had them," he said. "Starz was dirty rock 'n' roll, where every teenager hangs—suspended between great rock beats and pop melodies from hell." Eighteen years later, he tweeted that he would love to cover "Pull the Plug" someday: "Such a cool song with great lyrics." Rikki Rockett, the drummer of Poison, actually did cover Starz, recording for his 2003 solo album "Tear It Down," a Fallen Angels track that Starz redid on their debut LP. "I love all their shit," he says. "They were a torch-bearing band. They carried the torch for rock through the disco era, which was one of the most devastating eras for rock ever. If they would've been around a few years earlier, they would have been huge."

• • • •

**WHILE STARZ WERE IN** Los Angeles for a gig at the Santa Monica Civic Auditorium in May 1977, Aucoin arranged for them to film a couple of promotional clips at SIR, a rehearsal studio on Sunset Boulevard. Inside one of the darkened rooms, rows of colored lights surrounded a large stage. Dubé's kit, both of its bass drum heads emblazoned with a star, sat imposingly on a four-foot riser. First on the call sheet: a performance of "Cherry Baby," which was currently hanging low on *Billboard*'s Top 40 singles chart, the band's initial appearance there. Michael Lee Smith, in a dark, chest-exposing jumpsuit accented with his signature red sash, twirled as he lip-synced, while Ranno, wielding a double-neck guitar, and the others dutifully hit their marks.

"Sing It, Shout It," which ran more than five minutes on the album and was the proposed follow-up single, came next. After the band took their positions onstage, drums began to boom from the PA, followed by a gentle guitar line, steady throbbing bass, squelchy introductory solo, and Smith's first verse. Forty seconds in, the track on playback went straight to the bridge, skipping the second verse. The musicians, bewildered, stopped dead.

"What is this?" Ranno shouted at Aucoin, who was standing off camera.

"Oh, that's the edit," the manager responded.

"Can we hear the whole thing?" Ranno asked.

As the song played back, the band members seethed.

"*Who did this?*" Ranno screamed from the stage.

"Uh, Jack did it," Aucoin replied, referring to Douglas, the song's producer.

"What would possess him to do *this*?"

"Well, he submitted one after another, until I finally approved."

"*You* approved?"

With that, Dubé snapped. Leaping off his riser, he lunged toward his manager, knocking him to the floor, and wrapped his strong hands around the slight man's throat. "*What the fuck is this?*" he yelled. A few guys rushed over to pry him off. "It was a pretty crazy scene because Bill was not a physical guy," Ranno says. "He was freaked out. I don't know if there were apologies made."

Dubé admits he overreacted, but adds that due to the pressure of touring commitments, "we were all pretty high-strung at that point." The band understood that an edit might be necessary to get the song on the radio, but, Dubé says, "that's not the way to tell somebody—when there's a camera on them." After tempers cooled, the band agreed to power through and continue miming to the shortened song, as smoke machines coughed up plumes that mirrored the dark cloud that would soon loom over Starz. "I realized then that you can't trust anybody except the people you make the music with," Dubé says. "Everyone else has their hand in your pants, and not in a good way."

Harkin says it was well within Aucoin's purview to insist on the new edit. "We didn't have an agreement with anybody that every single thing had to get run by us," he says. "Certainly Aucoin had equal power and say-so about everything the band did, probably more so."

As far as Ranno was concerned, though, the manager had no right to make that creative decision, and soon called the person responsible for the edit. Jack Douglas, he says, insisted that he believed Aucoin had run the change by the band beforehand. "It wasn't his fault," Ranno says.

Whether it was kept secret out of shame or embarrassment, news of the commotion at SIR never made the twenty-eight-hundred-mile trip back to Aucoin's Manhattan offices. Production coordinator Stephanie Tudor, as well as publicists Carol Kaye and Carol Ross and promotion coordinator Gail Rodgers, hadn't heard about the assault until being informed of it more than forty years later. But Rodgers wasn't surprised. "Dubé was pretty expressive when things either weren't done the way he believed they should be done or in the way the group would want it done," she says. "It's an interesting relationship between artist and management. The artist comes in, and it's their creativity and their challenge. But it's the manager who spit-polishes, cuts the facets, and packages it, just that much better. Then it becomes, 'Whose band *is* this?'"

Both Ranno and Smith look back on the incident as a major turning point for the band, one that would impact everything that came after. "Right there, doing that video," Ranno says, "that was when our career actually ended."

A week or two after the altercation, Ranno, who would regularly call in to the office while on the road to inquire about the band's chart status, got Alan Miller on the line. The guitarist was surprised to hear that "Cherry Baby," after eight weeks on the *Billboard* chart, had stalled at No. 33, without a star (or bullet) to signify upward movement.

"Oh, we dropped the promotion on 'Cherry Baby,'" Miller told him. "We're kicking it."

"You're *what*? That makes no sense!"

"No, it does. We're putting all the money into 'Sing It, Shout It.'"

"Well, 'Sing It, Shout It' sucks!" Ranno replied. "You guys ruined it. You can't release that single like that."

"No, no, no. It's going to be great."

"Alan," Ranno said, "this is a *big* mistake."

"Sing It, Shout It," entered the Hot 100 at No. 83 on June 25. Three weeks later it had crawled to No. 66 and died.

• • • •

**THERE'S A LITANY OF** complaints artists typically pin on management when their careers aren't going exactly as planned—greed and neglect chief among them. The word "sabotage" is rarely uttered, but that's the accusation Ranno throws at Aucoin. It didn't strike him until years later, when distance brought some perspective. "Aucoin was a very powerful guy who loved using his power to make or break," he says. "I realized Aucoin never did forgive the choking incident."

Jonathan Daniel, Starz fan turned music-industry heavyweight, says that that's a very artist-like way of thinking. "It's a way to justify it, so I understand where the sentiment comes from," he says. "But if Aucoin dropped them after that, and *then* buried them, that would make sense. But to keep them and bury them, that feels like a weird thing to do. It feels like a lot of work."

Still, Ranno and Smith claim that's why Aucoin had Starz produce their third album themselves—not at the familiar Record Plant, but at the lesser-known Secret Sound—though others involved have vastly different recollections. With "Cherry Baby" plateauing not far from the Top 30, Starz's manager and label pushed them to try to write more hits in a similar vein. "Aucoin was steering us away from Jack Douglas, saying Jack wasn't ready," says Ranno, who adds that after he called Douglas to confirm, the producer told him, "I can't do it. I'm just finishing up the Aerosmith album. Just wait."

Aucoin told the band they couldn't; they needed to get a record out soon.

Since Starz were officially signed to Rock Steady, and not to Capitol, which funded the recording through Aucoin, Ranno suspects his manager was rushing them into the studio so he could secure the advance and was cutting costs in order to pocket some of the money that should have been going toward the budget. "Why didn't we do it at the Record Plant?" he says. "We did it at a shithole recording studio. They didn't have good playback speakers. No producer payments, no real engineer payments, and the studio was cheap." His gripes extended to the creative choices of his bandmates, whom he felt were acceding to the pressure to go pop. "I was really upset," he says. "I was going home from the studio every night, saying to my wife that I've got to quit the band now while I still have some integrity. I didn't want to be involved in this band, because I was establishing myself as a rock guitar player." Rock fans, he reckoned, were very loyal until they weren't. Veering off in a new direction could be fatal. "I was feeling like I was losing my grip on what I was doing. But I couldn't pull the trigger and quit. I had to stick it out and see what I could do."

Brendan Harkin says that the band had no qualms about self-producing after learning that Jack Douglas wouldn't be available. "Aucoin probably should have stood firm and said, 'No, wait for Jack,'" he says. "I just said, 'We know how to make a record.' And we had done a demo [for the album] at Secret Sound that everybody really liked.'"

Harkin still has affection for the LP that emerged from the sessions, but admits that it may have alienated fans who expected another heavy Douglas production. "Aucoin should have gotten us with Bob Ezrin," he says. "We should have written songs and recorded with him. That probably would have brought us over the top. Instead, they let us make this modest little record in this modest little studio. It was a mistake." A crisis of confidence may have contributed to what the band felt were lackluster results. "Richie was the one who knew how good we were," Harkin says. "Everybody else wasn't sure. I certainly wasn't sure. Michael wasn't sure."

Harkin, on a '70s-rock online forum in March 2009, elaborated on the recording's psychic cost. "Nobody will ever know what may have happened if we'd waited around for Jack to do the third album," he wrote, adding that constant touring and recording had taken their toll and the failure of *Violation* had everyone pointing fingers. "Aucoin blamed the band and Capitol and was in a cocaine and popper haze to boot, Capitol blamed Aucoin, the band blamed everybody but itself. . . . Of course, we had already done the best we could with *Violation* and that hadn't worked, so I'm not sure whatever we came up with would have done any better."

In a Facebook status update on March 1, 2019, Michael Lee Smith offered his recollection of the LP's origin. As the band prepped for their follow-up to *Violation*, Aucoin told him that despite having "a highly appreciated album and a Top 40 single . . . not one single producer in the world wanted to work with Starz!" which led to Harkin overseeing the recording. The frontman also suggested in the post that the band should have dedicated the album to their manager, given it an all-black cover, and called it *Death Sentence*. Jack Douglas later responded on the thread with his side of the story: "I wasn't asked or even approached to produce the third album. I always thought it was weird and it pissed off both Jay Messina and myself."

Jack Malken, the owner of Secret Sound, which was founded in Manhattan's Chelsea neighborhood by Todd Rundgren, engineered the sessions and recalls some awkwardness when he first met the band. "They said, 'When we fight, we really get into it,'" Malken says. They then had an unusual request: Could he set them up with an extra room? "And can you fill it with things that we can break?" Malken remembers Dubé asking. "Dishes, cups—anything we can throw at each other and break." The engineer indulged them by affixing padding to one of the three-story facility's rooms, but remembers the band being enthusiastic during their time there and keeping any drama they may have had to themselves. "I wasn't familiar with that request," Dubé says. "We weren't typically a bunch of throwers—maybe the occasional chair after a particularly rough show. Someone might have made the request as a joke to see if they would do it to accommodate any request we might have made."

In a move that trumpeted the accessible content within, while at the same time sounding not a little desperate, Starz titled their third album *Attention Shoppers!*—its front cover adorned with a flat red-and-yellow band logo on black, its grainy back cover featuring the previously stellar quintet clad in plaid pants, varsity jackets, and peasant blouses, hamming it up in a store window. That it was shot by famed David Bowie photographer Mick Rock makes it all the more peculiar. "I love that album," says Jonathan Daniel, who wrote an article in his high school newspaper about how it was a crime that Starz weren't big, "but I thought that was the worst album name and cover of all time. That was not cool or smart."

The packaging, designed by Capitol art director Roy Kohara, even confounded others at the label. "I thought, *This is a bad move*," says former promotion manager Ray Tusken. "This doesn't speak to the punk thing. It doesn't speak to the rocker. What is it? That, to me, was a deadly step."

Even if it does lack the beefiness of a Douglas production ("We forgot to turn on the echo," says Dubé), the album, released in January 1978, features some of the band's most appealing material, with "Hold On to the Night," "(Any Way That You Want It) I'll Be There," and "She" best capturing the poptastic "Cherry Baby" feel. "Bill said every single song has to be made for Top 40 radio," says Smith. "Every one of them. All I could do was say, 'Okay, let's try to write some friggin' Top 40 songs, but still try to keep the Starz fans happy.'"

Yet some compelling weirdness remains: "X-Ray Spex" sneeringly attempts to imitate the Sex Pistols, and the hilariously turgid "Good Ale We Seek" pokes fun at the pastoral Hobbit rock favored by Led Zeppelin and Jethro Tull ("I love no roast but a nut brown toast / And a crab laid in the fire"). With a softening of their sound came a rethink of their presentation, the dressing down on the back cover a conscious decision to put the music above all else. The leather look of the first album? That was Sean Delaney's doing, Ranno said in 1978. "Fleetwood Mac doesn't have an image," he said. "Foreigner doesn't have an image. What image does Boston have?" But then, what did those bands have that Starz didn't?

"I wanted that album to have, like, five hits," Jonathan Daniel says. "That was the thing about Starz. Everything else might have been slightly wrong—the logo is genius but a little corny, the name is a little corny with the z—but the songs were so good. I could not for the life of me understand why they weren't hits."

The subsequent tour found Starz opening for Foghat and Styx, among others, with a less-elaborate stage setup. "All of those gimmicks—the fog, the mirrored balls under the drum riser and the shooting sparks 30 feet in the air—were the right thing to do at that time," Ranno said in 1978. "They went well with the music."

Cracks began appearing in the shiny Starz façade on this tour, as some members felt Sweval's social life was beginning to take precedence over his responsibilities to the band. "Pieter was getting whole hog into the gay culture, which is fine, until it was impacting our music," Dubé says. "We would be in the dressing room half an hour before going on at eight, hadn't seen Pieter since we got to town. He'd get dressed, start rehearsing the warm-up, and he couldn't play the riff to [*Violation's*] 'Subway Terror' or something as clean and as hard and as hot as you had to in about twenty minutes. So if you can't do it here, how are you going to do it out there, when you're running around, looking cool, people throwing shit at you, and it's a hundred degrees?"

Harkin, having had the biggest hand in *Attention Shoppers'* production, bore the brunt of what the band perceived as its creative failure. Besides, with the traveling, the time-wasting, the constant ringing in his ears, he just wasn't enjoying himself anymore. He wanted instead to retreat to the studio and become a session player and producer. Ranno, Dubé, and Smith didn't fail to notice his unhappiness. So when the decision was made to let Sweval go, it became a twofer. "I showed up at the meeting," Harkin recalls, "and the guys said, 'Maybe you should leave too.' And I said, 'Okay, good. I'm done'— like, 'You can't fire me, I quit.' I was happy. I was free."

Sweval didn't take it so well. He left Smith's apartment, the site of the meeting, and went up to the Aucoin offices, where he proceeded to kick in a door. "I feel really bad to this day that Pieter just freaked out," Ranno says.

To replace Sweval, the band tapped Orville Davis, former bassist for Rex, a tough and tuneful hard-rock quintet led by Michael Lee Smith's brother Rex, before he became a pop idol and actor with the 1979 Top 10 hit "You Take My Breath Away." Leber-Krebs managed Rex (the band), who recorded their 1976 debut album, produced by Jack Douglas associate Eddie Leonetti, at the Record Plant while Cheap Trick were in the building doing their first-album demos with Douglas himself. Rex later shared a bill with Cheap Trick (and Be-Bop Deluxe) in 1977. Even with the fraternal connection between the lead singers, before he joined, Davis (who would later become Dubé's brother-in-law) wasn't all that familiar with Starz's music. "My attitude was, this is what I do," he says. "You want to kick ass? We're gonna kick ass." As the former bassist for Hydra, a superb Southern boogie outfit that opened for both KISS and Aerosmith, he had plenty of ass-kicking in his past.

Taking over for Harkin was Bobby Messano, a journeyman guitarist whom Ranno knew from Jersey. Before joining Starz, Messano hadn't yet quit Stanky Brown, a gloopy fondue of Steely Dan meat and Firefall cheese, managed by the Capitol Theatre's John Scher; Messano assumed (correctly, it turned out) that they would soon be dropped by their label, Sire. He had liked the first two Starz albums, especially the single "Cherry Baby," but Messano didn't know where they fit in the rock-and-roll food chain. "I knew they were on *Don Kirshner*," he says, "and I knew they were friends with KISS." And if there had been any negligence on Aucoin's part, Messano didn't see it. "I don't know where they would get the idea that he didn't believe in them," he says. "Maybe just for a momentary lapse of reason. In any conversation I had with Bill, it was clear that he loved the band, and he was telling me, the new guy. He didn't need to blow smoke up my butt."

Despite the nonperformance of *Attention Shoppers!*, Capitol decided to put more resources behind Starz's fourth album in three years. To help guide them, the band returned to the sure hand of a familiar Jack, not Douglas but Richardson, who thirteen years earlier produced the unreleased debut album by Fallen Angels.

To try out new material, the band played warm-up shows on July 21 and 22, 1978, at the small New York club Great Gildersleeves, where KISS cohorts the Brats opened. The following month, while recording in Toronto at Richardson's Soundstage Studios, the band scheduled a gig at the nearby El Mocambo club. In order to play, they had to drive down to Buffalo, New York, to pick up work visas, but at the border they learned that Dubé wasn't going to be allowed back in the country. "Some of us had previous 'experiences' with the legal system of the United States," says Dubé, "and that required some 'splaining to the customs folks."

The recording sessions otherwise proceeded fairly uneventfully. Until he was called in to track his vocals, Smith has said he "went around Toronto and hung out and had little flings and affairs and jogged and played stickball and had fun."

*Coliseum Rock* was released in the fall, shortly after it had been completed. As if to compensate for the chintziness of the *Attention Shoppers!* LP cover, the illustration on the front (which is repeated on the back and on both sides of the inner sleeve) impressively transforms the Starz logo into an open-air arena. Even the title suggests a newfound confidence or, some might say, delusion of grandeur. They'd go on to play coliseums, all right, but still as an opener for the familiar likes of Rush and Ted Nugent, never as the headliner. Sonically at least, the record stomps all over their previous effort, with Richardson imbuing the songs with a vigor that masks the weakness of some of the material. "Take Me" and "Don't Stop Now" coast on rote distorted riffs and easy, uninspired lyrics. But the pleasures come when Starz play up their utter crassness. A choppy guitar intro faintly reminiscent of Boston's "Peace of Mind" and a talkbox interlude that conjures peak Frampton are just two of the highlights of "So Young, So Bad," an ode to a fifteen-year-old who should be home playing with her dolls instead of here playing with Smith's balls. And on the blustery glam-pop nugget "Outfit," the singer assumes the role of fashion cop, complimenting a woman on the way her pants fit across her hips, adding, "I can't believe that those things don't rip." (In concert and uncensored, Smith smuttily substituted that last bit with "I can see your little pussy lips.")

"It was gelling into what turned into '80s rock," Messano says. "Not as mainstream as Foreigner, but it was moving in this really cool direction. I loved Michael Lee's voice. I wasn't always into his lyrics, because he's dark and strange sometimes. But he's an incredibly intelligent man."

To promote the release, Capitol sponsored a half dozen free radio tie-in gigs in theaters throughout the Midwest, an unusual Hail Mary for a band already on their fourth album and who had been launched in a similar fashion two years earlier. "We felt they were a really strong live band," says Bruce Ravid, former AOR promotion coordinator at Capitol, "and it was a way to try to create major buzz, which radio could do back then."

When Marc Ferrari, lead guitarist for the L.A. glam-metal band Keel, saw Starz open for Rush on January 24, 1979, in Buffalo, New York, he couldn't help but gawk at Richie Ranno's double-neck guitar. "That was the first time I ever saw one onstage," says Ferrari, who later wrote the liner notes for one of Starz's reissues. "I was like, 'Oh my God, what's that?'" He has his own theory about why the band never broke out. "Those songs could have been just as big as anything," he says. "But they have interesting arrangements—they don't just go from A to B to C. There's a left-hand turn in some of their arrangements, and that may have worked against them when trying to get stuff on the radio."

Indeed, when *Coliseum Rock* failed to gain much radio interest, or even make an appearance on the *Billboard* albums chart, the label and the band agreed to part. "The guys at Capitol I don't think knew quite what to do with us," Dubé says. "We had a couple of songs that got close, and Capitol certainly poured a ton of dough into it, but I don't know if they completely understood what they were listening to or looking at."

"I sympathize with Starz," says Ferrari, "because Keel was in the same boat." Black 'N Blue, featuring his good friend Tommy Thayer, were big Starz fans too, and fared similarly. "They had everything," Ferrari says. "They were on Geffen, they had a great-looking singer, great songs and musicianship—tight as nails. But it didn't happen for them." But eventually it would happen for Tommy Thayer.

Likewise, Steve West sees a lot of Starz in Danger Danger, which released two albums on Epic, a handful on an indie, and never made the leap from arena opener to headliner. "We're the Starz of the hair-metal scene," he says, sanguine about his band's box on the org chart of rock. "You've got all the big bands—the Mötleys, the Poisons, the Bon Jovis. We're the also-rans we grew up loving: 'Those guys were good. Why weren't they bigger?'"

· · · ·

MICHAEL LEE SMITH MOVED to Los Angeles when his wife, Lynda Lee Lawley, who had been touring with Petula Clark, signed with power-pop gurus Nicky Chinn and Mike Chapman as a member of the group Thieves. Starz's day-to-day manager, Alan Miller, who had also moved out there, told Ranno, "I'm going to talk to Aucoin. I'm gonna get you guys off of him, and I'll manage you."

"Aucoin wouldn't let us go," Ranno says. So the band stayed out there for nearly two months in 1979, writing and playing, including a three-night stint in March headlining the Starwood with Valentino, featuring Micki Free—a Gene Simmons protégé—and future Cheap Trick members Pete Comita and Jon Brant. "We were bouncing around," says David Rule, a former Starz roadie, "picking up club gigs here and there, and just trying to work it as long as we could."

"The only income we had was if we played live," says Ranno. "It was a strange new arrangement for us." And it wasn't working.

One day, Ranno went with his wife to Smith's apartment, where the singer told him he wanted out. "His wife kept saying, 'Michael has to leave in order to get his career back on track.' And I said, 'No, Lynda. If Michael quits this band and Starz breaks up, Michael will never have a career again because we're quitting at the bottom. We've got to keep going and get ourselves back. We could do another album. We can get it back.' 'No,' she said. 'This band is ruining him.' Michael just sat there: he wanted his marriage to continue. And he just listened to everything she said and said, 'She's right.'"

"I honestly don't remember this happening," says Smith. "I know Richie remembers that time way better than me. As far as Lynda saying I needed my career back on track, when was it ever on track?"

The band split up eight months after their fourth album arrived. "If we had been smarter," says Dubé, "we would have said, 'Let's take a six-month hiatus, figure out what we want to do, then reconvene.' But no, we were not that bright."

"Once we quit at the bottom," Ranno says. "I should've just thrown all my guitars into the ocean."

Messano remembers being taken aback when it came time to sign his contract to join the band. "I was sitting there, initialing page after page," he says. "I was reading them and asking questions. I saw this number in excess of nine hundred thousand dollars and asked, 'What is this?' 'That's what the band owes,' the lawyer said. 'If you want to be in the band, you owe a million dollars.' So I said, 'What does it mean?' 'It means absolutely nothing. If you recoup that, then you're making a lot of money and you're going to be fine. If you make no money, it's just going to vaporize and it doesn't exist anymore.' 'You sure it's gonna vaporize?' 'Yeah, it'll just disappear.' 'Promise?' 'Sure, kid, give me my three hundred dollars per hour.' But for all intents and purposes, it did vaporize, even though there was an audit done later by Capitol, and I heard rumors that we had sold well over gold and never gotten paid for it."

According to the label, the numbers were significantly smaller. Rupert Perry, the former Capitol A&R executive, citing an internal company memo from January 1979, says that in 1976 the band sold 119,000 albums, a combined 213,000 in 1977, and a total of 184,000 in 1978, the year they released both *Attention Shoppers!* and *Coliseum Rock*. (It must be said, too, that labels have been known to underreport these kinds of figures.)

When he returned to New Jersey in early 1980, Messano felt lost. "What am I going to do here?" he remembers thinking. "I was in this great band. We were just on the road playing arenas. Now what?" Through his friendship with producer Vini Poncia, for whom he played on the second album by Toto-esque rockers Tycoon, he appeared, like his Starz predecessor Brendan Harkin, on a Peter Criss solo album: 1982's *Let Me Rock You*. He also tried to get a band going with Boston singer Brad Delp and Aerosmith drummer Joey Kramer, with whom he was tight for a few years "when Aerosmith were in that weird mode," he says.

"Everybody sort of disappears after a while in Rock Land," he adds, ruefully. "If you're not happening, nobody talks to you. And you don't want to talk to anybody."

*Cash Box* announced in its June 30, 1979, issue that Aucoin had dropped Starz from his management roster. "I wanted to get out of my contract with him right away, and so did everybody else," Ranno says. "We got back together a year later without him, thank God, in our lives."

In a 2007 podcast interview, Aucoin said nothing about the SIR incident, but echoed the band's suspicion that the label never fully supported them, conceding that by the time of the third album, it was all pretty much over. "We put about a half million dollars behind them in touring and everything else that Capitol didn't," he said. That they even got the chance to make *Coliseum Rock*, he claimed, was due to his political pull at the label. "They said, 'Well, maybe let's give them one more shot.' But I think by that time the promotion department had written us off." Looking back, he felt he probably gave Starz too much, too soon. "I would do it slower," he said. "I'd let them start in smaller clubs and let the fans build up before I would go as far as I did."

## CHAPTER 14

# UP THE CREEK

LIKE AEROSMITH AND KISS—and the Beatles before them—Cheap Trick seemed a natural fit for the movies. Filmmakers thought so too, and the band believed they'd get their first major exposure with four songs on the soundtrack of 1979's *Over the Edge*, a compelling teen-angst melodrama that became one of the favorite movies of Kurt Cobain, who more than a decade later would help turn compelling teen-angst melodrama into a mega-successful rock genre. The movie's limited theatrical run didn't do much to get the word out, but over time the band expanded their discography by contributing several songs to motion pictures of varying quality, including *Roadie*, *Heavy Metal*, *Rock & Rule*, *Spring Break*, *Up the Creek*, and *Top Gun*.

It wasn't a lack of enthusiasm that kept the photogenic band from actually appearing on-screen. In 1978, director Allan Arkush was developing a teensploitation comedy called *Disco High* for B-movie producer Roger Corman, who wanted to cash in on the back-to-back John Travolta successes *Saturday Night Fever* and *Grease*. Arkush originally envisioned Todd Rundgren as the featured artist, perky Riff Randell's object of adoration. Rundgren read the script, liked that the high school got blown up, but preferred more serious fare such as Lindsay Anderson's *if*. . . . .

When Arkush heard Rodney Bingenheimer spin the not-yet-released *Budokan* on the radio, he thought he had found his band. Wowed by Cheap Trick's intensity, strong but never saccharine melodic sense, and humorous lyrics, he met the band at a taping of the TV concert show *Midnight Special* and pitched the concept. "They liked the idea and were very interested," says Arkush, who found Nielsen's signature look and the band's comical self-awareness perfectly aligned with his vision for the film. As the director petitioned Corman to change the title to *Rock 'n' Roll High School*, Corman's lawyer was encouraging Arkush to meet with Warner Bros. to explore the label's roster. Two new artists were considered, then dismissed: Van Halen (too early and, Arkush was warned, too nuts) and Devo (too, well, sui generis). Warner Bros. then suggested a band on its Sire label that were already a few albums into their career but desperate for some traction: the leather-jacketed New York City crew known as the Ramones.

The filmmakers initially offered Cheap Trick $15,000 for three weeks' work, a pittance for a self-sustaining band with a substantial overhead. "We said, 'We can't do that. We'll go out of business,'" Carlos says. "Fifteen grand doesn't pay for anybody for three weeks, much less the crew, the buses, and everything else we would have had to stop but still pay for."

The band countered with $50,000, nearly one-third of the film's initial budget, which included the rights to use songs from *Budokan*—a boon for the soundtrack—but Cheap Trick still would have needed to record a theme song. The Ramones required half that amount. Equipped with images of each band, including pages of singer Joey Ramone from a *Punk* magazine *fumetti* called "Mutant Monster Beach Party" (which, incidentally, included a cameo by the Starz logo), Arkush presented the groups to Corman, who immediately responded to the photo-comic, a parody of movies with which he was intimately familiar.

Corman then asked the director what the bands would cost. "I said, 'Fifty thousand dollars and twenty-five thousand dollars,'" Arkush recalls. "He points to the twenty-five-thousand-dollar band and says, 'These are our boys!'"

The effervescent, smart, yet deeply silly *Rock 'n' Roll High School* ended up giving a huge boost to the Ramones and brought forth one of their most recognizable songs. Encouraged by Cheap Trick's positive response to their script, screenwriters Russ Dvonch and Richard Whitley followed up with a treatment for a film specifically designed to showcase the band. Titled *The Big Broadcast of 1999*, it was intended to be the directorial debut of Rob Bottin, the special-effects wizard who created a giant mouse for *Rock 'n' Roll High School*.

The premise: Twenty years into the future, Las Vegas is the hot new vacation resort on the now-colonized moon, which sets in motion a race between a sleek spaceship commandeered by the villains (parts earmarked for *Rock 'n' Roll High School*'s Paul Bartel and Mary Woronov) and a steampunky *Queen Mary* encased in a giant clear shell. "The secret," says Whitley, "is that the

*Queen Mary* is powered by rock and roll. All of these famous acts are performing on this ocean liner to the moon, and Cheap Trick needs to sneak on to perform, get notoriety, and be discovered." Their aide de camp? A busboy to be played by none other than Huntz Hall, whom the writers envisioned as an older relative of Rick Nielsen. The project never moved past the script stage ("We did not get paid," Whitley says), but it would hardly be the band's last dance with Hollywood.

In 1979, Adamany was juggling six different proposals from such machers as Ken Ehrlich (which would have put the band together with the Cars and Earth, Wind & Fire) and Marty Erlichman (best known as Barbra Streisand's manager). Nielsen has said that the writer of *Bonnie and Clyde* and *Superman*—presumably either Robert Benton or David Newman—was working on a screenplay for them. For one of these projects, a writer was sent on tour with the band. One night on the bus, he showed what he was working on and asked for feedback. Carlos was characteristically forthright in his assessment: "I said, 'It's like if Jack Nicholson tried to do a rock-and-roll record. How stupid would that be? Us trying to do a movie makes about as much fucking sense.' And the other guys in the band went, 'Yup.' And the guy said, 'I see what you mean.' And that was the end of that."

Yet another deal involved Jack Douglas, his wife Kristine Desautels, and his manager Stan Vincent producing a film tentatively titled *Cheap Trick Flick*. Douglas was confident he could get it made with Mace Neufeld—the Captain & Tennille manager turned producer of *The Omen* movies—but it never materialized. "Although we did receive an advance payment," says Adamany, "I don't think they were able to raise the funds to continue with it."

Nielsen also had another project in mind, a screenplay collaboration with Christopher Crowe, Cameron Crowe, and Eric Van Lustbader, which he described as *"The Rocky Horror Picture Show* meets Cheap Trick in a dark alley." Though the band did do some (very bad) acting on Christopher Crowe's short-lived TV drama *The Watcher* in 1995, it wasn't until 2003 that they finally got their shot on the big screen, some thirty years into their career, playing "Surrender" at an outdoor concert for kids in the Eddie Murphy comedy *Daddy Day Care*.

· · · ·

IN 1979, GENE SIMMONS reached out to Cheap Trick, looking for a favor. KISS had booked a show on the Dynasty tour for July 13 at the Pontiac Mini-Dome—essentially a 35,000-capacity, half-size configuration of the

Silverdome—and tickets weren't moving. "It's pretty dead," he told the band. "We need you guys on the bill."

"It was like payback," Adamany says, "because we were really popular then. It was for a lot of money too. But we always liked those guys, so it was fine."

Mark Cicchini, a Detroit-based fan of both bands who was in the audience that night, remembers Cheap Trick playing a typically fine set, with one hitch: Someone pelted Nielsen with a bottle, prompting Petersson to leave the stage momentarily. He returned wielding Simmons's AXE—a bass named for its resemblance to a barbarian's weapon—walked up to a mic, and, Cicchini says, "threatened to remove the testicles of the person who threw it." It was the last time Cheap Trick would open a KISS concert, but it would not be the last time they helped the band out.

Sebastian Bach saw KISS in concert for the first time, from the front row, during that stretch. "Paul Stanley says that tour was awkward because there were so many kids with their parents," he says. "*Hello!* That was me. And that was Dimebag Darrell, Tom Morello, Poison, Steven Adler, Slash, and Lenny Kravitz. We were all little-kid KISS fanatics. Kravitz, when I see him, we are KISS geeks. He talks to me about the production on *Dressed to Kill*. We don't talk about their boots. We talk about their music."

## CHAPTER 15

# WALK THE NIGHT

DESPITE THE KISS SOLO-ALBUM debacle the previous year, Casablanca put some sixty-nine albums in the distribution pipeline for 1979, up from forty-three. In the grand scheme, this number was not unusual. As Fredric Dannen wrote in *Hit Men*, that year the labels, reacting to the runaway popularity of disco, "force-fed millions of albums to retailers and booked them as sales. But they weren't." The resultant enormity of returns was catastrophic, leading to an 11 percent slump in record sales "to $3.7 billion, the first decline since World War II."

Larry Harris, then Casablanca's senior vice president and managing director, later characterized the label's tsunami of product, most of it disco, as a "rash of cheap signings that held little hope of long-term profit." Among such no-hit wonders as Beckmeier Brothers, Sam the Band, and Harlem Globetrotter Meadowlark Lemon were two albums featuring the musical talents of a longtime label associate, Sean Delaney.

Having produced Gene Simmons's album, as well as records for Aucoin charges Piper and Toby Beau, Delaney was no stranger to the recording studio, but it had to seem unreal when Casablanca designated his debut solo effort, *Highway*, as its first release of the year. Produced with Mike Stone, who engineered Paul Stanley's 1978 solo LP and helped Delaney remix the KISS greatest-hits package *Double Platinum*, *Highway* featured many of the session aces Delaney had worked with on Simmons's record, including guitarist Elliott Randall, bassist Neil Jason, and drummer Allan Schwartzberg, along with keyboards by Paul Shaffer and backing vocals from a pre-stardom Luther Vandross. Shaffer had met Delaney when the *Saturday Night Live* house-band member was hired to fill in for Bob Dylan pianist Paul Griffin on a demo session with Delaney and Pattie Darcy, then wife of Starz guitarist Brendan Harkin, who'd later sing backup for Cher and Rosanne Cash. "I hadn't heard of him before," Shaffer says. "But he had these connections with the older studio cats. He was coming into it from a traditional point of view."

Shaffer reciprocated by getting Delaney hired to choreograph a skit on a season two episode of *SNL*, featuring a Runaways-like all-girl band called the Video Vixens, made up of host Shelley Duvall and regulars Jane Curtin, Gilda Radner, and Laraine Newman. "The girls needed a little help in the swagger department," Shaffer says. So he suggested the producers bring in Delaney, "the guy who does KISS, choreographs them, stages them." Delaney worked with the women for a week, teaching them how to move with Flying Vs, work among flash pots, gesticulate like rock stars. "Everybody loved it," Shaffer says, though he recalls Delaney seeming extremely insecure. "We were doing a little comedy show, but this guy did KISS. I thought, *What does he got to worry about?* But he was telling me later how nervous he was. He used a fake Southern accent just to give himself more confidence."

For Delaney, one of the perks of working on *SNL* was hooking up with the show's chief party animal. "Sean was so wild at the time," Shaffer says, "but he met his match when he came upon John Belushi. Those guys hit it off and were tight for a while. You can only imagine."

While Delaney's contributions to KISS and Starz records hewed carefully to those bands' identities, his own work embodied a decidedly echt-'70s aesthetic: earnest, piano-heavy soft rock packed with melodrama; Paul Williamsy whimsy; blue-eyed gospel (the stirring "Walk on Water," written with Starz's Pieter Sweval); and countrified pop not so different from that of Toby Beau, a Texas band Delaney discovered and for whom he produced the 1978 AM-radio hit "My Angel Baby." "Sean was very naturally production oriented," Neil Jason says. "He would see the big-picture stuff. He had that thing that I've seen in a couple of people, where they just know if the song—it could have been perfectly played—was missing *the vibe*."

On *Highway*, with his limited but not unpleasant rasp front and center, Delaney revealed himself to be a songwriter of surprising depth and ambition. Album opener "Welcome to the Circus" suggests Three Dog Night's "The Show Must Go On" as reconceived by Jim Steinman, and the symphonic closing track "Dreams" echoes the three-ring theme with bonus anamorphic hugeness. "Everything had to be big and lush and theatrical with Sean," says

Jason. "Even if it was two instruments, one of them had to freak you out, like, *Holy cow, I never heard it like that before!*"

Lyrically, Delaney tended to wax a very rich purple—on "Dreams" he shouts out to "those high-stepping sexy witches, sons of satin, sons of bitches." But that suited Jefferson Starship's Grace Slick just fine; she covered it as the title track of her 1980 solo album, produced by *Highway* orchestrator Ron Frangipane and featuring Schwartzberg and Jason reprising their roles in the rhythm section.

In its capsule review of *Highway*, *Cash Box* predicted that Delaney, an "infectious mainstream rocker . . . should be on his way to both Top 40 and AOR success with this LP." In reality, the album beat a swift retreat to cut-out bins everywhere. For Casablanca, it had to have been a tough sell: If KISS diehards weren't going to care, why on earth would anyone else?

. . . .

WILLI MORRISON WAS ENJOYING lunch in a Los Angeles restaurant with his production partner Ian Guenther when a bottle of champagne they had not ordered suddenly arrived at their table. The Toronto-based duo had recently completed the debut album by a disco act called the Duncan Sisters and just delivered it to EarMarc Records, a custom imprint at Casablanca, overseen by marketing and promotion whiz Marc Paul Simon. The gift, they soon discovered, came from Sean Delaney, who had gotten a sneak peek at the LP and instantly flipped, tracked the pair down, and wanted to show his appreciation. Naturally, he had another motive. "When he said, 'I'd like you to do my album,' we said, 'Of course, thank you very much,'" Morrison remembers, not thinking for a minute they'd ever get the call. But a few weeks later a request came in from Casablanca: How quickly could they start on Delaney's second album?

Working under the assumption that Delaney wanted to depart from the histrionics of *Highway* and make a proper disco record, Morrison and Guenther, who as Three Hats Productions were one of Canada's most successful purveyors of dance music, began preparing backing tracks for some of Delaney's songs with their usual crew of crack session players. The two men were more than a little confused when the artist soon arrived in Toronto with a full band in tow. At the time, Morrison and Guenther ran their own show and had limited experience producing rock acts—one, called Thor, was fronted by a blond bodybuilder whose concert highlight had him showing off his lung power by blowing into a hot water bottle until it burst. "We asked Sean, 'Who are these guys?' He said, 'Oh, they're here for the Skatt Bros. album,'" Morrison recalls. "And we said, 'No, Sean, we're doing a Sean Delaney album. That's what our contract with Casablanca says.'"

Richie Fontana, drummer of the then recently disbanded Piper, whose second album Delaney coproduced in 1977, remembers receiving a frantic phone call from him: *Get to the airport! We've got a flight for you to Toronto and we're going to make a record!*

In addition to Fontana, Delaney, who sang and played keyboards, assembled a group of musicians with impressive pedigrees. His buddy Pieter Sweval, who had been booted from Starz, played bass and sang. David Andez, a guitarist and singer with a freakishly versatile four-octave vocal range, worked with the Village People and had known Delaney for years: he costarred in *Lovers*, produced by TOSOS, which shared a basement space in downtown Manhattan with KISS in the early '70s. (Coincidentally, as a teenager, he played in bands with Peter Oreckinto, who later became KISS's first roadie.) Another singer-guitarist, Richard Martin-Ross, had worked with blues-rock maestro Harvey Mandel. A second drummer, Craig Krampf, recorded with Nick Gilder (and can be heard on his No. 1 hit, "Hot Child in the City"). Like Fontana, Krampf had recently played on Paul Stanley's solo album. "When we met," Fontana remembers, "the first thing Craig said to me was, 'You're the guy on side 1!' I said, 'You're the guy on side 2!'"

With the arrival of the band, the recording process took an unorthodox turn. "So, we got up there, the session guys were pushed away, we erased some of their tracks, kept some of them, overdubbed things, pieced it together," Fontana says. "And then we had the basic tracks without vocals."

From Toronto, the musicians flew to Los Angeles. Bill Aucoin had set up a meeting with Neil Bogart, who was expecting to hear songs from Delaney's second solo album. Walking past the palm trees and giant promo pieces for KISS and Donna Summer, they entered Bogart's office at 8255 Sunset Boulevard and stood around the label chief's desk. Aucoin placed a reel on Bogart's tape deck. After he hit PLAY, the group proceeded to croon to an unfinished midtempo track. "Sean's on one knee, singing to Neil, and we're doing this killer harmony," Fontana says. "The song ends. Sean pleads with Neil, 'Please change the contract! I want this to be a band. I don't want it to be a solo thing.'"

Bogart didn't need any more convincing.

Gail Rodgers, who worked in promotion at Aucoin, believes this was all about Delaney getting in the game after years of working on the sidelines. "I think he tried to put his hands in a figurative sense on every band in Aucoin's stable," she says. "Some said, *Yes please.* Others said, *Get your hands out of here.* The Skatt Bros. was really about, *This is now my time.*"

While he always pushed the idea of a band looking like a gang, Delaney was initially reticent about being part of one. Fontana remembers seeing him always at the piano up at the Aucoin offices: "But when we formed the Skatt Bros., he goes, 'Oh, shit! I've got to really play now'—within the context of a band, in time, in key." Delaney had handpicked guys who were solid professionals. Now he had to be one too.

The group were soon back in Toronto to finish recording.

"From our point of view," Morrison says, "what they were singing about was not nearly as important as how it was sounding. We were using Duane Eddy guitars, which was unheard of in disco. So part of what Sean liked was that we were pushing the boundaries." He remembers Delaney as an endlessly energetic and clever personality. "Because of the time he spent working with KISS, he had gotten used to big ideas," Morrison says. "We weren't guiding an artist or a group that never had any experience in the music business. They were seasoned, and these were very intense sessions."

Guenther recalls a very determined artist who liked to control the environment in which he was working. "My memories of him are simply that he was very macho and angry," he says. "It had been a very intense experience."

The fact that the band had four lead singers made it feel to the producers as though they were working with at least as many separate acts. And since those members had temporarily relocated to Toronto, it wasn't as if they were going to a day job, then returning home, keeping everything separate. "It was *full on*, all the time," Morrison says. "There was stuff that they would get up to outside the studio and we would hear stories afterwards."

Fontana admits that the group, led by "bulldozer" Delaney, did come on "like gangbusters," but since the producers were comparatively laid-back, it all probably seemed more extreme than it really was. "Sean was irresponsible in some ways. He was a genius in others," says Fontana. "But when you were around Sean, you felt like something good was going to happen." Delaney had a mantra: *You're shit without the hit.* "And everything we wrote, we tried to make radio friendly," Fontana says. "Whether or not it made it to radio is another story."

Barry Keane, a member of Morrison and Guenther's THP Orchestra, who for decades also drummed for Canadian folk superstar Gordon Lightfoot, is credited on the Skatt Bros. debut as an "auxiliary musician." He recalls meeting some of the band members at Toronto's Phase One Studios but insists that it was actually the session players who banged out most of the album over a four- or five-day period. "We played all of the music on *Strange Spirits*," he says. "They wrote the songs and sang on them and they may have done a few overdubs after the main band left."

Though Guenther and Morrison can't recall the exact division of labor, Fontana doesn't dispute Keane's account. "We didn't redo very much of what the session players recorded," he says. "I don't remember playing a full kit on a lot of that album. I did a lot of overdubs, snare fills, tom bashes, and percussion things. I remember Sweval redoing bass parts. Lead guitar work? None of that's theirs. But are some of the rhythm parts theirs? Yes."

. . . .

**STRANGE SPIRITS BY THE** Skatt Bros. was released with little ballyhoo in November 1979. It's hard not to see and hear it as not only a celebration of the lifestyle that Delaney, Sweval, and Andez fully embraced, but also as a calculated attempt at a sleazier, more extreme Village People, who at the time were one of Casablanca's best-selling acts. First, there's the band name, which suggests an unholy fellowship bound by both improvisational jazz singing and a sexual preoccupation with poop. Then there's the cover: six dudes—four with bushy mustaches, some holding cigarettes, clad in muscle tees and leather—posing in a bar as backlit smoke billows out from behind them. (In an overt nod to Delaney's earlier success, on the back cover he's playing a KISS pinball machine.) Then there are the messages etched into the run-out grooves: MUSIC FOR MISS THING (side 1) and I LOVE PAUL (side 2).

The album opens with "Dancin' for the Man," written by Delaney and sung by Martin-Ross in a remarkable soul-man growl. Punctuated by anachronistic *wah-ooohs*, it's like a discofied update of the early-'60s chestnut "Mashed Potato Time." "Fear of Flying," written by Morrison, is a sticky hunk of dense bubbleglam that surprisingly squanders the opportunity to promote the zipless fucks of Erica Jong's namesake 1973 feminist novel, an omission that is swiftly redressed when Sweval takes the mic for the next song. A soaring, overripe SoCal country ballad, cowritten by Delaney, "Midnight Companion" begins with a trucker cruising for an anonymous encounter at a rest stop just north of the Valley and ends with him begging for a hitchhiker, biker—someone, anyone—who wants to play. If Fallen Angels' "Elouisa" represents his tentative coming out, and his stint in overtly hetero Starz the suppression of his queerness, on this song Sweval positively revels in his newfound and hard-won freedom to explore his sexuality through his art.

After this unexpectedly moving orchestral schmaltz comes the album's centerpiece, the sinister and sublime rough-trade anthem "Walk the Night," which may be the most pungent fusion of hard rock and disco ever recorded. Over a thumping foundation that combines an ominous bassline, handclaps, ribbits, a villain's chuckle, and a victim's scream, a spaghetti western guitar riff conjures up the stink of illicit sex mixed with the smoke of a thousand unfiltered Marlboros and fetid lakes of spilled Budweisers. The song's highlight: Andez's absurdly deep-voiced rap interlude, during which he warns, "He's got a rod beneath his coat he's gonna ram right down your throat!" Released a full year before Blondie's "Rapture" brought rap into the rock mainstream, the track had its origins in "Creeper," a song by one of Andez's earlier groups, the short-lived funk-rock Manhole—four Freddie Mercury clones who parted ways when one of them tired of the act and decided to grow a beard. Bobby Locke, Manhole's drummer, recalls pitching the song to Delaney at his Manhattan high-rise one frigid night in December 1977. "He quickly turned it off after about a minute and said, 'I want you to listen to a new project we've got,'" he says. "Sure enough, he put on 'My Angel Baby' by Toby Beau. It's typical: the ego-driven producers always want to shut the music off and play their latest project. *Forget you, here's me.*"

"'Walk the Night' was David's baby," says Fontana, who helped the guitarist finish it off in a Toronto bar by adding such genius lyrical imagery as "venom kiss of love insane."

"Old Enough," *Strange Spirits'* most unabashed shot of pure porno-disco, tells the tawdry story of a runaway named Sally, caged at the tender age of twelve, who was last seen showing pink in a skin magazine. In "Life at the Outpost," a sergeant at arms with masculine charms teases the ladies when he's not using his black leather boots to kick the butts of recruits. When the gang vocals of the chorus urge the listener to "Give your love to a cowboy man / He's gonna love you hard as he can," the promise (or threat) of rough sex is palpable. It's the aural equivalent of a Tom of Finland poster, though, according to Sweval, some of the group's inspiration came from more genteel places. "There's a lot of influence from people like the Andrews Sisters and the Mills Brothers," he said at the time, "in the way we stack our harmonies."

The album stayed pretty much under the radar in the Casablanca offices, not least because the sheer tonnage of product made it impossible for every record to get the TLC it deserved. The label's hands-off approach apparently extended to the cover art. Dean Tokuno was a young photographer, specializing in celebrity and fashion, when he got the gig to shoot the band at Griff's, one of Delaney and Sweval's favorite Hollywood leather bars. "I remember the creative team at Casablanca being very weak, and I'm going to have to assume that it had something to do with their lack of commitment to the band," Tokuno says. He had done a lot of work with A&M Records at that time, for which he was thoroughly briefed. With the Skatt Bros., he remembers being surprised at how little information was on offer.

"It was an extremely gay set," Tokuno adds. "My creative team—stylist, hair, makeup, everybody—they were gay. No big deal. I think the group felt very comfortable." In his studio for some promo shots, they were so comfortable that, as introductions were made, one of the band members—Tokuno doesn't recall whom—grabbed his face and kissed him on the mouth. "I thought, *Oh, okay we're having fun here but* . . . It was weird. I don't know what they were on, but they were pretty loose when they came in."

Upon its release, the record garnered little press, and the reviews it managed to get were mixed at best. One gay magazine, *The Advocate*, wrote at the time, "For those of our kind who do spend late night hours in sleazy bars, cruisin' and cavortin', they hit a few responsive chords. . . . It is altogether relentlessly masculine." Another, *In Touch for Men*, described them as "a gale-force rock band with a strong leaning toward both danceability and romance in their music." Calling the album "a strong debut for several tastes," *Record World* went with this generic boilerplate: "The rock is just hard enough for AOR, while a number of tunes have Top 40 perfect hooks." The *Santa Cruz Sentinel*, on the other hand, led off its capsule appraisal with the words "Here comes some more bad wave . . ."

Jim Farber was a young New York City–based music critic in the '70s when he wrote about the burgeoning rock-disco scene for the gay-leaning entertainment magazine *After Dark*. Although he loved camp, he was deeply suspicious of the Skatt Bros. "I mainly remember the album cover because I thought it was so unbelievably ridiculous," he says. "It seemed like such a niche thing they were trying to market: gay rock-disco. Casablanca had some great stuff, but there was always that whiff of exploitation." The group, particularly the unpleasant connotation of their name, also managed to turn off Paul Stanley, who saw his former collaborators embark on a project that he views as a sort of unsuccessful precursor to Frankie Goes to Hollywood. "It was uncomfortable," he says. "It was too edgy and dark and represented something that most people couldn't relate to."

Farber recalls hearing deejays spin "Walk the Night" at Manhattan leather bars like the Spike. "It was meant to be the soundtrack to people fucking in the trucks," he says, referring to the often-anonymous public sex that would occur in empty, unlocked vehicles parked off the West Side Highway. As if to remove all doubt, in a 1997 study of "music of the baths" (i.e., "music programmed to enhance S/M or fistfucking"), cultural anthropologist Gayle Rubin cited "Walk the Night" as "a particular anthem of late '70s gay male S/M" that was popular at the Catacombs, a fisting club in San Francisco. And in an unofficial YouTube video, the song plays over footage from the scandalous thriller *Cruising*, in which Al Pacino, as an undercover detective, dances sweatily in a dank basement club while huffing a bandana presumably soaked in poppers, the sex stimulant amyl nitrate, as severe shenanigans go on all around him.

On a January 1980 episode of Dinah Shore's talk show, the Skatt Bros. performed "Dancin' for the Man" and "Midnight Companion," likely the first and only time a song about furtive trucker sex has aired on daytime TV. As Shore signed off, the band presented the host, a genuine America's sweetheart, with a black satin jacket adorned with their incongruously cartoonish logo—reminiscent of KISS's. Above it was the album's title, drafted in letters that resembled dripping ejaculate.

"Walk the Night" (backed with "Life at the Outpost" and "Dancin' for the Man") ended up spending eleven weeks on *Billboard*'s Disco Top 100 chart, peaking at No. 9 in April 1980 and becoming the group's only U.S. hit. The song has since experienced an extraordinary afterlife: dance remixes by the likes of superstar deejay Frankie Knuckles, an appearance in the video game *Grand Theft Auto IV*, a 2012 gender-switched cover by Peaches and the Phenomenal Handclap Band for a Casablanca tribute album. Jake Shears, of nu-disco extroverts Scissors Sisters, has said that hearing "Walk the Night" at a "disgusting" German sex party inspired the sound of his group's 2010 album, *Night Work*. One of that record's highlights, "Harder You Get," drops so many blatant sonic references to the Skatt Bros. classic, it's nothing short of a tribute. Hard rockers Queens of the Stone Age and alt-dance act LCD Soundsystem used the song as walk-on music during their respective 2017 world tours. And it played over the end credits of a 2019 episode of the HBO comedy series *The Righteous Gemstones*.

*Strange Spirits* is a favorite of rock critic Chuck Eddy, though he admits he didn't discover the album until years after its release. "Half of it is as catchy as any record I own," he says, reserving the most praise for "Walk the Night." "As far as a metal-disco mix or a rock-disco mix, it's hard to think of a song that's just got more punch to it."

"That leather-bar stuff, it's a foreign world to me," he continues. "So I hope I'm not being condescending by thinking it's so funny. But it seems like they were trying to be funny in those songs. That's why they're so clever. And as I understand it, that's what camp is. It's tongue-in-cheek and serious at the same time, and it's a coded language."

Though the Skatt Bros. never did a full-blown tour of the States—gigging sporadically at the Starwood and Hong Kong Café in L.A., and at venues in Portland, New York, and Boston—they are surely the only band to have opened for both Gamma (featuring Ronnie Montrose) and Natalie Cole. "We played some gay gigs," says Fontana, "but we were a rock-and-roll band." One of those gigs, at the West Hollywood disco Studio One, saw the group members lining up on a scaffold—no instruments, just microphones—singing to backing tracks. "It was almost like the '60s," Fontana recalls, "like [the NBC TV series] *Hullabaloo*."

A few months after the album sessions, Casablanca sent the group to the Record Plant in L.A. to cut a clamorous cover of Elvis Presley and Otis Blackwell's "Don't Be Cruel" (eight years before Cheap Trick hit No. 4 with a much nimbler version). Sung by Richard Martin-Ross and recorded live in the studio by Lee DeCarlo—who worked with Aerosmith, Rex, and Angel— the single "was a powerful track, a fucking rock-and-roll song," Fontana says. It was also a move, he believes, that further confounded the audience's perception of the band. "David's playing lead guitar like Hendrix," he says. "People would think, 'Are they gay? Are they not?' "

• • • •

ON JULY 18, 2016, for a segment called "Do Not Watch," *Tonight Show* host Jimmy Fallon introduced a vintage music video by announcing, "This is from an '80s band called the Skatt Bros., and they're like a country-rock band. The song is called 'Life at the Outpost,' and according to them, it's for all the ladies out there. Take a look." The screen cut to a bunch of musclebound guys in butch cowboy hats and berets leaning against a bar. Next: Those fellas, now set in two rows, dance stiffly and shirtlessly near a pool table. Awkward hip-swiveling and perspiration-slicked pleading ensue. As they mime to the couplet "Give your love to a cowboy man / He's gonna love you hard as he can," a Sean Delaney lookalike methodically thrusts his fist up, as if it's been slathered in Crisco.

"Should've been a hit," Fallon mumbled back in the studio. No doubt he would have been surprised to learn that, some thirty-five years earlier, it had indeed been one. Ten thousand miles away maybe, but still . . .

In 1980, Bob Aird was the manager of Casablanca and other PolyGram-affiliated labels in Australia. His job was to evaluate records coming in from overseas to see what might work in his territories. Knowing nothing at all about the band, he decided to push the Skatt Bros.' "Life at the Outpost," seeing as it capitalized on the largely gay disco scene raging there at the time. He marketed a twelve-inch single through the clubs and it became an immediate dance-floor sensation. When radio became interested and mainstream exposure seemed imminent, the label requested a video from the band's management to help sustain the momentum. But since the song was never a hit anywhere else, one hadn't been made. So, with the understanding that Bill Aucoin had veto power, PolyGram commissioned a clip in-house using actors (including Sweval and Delaney doppelgängers) who'd lip-sync to the track. "I never heard if the band liked it," Aird says. "But since Bill approved it, I guess the band endured it." The group were in Toronto recording their second album when the song hit No. 13 in Australia, eventually getting certified gold there by selling in excess of 50,000 copies.

Although thrilled with the success, the musicians could not have been more appalled by the video. "Even the guys in the band who were gay didn't like it because it was a total misrepresentation of what we were," Fontana says. "PolyGram went with what they thought was the image of the band. People thought it was us. It wasn't us."

The Skatt Bros. followed up *Strange Spirits* with 1981's *Rico & the Ravens*, again recorded with Guenther and Morrison, this time without any session players. The producers debated whether or not they should get involved again. "Because we knew them, that made it slightly easier," Morrison says. "But they were still crazy and manic. That hadn't calmed down at all."

If the LP's title sounds more like a band name, that's because it refers to one of Richard Martin-Ross's previous groups, which had a local hit in Philadelphia in the early '60s with "Don't You Know," an untamed howl of garage soul. Consciously avoiding the overtly gay content of the debut, the Skatt Bros. also abandoned disco in favor of mostly de rigueur new wave and glittery power pop—with terrific results. The infectious "Oh, Those Girls" comes off as a catalog of gripes against women so comical in its bitchiness and with a bridge so gloriously random ("What can you do, every girl's got a mind of her own / What does it take to awake an erogenous zone"), it's just got to be a goof—until you realize it was written by two gay men about other gay men.

Andez's creepy-crawly basso returns in "Heat of Passion," a disturbing serial-killer fantasy that begins sunnily enough before interjecting some of the operatic pomposity from Delaney's solo album. Similarly, the showy, piano-led "Wait Till Tonight" resembles leftover Meat Loaf that still tastes delicious after reheating. "If It's Alright" appropriates the grumbling sixteenth-note rhythm of KISS's "I Was Made for Lovin' You" to excellent effect, while the gospel-tinged "Rain" and peaceful-easy "Eternity" recall *Highway*'s overtly middle-of-the-road bits. But it's Sweval's transcendent "Kiss Rock 'N' Roll Goodbye," with its Raspberries-sweet melody and hyper-anthemic chorus, that secures *Rico & the Ravens*' place in the pantheon of great lost albums of the 1980s.

Krampf left the band before the second album, preferring to return to session work and joining up with Kim Carnes and Alice Cooper. Andez split soon after recording *Rico & the Ravens* over a dispute about finances, having lost trust in his old friend Delaney and demanding to review Aucoin's books. "We didn't have enough hit records for any mega-money to be coming in," Fontana says. "But we were getting advances. We would hit up Casablanca for, say, another fifty grand for salaries and things."

Guitarist Danny Brant—who appears on the album cover despite not playing a note—stepped in when Delaney decided to take advantage of their antipodean success and organize a trip to Australia, including a few dates in Tasmania. At the time, the Texas-bred Brant was a struggling gun for hire, who'd sometimes fill in for musicians who for whatever reason—say, an arrest record—couldn't get into Canada to tour. It didn't hurt that he could also mimic virtually any style of singer, from Michael McDonald to Donald Duck. When he groused to a friend who worked at Barney's Beanery on Santa Monica Boulevard that he was having trouble finding a gig, she introduced him to a bunch of guys huddled at the opposite end of the bar who were looking for a singing guitarist. After he auditioned, they had just one question: "How do you feel about members of this band being gay?"

"I looked at them and said, 'Whatever blows your fucking dress up,'" Brant recalls. "They burst out laughing." He took the job, figuring it would tide him over until the next one. The Skatt Bros. hadn't mixed the second album yet, but when Brant heard it, he thought, *Okay, it's music. I play music.*

*What does it pay?* They rehearsed and gigged at local bars and clubs for about two months before landing in Australia.

"Down there, it was a full-blown rock-and-roll tour," says Fontana of the summer 1981 dates, which found the Skatt Bros. playing clubs, private parties, even a racetrack, and featured support from the young Aussie bands Men at Work and the Church. "That whole gay thing went away," he says. "But it went away only in Australia."

Down under, Delaney ran the show while he and his bandmates also ran wild. "The other guys generally acquiesced to him because he was very strong in his opinions, and maybe they were afraid of him physically," Brant says. "Some members, when they got out of line, there were times they got punched."

Brant remembers the group constantly getting hit on "by everybody and everything." "If you weren't getting three at a time," he says, "you weren't doing your job. We were young. We still had our hair. And I loved every minute of it." The partying extended to irresponsible joyrides, which resulted in Delaney totaling two cars, leading their tour manager to tell Brant, "From now on, you're the only one who gets to drive."

PolyGram's Bob Aird recalls the shows going down less than successfully. "The band only had one hit single and it's difficult to sell a tour on that," he says. "The audience expected disco music similar to 'Outpost,' but the band essentially played rock. Predictably, much of the audience thought the actors in the video were the band and didn't relate to the real band."

Casablanca declined to distribute *Rico & the Ravens* in the U.S. Neil Bogart, perhaps the group's biggest champion, had left the label in 1980. It was released, on Mercury, only in Australia and, all told, sold fewer than 5,000 copies, which makes its appearance on record-collector sites like Discogs a rare, not to mention pricey, occurrence.

Three weeks after returning to the states, the Skatt Bros. were done. Brant says the breakup had nothing to do with any intra-band conflicts but everything to do with Bill Aucoin and a lack of funds. "The first album had done well," he says. "They were having success, and they couldn't figure out why there wasn't any money." He recalls dental bills popping up for one member who hadn't even been to a dentist.

"It fell apart basically because they were wild," Aucoin's Stephanie Tudor says. "They were going in different directions toward the end. And if I remember correctly, they spent a lot."

After the group's demise, Brant went on to work with soul-pop band Carrera and "Weird Al" Yankovic. Fontana kicked around L.A. for a bit with Martin-Ross before returning to New York, where he networked his way into a gig touring with Laura Branigan, who was then riding high on the pop hit "Gloria." He and Delaney hadn't spoken in around fifteen years when his former bandmate called out of the blue in 2001 to invite Fontana to a gathering at the home of Lydia Criss, who'd divorced Peter in 1979, where he had been staying for a few weeks. "It was like old times," Fontana says, "and when I'm about to leave he goes, 'Come back tomorrow night for New Year's Eve.'" The next evening, Fontana was pleasantly surprised to see two other guests from the Aucoin extended family, Peter Oreckinto and J.R. Smalling, original KISS crew members. Three weeks later, he and Lydia Criss were inseparable.

A flyer promotes a gig featuring Bun E. Carlos's Paegans and Rick Nielsen's Grim Reapers at Sherwood Lodge in Loves Park, Illinois, 1967.

After Looking Glass and before Starz, there were Fallen Angels, 1975. Top, from left: Joe X. Dubé, Larry Gonsky, and Brendan Harkin. Bottom: Pieter Sweval and Michael Lee Smith.

*Photo: Benno Friedman*

KISS and Starz at the Toledo Sports Arena, July 31, 1976, the only time the bands shared a concert stage. From left: Paul Stanley, Smith, Harkin, Dubé, Peter Criss, Richie Ranno, Gene Simmons, Sweval, and Ace Frehley.

*Photo: John Gibbs Rockwood*

An ad for one of Starz and Aerosmith's many gigs together, from the *Los Angeles Times*, 1976.

Stanley, in an ape mask, flanked by Dubé and Harkin at a party in 1976.

*Photo: Jeffrey Grob / Joe X. Dubé*

This 1976 porn film features Fallen Angels songs on its soundtrack.

Starz's Ranno (above), Harkin, and Smith in Tulsa, Oklahoma, 1976. *Photos: Richard Galbraith*

Cheap Trick's Robin Zander, Carlos, Nielsen, and Tom Petersson visit KISS's Stanley and Simmons backstage at the Dane County Memorial Coliseum in Madison, Wisconsin, February 4, 1977. *Photo: © Thomas W. Giles & ClassicRock-Photos.com*

An ad for the Love Gun tour from the *Los Angeles Times*, 1977.

Starz bend over backward to please the crowd at Rich Stadium in Buffalo, New York, on a bill with Blue Öyster Cult, Lynyrd Skynyrd, and Ted Nugent, June 19, 1977.

*Photo: Steve Waxman*

Cheap Trick and Aerosmith highlight the Florrida Jam, 1979.

Carlos, steadied by Petersson and Zander, wears Paul Stanley's KISS boots and jacket, 1979.

*Photo: Lynn Goldsmith/Corbis Premium Historical via Getty Images*

In 1979, Casablanca released the debut album by the Skatt Bros., who had KISS and Starz connections. From left: Sweval, David Andez, Sean Delaney, Richie Fontana, and Craig Krampf. Seated, front: Richard Martin-Ross.

*Photo: Author's collection*

Aerosmith's Steven Tyler, Ratt's Stephen Pearcy, and Stanley, 1986.

Zander's got his KISS record out, 1980.  *Photo: © Mark Weiss*

Kurt Cobain drew the portrait of KISS that adorns the Melvins' early touring van.
*Photo: Angie Holmquist*

Tyler and Nielsen team up on tour, October 2001. *Photo: © Mike Graham*

Stanley and Zander hang backstage, 1988.

Joe Perry performs with KISS at the Forum in Inglewood, California, December 18, 2003. *Photo: © Michael Zito*

A poster for the Japanese Cheap Trick and KISS cover band CheaSS, 2007.

Aerosmith's Brad Whitford plays with Cheap Trick, December 2012. *Photo: Jeff Daly*

Nielsen guests with Stanley and KISS in Rockford, Illinois, July 20, 2016. **Photo: © Mike Graham**

Simmons and Nielsen with Flipp's Brynn Arens at CHS Field in St. Paul, Minnesota, September 20, 2017. **Photo: Kyle Hansen/RKH Images**

Zander helps Perry celebrate the release of *Sweetzerlund Manifesto* at the Roxy on the Sunset Strip, January 16, 2018. *Photo: Alex Kluft Photography*

Carlos plays with his Monday Night Band, featuring Daniel MacMahon (left) and Andrew Scarpaci, at Mary's Place bar in Rockford, Illinois, October 29, 2018. *Photo: Doug Brod*

Starz, featuring Alex Kane (far left), George DiAna, Dubé, Smith, and Ranno, open for Angel at Debonair Music Hall in Teaneck, New Jersey, April 13, 2019. *Photo: Doug Brod*

## CHAPTER 16

# I WAS MADE
# FOR LOVIN' YOU

IN THEIR BRIEF, FOUR-STUDIO-ALBUM, major-label career, Starz rarely needed to reach outside their ranks for songwriting assistance. KISS did, and early on had no problem crediting the likes of Sean Delaney, Bob Ezrin, Wicked Lester's Stephen Coronel, and Peter Criss's buddy Stan Penridge. But it was Desmond Child who became the band's most consequential collaborator, and in 1979, his partnership with Paul Stanley yielded a song that became a crossover hit for KISS seemingly more controversial than the mushy "Beth."

Right from the start, Desmond Child & Rouge defied categories. Here was a skinny, half-Cuban pretty-and-pouty frontman, with a mop of blond curls, carousing with three female singers in various stages of brunette, putting a rock/Latin/dance spin on the Tony Orlando & Dawn pop template. After stalking the New York cabaret circuit in the late '70s, they eventually moved to hipper rooms like Trax and the Bottom Line, where Stanley, who had seen a gig flyer, began following them. "He was intrigued by the androgyny in our presentation," Child says, though Stanley has characterized his initial attraction a bit more libidinously. "The girls," he wrote, "looked kind of sleazy and cool."

Child, an acolyte of Laura Nyro and Joni Mitchell, wasn't all that familiar with KISS—he thought they were for little kids. "Our group was using R&B rhythms and rock chords, but telling singer-songwriter stories over that dance beat," he says by way of distinction. It seemed a foregone conclusion that Stanley would ask the girls to add backing vocals to his 1978 solo album, but

Child was surprised when he also suggested the two men attempt to write together. Child agreed on the condition that the song would be for *his* group, because, he says, "I really didn't understand who I was talking to." Their initial collaboration, "The Fight," appeared on Rouge's self-titled debut album (backed by players from the New York session mafia that worked on Gene Simmons's and Sean Delaney's solo LPs).

Around that time, Stanley was spending evenings and early mornings entranced by the decadent scene at Studio 54, thinking he could compose a track just like the pumping disco anthems that made the nightclub sweat. He came up with some rudiments at home before asking Child to meet him at Manhattan's SIR Studios, where KISS were rehearsing. "They had a big grand piano," Child says, "and on one of their breaks, Paul and I sat on opposite sides and we wrote the song. It wasn't even on guitar."

Creating a slow song with big power chords over a fast dance beat inspired Stanley, and he took it to producer Vini Poncia to finish off the chorus. (Peter Criss had insisted they hire Poncia, who had overseen the drummer's solo LP, to helm *Dynasty*, the band's seventh studio album.) The result of the collaboration, the throbbing, undeniable "I Was Made for Lovin' You," peaked at No. 11 on *Billboard*'s pop singles chart on August 11, 1979, just one month after Disco Demolition Night devastated Chicago's Comiskey Park, home of baseball's White Sox. At that event—which drew some 70,000 fans to the stadium for a team that had been averaging 18,000 per game—popular rock-radio deejay Steve Dahl blew up a giant crate of disco records during the break in a White Sox–Detroit Tigers twi-night doubleheader. It prompted mobs to storm the playing field, setting fires and damaging the grounds, causing the home team to cancel and forfeit the second game. The protest has since become recognized as the moment that exposed the implied racism, sexism, and homophobia that often dogged the opposition to disco—as resentments fomented by economic uncertainty and an imminent recession led to attacks on a musical genre that gave cultural clout to previously marginalized groups. Drunken rowdies also saw it as an opportunity to break stuff. "That evening was a declaration of independence from a tyranny of sophistication," Dahl later said. "We were just kids pissing on a musical genre." An oversimplification, to be sure, but back then it was sometimes tough being a rock-and-roll denizen in a dance-music world.

"There's a variety of ways to unpack the objection to the disco era," says journalist Ira Robbins. "But one of the real problems for people like me was this feeling of being overwhelmed by something. Top 40 radio suddenly stopped playing the music that we liked and was only playing songs that went [*imitates a disco hi-hat cymbal sound*]. It didn't seem like they were challenging intellectually or artistically. They all sounded like the same song. Obviously, that's not the way I feel about it now, but it was at the time."

The KISS single's success only proved that despite the hostility, a big part of the rock audience could be accepting of dance music, and vice versa. "KISS or the Stones or Rod Stewart would not have put a disco song on their albums if they thought that their entire audience would be turned off," says critic Chuck Eddy. Still, "I Was Made for Lovin' You" ended up alienating KISS's vocal "disco sucks" contingent and at least one of the band members: Simmons simply hated that in concert he had to sing the fey *doo-doo-doo* backing vocals.

"They were surprised at how successful 'I Was Made for Lovin' You' became," Child says. "Gene has always said he never liked the song, but he says they perform it because it gives the audience what they want."

· · · ·

**"PRETTY CRAPPY," "WIMPY," "NEUTERED,"** and "ball-less" are just a few of the words Paul Stanley has used to describe *Unmasked*, KISS's eighth studio LP. On the contrary. Some would say it takes balls the size of Jupiter to feature a comic strip on your album cover that ends on a word balloon reading, "I still say they stink!"

Released in May 1980, KISS's attempt to go pop may be the oddest and most experimental album in their catalog and, until 1997's *Carnival of Souls*, the one that least resembles classic KISS. But it's far from their worst. (And no, despite the teasing title and cover, the band would remain masked for two more album cycles after this one.) Though they no longer had to appease Peter Criss, who sat out the entire record, the band nevertheless rehired Vini Poncia to produce. And as he did on *Dynasty* and *Destroyer*, Jay Messina sat in the engineer's seat. This time around, Poncia's stamp, Messina says, was to put more emphasis on the vocals.

Stanley later complained that his stamp was more conspicuous than that. "Vini's input at that point was taking us in a direction that we weren't comfortable with," Stanley has said. "But . . . nobody protested very loudly because we were beginning to lose sight of who we were."

Ace Frehley's pal Anton Fig—who played drums on most of *Dynasty* and whose band Spider, also managed by Bill Aucoin, would release their debut album that same year—again ghosted for Criss. Likely due to Simmons and

Stanley's collective disinterest and distraction, the lead guitarist managed to have three of his compositions, with his lead vocals, accepted for inclusion, his best showing on a KISS studio album. But where Poncia shot *Dynasty* through with a punchy soullessness, here the band just sound defeated and deflated and unsure of who exactly was listening, the mostly half-baked ideas slathered with gooey harmonies and sprinkled with icy keyboards.

The best songs, however, would sound like lost classics had they been doled out as bonus tracks on reissues of other albums. "Is That You?" (written by Gerard McMahon, who later had a hit with "Cry Little Sister" from the teen-vampire movie *The Lost Boys*) is a righteous striptease strut that presages Robert Palmer's "Addicted to Love" by a full half decade. And one could imagine hearing or, better yet, seeing "Tomorrow" soundtracking a locker-room montage in some high-school T&A comedy. Likewise, Frehley's thuddingly simplistic "Talk to Me," with its slurry Keith Richards–like lead work, and the Simmons-sung new-wave trifle "She's So European" exert a certain bumbling charm. But then there's "Shandi," as feeble a song as KISS ever attempted—difficult to imagine, when the same album features "Torpedo Girl"—which suggests the direction Wicked Lester might have taken had Simmons and Stanley decided to satisfy their soft-rock jones and occupy the soporific purgatory between Player and Pablo Cruise. Considering its similar title and chorus, "Shandi," written by Stanley and Poncia, is clearly indebted to the Hollies' version of Bruce Springsteen's "4th of July, Asbury Park (Sandy)." One could say, then, that when the Boss purloined the riff from "I Was Made for Lovin' You" for his song "Outlaw Pete" thirty years later, he paid them back with interest.

• • • •

AFTER THE INCREASINGLY ERRATIC drummer sabotaged a number of live gigs in December 1979, by early 1980, Peter Criss was no longer in the band. "Maybe they thought by firing me, they were scaring me straight," Criss wrote. "I don't know. But I did know that I hated them even more after they fired me."

"I wanted to give him another chance, but my hands were tied," Frehley wrote. "I was outvoted and the decision was made to move forward without him, so I accepted the decision reluctantly." But before heading out to tour *Unmasked*, the band decided to bring Criss in for a rehearsal just to confirm they were making the right decision. They realized they were, all right, and Criss was soon arranging the terms of his exit. "Our family is no different than any other," Simmons says. "There's dysfunction and people get drunk and high. The only difference with our family is, we kick their asses out."

During all this turmoil within the band, PolyGram was in the process of buying out Casablanca, and since KISS had a key-man clause in their contract and their key man, Neil Bogart, would be leaving the label, they were able to negotiate a fruitful new pact.

Criss ended up retaining a 25 percent interest in the band, and PolyGram, wanting to remain all-in with KISS after the platinum success of *Dynasty*, immediately signed him to his own deal. His second solo album, *Out of Control*, made little noise when it was barely released in September 1980, but two songs distinguish the otherwise ho-hum effort: one, a virtual rewrite of *Rock and Roll Over*'s "Calling Dr. Love" titled "In Trouble Again"; the other, a rugged cover of the Young Rascals' "You Better Run," whose release couldn't have been timed worse, as Pat Benatar had had a hit with her version just months earlier.

Despite the renewed attention from PolyGram, KISS saw their fortunes severely diminish Stateside, as their strategy to go pop made much of their hard-core appeal go *POP!* With *Unmasked* taking nearly three months to sell 500,000 copies at home, the band decided to tour the album exclusively in Europe and Australasia, where "Shandi" had become something of a hit.

To replace Criss, the band hired Paul Caravallo, a thirty-year-old unknown, also from Brooklyn, who could sing and play double kick drums. (In a bizarre coincidence, as a member of the disco band Lightning, he appeared on a 1979 album released by Casablanca that was coproduced by Lewis Merenstein, who had overseen the debut album by Criss's band Chelsea.) Renamed Eric Carr—two Pauls in the band apparently being enough—he took on the persona of the Fox.

KISS played their sole 1980 U.S. gig at the Palladium, a Manhattan theater, on July 25, in essence a coming-out party for Carr (the band had performed there on New Year's Eve 1973, when it was known as the Academy of Music). In reality, it was a significant comedown from their two previous hometown gigs the year before, at Madison Square Garden, and KISS wouldn't do another full concert in the U.S. for two years. A few days after the Palladium gig, to introduce Carr to a national audience, the band taped an appearance on the children's show *Kids Are People Too*. They had to have been embarrassed when, after being asked by the host to name his favorite KISS member, one young fan in the audience answered, "Peter Criss."

The Unmasked tour began on August 29 in Italy and concluded on December 3 in Auckland, New Zealand, which would also be Ace Frehley's last live performance with KISS for sixteen years. He played on 1981's *Music from "The Elder,"* an overblown and undercooked attempt at a Hobbit-rock concept album, which reunited KISS with *Destroyer* producer Bob Ezrin but pushed the lead guitarist further away. In 1982, "in a blur of drinking and drugging," Frehley lost interest in the band he had given nine years of his life to and jumped. That same year, upset at the bad decisions the freebase-addicted Bill Aucoin had been making on their behalf—and who initially took 25 percent of the band's gross when most managers took 15—Simmons and Stanley let him go. "He was effective in the beginning, and then fame and power corrupt," Simmons said. "Machiavelli and all that."

His replacements: KISS's longtime business managers Howard Marks and Carl Glickman, who had begun exerting more influence and directing their career. Since they were essentially money guys, they needed somebody to come up with strategy and liaise with the label and the media, particularly since a fledgling cable channel was beginning to play a big role in creating new superstars and extending and expanding the popularity of veterans. They hired respected industry veteran Danny Goldberg, who wrote for *Circus* early in his career and briefly helped out with KISS's publicity efforts in 1973, as creative consultant, a quasi-management position. With his guidance, the band would undergo a controversial transformation that would for several years alter the course of their career.

## CHAPTER 17

# NO SURPRIZE

IN JANUARY 1980, AT the request of their publisher, Cheap Trick entered the Record Plant in L.A. to cut demos of a few older songs with engineer Gary Ladinsky, in hopes of getting other artists to cover them. "We rented some gear because ours was on its way to some other town, smoked a joint in the booth, and went out and cut, like, nine basic tracks," says Bun E. Carlos. Robin Zander came in the following week to add vocals. One track, the rollicking "Ain't Got You," also had been demoed eight years earlier by Sick Man of Europe. Another, the elegant "Take Me I'm Yours," had been earmarked for Bryan Ferry—in fact, at moments Zander's inflections practically replicate his—though it's hard to imagine the urbane Roxy Music frontman crooning the line "come six with my nine." Linda Ronstadt expressed interest in the buoyant "Oh Boy." Ultimately, no covers were forthcoming, although "Take Me I'm Yours" and "Such a Good Girl" appeared on *Found All the Parts*, a ten-inch EP that Epic released that year as part of its Nu Disk series, and a rerecording of "You Talk Too Much" ended up as a bonus track on the CD and cassette editions of 1983's *Next Position Please*.

Rick Nielsen's fecundity as a songwriter led him to offer "Need a Little Girl (Just Like You)" and "It Must Be Love" to Rick Derringer, whose 1979 album *Guitars and Women* Todd Rundgren was producing. He also contributed "Heart on the Line" to House of Lords, a band led by former Angel keyboardist Gregg Giuffria that was managed by Ken Adamany and signed to a label Gene Simmons began in the late '80s. That Cheap Trick would include their own, remarkably similar version on an album recorded a quarter century later speaks both to the timelessness of Nielsen's writing and the consistency of his band. The song was a vast improvement over Nielsen's previous collaboration with House of Lords, for their 1988 debut album, a galumphing metallic paean to cunnilingus called—what else?—"Slip of the Tongue."

The songwriting association with Simmons began years earlier, when the KISS bassist offered Cheap Trick eight numbers that were in various stages of development. Among them: "Mongoloid Man" (which he demoed in 1978 with Joe Perry); "I've Just Begun to Fight" (recorded with members of Virgin, an Aucoin band he was producing); "Nobody's Perfect" (no relation to a similarly titled song KISS put on 2009's *Sonic Boom*); "We Won't Take It Anymore" (a cowrite with Eric Carr that was also sent to Scottish rockers Heavy Pettin); "So Many Girls, So Little Time" and "Sooner Said Than Done" (both of which ultimately went to Marc Ferrari's band Keel, whom Simmons produced); "Hello Hello"; and "Secretly Cruel" (which KISS recorded for 1985's *Asylum*). Simmons later suggested that his "What You See Is What You Get" would get Cheap Trick back on the radio. But the band had to wonder what on earth he was thinking, as none of the demos in circulation— typical Demon bluster and say-nothing almost-anthems—sound remotely appropriate for Cheap Trick.

In April 1990, CBS Music Publishing sent a tape to Adamany promoting the services of a songwriter the company had just signed: Paul Stanley, who was riding high after the success of the KISS power ballad "Forever." Stanley was never made aware of the outreach to Cheap Trick, but "Wouldn't You Like to Know Me" from his 1978 solo album and his KISS songs "Comin' Home" and "Anything for My Baby" indicate that his work might connect more than Simmons's would. Alas, nothing came of the solicitation.

In October 1991, Adamany sent Simmons two Cheap Trick compositions to consider for KISS: "Burn Down the Night" and "Right Between the Eyes" (an outtake from the *Lap of Luxury* sessions). As an aside, he also included on the tape "Mystery of Love," a Nielsen/Zander composition that New Jersey rock mononym Fiona would be covering on her 1992 album *Squeeze*. KISS passed.

• • • •

**WITH NO NEW ORIGINAL** material since *Draw the Line*, Aerosmith—more specifically, Columbia Records—were desperate for a hit. Jack Douglas was out, replaced by Foreigner producer Gary Lyons. In April and July 1979, between sessions for their sixth studio album, *Night in the Ruts*, the band, in a brazen cash grab, headlined a few major North American festivals. One, another World Series of Rock, this time at Cleveland's Lakefront Stadium, featured Scorpions, AC/DC, Thin Lizzy, Journey, Ted Nugent, gang violence, and two fatalities. But for the band, the biggest drama played out backstage, where the Toxic Twins screamed at each other as the wives of Tom Hamilton and Joe Perry also got into it. "Being in Aerosmith," Brad Whitford has said, "was like walking into a dogfight and both dogs bite you." Perry, finally tired of all the bullshit and eyeing a solo career, walked out of the dogfight.

"I swore that night I'd never play onstage with Joe Perry again as long as I lived," Tyler has said. "The drugs won."

"We were pretty burned out," Perry later said. "We had been busting our asses for eight or nine years, playing everywhere, trying to make it. If we had been a little wiser, we would have just taken a vacation. We just kept going until basically we had a meltdown." When *Night in the Ruts* finally came out—featuring two Perry/Tyler cowrites, "Chiquita" and "No Surprize," that were among their best—the band, now featuring Jimmy Crespo on lead guitar, still managed to play arenas, but the crowds were beginning to shrink.

After leaving Aucoin, publicist Carol Kaye worked at Elektra Records before starting up an in-house PR department for Leber-Krebs in 1979. Behind the scenes at one Aerosmith concert, she saw just how out of control and difficult Tyler could be. She had shuttled journalists in limos to see the show, which was supposed to be followed by a press conference with the band. "Everything was set up and I went into the dressing room and Steven went crazy," she says. "He literally picked up a big steel garbage pail, threw it, and it just missed my head. At that point I just said, 'This is not what I signed up for.'" She soon told Krebs, "I can't continue to work like this. I can't work with Steven. He needs help."

In November 1980, smarting from *Night in the Ruts*' disappointing sales, Columbia released Aerosmith's *Greatest Hits*, which eventually sold some eleven million copies, becoming their biggest album. After leaving the band, Perry fired Leber-Krebs and started the Joe Perry Project, enlisting Jack Douglas to coproduce their first LP, *Let the Music Do the Talking*, for Columbia. He always suspected that the label signed on to keep him in the family and purposely allowed the album to fail, expecting one day he'd return to Aerosmith.

Whitford left the band in 1981 to start Whitford/St. Holmes with Derek St. Holmes, who had sung with Ted Nugent, and drummer Steve Pace, who had played in Hydra with Starz bassist Orville Davis. His replacement in Aerosmith was Rick Dufay, whom Tyler described as "a friend of Jack's, a guitar player, a total asshole, and we loved him."

• • • •

**PEOPLE ALWAYS TOLD MARC** Ferrari that he looked like Joe Perry. So in 1982, at age twenty, the guitarist put his resemblance to good use—even dyeing a skunky white streak in his dark hair—and formed an Aerosmith tribute band in Boston called Last Child, comanaged by Ray Tabano, the guitar player Brad Whitford succeeded in 1971. This being the band's home turf, Ferrari ran into and befriended Tim Collins, who was then managing the Joe Perry Project. Deepening his connection to Aerosmith, Ferrari, at the time, was dating Joe Perry's then sister-in-law. A few years later, two of Ferrari's subsequent bands, Keel and Cold Sweat, would open for the real thing. Of *Rocks*, his all-time favorite album, he says, "Whatever they were smoking, drinking, or doing back then, it just all came together." The guitarist, who first saw them live on the Draw the Line tour, reckons he's attended Aerosmith shows in five different decades: "Being on the same bill with them was a dream come true for a kid like me."

## CHAPTER 18

# STOP THIS GAME

WHEN CHEAP TRICK STEPPED onstage at the Winnipeg Arena in Manitoba, Canada, on August 7, 1980, it probably took fans a few moments to realize something was amiss. The bass player was carrying the usual monster twelve-string, but he looked just slightly off. The hair seemed about right: big brown curls framed a jaw carved out of quartz and cascaded toward hard-angled shoulders. But where was that dimpled chin you could park a bicycle in? Who was this imposter? And what had they done to Tom Petersson?

The official line was that Petersson had fallen ill, having contracted an incapacitating viral infection that made his hands and teeth numb and caused him to vomit blood. On doctor's orders he needed to miss scheduled shows in Canada and Japan. "He left for medical reasons," Rick Nielsen quipped in 1988. "He made us sick." What went unsaid was the fact that for months the bassist had been checking out of the band. Soon after Petersson met a model named Dagmar in Germany and quickly married her, straws began to weigh down the camel. "Every week, he'd tell us what was wrong with us," Bun E. Carlos says. "Stuff he'd been hearing from his wife: 'All of the songs should be about sex. Rick and Bun E., you guys look terrible onstage. You should be in the back and dark, and it should be me and Robin out front. And I should be singing half the songs.'"

The camel finally collapsed at AIR Studios on the Caribbean island of Montserrat, during the recording of *All Shook Up*. Despite the success of *Dream Police*, the band felt it was time to move on from Tom Werman. "We had done this L.A. drum and guitar sound," Carlos says. "We wanted to get better sounds." He says the decision to hire George Martin was easy: "Who's the greatest producer in the world? The guy that did the Beatles, obviously."

The executives at Epic bristled at the mention of Martin, whose last "hit" was the successful but widely derided soundtrack to the movie *Sgt. Pepper's Lonely Hearts Club Band*, which featured Aerosmith's version of "Come Together." Carlos remembers the label's chorus of nays: "George Martin? That old guy? Forget it. No way."

"The more they said that, the more we said, 'We're using George Martin,'" he recalls. "The label won't support George Martin? No problem. We'll give him the fucking money. The label by then was getting a little toxic." So too were relationships among some of the musicians. After they finished recording basic tracks, which took around three weeks, the bassist told his bandmates he needed to fly to Los Angeles, where he and his wife were living, to deal with mud in their swimming pool. The band completed the album at Martin's London studio without him.

Cheap Trick saw the opportunity to work with Martin and his beloved engineer, Geoff Emerick, as a chance to indulge their Beatles fanaticism and cut a record that sonically at least would resemble one of the Fab Four's. "We used the Beatles as a point of reference because they worked with the Beatles and we knew the Beatles," says Carlos, who remembers the musicians constantly asking, "So how do we get it to sound like *that* right there?" When Petersson was laying down the bass track for "Stop This Game," he asked Emerick what Paul McCartney used on "Rain" and tried to replicate that sound. He succeeded.

Released in October 1980, the album revealed a band unsure of where they fit in or even who they were, as they baldly aped a bunch of groups that were not necessarily named the Beatles. The LP's surreal cover collage, with Nielsen in a checkerboard getup staring bug-eyed at a flying locomotive and Carlos in a black trench coat and fedora, clearly pitched Cheap Trick as a new wave band—and it may even have inspired the design of the Cars' "You Might Think" video four years later—but, with the exception of the dystopic vocoder on "High Priest of Rhythmic Noise," they didn't much sound like one. And the divide in quality between the songs on side 1 (*blam!*) and those on side 2 (blah) had till that point never been so pronounced. Of the bright spots, the symphonic wall of sound on "Stop This Game" harkens back to the best of *Dream Police*, and "Just Got Back," as powerful and playful a statement of intent as they've recorded, is "Lust for Life" as played by the Royal Drummers of Burundi.

"Baby Loves to Rock," essentially a rewrite of the Yardbirds' "Psycho Daisies," is a delirious Chuck Berry duckwalkathon that flaunts the comical elements apparent not just in Nielsen's lyrics but also in his music—with a rooster crowing after Robin Zander sings "in the morning" and crickets chirping after "in the evening." "That was George Martin saying, 'Let's dress this thing up. Let's go all the way,'" says Carlos. The humor extended to the guitarist's technique: for this track Nielsen used an instrument equipped with a string bender so that any duffer attempting to learn it at home on a regular guitar would go nuts trying.

"Love Comes A-Tumblin' Down," with its memorable, AC/DC-style riffing, became a tribute to that band's singer after Bon Scott choked on his vomit and died during the album's recording. The track had already been cut, but, Carlos says, "the lyrics suddenly became more about Bon dying in the back seat of a car."

Once while occupying a stall at the studio's bathroom, Carlos listened as Martin and Emerick discussed what they had in store for one song.

"Well, Geoffrey, 'World's Greatest Lover'—I think I know what we're going to be doing on that," Martin said. "We're going to give it the George Harrison treatment."

"Everything but the kitchen sink?"

"That's right."

Carlos was thrilled to overhear the plan: "I was like, 'Ooh, we're going to do the George Harrison treatment—triple drums and everything.' We did a triple drum track and double piano track and nine of these and eight of those."

A villainous silent-movie piano bit—that resembles the beginning of AC/DC's "Big Balls"—introduces "World's Greatest Lover," which in addition to its regal, Harrisonian air, stands as the epitome of Cheap Trick's Lennonphilia. Over a deliberate, pulsating melody, Zander perfectly captures in his enraptured "Imagine" vocals his yearning for the title paramour, before a crisp Nielsen guitar solo vigorously sings a verse. (Nielsen and Carlos finally got to work with Lennon himself in August 1980, when Jack Douglas brought them in to play on two songs for *Double Fantasy*. Their contributions, deemed too heavy, didn't make it onto the finished album.)

The best track on *All Shook Up*'s flip, "I Love You Honey but I Hate Your Friends," sounds very little like Cheap Trick, but in its slack, go-nowhere way could pass for secondhand Stones or artificial Aerosmith. The weirdest, a novelty drumline-cum-chant called "Who D' King," closes the album but was initially intended as a non-LP B side. Martin worked hard to fit a Petersson song, "Machines Make Money," into the overall picture and slotted it onto side 2. But after the bassist decided to take it with him when he left the band, "Who D' King" made the cut.

With no hit single—"Stop This Game" couldn't even muster a Top 40 showing—the album fizzled after going gold. But it did give Tom Werman the opportunity to bask in some schadenfreude. "I spent some time with George Martin and thought he was a wonderful gentleman, one of the greatest producers in the world," he says. "At the same time, I got some satisfaction out of the fact that that was a stiff album and that I could make a hit with a band that George Martin couldn't."

As of August 26, 1980, two months before the album's release and nearly three weeks after Pete Comita replaced him, Petersson was officially out of the band. He later said that it was playing three hundred nights a year and recording two albums a year during their time off that did him in. "After a while, we'd gotten to the point where we were successful, but we were still on this schedule and still doing albums in two or three weeks," he said. "We needed more time to think, to air out and encourage the creativity to write. Nobody wanted to do that."

Forty years later, Carlos regrets the decision to fire the bassist: "We should've called the office and gone, 'We need some time off.' 'You'll go bankrupt! You've got to work or you're gonna die.' There was always that from Ken and the label." The drummer wishes that counseling had been available to the band. "The only way we knew how to deal with it was, 'Let's get this guy out of here.' And that was a big mistake."

According to Nielsen, "We should never have gotten into the position"— one that he says was brought on by Adamany and Dagmar, whom he felt tried to divide and conquer the band. Petersson's restlessness, he believed, could have been better handled. "A creative manager," he said, "would figure out how to do it and keep the core going at the same time."

With a few gigs upcoming in Canada and a return to Tokyo imminent, Adamany drafted Comita—a guitarist, formerly of the Chicago band d'Thumbs, whom he had managed a few years earlier—to quickly learn the set. Although a talented songwriter in his own right—"Reach Out," a catchy new wavey number he cowrote that Cheap Trick recorded for the 1981 animated science-fiction movie *Heavy Metal*, is one of their best from the period—Comita displayed capricious behavior that soon eclipsed his usefulness. Comita has said his free-spirited, happy-go-lucky personality rubbed the band the wrong way, but the band saw things differently. "We knew Pete was a party dog," says Carlos. "But we didn't know how much of a party dog he was."

. . . .

ON FEBRUARY 28, 1981, Cheap Trick headlined the Boston Garden with Comita, offering a set that included songs from the recently released *All Shook Up*. The show found the band in fine form, with Zander taking his KISS record out—in this case, a copy of *Dynasty*—and throwing it into the crowd during "Surrender." ("There's no fire or blood and the drum set doesn't levitate or turn upside down, but here was a simple prop that we incorporated into the show," said Nielsen, who would ultimately take charge of the KISS-tossing.) The audience was also treated to the added spectacle of a drum choir during "Who D' King"—two drummers flanked Carlos, while a dozen fans and contest winners wearing Bun E. Carlos masks played along.

Carl Plaster, a Boston-based engineer and drum tech who has worked with the Lemonheads, Yo La Tengo, and Buffalo Tom, was sixteen when he attended the show. "Cheap Trick were great," he says, "although they had a tendency to always be ridiculously loud, way louder than you'd expect. The sound at Boston Garden, unless you were up close, was pretty awful." Before one of the encores, Zander announced that they'd like to bring out some friends. And with that, Joe Perry walked onstage to share leads with Nielsen on the Beatles' "Day Tripper" (which Cheap Trick had covered on the *Found All the Parts* EP the previous year), and then Steven Tyler emerged to rapturous cheers as they all launched into the Rolling Stones' "The Last Time."

Plaster describes this as occurring during Aerosmith's "jury's out" period, "because it seemed like they were in the process of just starting to suck, because they were fucked up all the time." The Perry-free Aerosmith had been playing shows, and Tyler himself had experienced an eventful few months, passing out onstage in Portland, Maine, and tearing off one of his heels in a drunken motorcycle accident the previous fall. "But they were still Boston heroes, so people were pulling for them," Plaster says. "At least for those fifteen minutes, they seemed pretty coherent. They came out and had a good time, and that was that."

"We'd go to Boston and then one or two of them would come to the gig and, of course, you've got to get up and play with us," Carlos says. "I don't know where they went afterwards, probably their separate ways. A few years later in interviews Rick would say, 'We got Aerosmith back together!'"

"They started speaking again," Nielsen says proudly. "And they never sent me a gold or platinum album either, the bums. I didn't want a thank-you card, I wanted a gold or platinum album."

. . . .

PLAYING SOLO LIBERATED JOE Perry. He called the shots, he hired the players, he got to rock out in clubs where he could hear everything and see everyone. "But then it became a grind and he needed the money," says Tim Collins, his manager at the time. "He kept living like he was in Aerosmith."

By the third Project album, Perry had split from his wife and, he has said, "I went berserk for the first time in my life. Wine, women, and song." He was still traveling in a van, playing joints like West L.A.'s Music Machine, where on March 29, 1984, Steven McDonald, bassist for Redd Kross, opened with his side project DC3, led by Black Flag's Dez Cadena. "We all had respect for Joe Perry's musicianship," McDonald says. "Then we were confused, because I think he has since called it his bottom, his clarity moment. He complained that his tech kept handing him out-of-tune guitars, but I'm sure that Joe probably didn't deserve much better." Maybe a hundred people showed up at a club that held roughly two hundred fifty. "It was kind of a bummer."

Just a month earlier, on February 14, Aerosmith had played an intimate gig at the Orpheum Theater in Boston, at the tail end of their Rock in a Hard Place tour. "Nitebob" Czaykowski, who'd left their steady employ in late 1977 when he got fed up with all the drugs and observed "weird shit going on internally with the crew," had reluctantly agreed to mix a few weeks of shows. "I just stayed far away from the band, although they were actually okay," he says. "Steven was a bit of a mess, but I'd seen him way worse." Czaykowski was on the Orpheum stage with Jimmy Crespo and Rick Dufay during soundcheck when, to their surprise, Perry and Whitford showed up. "[Jimmy and Rick] see the two of them walk in and they see Tom, Steven, and Joey go into the dressing room, and Crespo says to Dufay, 'I think we better look for a new job.'"

During the waning days of the Project, Collins would check in once in a while with Steven Tyler's roadie, who was taking care of the singer, because, the manager says, "we knew sooner or later they were going to get back together. The problem was that Joe and Steven both hated each other. We had explored all these other things for Joe to do that didn't come together. He had to do something, or else he was going to have to change his lifestyle drastically."

Perry and Collins went to New York to meet Tyler, then living in a run-down hotel on $30 a day. Perry's big ask of his former partner: Collins was going to manage the reconstructed Aerosmith; they had to can Leber and Krebs. "David and I went to war because the band said he cheated them out of money," Collins says of the two-year process it took to extricate the managers. "But when we finally got to see the books, we owed *him* money."

• • • •

"IF THE RECORD COMPANY didn't like it, you were fucked," Bun E. Carlos says. "You and the record company had to work together on this stuff. It was a big dance you all had to do."

Epic skimped on the foreplay when in July 1981 its parent company CBS Records sued Cheap Trick and Adamany for $12 million each to prevent them from signing to another label. The brief alleged that the band breached their recording contract by refusing to record for Epic two more albums by December 1981.

In response, the band countersued CBS and Tom Werman for $28 million in damages, citing, according to *Billboard*, "breach of contract, interference with prospective business associates, improper accounting, and inducement to breach," claiming the label failed to market the band appropriately, paid Werman money owed to them, and manufactured inferior product.

"Adamany was getting frustrated with them, and they weren't working with him either," says Carlos of the fraught period. "Adamany had a band meeting and goes, 'It's all fucked up with CBS, and they hate the new record.' Then we were on the road literally making our living because all of the royalty streams had stopped."

"The band was fed up with Adamany, the band was fed up with Epic, and Epic was fed up with the band and Adamany," says Ira Robbins, who was close with the group at the time. To Adamany, this type of disgruntlement was nothing out of the ordinary. "The management and the bands are always wanting more," he says. "We wanted more promotion money, and the argument was, 'It's not a hit.' Well, wait a minute, some of these songs are really good." He also had issues with Epic's marketing, noticing on tour stops, for example, that local stores were not stocked with albums. And he was indeed looking to sign elsewhere. "We had Elektra come in and see the band in Ann Arbor," he says, "because we thought we'd be able to get off of the label."

The parties resolved the issues not long after and Cheap Trick re-upped with Epic, but for the next few years the band remained in the wilderness.

When it came time to make their next album, *One on One*, with Roy Thomas Baker, producer of Queen and the Cars, the band recorded in Evanston, Illinois, not too far from home. "Because of the fight with the label, we didn't have the budget to take it to L.A. or New York," Carlos says. "Time dragged out, a million takes of this, and parts of it went south."

One of those parts, apparently, was their new bass player. "Pete got in the studio and couldn't play," Nielsen has said. "He was a screwball anyhow. He was the sweetest guy, nice guy." Before the band could fire him, Comita quit. (He segued right into U.S.S.A., which featured members of Montrose and Pezband and were managed by Adamany, and then, for a short time, joined budding Cheap Trick acolytes Enuff Z'Nuff.) To replace Comita, the group hired Jon Brant, one of his former bandmates in d'Thumbs, who also bore a striking resemblance to Petersson. Nielsen ended up playing most of the bass parts on the album, whose loud, burnished iciness and clutch of strong songs seemed a calculated rebuke of *All Shook Up*'s iffy experimentation.

"I don't enjoy sitting down with that record," Carlos says of *One on One*. "There's a lot of noise on it and a lot of bad notes in the mix." To encourage audience participation at their concerts, Nielsen began writing songs with gang vocals. "So some of the songs got written for the wrong reasons," Carlos says. "'Let's do this because it'll go over great live and be an arena hit. It'll look beautiful from the fortieth row.' That's no reason to do a song."

*One on One* did manage to generate a couple of minor hits—the bright but boorishly lecherous "She's Tight," and the ravishing "If You Want My Love," as perfect a Beatles homage as they've recorded. But neither *One on One*, nor its follow-up, the ecstatically tune-packed yet thin-sounding *Next Position Please*, produced by Todd Rundgren, were the returns to form the label had hoped for.

On July 15, 1984, a rare day off, Carlos went to Rockford's MetroCentre to see the reunited Aerosmith on their Back in the Saddle tour. With no album to push, but a hell of a lot to prove, they had become a dangerous band again. "Not only onstage," Tim Collins says, "but leading up to every show. The band almost broke up several times. I would sit them down and say, 'Listen, nobody pays a hundred dollars'"—though tickets were usually priced around $15—"'to see a sane guy. They love the craziness.' Steven would come up behind Brad and bite the back of his head, or make like he was fucking him. He thought Brad and Tom were very uptight and he was trying to loosen them up. People would say, 'You gotta rein him in. You're not a strong enough manager.' 'No! We gotta let him do his thing.'" The previous night in Springfield, Illinois, a stumbling Tyler did more than his thing: fucked up on heroin and coke, he collapsed into the audience.

Before the Rockford show, Carlos went backstage to say hi and was struck by the dysfunction. "I saw Steven in the hallway," he says, "and he's like, 'Yeah, Joey's got his own dressing room. The band's down here. Here's my dressing room up the hall here. No one's speaking to me because I got fucked up and fell off stage.'"

When Carlos saw Kramer, the drummer told him, "Yeah, I want to kill Steven, but, boy, the band sounds great." Then Whitford came by with a request. "You got a joint? I'm dying to get high," he told Carlos. "Suddenly we're trying to do no drugs. This is driving me fucking nuts." Carlos shared some pot with him.

"That was the best show I've played since I've been back in the band," Whitford told him afterward. Carlos couldn't argue: "They were just fucking great."

At the same time, Carlos's own band were slogging it out, doing theaters, clubs, dumps, anything to stay on the road. "At the end of the tour," Carlos says, "we got the breakdown from the office and the tour made three dollars or something, for the whole year. We managed to spend every penny on the road that we made on the road. What a total waste of a year."

· · · ·

AS THEIR RECORDS BECAME more elaborate-sounding, Cheap Trick hired their first touring keyboardist. Phil Cristian (who'd come to be dubbed Magic Cristian, likely the first rock nickname to reference a Terry Southern book) had been a member of Fortress, which had had a production deal with MCA Records that went kaput and eventually became a cover band called Front Page, featuring guitarist Mark Norton. In 1981, at one of his gigs in Orange County, California, Cristian was approached by members of Micki Free's band, which included bassist Jon Brant, to see if he'd be interested in touring with them. Gene Simmons had discovered Free in 1975 when the Native American guitarist opened for KISS as a member of the flashy Illinois-based power trio Smokehouse. Soon after Mercury Records and producer Eddie Kramer began to show interest in them, Free left the group and moved to California.

In 1981, Simmons was dating Diana Ross, whom he hooked up with while living with her best friend, Cher. When Cristian showed up at the audition studio, he was surprised to see the pair sitting there. Ross, he soon learned, was managing Free and wanted to take him out to open her tour. Tod Howarth, Free's previous keyboardist, had recently left to join 707, a bland rock act that moved with Neil Bogart when the label chief left Casablanca and started Boardwalk. After Cristian joined, Free's band ended up doing only a handful of concerts with Ross, for which Simmons helped mix the sound. Afterward, there was some discussion about recording either a demo or an album that Simmons would produce. "As usual," Cristian says, "nothing really came of that."

Simmons would later encourage Free to join the funk-pop group Shalamar and work with him on an album for Wendy O. Williams, former screecher for theatrical shock-punks Plasmatics. Paul Stanley would coproduce songs for Free's band Crown of Thorns, which also featured KISS collaborator and ex-Plasmatics bassist Jean Beauvoir. Mark Norton changed his last name to St. John and joined KISS after Ace Frehley's replacement, Vinnie Vincent, left in 1984.

When Jon Brant succeeded Pete Comita in Cheap Trick and the band were considering adding a singing keyboard player for 1982's One on One tour, he mentioned Cristian. "The main reason we got a keyboard player was to do all the high parts," Bun E. Carlos says. "Robin goes in to make a record and he does ten or fifteen tracks of vocals and then you've got to go out and play the thing live."

For the better part of a year, Cristian traveled on a tour bus, not with the band but with the crew ("It was cheaper," he says), beginning with a fireworks display/concert in front of tens of thousands at Jack Murphy Stadium, organized by San Diego radio station KGB-FM and featuring Chuck Berry and Joan Jett and the Blackhearts. Like a number of heavy bands of that era—including KISS, Black Sabbath, Judas Priest, and Iron Maiden—who didn't want to reveal that they were supplementing their sound, Cheap Trick relegated Cristian to the side of the stage, mostly hidden from view. "That was just the image they wanted," he says. "They didn't want the keyboards to be a visual part." To most of the crowd in a stadium or theater, it was as if he didn't exist, but sometimes in smaller clubs, he was hard to hide.

In 1983, Cristian moved to Rockford from L.A., hoping his proximity to the band would eventually lead to his writing and recording with them, an endeavor that proved fruitless. "They just didn't use the touring keyboard players in the studio," he says. "I came to learn that producers have a gaggle of guys that they like. So while I took it personally back then, I don't take it so personally anymore." He did manage to play, uncredited, on "Love Comes," from their 1985 album *Standing on the Edge* and on the band's theme song to the teen comedy *Up the Creek*, and he appears in the inane video for the latter. After a few guest spots over the ensuing years, Cristian would reenter the Cheap Trick fold in a big way in 2009, playing on their North American tour with Def Leppard and Poison.

• • • •

FOUR YEARS AFTER CONQUERING Japan, Tom Petersson returned to Budokan in March 1982, as a member of Carmine Appice & Friends. In this sort of proto–All-Starr Band (sans Ringo) revue—featuring drummer Appice (whose KISS ties include playing on one track on Paul Stanley's 1978 solo album and recording Stanley and Simmons songs in his band King Kobra, which also toured with KISS), Raspberries singer Eric Carmen, guitarist Rick Derringer, and keyboardist Duane Hitchings—the bassist took the lead for Cheap Trick's "I Know What I Want" and the *All Shook Up* outtake "Machines Make Money."

"Seemingly, from the minute we arrived in Japan, the rock press divided us into two different groups," Carmen later wrote on his website. "Carmine, Duane, and Rick were seen as 'serious musicians,' while Tom and I were seen more like 'teen idols.' When the elevator in the hotel arrived in the lobby every day, Carmine would walk out with serious mascara, the Fu-Manchu mustache, a large cloak, pirate earrings, and tri-colored hair. I think the Japanese girls thought he was kind of scary. He was hoping to be mobbed, but it wasn't happening. Then Tom and I would come down, and 500 girls would rush the elevator. Carmine was not pleased."

At the time, Appice was managed by Alan Miller, who had just a few years earlier parted ways with Starz. Miller brought in one of Starz's former road managers, Arnie Silver, to mix the sound and run the tour. "Before they rehearsed one note, how bad could they be?" Silver says. "But they had no direction. Every night they played, they played their hits. But what were you going to do with it?"

After leaving Cheap Trick, Petersson also reconnected with former Nazz and Fuse drummer Thom Mooney to record a few tracks, before Dagmar became involved as the singer. The solo project Petersson had been threatening in his waning days as a member of Cheap Trick materialized in 1984 with the release of an EP called *Tom Peterson and Another Language*. "It turned into another bad-news experience," Mooney said. "He would bring her to meetings with potential record companies. With her presence and her strange accent, she would stand up and tell these record execs, 'We want $300,000 each to go any further with the conversation.'"

Aside from the restored spelling of his surname (which he introduced on the back cover of *All Shook Up*), the EP offers little in the way of innovation, its generic new wave resembling nothing so much as a goth Missing Persons or a more guitar-focused Berlin. "That's a piece of shit, isn't it?" Nielsen said in 1990. "I couldn't even listen to it. You could give me a hundred dollars today, I still won't even listen to it." The project did, however, secure Dagmar and the band exposure on *Playboy's Girls of Rock & Roll* home video collection. In 1984, Petersson also played on sessions with Jeff Beck for Mick Jagger's solo album *She's the Boss*, though his work didn't make it onto the album. While living in L.A. he talked with Joe Perry about starting a band with neo-rockabilly singer-guitarist Rocky Burnette and his cousin Billy Burnette, but Perry rejoined Aerosmith before they were able to play together. In early 1985, he split from Dagmar and moved to New York where he reignited Sick Man of Europe (later renamed on at least one club invite, Spuyten Dyval), this time with Janna Allen, his girlfriend at the time, drummer Lon Monroe, and on guitar Pete Comita, who'd replaced him in Cheap Trick, playing what Petersson described as a cross between Cocteau Twins and AC/DC.

Interviewed in 1990, Robin Zander sounded philosophical about the bassist's departure. "He just took off on a part of his life that he needed to do," the singer said. "And it was definitely a good thing to happen at the time for all of us. Financially it didn't help. But we made some fine records."

# SHOUT IT OUT LOUD

**WHAT EXACTLY IS IT** that the fans of KISS, Cheap Trick, Aerosmith, and Starz latched on to? What made these four bands seem, to many, to be of a piece?

For one thing, all of them are just a bit . . . different. So were a few other American bands at the time. Alice Cooper, the Tubes, and Sparks, to name three, all trafficked in theatrics and humor. But with the exception of Cooper's, their music was too brainy and their appearance too outré to garner any lasting mass success. The kids didn't want their rock in quotation marks or, in the case of Sparks' Ron Mael, a Hitler mustache. They were, however, ready to embrace maximum exaggeration. KISS might have seemed like supernatural comic-book beasties, but anyone could tart themselves up to look just like them (and many still do), in defiance of peers who'd mock the band and, by extension, their devotees. The two studs and two duds in Cheap Trick did nothing if not upend the traditional notion that all members of a band had to *look* cool to *be* cool. Aerosmith, with their striped unitards, flouncy scarves, and gonad-squishing dungarees, took stereotypical hard-rock chic to its logical illogical extreme. As for Starz, they were ultimately an endearing composite—KISS and Aerosmith fighting to the death, armed with Cheap Trick's pointed hooks—spangled perpetual openers punching the clock for rock and roll.

To put it another way, these bands acted as mirrors to impressionable young fantasists. "They were so much like their fans," says former *Creem* senior editor Jaan Uhelszki. "The commonality among them is that they were all accessible. That could actually be *you* up there." With the exception of Steven Tyler, whose monkey jaw and twig-hipped Jagger mien make him resemble nothing less than a creature conceived in a test tube labeled ROCK STAR, there's something very normal about them that somehow humanizes their existence. "Robin Zander and Ace Frehley didn't reside in Valhalla like Jimmy Page," Uhelszki says. "Our Letters to the Editor showed that readers liked the people they thought they could be like. Music at the time helped kids forge their identities. These were all bands for nerdy middle-of-the-road types who weren't popular. Every single one of those bands was really empowering."

The '70s was a time of pop-culture deviance, when lurid or esoteric phenomena—UFOs and Death Stars, man-eating sharks and Pet Rocks, exorcisms and Kool-Aid cults—captured the mainstream imagination in a significant way. But even to kids who weren't into comic books, horror, or science fiction, KISS struck an uncommon chord. Sure, the fantastical visual trappings gave rise to countless bands characterized by Freddy Krueger vocals and illegible logos. But aside from the occasional self-actualizing rallying cry, KISS's songs tended to wallow in rock-and-roll debauchery, their objectification and subjugation of hot women no doubt tapping into the simultaneous lust and distrust felt by confused pubescent boys—all rather grubby stuff for albums that came packaged with posters, stickers, temporary tattoos, and cardboard guns.

Still, says Redd Kross's Steven McDonald, "All the fantasies they encouraged totally worked on me early on. KISS inspired kids to put the makeup on for the school talent show. If you put that costume on, you would feel different, like you had some kind of superpower."

Led Zeppelin, on the other hand, didn't give a fuck about empowerment. "They got channeled information from Aleister Crowley," says Uhelszki. "There was never a sense that they were like you, and I'm not even sure they were people you aspired to be. But you actually thought you could be a member of KISS or Starz. Ace Frehley used to always say, 'We are our fans.' And that was true for all of them."

Scott Ian of Anthrax, born on the last day of 1963, never saw the bands as all that similar sonically. The attraction, for him, was generational. They were *his* groups, not some older sibling's Pink Floyd or the Allman Brothers. "I liked that stuff," he says, "but I didn't connect with it when I was twelve."

The first time Dale Crover encountered KISS, being introduced by *H.R. Pufnstuf's* Witchiepoo before vigorously miming to "Detroit Rock City" on *The Paul Lynde Halloween Special* in 1976, he was nine. "That was my Beatles on *Ed Sullivan* moment,'" he says. "It was just like, *What the fuck is this?* I didn't know if I liked it, but I was totally intrigued. The first record I had was *Love Gun*, probably because it was cheaper than *Alive!* or *Alive II*. And for a good two-year period, I was into nothing but KISS. I didn't care about any other band. My room was adorned with every KISS poster I could buy." In the sixth grade, when he bought a drum kit, he emulated Peter Criss because it was easy to play along to "Rock and Roll All Nite." "KISS," he says, "was my gateway to everything else." Once he joined grunge pioneers the Melvins in 1984, Crover was surprised to find that bandmates Buzz Osborne and Matt Lukin liked KISS and still listened to their old records. "I had stopped," he says, "but I remembered these guys did write really good songs, like 'Goin' Blind,' which we covered."

Steven McDonald, who himself became a Melvin in 2015, sees as the link between KISS, Cheap Trick, Aerosmith, and Starz the aftershocks of a cultural earthquake that his own generation had missed. All four were indebted to the Beatles, it became obvious, while Aerosmith also clearly embraced the Rolling Stones. "They continued the great tradition of British Invasion rock that came to America in the '60s, before my time," he says. "They modernized it and took it into the arenas. They were taking it to the next level: 'What can be done with the technology at hand? What can we do with a loud show?'"

That detachment from an earlier era had a similarly profound effect on Butch Walker. "When I was really young, all I knew was the trifecta of KISS, Aerosmith, and Cheap Trick," he says. "I didn't know the Beatles. I was born in '69, and my first musical memories were Elvis Presley, my mom's records, and then the Monkees. I didn't even know the Monkees were a spoof of the Beatles." Unlike Scott Ian, Walker noticed a similar musical thread shared by the three groups: "It was not quite dark or Sabbathy, and not pop rock or power pop, like the Raspberries. It had teeth, but it was blues-inspired, and there was a tightness in the production, which I suppose spoke to me as an aspiring producer. Those were the things that mattered to me: the sonics of the records, the sound of the guitars and drums. And then the pop structures of the songs, which for all of these bands obviously go back to the Beatles."

Radio personality and former record executive Eddie Trunk says that word of mouth often pointed him toward many of the bands he eventually fell in love with, but other factors were just as important. "I would get all the magazines—*Circus* and *Creem*—and see the ads, and if the band or the logo looked cool, I'd have to check them out," he says, adding that "the whole packaging of a record, or maybe an appearance on *Don Kirshner's Rock Concert* or *Midnight Special*" also mattered. But at the core, it was always about big, guitar-driven music and ineffable vocals. "KISS obviously had that and all the theatrics, as did Aerosmith, Cheap Trick, and Starz. The common thread between those four bands is that I've got to like the singing. They don't have to be the most incredible vocals in the world, but I've got to like the singing."

Alex Kane, who replaced Pete Comita in Enuff Z'Nuff, played with Anti-Product and Life, Sex & Death, and joined Starz for reunion shows in 2013, was a kid in Chicago when he discovered them. "In those days, you had no access to bands," he says. "They were these mythological beings that did not roam the same plains as we did." So when he saw Starz on a bill with Angel and the Runaways in 1977, it was as though Bigfoot, the Yeti, and the chupacabra had all gathered to cavort in the Aragon Ballroom.

Amid the low hum of the PA, glowing amps, and plumes of artificial fog, the band appeared. Michael Lee Smith, who until then had just been someone Kane saw on TV, began pacing across the front of the stage. "All of a sudden, the energy in the room starts to rev up," Kane says. "It becomes this palpable thing. And while the lights are still off, he stops in the center of the stage—the natural heir to the Steven Tyler/Jim Morrison crown—and he says something like, 'If you love rock and roll, *get the fuck up!*' It wasn't a question. It was 'This is what we're all going to do now.' And then they rip into the opening chords to 'Fallen Angel.' The stage lights come on, and there's the huge elaborate band logo suspended in the air.

"I had seen KISS already," Kane continues. "Somehow this was more for me. Starz were directly mine because I found them, the way I found Cheap Trick. Aerosmith and KISS were already existent when I came to know them. Starz and Cheap Trick were the first bands I got to discover in their nascent stages."

For Ginger Wildheart, frontman of the acclaimed British hard rockers the Wildhearts, whose band is essentially a boisterous amalgam of the best parts of all four groups, KISS motivated him to become a musician. "I wanted to play in a band since 1973, when I first saw the Sweet on TV," he says. "KISS galvanized that desire and made me pick up the guitar and wrestle with it until something decent came out." For him, their appeal lay in the idea that the music was simple enough for kids to digest and bombastic enough to inspire them. "I didn't need Rush to tell me that it would take ten years of practice to get onstage," he adds. "I wanted KISS to tell me that I could get up there with very rudimentary skills and enjoy being in a band."

Seeing Cheap Trick open for Mötley Crüe in 1986 taught him something different but no less valuable. "It was the first time I'd seen a support band completely blow the headliner off the stage, and that set wheels in motion," he says. "I didn't just want to be in a band anymore. I wanted to be in a band that could challenge the bigger bands. That was a crucial moment for me. I could have ended up playing cover versions if I hadn't seen Cheap Trick annihilate their competition with killer songs." Having been a fan since *Dream Police*, he even wrote to the band in 1982, after getting a copy of *One on One*, volunteering to play bass should they ever need another fill-in. "Rick wrote back with a postcard that said something like, 'Pack your bags, you're in for an audition.' The next day another postcard arrived, saying, 'Only kidding.'"

*Live! Bootleg*, the first Aerosmith album Ginger heard, held another kind of appeal, showing him that playing sloppy could be far more exciting than playing safe. "It made rock music seem as dangerous as punk," he says. "They looked like trouble and they sounded like it too." What attracted him to Starz were the songs, particularly the lyrics. "Dirty, funny, and clever, like Steven Tyler or Bon Scott," says Ginger, whose own song "29 x the Pain" name-checks Starz along with KISS, Cheap Trick, and a bunch of other outstanding bands. "Michael Lee Smith doesn't get anywhere near the credit he should as one of the greatest rock lyricists of all time." Taken together, he says, the four bands' allure is, simply, more geographical than anything else: "They're a snapshot of America when it was the sexiest, coolest, most vital country in the world."

CHAPTER 20

# WAITIN' ON YOU

RICHIE RANNO IS CERTAIN that Starz made a real impact. He knows this because of all the musicians who've gone on about how much his band inspired them: Jon Bon Jovi, Lars Ulrich, Sebastian Bach, Nikki Sixx, the guys in Warrant, so many others. Why, then, have Starz been forgotten or, for that matter, never even been known? He lays some of the blame at the feet of one man who, for better or worse, set the stage for what is now considered classic rock, those songs and artists that are still played on the radio some forty or fifty years after peaking, a man named Lee Abrams.

"There are groups," Ranno says, "that didn't have hits as big as ours and didn't have an impact nearly as big as ours, like Motörhead, that are considered classic rock but weren't really classic." He believes radio never latched on to Starz because Abrams, one of the most significant figures in the business, didn't like them. "That's okay. You don't like us, you still should play us. But he didn't," Ranno says. "So now, classic rock just feeds on itself, and that's what keeps groups popular. That's what's kept Foreigner and Journey popular. Don't get me wrong: They're ten times bigger than we ever were. I'm not delusional. But we should still have had our place. He wrote us out of rock history, that guy."

While that last part is certainly up for debate, there's no denying that guy had some pretty radical ideas. In the late '60s, as teenagers began to reject mainstream Top 40 radio and show an interest in bands like the Yardbirds, the Rolling Stones, and Cream, not only were there hardly any periodicals reporting on these acts, but also folks had few places to tune in to hear this music exclusively without being subjected to the whims of snobbish disc jockeys. Abrams, then based in Chicago, discovered a way to pinpoint what listeners wanted and to serve them—subverting the idea of freeform radio—while making stations very rich, by employing research tools that were primitive at first but evolved into the industry's gold standard. Sure, his inflexible playlists became the soundtrack to many a boomer and post-boomer's life. But other listeners, like Ranno, have rejected his innovations, which they say led to a homogenization of FM rock in the '80s, encouraging stations to play only that which tested well and leaving worthy artists like KISS, Cheap Trick, and other hard rockers of a certain vintage confined to the margins, with only a song (or two) that audiences still remember. "Unfortunately for Cheap Trick," says Eddie Trunk, "although real fans know they've had a good amount of hits, in the end, it really comes down to 'I Want You to Want Me' and 'Surrender.' Those are the big songs that get played on classic rock radio all the time. They don't have five or six like that. They have two."

Early into his career as a radio consultant, Abrams walked through parking lots to see what stations car radios were tuned to, polled kids as they left concerts, and conducted what he calls "hitchhiking studies"—he'd wake up early, stick out his thumb on the side of the road, and report on the listening habits of the folks who'd pick him up. He noticed that often when a disc jockey would talk through the beginning of a record, his frustrated drivers would complain, "God, get that guy to shut up! I want to hear the song." Traditional radio people thought "hitting the post," shutting up only when the vocal started, was a cool move. "It was actually a huge distraction," Abrams says.

Abrams's first great success came in 1971 when, a year after graduating high school, he created a format aimed at people who loved hearing, say, Jimi Hendrix or Jethro Tull come on, but got turned off when the next song was by Bread or the Carpenters. With the focus now on these new, flashier artists, the age of album-oriented rock was born. "The big idea behind it," Abrams says, "was to create something very familiar, but to change the familiarity factor from song title to artist's name." Traditionally, pop stations relied on well-known singles to breed a repeat audience. Abrams wanted to concentrate on album cuts. "We called it the 'oh wow' factor," he says. "It'd be like, *Well, that's Santana, but oh wow, that's not 'Black Magic Woman' again. It'd be another track.* We had the advantage of going very deep into artists but maintaining a level of familiarity." The first station to adopt the format, WQDR-FM in Raleigh, North Carolina, a college town, dramatically increased its share—the percentage of listeners tuned into a station at a given time—from 1 to 11 percent in one three-month ratings period.

The revolution could not have been timed more perfectly. Back then, some radio stations owned both AM and FM channels: AM, which was cheaper and could be carried over long distances, was where the money was; higher-fidelity FM transmission, better for broadcasting music but impacted by physical obstructions, was almost an afterthought. "All these big AM stations had these FMs, which literally were stuck in closets, playing dentist-office music," Abrams says. "I'd go in and say, 'Look, you have this FM station with a big signal, you're making no money, and for a pretty reasonable price'—because we're not talking about hiring new huge talent and having big news departments—'you could turn that FM into a station that focuses on this new generation of rock that's not going away.'"

All that was required was a program director who could spend a few days in Atlanta, where he and his partner, Kent Burkhart, set up shop, and learn the theory. Abrams would accompany them back to the station and implement the new format, hiring and training staffers. He'd follow up with the program director every week and fill them in on what was happening nationally. Abrams remembers being skeptical when one of his programmers in Seattle told him that a local band called Heart had the makings of a very big act. "I said, 'Well, go ahead and play them,'" he recalls. "The next week it was No. 1 in phone requests." Convinced, he soon became a loud evangelist for the group.

It was a devastatingly effective formula. AOR became the No. 1 format in its demographic target, ages eighteen to twenty-four, almost instantaneously, just about everywhere it was implemented. Rather than spend tens of thousands of dollars on TV ads, Abrams and his followers made the most of cosponsoring radio concerts and being on the street. AOR turned occasional listeners into ardent fans who in turn bought more albums, more concert tickets, more merch, and more of whatever it was the stations were advertising. To make the format sound palatable to the corporate radio overlords, Abrams named it "Superstars."

"They said, 'What does *that* mean?'" Abrams recalls.

"These are the guys selling out twenty thousand seats a night," he'd respond.

"Oh, okay. There must be an audience for it, then."

One of Abrams's premier concepts was the use of callback cards to determine which album tracks to spotlight. He'd stock participating stores with cards that customers would fill out with their name, age, phone number, and the title of the record purchased. A week later, Abrams's team would call around 5,000 respondents and have them evaluate the record. "Because you lived with it," he says. "You'd spend four ninety-eight for an album and you'd play it over and over again. That's how we often found out what the best one, two, three, four, five cuts were. That's how we found 'Free Bird,' which none of us really got. But we called back these people who bought the Lynyrd Skynyrd record and they said, 'Oh my God, it's the anthem of life.' It wasn't one person. It was one after another. So we knew to play that.

"'Stairway to Heaven' was the same thing," he continues. "Because it was Led Zeppelin, we'd play just about everything. But you'd know that after reading these callback cards, talking to the people, that 'Stairway to Heaven' was just a timeless anthem."

The label promo people were for the most part thrilled at this new development—if they could secure a spot. "We were very selective," Abrams says. "But once we did add a record, we played it a lot. One of the problems with underground or freeform radio was, they'd add a hundred records a week and you'd hear it or you wouldn't hear it. It would come up once or twice a week, where a record that got added to one of our client's stations got played several times a day—not the same cut, but the artist and the album."

Though he was able to expand the format to more than one hundred stations by the mid-'80s, Abrams did encounter resistance from some established rock outlets. "They thought they owned it all, but their ratings were like nothing," he says. "So that's why their management/ownership would call us. And they'd be pissed off that there was some outside guy coming in to tell them what to do. The best stations were the ones where we had a clean slate. They were going from Mantovani to rock. But of the existing album rock stations we would go into, half to sixty percent were fine. It was like, 'The more ratings we get, the more salary we'll make. Let's get in the game.'"

In Abrams's vision, AOR was the soundtrack of the city: "Let's get as many listeners as we can get, and everybody's happy." He was, however, often chided for being slow to present new music or shutting it out altogether. "But if you look back," he says, "the records we played generally, not exclusively, became hits, and part of that is because we played them a lot. Once we added a record, we committed to it."

Abrams admits that for the longest time he couldn't elevate Aerosmith. "The reason it took them so long was that very few people were playing them," he says. "We were, but at that time we weren't powerful enough to break a record nationally. I thought people in the industry might have looked at them as just another rock band: 'They'll be gone next year.' But they proved themselves. And once Steven Tyler showed himself to be the showman he is, all of a sudden girls became infatuated with them.

"A lot of bands back then took three records to break," he continues. "They'd get a cult base, then they'd get some exposure, and then that cult would turn into more of a mainstream thing. And if they kept coming out with good music, that mainstream thing made them superstars."

While consultancies like Abrams's branched out and ultimately would come to dominate the field, local radio still had a heavy hand in building acts like KISS. Century Broadcasting, which owned St. Louis's KSHE-FM and Detroit's WABX, was run by brothers Shelly and Howard Grafman, who also promoted concerts. "So," says Ray Tusken, Capitol's former national AOR promotion manager, "if you went into a market like that—and this is one of the ways Bob Seger broke—they could, just through the radio station, sell 40,000 tickets to a concert for an artist who brought 10,000 or maybe even 1,000 in L.A. It was a phenomenon that the local radio stations, working with the artists' management and the record companies, could break an artist."

Capitol, Starz's label, often collaborated with Abrams's network to test the viability at radio for its AOR artists. "Superstars hasn't limited our musical growth," Tusken told *Cash Box* in 1978. "It's only endorsed the material that has great mass-appeal potential." The article went on to name Starz as an example of a band that benefited from the Abrams testing, citing two stations—WGRQ in Buffalo, New York, and WLRS in Louisville, Kentucky—as particularly receptive to the group. Tusken also mentioned that the label would soon issue a live Starz promo album that would be released to Superstars Radio Network stations.

So while Ranno's complaint that his band were shut out of the broader airplay equation may be true, Abrams says it was research that did Starz in, not his personal taste. "When some of those bands like Starz and Angel came out," he says, "there was a real emphasis on twenty-five- to thirty-four-year-olds, assuming the audience was growing up, and there was a reticence to play anything too hard." In this limited view, Led Zeppelin "hard" was okay, but programmers feared new and unproven "hard." According to Abrams, some station owners believed that once listeners aged out, they would say, *Bring on the Neil Diamond, because I'm now twenty-five to thirty-four.* "You know, an ad agency definition," he says. "These bands did get their shots, but they didn't have that one killer song."

It's a belief seconded by Bruce Wendell, Capitol's former vice president of promotion. "We had so many things going on in those days," he says, "that unless you were a really big act, there was only so much you could do." As for Starz, he says, "They had good promotion. If it got played on the radio and we could sell it, we would have. I guess the radio people just didn't go for it."

## CHAPTER 21

# STANDING ON THE EDGE

MARK RADICE WAS TEN years old in 1968 when Decca Records released the musical prodigy's third major-label single, "Ten Thousand Year Old Blues," featuring a young man named Steven Tallarico. Radice's dad, Gene, a well-connected engineer who had worked with Jimi Hendrix and the Velvet Underground, had been recording Tallarico's band Chain Reaction at the time and hired the twenty-year-old to add drums and bass marimba to the track, on which Radice played acoustic guitar and sang. "Steven would be in the studio a lot just absorbing stuff," says Radice, "even when he wasn't booked there."

In 1972, Paramount Records released Radice's self-titled debut album, a collection of gorgeous balladry and robust sunshine pop that suggested a melodic ear and lyrical prowess of an artist much older than fourteen. Despite the novelty, the album went nowhere, and two years later Radice was playing keyboards and singing backup for Donovan on the "Mellow Yellow" troubadour's U.S. tour. He had just walked into the lobby of an L.A. hotel when he spotted a familiar face in an elevator as its doors began to close. "Radice!" yelled the occupant. The teen heard the ping of the conveyor opening on the second floor followed by footsteps racing down the spiral staircase. "Radice, what are you doing here?" asked the man, now going by the surname Tyler.

"I'm touring with Don," Radice responded. "What are you doing here?"

"I'm with my band, man. We're about to do a big tour and we're looking for keys."

In 1976, when the talks with Aerosmith got serious, Radice had already moved on to something completely different—touring with a twelve-piece funk band to promote his album *Ain't Nothin' but a Party*—and if he were going to break it up, he needed a good reason. Sure, Aerosmith were one of the biggest bands on earth, but just adding keyboards and vocals while staying hidden behind a humongous PA held little appeal. He agreed to join the Aerosmith Express tour on one condition: at some point he'd be able to write with Tyler. Radice ended up touring with the band throughout 1978, including playing in front of more than 300,000 people when Aerosmith headlined California Jam 2 on March 18.

Radice sang a lot at the shows. "Sometimes I sang the high harmony of the 'Walk This Way' hook if Steven didn't want to hit it that night," he recalls. "He always could—it was just about resting his voice." Every now and then, when the keyboardist was harmonizing, Joe Perry would step up to Tyler's mic and pretend it was he who was singing, and as a joke Radice would stop cold in the middle of a line. "It was pretty funny," he says. And it would never fail to piss Perry off.

Radice's tenure with the band, documented on Aerosmith's *Live! Bootleg*, ran through their *Draw the Line* plateau and right before their crash, at the height of their bad behavior. "For me, the whole thing was a beer-soaked, nose-in-the-bag blur," he says. And to his disappointment, the cowrites never materialized. "We tried one morning, but nothing ever came of it." All told, Radice looks back on his days and nights in Aerosmith as "a waste of my time and bad for my health."

Radice, who claims to have composed more than 5,000 songs, was signed to CBS Songs, the company's publishing arm, when he got word in 1984 that Epic was nudging Rick Nielsen to find an outside writer for the follow-up to *Next Position Please*. "Epic called us up and said, 'We don't think Rick can write a hit record anymore,'" Bun E. Carlos says. "They destroyed Rick's confidence. That was like a knife to the heart of Rick and the band."

"I was like, 'I don't think outside writers would help,'" Nielsen says. "That kicked the snot out of me."

Technically, the label had a point. Nielsen was writing songs, but they weren't becoming hits. "The band didn't necessarily believe that they couldn't write hits," says Ira Robbins. "They believed that, for a variety of reasons, they weren't *getting* hits." Robbins thinks this feeling of inadequacy is not uncommon among bands from the Midwest: "At every point there's this degree of humility, shyness, modesty, and insecurity that combines. Only when it's impacted by the outside—like when somebody from New York says, 'You guys suck!'—all of a sudden, it's a problem."

This wasn't the first time the label would suggest the band needed help, and as Ken Adamany says, "Mark was a good writer and I think he got along with the band. But there were a lot of other problems with that record." Chief among them, the unreliability of Jack Douglas, whom the band brought on to oversee the recording. They were eager to reteam with the guy who harnessed their raw power for the debut album and helped piece together their live breakthrough. But John Lennon's murder had sent the producer spiraling into heroin addiction, and he had been engaged in a legal battle with Yoko Ono over unpaid royalties from his work on her and Lennon's *Double Fantasy*. He literally wasn't all there.

Radice admits to entering this scenario with some trepidation: "Rick didn't like it one bit." He had met Nielsen on tour years before, "so he most likely looked at me as the path of least resistance," he supposes. "Truth is, there's something to be said about writing while still hungry and eager to make an impression, as opposed to being a major band that has already proven themselves." After arriving in Rockford for his two-month stint, Radice initially asked each member what they wanted the band to sound like now. Carlos gave him a cassette of drum patterns. Nielsen would show up at Radice's place on Shaw Street and say, in reference to a writing session the night before, "That settles it. I'm never gonna drink or take drugs again," Radice recalls. Then Radice would offer a beer, Nielsen would accept, and they'd start all over again.

Radice spent some time in Robin Zander's basement with two TEAC four-track cassette recorders that he'd start simultaneously so the band could hear eight tracks when he played back his work. He composed nearly two dozen bits, recording drums, bass, and two guitars on one machine while leaving room for vocals on the remaining four tracks. Some were ideas for hooks. Some were what he considered cool riffs that sounded like Cheap Trick. Others he left open to Zander's interpretation, including one that became the album's only single, "Tonight It's You," a soaring midtempo number with a goose-bump-raising chorus. Listening to the then-untitled track, Zander started singing, "Time's not sleeping and time can't lose / You can't win 'cause time can't lose"—which prompted Radice to exclaim, "That doesn't make any sense and you just rhymed 'lose' with 'lose.' It's perfect!"

Still, Carlos was not exactly thrilled by the new setup. "We would take home Mark's cassettes and play them and go, 'Oh, they're all songs. And they're played nice. But that's not our kind of stuff,'" he says. "And we were just trapped in that world for a while.

"Jack had personal issues and didn't finish the mix," Carlos continues, marveling that one day the recording was disrupted when Douglas received in the studio a multimillion-dollar check, his settlement from the dispute with Ono.

When the band left in the spring to do a USO tour of Europe with members of Kansas and Santana, among others, Adamany brought in Tony Platt—who had worked with AC/DC on *Back in Black* and with Patto, a forgotten early-'70s band Carlos and Nielsen admired—to put together a mix. "We got like twenty mixes on cassette in the mail one day," Carlos says. "And they all sounded like a tin can. We had demo-itis on that album. We couldn't beat the demos."

In an MTV interview for the album's release, Zander told veejay Nina Blackwood that it took about four weeks to record the basic tracks. "The mix took a little longer than that," he said with a laugh. "It was a four-month mix," Nielsen chimed in, before adding sarcastically, "the studios, I guess, needed the work." When asked why they used Tony Platt, Nielsen deadpanned, "He's an English guy. He was out of work. Felt sorry for him."

For all its dated production tricks—clackety electronic drums, ostentatious keyboard blasts, and heavy, heavy echo—*Standing on the Edge* remains one of the band's strongest '80s collections, notable for the consummate single-mindedness of the lyrics, which tackle such road-worn rock clichés as hot chicks ("Cover Girl," "Wild Wild Women," "She's Got Motion"), one-night stands ("Tonight It's You"), little sisters ("Little Sister"), and on the title track, a blow job by "Sweet" Connie Hamzy, the legendary Little Rock, Arkansas, groupie previously immortalized in Grand Funk Railroad's "We're an American Band." "She had quite the reputation," Nielsen says. "It's like, you're looking at a girlie magazine and you're thinking, 'I don't know anybody who wants to take their clothes off in this. But thank God they do.'"

Zander has called *Standing on the Edge* one of his favorites of their albums. "I love about half of it," Carlos hedges, believing the other half just panders. In the case of "Wild Wild Women," the drummer asked Nielsen to write a song in the vein of AC/DC's "Highway to Hell" or Free's "All Right Now"—three chords and a chorus every kid can sing. When Carlos heard the finished version, he remembers thinking, "I'll never do *that* again—tell Rick what he should do. I don't know what the fuck I'm talking about when it comes to songwriting."

Radice, who went on to compose dozens of songs for the Muppets and one hundred sixty for *Sesame Street*, also had a KISS connection. In the mid-'80s, he was sent out by CBS Songs to spend a day writing with Gene Simmons. "He played me a bunch of tracks, no vocals—and I was thinking to myself, *So what? It's a bunch of power chords with no words*," says Radice, who took the tapes home, then met Simmons in a studio a few days later. "I gave him a track of his called 'Shake It' that I sang my words on. He said, 'That's excellent,' left, and I never heard from him again."

Not long before the recording of *Standing on the Edge* began, Gene Simmons contacted Ken Adamany, confirming his receipt of a tape of demos, including a song called "X-Rated," sent to him by Rick Nielsen, apparently for a critical evaluation. Simmons thought the material was too poppy and needed to be harder, a la Def Leppard. Cheap Trick never did officially release "X-Rated," whose herky-jerky verse riff manages to evoke both "My Sharona" and "Whip It." It ended up becoming an outtake from the *Standing on the Edge* sessions. But the band seemed to heed Simmons's advice on "Rock All Night," a gleefully hamfist-punching shout-along tailor-made for seventh-inning stretches at minor-league stadia nationwide, which appears on the album: it's positively Leppardian.

To support the LP, Cheap Trick opened for the likes of REO Speedwagon and Night Ranger in arenas and amphitheaters as well as headlining smaller venues on their own. When Adamany stablemates the Elvis Brothers did some dates with them, drummer Brad Elvis noticed the band's dissatisfaction with their current situation. "They were bummed," he says, "but they didn't really let it on." One gig, at the Kellogg Center in Battle Creek, Michigan, on December 30, 1985, was a particular lowlight. It was freezing, snow everywhere, and few tickets had been sold. "They were debating whether to cancel," Elvis says. "Then they decided, 'Nah, let's just play for the people who did buy tickets.' I swear, in this big hall there were two hundred people standing in front of the stage loosely when we opened. By the time Cheap Trick went on, around three hundred people were there."

At that show Elvis witnessed Nielsen doing something surprisingly odd and arguably passive-aggressive, performing 'Rudolph the Red-Nosed Reindeer' in the style of the Sex Pistols: "He was singing, 'Fuck this and fuck that, and fuck you, Rudolph!'" The next night, when Cheap Trick and the Elvis Brothers played New Year's Eve at Chicago's Vic Theatre, they drew a significantly larger crowd.

· · · ·

TOD HOWARTH REPLACED PHIL Cristian as Cheap Trick's touring key-boardist and backing vocalist in 1985. After leaving 707, Howarth toured with Ted Nugent, then connected with Cheap Trick through Jon Brant, Pete Comita, and Jai Winding, producer of *The Second Album* (707's inven-tively titled second album), who had played keyboards on *Heaven Tonight* and *Dream Police* (and, as it happens, Peter Criss's third solo effort, 1982's *Let Me Rock You*). While out with Cheap Trick, Howarth befriended John Regan, the bassist in John Waite's band, when the groups shared a string of dates in the fall of 1985. After letting Regan know that he was also a songwriter, lead singer, and guitarist, Howarth piqued the bassist's interest. Regan had been working on a secretive project that was ideal for How-arth, but couldn't say any more. A few months later, Regan invited him to audition for this new band, called Frehley's Comet, featuring the former KISS guitarist. His first tryout went okay, Howarth recalls, though Frehley was not overly excited by his lead guitar work. He was, however, sold on Howarth's singing and songwriting abilities. "The second time I played with them locked it up," Howarth says, "and I joined them right in the studio in January of 1987."

When they first got together, Howarth saw how much Frehley seemed committed to the group. "One would be, after spending virtually a musician's lifetime in a huge band and then getting out to play on his own," he says. "He was very energized and he had high hopes, because all the elements were behind him to make it happen. He did all the right moves." Howarth appreci-ated that Frehley, never the most confident singer, gave him plenty of room to write and perform, including lead vocals on three songs on their debut album. One of them, "Calling to You," a credited rewrite of 707's "Mega Force" (orig-inally written as the theme to a 1982 sci-fi movie, a gig that Rick Nielsen had rejected), incidentally contains echoes of Cheap Trick's "Reach Out" from the *Heavy Metal* soundtrack.

On the second Frehley's Comet album, Howarth landed even more songs, or cowrites, and lead vocal spots, this time five. One of them, "It's Over Now," he originally wrote for Cheap Trick while staying in an apartment over Rick Nielsen's parents' music store in Rockford. His instincts weren't too far off, as the song—a soaring midtempo number with a superb vocal—resembles some of the more endearingly schlocky/lovely moments Cheap Trick would later feature on their albums *Lap of Luxury* and *Busted*. "They said, 'You should write some songs and you can tell us what to do,'" Howarth recalls, "so I did."

After demoing it, he passed it along to Carlos, who listened, shook his head, and said, "You need to edit it." "He was right," says Howarth, "because some of the parts were too long. So I chopped it. It was a little bit darker and more brooding than it is now. I think they didn't do it because it was a big keyboard tune and they're not a keyboard band."

Howarth hooked back up with Cheap Trick from 1990 to 1996, after having left Frehley's Comet in late 1988 when he saw the band dynamic beginning to change. "Unfortunately, everything didn't come quickly enough, like it had with KISS," he says. "And that's a slap in the face when you're used to snapping your fingers. It just didn't happen for Frehley's Comet, so that was probably a rude awakening."

．．．．

**IT'S HARD TO OVERSTATE** the extent to which MTV revitalized the music business and revolutionized pop culture, by bringing artists into living rooms 24/7 and, to put it bluntly, ingeniously packaging promotional material as original programming. No longer did an artist have to traipse through region after region to be heard. MTV had the power to break a song nationally, immediately. In the '70s, many bands made it clear that their goal was to become wealthy and famous, with all the drugs, chicks, chartered planes, and private Caribbean islands that dream entailed. No one would question these motivations, least of all fans. MTV made that attitude suspect, offering the chance for worldwide stardom and riches, provided that bands were willing to play the game. They could still have it all; they just couldn't say it. Some hard rockers sought to capitalize on the potentially broader audience by actively courting female fans to join what was formerly mostly a boys' club. They began to rethink and soften their approaches, as their appearance became key to selling their (often newly glossy) sound.

By 1983, this outlook would begin to create a whole new race of rockers—one that favored heavily made-up, androgynous pusses; sky-high hair; skintight jeans, spandex tights, or leather trousers (codpiece optional)— who performed acrobatic stage runs and twirls, all while relentlessly mugging for a whip-panning camera. Many in the cream of this garish crop—Bon Jovi, Cinderella, Dokken, Mötley Crüe, Poison, Ratt, Skid Row, Slaughter, Warrant, White Lion, and Winger—acknowledged their heavy debt to the likes of KISS, Cheap Trick, Aerosmith, and Starz. And it didn't go unnoticed.

KISS, for one, cannily seized the opportunity to expose themselves, quite literally, to the channel's young viewership. On September 18, 1983, ten years after they first applied their makeup, KISS revealed their true faces for the first time, which made the band, now featuring Vinnie Vincent on lead guitar, an MTV fixture. The video for "Lick It Up," which they timed to the unmasking, found them lip-syncing in animal prints while ravaging a postapocalyptic wasteland lousy with torn-shirted babes sporting leotard wedgies. In other words, the band unabashedly adopted all the tacky trappings of the subgenre they had helped spark. "From what I understood," says Bruce Kulick, who would join KISS the following year, "Gene was always the most reluctant, but Paul was very adamant that they needed to do that. And I think Paul was right. Music and fashion, which seem to run somewhat parallel at times, needed the band to be very glammy, but not the KISS version of glam. This was more flamboyant and colorful, and Gene definitely was not in his Demon element."

Many invested observers cringed at what they saw as a desperate band waving a tattered white flag, capitulating to forces both internal and external that KISS should have had the strength to resist. These were the most recognizable pop specters on the planet, nearing their midthirties, whose face paint rendered them ageless. And now that their competitors are ten years younger, they decide to wash their faces? To look like everybody else? It was only a matter of time before Day-Glo kaftans, pink elbow-high gloves, and puffy high-tops came into the retina-singeing picture. "It was bizarre how they dressed when they took the makeup off," says Tracii Guns, "like a Sunset Strip band that no one's ever going to see. They had all the clichés, which was really strange."

"The fans were bummed out beyond belief," says Chip Z'Nuff. "Because once you see this beautiful model—she's posing in front of you, you admire her strut—and then you see her when she wakes up in the morning and it's a different person, you don't look the same way at her. KISS weren't easy enough on the eyes to make it that way."

As a kid, Taime Downe, of sleaze-rock stalwarts Faster Pussycat, graduated from modifying his KISS sleeping bag into a comforter in elementary school to shoplifting KISS posters in junior high. "I credit KISS for fucking my shit up, for turning me into a degenerate rock and roller," he says. "After I saw a KISS show, I didn't want to do anything else." But by the time his band opened for KISS, in 1991 and 1992, he felt the need to adjust his appreciation. "I was a fan of the makeup, not of the white LA Gear sneakers," he says. "I'd just close my eyes, listen to 'God of Thunder,' and go back to my dazed and confused days."

Others appreciated seeing for the first time the band stripped of artifice and committing to the merits of the music. "I was fine with it," says radio personality Eddie Trunk. "I don't think people realize how rock bottom KISS were in their career at that time. They definitely needed to do something to shake things up." Even so, Trunk resigned himself to the fact that a denuded KISS would never reach the band's previous commercial heights. "There was an ad in *Billboard* in '83 celebrating the fact that *Lick It Up* became a gold record, while a few years before, anything they put out would have gone platinum."

Desmond Child, who cowrote "I Was Made for Lovin' You" and some of KISS's biggest unmasked-era hits, understood their need to go naked, as it were. "People always made fun of them and didn't take them seriously," he says. "Also, when they were out in public, they would always have to hide their faces. It was a desire to show that they were more than just the image they had created."

## CHAPTER 22

# WALK THIS WAY

LIKE MANY BANDS THAT saw their creativity ebb and fortunes wane in the mid-'80s, KISS, Cheap Trick, and Aerosmith, sometimes willingly, sometimes kicking-and-screamingly, began fielding requests both to entertain songs submitted by proven hitmakers and to join forces with said proven hitmakers. KISS's team-up with Desmond Child not only helped resuscitate them during their makeup-free days, but was also directly responsible for the artistic and commercial rebirth of Aerosmith, the band's biggest competitor from back in the day.

Child recalls that years after KISS recorded "I Was Made for Lovin' You," during one of the band's promotional blitzes, Simmons told an interviewer that KISS didn't need cowriters, and that they were putting guards at the studio door to keep Child out. "He said it not just the one time. He said it in, like, a hundred interviews," says Child, who phoned Paul Stanley, furious.

"Why don't you attack your enemies?" he said. "Not the people that made you money and who are your friends."

"Oh no, it wasn't me, it was Gene," Stanley responded. "I can't control Gene."

"You know what?" Child said. "You can tell Gene Simmons to go fuck himself."

Later that day, Child returned home to find a pithy message on his answering machine from a man seemingly never at a loss for words: "It's Gene. Sorry."

Child and Stanley went on to write many more songs together. When working with KISS, Child quickly learned that the band had rules about how they wanted to be portrayed. First, KISS couldn't ever be seen as victims. "You always have to be the winner," Child says. "Also, the music inherently is very upbeat and fun and a little naughty. Sometimes we wrote serious songs, like 'Who Wants to Be Lonely.' But for the most part, we were writing fun songs because the band understood what it meant to perform for a stadium full of people who are going to sing along. They have to be able to sing to easy, monolithic things."

Child never worked with Simmons—he was always Stanley's guy—and he brought to the sessions a meticulous technique he learned from apprenticing with Bob Crewe, cowriter of many of the Four Seasons' hits. Child would go through every word, every syllable, and try to dig deeper and deeper and scratch away at what they had written to look for even more alliteration, more inner rhyming, more meaning. "Sometimes we'd come up with a brilliant line," he says. "But now the line before it wasn't as good. We would have to go back and make it worthy. I can drill down, laser-focus on one little syllable, sometimes to the frustration of the people I work with."

Bon Jovi were opening for KISS in Europe in October and November 1984 when Doc McGhee, the New Jersey band's manager, asked Stanley if he would be interested in writing with them. Stanley instead suggested that they give Child a call. "That was the turning point to superstardom for them." Stanley says. "It just seemed like a perfect fit."

Bon Jovi already had some of KISS's DNA in their music—the chorus riff from "In and Out of Love," from their second album, sounds maybe once removed from Stanley and Child's "Heaven's on Fire"—so bringing the songwriter in made a lot of sense. The resulting collaboration, Bon Jovi's third album, *Slippery When Wet*, featured four Child cowrites. Child had been working with Stanley when he brought the KISS frontman rough mixes of the young band's "You Give Love a Bad Name" and "Livin' on a Prayer." "We went into his car and he took me around in this kind of Batmobile," Child says. "It was black and it had all these corners and it was low. Who has a car like this in Manhattan? I played him the songs and he was like, 'Hmm. It's good but I don't think these are hits.'" Both songs ended up at No. 1 on *Billboard*'s Hot 100 in 1986, helping *Slippery When Wet* to sell more than twelve million copies in the U.S. alone. The following summer Bon Jovi were booked to headline the U.K.'s Monsters of Rock festival at Donington Park, an event that would draw 80,000 people. When KISS got an offer to open for the band they had taken out just three years before, they passed.

Simmons and Stanley did, however, attend the concert, where Scott Ian played with his band Anthrax. Ian, who sports a massive tattoo of Simmons's face and tongue on his right leg, saw KISS twice ten years earlier, at age thirteen, including once at Madison Square Garden. "It was everything I hoped and dreamed it would be," he says. "That was the beginning of the path I was going to take with my life, which was to be in a band.

"That period from '75 to '78 still means as much to me as it did then," he adds. "In 1996, when they put the makeup back on for the reunion, I went ten times and I cried every night."

Ian and Metallica's Kirk Hammett were hanging out at Donington after their bands performed and heard that Simmons and Stanley were watching Bon Jovi from a monitor in a tent backstage. "There they are, standing larger than life," Ian says. "We were drunk and didn't know what to do. We finally got the balls to walk over. I started talking: 'Excuse me, we don't mean to bother you, but we just wanted to say hi.' Before I could even finish the sentence, Simmons points at me and says, 'You are Scott Ian from Anthrax and you are Kirk Hammett from Metallica, and you both played terrific today. Congratulations!' I literally peed my pants. My name came out of Gene Simmons's mouth! In what fucking alternate universe can that be possibly happening?"

KISS returned the following year, but not as the headliner, agreeing to support Iron Maiden at Donington and on a brief European festival tour. During their career, KISS opened for, then headlined over, such bands as Jo Jo Gunne, Blue Öyster Cult, Nazareth, REO Speedwagon, and Uriah Heep. Iron Maiden would become the first support band to leapfrog over KISS.

• • • •

IN EARLY 1985, AEROSMITH flew to Berkeley, California, to begin work on *Done with Mirrors*, the band's first album in their new deal with Geffen Records. There, at the suggestion of John David Kalodner, the A&R executive who signed them, they teamed up with Ted Templeman, who produced the first six albums by Van Halen. (Gene Simmons had produced an early demo for Van Halen; his manager, Bill Aucoin, didn't see or hear stars and turned them down.)

Berkeley was chosen to keep the band away from easily accessible big-city vices, an admirable, if naïve, endeavor. Templeman's technique, recording whatever the band was playing in the studio, not necessarily calling for takes, initially freed the band up to get loose and into a groove. "But it turned into all drinking and drugging, which was allowed to get in the way," Joey Kramer has said. "After the studio, it was back to our rooms in the hotel, doing coke and isolated from each other, like the old days and old ways."

"Kalodner would walk into the studio, listen to some of the music and say, 'That's a piece of shit,'" says then manager Tim Collins. "You can only say that to Steven Tyler once."

If any one person is to blame for the record's artistic failure, Templeman says it is he. For one thing, the producer was distracted by his own personal problems, which required him to fly back and forth from the studio to his home in Southern California. "Consequently, the band suffered," he says, "because they had to wait for me." His deep admiration for the musicians led him to feel intimidated by them. Tyler was writing great lyrics and Perry was coming up with incredible riffs, but Templeman says he couldn't get the guitarist comfortable enough to stretch out and blamed the unfamiliar studio for his inability to nail the sound he wanted for Kramer's drums. "Anything that's wrong with that record is my fault," he says. "It's a matter of a great band with a producer that didn't do a good enough job."

Kramer later lamented that the record sounded incomplete, "without the finishing touches, the nuances, the personalities. Because we weren't all there." Upon the album's release at the end of 1985, neither were their fans. *Done with Mirrors* didn't do much commercially, even with the exquisitely brutal "My Fist Your Face" and the first single, a blazing redo of the Joe Perry Project's "Let the Music Do the Talking."

Despite his admittedly lackluster job, Templeman says the band asked him to produce their next album, an offer he had to refuse since he promised to reteam with David Lee Roth on the follow-up to the Van Halen singer's solo smash, *Eat 'Em and Smile*. "Then Dave calls me over to his crummy little fucking dump office," Templeman recalls. "He says, 'Ted, I think I need another producer.' I said, 'I blew off an Aerosmith record I wanted to do, and the album I just did with you is double platinum, and you're going to fire me? Well, fuck you!'

"Comparing what he's done on his own in the studio to what he did with me, it's like Gomer Pyle firing Douglas MacArthur," Templeman adds. "I'm still pissed off at him for that, because I missed my shot to redeem myself with Aerosmith. I knew where I wanted to go with them. You really don't know a band till you've done one record with them."

Kalodner, who had had enormous success with Foreigner and Asia, felt he handed the band the keys on *Done with Mirrors*, and they went ahead and wrecked it. The tour that followed took them back into arenas, but the clip for the single—a graceless combination of performance footage and a video bootlegger storyline—made no headway on MTV, which at that point was beginning to feature the big-haired likes of Mötley Crüe and Ratt, bands that owed their very existences to Aerosmith.

Collins, Kalodner, Tyler, and Perry were all initially leery when they got a call from hip-hop producer Rick Rubin in early 1986 asking the singer and guitarist to perform on a cover of "Walk This Way" with Run-DMC. The Queens-based rap trio had grown up with that song's indelible stuttering kick, snare, and hi-hat pattern, which had been a favorite of early turntablists. And Rubin wanted to expand their audience into the white suburbs. The subsequent music video, which depicted the two sides literally breaking down the wall (or, figuratively, the racial divide) between them, finally got Aerosmith into heavy rotation on MTV and back in the Top 10, for the first time since the original "Walk This Way" nearly ten years earlier. The collaboration, while hardly the first rap-rock hybrid, would prove monumental and consequential, not only bestowing superstardom onto both groups, but also sparking a genre that—for better, or mostly worse—would continue to bring the funk, and the clunk, to radios and arenas for another couple of decades.

Aerosmith, having returned to drink and drugs while on the Done with Mirrors tour, were in terrible shape by the time they got home. To capitalize on the Run-DMC success and to keep Geffen from dropping his band, Collins knew he had to take action. The manager, who had recently gotten sober himself, led a comprehensive effort to clean them up, which included staging an intervention with Tyler and helping Perry kick heroin. "That was my young ego," Collins says ruefully. "Nobody ever gets anyone else sober."

He also issued a warning to the road crew: *If you want a job, we'll send you to rehab. Otherwise, see you later.* "There are a lot of road guys who want to kill me," he says, "because they thought they had a job for life. When I signed Aerosmith, they had roadies who had roadies. There was so much fat in their business, it was ridiculous."

Joey Kramer has described Collins as a "control addict with an insatiable appetite for ruling the world and people around him, using fear, shame, and what felt like a twisted version of the principles of 12-step recovery as his tools for manipulation." The new manager, who had been enabling

Tyler, took on much of the heavy lifting to help save their lives, but it was Kalodner's mission to salvage their career. To do that he needed to take charge. Their songwriting well had run dry, a problem that became even more apparent during the initial stages of what would ultimately become their ninth studio album, *Permanent Vacation*. When Kalodner suggested to Collins that it was time to call in outsiders to help the band write, even the manager was initially skeptical, thinking the idea sounded "a little Elvisy." Kalodner, who around that time had also begun working with Bon Jovi, convinced Collins that they needed someone to help prime the pump. He suggested Desmond Child.

"I told [Kalodner] if he knew someone I could write lyrics with and have as much fun as when I'm writing songs with Joe Perry," Tyler said, "then *please* bring 'em in."

Collins remembers Tyler being reluctant at first. "Steven was afraid to let people in to cocreate," he says. "He only wanted Joe to do that. So Desmond came in and John said, 'Pretend you're Steven Tyler. Write your Steven Tyler song.'"

Child flew to Boston, met the band at their warehouse-cum–rehearsal space, and was immediately awed by what he saw. "To the right, there must have been literally a hundred guitars, all different, sparkling," he says. "Then there was a big performance stage with a microphone, scarves hanging off, giant Marshall amps." After Tyler came by to introduce himself, Child saw Perry working on a backward guitar loop, singing, "Down Sunset Strip, cruisin' for the ladies."

"It was like a bad Van Halen song that even *they* wouldn't put on a record," Child recalls. "I said, 'I think that's really bad.' That's, like, the first thing out of my mouth, and Joe looked at me sideways, with his arms crossed and head tilted back."

Tyler, forever the people pleaser, interjected, "Well, you know, when I first came up with that riff, I was singing, 'Dude looks like a lady.'"

"I just went crazy and said, 'That's a hit title!'" Child remembers. "Joe was like, 'We don't know what that means.' I said, 'I know what that means. Just go with me.' And we started writing the song about a guy who goes into a strip joint and there's a performer onstage who looks exactly like what he would want. Then he goes backstage and figures out that it's really a guy. But instead of running away, he says, 'Never judge a book by its cover, or who you gonna love by your lover.' The song was completely a transgender anthem."

At the time, the band members were all involved in meetings to address their sobriety, which Child says, manifested itself in a lot of twelve-step truth-telling: "It helped them to get it together and put all their frustrations—everything—into the music." "Dude (Looks Like a Lady)," written that first day, spurred a whole new wave of creativity, because they finally saw they could have fun again.

Perry didn't show up to the next day's songwriting session, so Child took the opportunity to get personal with the singer. "He overshared with strangers easily," says Child, who recalls Tyler going deep about Teresa Barrick, the woman he would soon marry. The two men were sitting together, their faces barely a foot apart, when Child had an epiphany: "I'm looking at those liver lips and I'm thinking, 'My God, it's so much like Mick Jagger.'" Child had always liked the Rolling Stones song "Angie," particularly the way Jagger's mouth resembled a sea creature when he enunciated the woman's name in the song's video. "I just want to see Steven say that kind of word and see if his lips do the same thing," Child says. When he proposed they write a song called "Angel" about Teresa, it took them all of forty-five minutes to finish it.

After hearing the results, Perry came around and asked to work with Child. "I was never in the room when they were writing," Collins says. "But I would debrief with [Child] and Joe Perry and I would know what was going on. It was getting them back on track."

"Tyler says I ruined his career by making him write 'Angel' with Desmond," Kalodner has said. Child suspects that's because it was such an extreme departure into pop. "It was not maintaining the hard-edge rocker ideal," he says.

One thing that struck Child about his days working with both Tyler and Perry was how much their homes were alike. "Joe and his wife have a certain taste—hippie-ish style, very natural, and very high-end," he says, adding that once when he arrived at Tyler's, "We pulled up at a house that looked identical. I go inside and—*oh my God!*—it's decorated exactly the same.

"He had a studio above the garage and we started something there," he continues. "While we were writing, a hurricane hit and all the trees started coming down around us and we had to run for our lives, like in *The Wizard of Oz* when the tornado came. We had to run into the main house and everything was shaking. It was crazy. I don't know if that was the start of 'What It Takes,' maybe it was. Or maybe it was the start of another song we wrote called 'Another Last Goodbye,' which we finished years later."

Kalodner brought in Bruce Fairbairn, who oversaw *Slippery When Wet*, to produce the album. (A couple of years before, Fairbairn worked on *Without Love*, the second album by Black 'N Blue, one of KISS guitarist Tommy Thayer's earlier bands, on which they covered Aerosmith's "Same Old Song and Dance." Fairbairn would later produce KISS's 1998 *Psycho Circus*, featuring an uncredited Thayer, who was not yet in the band.) On the strength of the singles "Dude (Looks Like a Lady)," "Angel," and "Rag Doll," and their attendant expensive, super-slick videos, Aerosmith once again took flight. With their next four albums going platinum or multi-platinum and "I Don't Want to Miss a Thing," a Diane Warren power ballad from the soundtrack to 1998's *Armageddon* (which costarred Tyler's daughter Liv), becoming the band's first and only No. 1 single, they were back to being one of the biggest rock bands in the world.

A few of Child's subsequent cowrites, "What It Takes" and "Crazy," helped them to achieve that standing. Along the way, he became a party to the band's dysfunctional work process. "I loved writing with Desmond Child," Tyler has said, "because we always got into arguments." Child remembers Tyler once becoming so frustrated during a session because the songwriting mojo had failed to materialize that he declared, "Wow, I wish Diane Warren was here."

"Why don't you just go ahead and call her?" Child told him, before grabbing his things and phoning for a car to pick him up.

"Hey, man, I didn't mean anything by it," Tyler said.

Child lit into him: "You're really fucked up, man. If you want Diane Warren, then call Diane Warren. Get her over here if you think your song is going to be better with her."

Tyler quickly apologized.

"I showed him that I wouldn't take that shit," says Child, who believes that Tyler sparred with him so he'd have someone to fight with who was not named Joe Perry and that by teaming up with Perry to fight Child, they could be more together.

Of Child's hot streak in the late '80s and '90s, Paul Stanley says, "Desmond went on to be the hit machine for many bands, less so for us. We certainly didn't have the abundance of radio hits that some other bands had." Regardless of the massive success he achieved with others, Child credits Stanley as his most important collaborator. "I owe everything to Paul," he says. "I could never have written the songs I did with Bon Jovi or Aerosmith had I not learned from Paul's mentorship."

As to the effect Child had on his and Aerosmith's careers, Stanley says, "I guess the only parallel would be that we both started out pretty much at the same time and we're both still alive and kicking."

· · · ·

THE DOCTOR, CHEAP TRICK'S 1986 follow-up to *Standing on the Edge*, is a mess—a collection of mostly fine songs (nearly all of them attributed to Nielsen and Zander), crippled by atrociously boomy production by Tony Platt (credited with rescuing their previous album), that, for the listener, simulates the experience of being in an MRI machine operated by the ape-men of *2001: A Space Odyssey*. Widely cited as the band's creative nadir, it also could be seen as a metaphor for their frayed relationship with Epic Records.

So the label's renewed interest in Cheap Trick the following year, while welcome, did not come without challenges. Don Grierson had been an executive at Capitol before joining Epic to head up its A&R department and was known as something of a power-ballad guru, after resurrecting the career of Heart by presenting them with "What About Love" (originally recorded by a Canadian band called Toronto) in all its Aqua Netted, lace-gloved glory. And he made it one of his missions to reanimate a moribund Cheap Trick.

"One of the main reasons why I came back to Epic was because of you guys," he told the band. "It's not been going right and I'd like to help turn your career around."

At some point during the recording of Cheap Trick's tenth studio album, Grierson presented the band with demos of two songs, saying, "One's for you and one's for Chicago," the long-running soft rockers who were also in need of a career boost. "I'll give you first pick."

He played them "Look Away," by Diane Warren, and "The Flame," by British songwriters Nick Graham (formerly of prog rockers Atomic Rooster) and Bob Mitchell (who had coproduced a Eurodisco cover of KISS's "I Was Made for Lovin' You"). Richie Zito, the album's producer, says it's possible that the band were presented with a choice, but in his recollection, "We couldn't pry that song away from Diane Warren and Chicago."

Nielsen immediately pegged the strummy intro to "The Flame" as very similar to "Nature's Way" by Spirit, but faced with what they perceived as two evils, the band chose the lesser one. "We all hated it," Carlos says of the song. "We didn't consider ourselves a ballad band."

When "The Flame" came along, Zito says, "I think Rick instinctively knew that this might be a song that could be very important to them. He rebelled the most against it." Zito remembers the guitarist taking the tape out of a machine and flinging it across the room. Ultimately the band members filed in one by one and begrudgingly recorded their parts. "Everybody did a little more, filling it out, overdubbing, putting more of their personality into it," Zito says. "And that was how that record came to be."

Robin Zander was surer of the track's potential. "I knew it could be a big song," he has said. "I thought the lyric was middle-of-the-road stuff and musically it was okay."

In what was surely for Zito the sweetest of ironies, "The Flame" became the band's first and only No. 1 pop hit, and *Lap of Luxury* their best-selling album since *Dream Police*. "Sometimes success is a double-edged sword. It was successful to the point where it almost annoyed them," the producer says. "I was there for them to blame, which is fine."

Cheap Trick had reluctantly accepted outside help before, but with the lawsuits behind them and the new commitment from Epic, they acquiesced to having nine of the ten songs either written by others or cowritten with the band. Significantly, the only Cheap Trick original not to get an outside cowrite, Petersson and Zander's "Never Had a Lot to Lose," wasn't even by Nielsen, the band's chief songwriter. Still, Nielsen's justification for caving to the pressure—"We can take a crappy song, and because we're good, we can turn it into something"—couldn't have rung truer.

Even though the band rejected her "Look Away" (which, thanks in part to Cheap Trick, became Chicago's biggest-selling single), Nielsen let Warren finish his composition "Ghost Town" for *Lap of Luxury* and reluctantly recorded her "Wherever Would I Be" for their next album, *Busted*. But the band hated her songs and were unhappy with their recordings of them. "They sounded stupid," Petersson has said, "like Starship."

"She was aggressive and tenacious," Zito says of Warren. "She was so enthusiastic about getting people to listen to her and record her songs. It was a combination of salesmanship and outright talent." Nielsen could not have cared less. "We didn't want any of those people," he said. "They're good songwriters, but so what? They're good songwriters for other people." Nielsen understood the inclination to supplement a band's songwriting, but wondered if the label just didn't know how to promote Cheap Trick. One example Nielsen has cited, *One on One*'s "If You Want My Love," went to No. 2 in Australia. "It didn't do anything here," he said. "What does that mean? I don't get it. It was a good song, so what more can I do? If it did well or charted well and they don't know what to do with it, then I think they don't know what to do with us."

L.A. Guns opened for Cheap Trick in clubs and small theaters in 1988. By the time the tour was over, the headliners were on the upswing again, thanks to "The Flame." "But during the tour," says guitarist Tracii Guns, "we were all staying in the same Motel 6, and it was fucking awesome. The first day of the tour, me and Mick, the other guitar player, go into the catering area. Rick and Bun E. are in there with the catering girls. We didn't dare go up to them, we hadn't met them yet. We walk in for food, and they've destroyed the catering area. But they were the big dogs pissing on the tree and letting us know 'You're not going to fuck with us,' because we were on fire. So we didn't meet them then. We played, they played, no hello, no goodbye."

The next night, after Nielsen stood on Guns's side of the stage, watching the younger man play, his guitar tech allowed Guns to view him from the same vantage point. "The night before," Guns recalls, "he did a little guitar solo in the set. But the second night, when I was standing over there, he terrorized his guitar. We all want to be guitar heroes, and Rick, every night, is a guitar hero. He's as much of a guitar hero as Hendrix."

From then on, after the ice broke, the jokes never stopped. "I had fallen in love with a girl named [redacted], and they got wind of it," says Guns, whose main guitar is a Rick Nielsen model Les Paul. "One night, Tom Petersson says, 'Hey, we heard about [redacted] in Rockford. Is she your girlfriend?' And I'm like, 'Yeah, I think so.' I mean, I'm twenty-two at the time. I'm in love. Then Tom looks over at Rick and goes, 'Uh-oh!' And Rick goes, 'I know [redacted]. Sit down, Tracii. I've got to tell you: she's been making the rounds since she was fifteen.' He was freaking me out. *Oh my God. This beautiful, sweet young girl with these horrible men in a small town called Rockford, Illinois.* They let me stew on that for twenty-four hours before Tom came up and said, 'Oh, just kidding, man.'"

With the success of "The Flame" and their cover of "Don't Be Cruel," also from *Lap of Luxury*, Cheap Trick were, for a while at least, headlining small arenas and still supporting the likes of Heart and Robert Plant. For Zander, touring with one of rock's greatest frontmen was particularly validating, as it came at a time when his own band were inching their way back up the ladder and even helping the headliners to sell a few tickets. "It gave us a pretty good feeling," Zander recalled. "I remember Robert Plant coming backstage after the first show saying, 'Hey, boys, I should be opening for you.'"

· · · ·

THE UNMASKED '80S SAW KISS fighting to stay relevant as the spotlight shifted to the bands they helped spawn and significant personnel changes shook their very foundation. Ace Frehley's replacement, Vinnie Vincent, lasted fewer than three years. *His* replacement, Mark St. John, lasted just eight months (though he'd later join the extended family, playing briefly with Peter Criss). Bruce Kulick, who took over in 1984, remained a member until 1996.

Not long after Kulick came in, Gene Simmons, by his own admission, had essentially checked out, having become more interested in pursuing a movie career (who can forget his sublime performance as murderous hermaphrodite Velvet Von Ragnar in *Never Too Young to Die?*), running a record label, working with other bands (including Keel and Black 'N Blue), and managing, of all people, Liza Minnelli—leaving Paul Stanley to take creative control of KISS. "From the second I walked in," says Kulick. "Paul was clearly in charge." By the time he started writing with Simmons, for 1985's *Asylum*, Kulick found that they'd have to work around the bassist's movie schedule. "I wasn't as aware of it until time went on how annoying that was for Paul," he adds. "Then again, Paul was comfortable in his element and quite capable of steering the ship. Of course, Gene's songs were directed by Gene, and if Paul was needed to massage them a bit, he was there. Sometimes, when they would compromise, the best result did not necessarily come about."

*Crazy Nights*, their 1987 album, had gone platinum, but the arena tour fizzled; the average attendance of 5,691 (with some shows drawing fewer than 3,000) represented an 8 percent drop from their previous outing. Faced with a multimillion-dollar tax debt and having learned of dubious investments, by 1989 the band had canned business managers Glickman/Marks and hired Paul Stanley's psychotherapist, Jesse Hilsen, to run the show, thinking a neophyte with no preconceived notions could align them with unconventional partners and get them back on track.

KISS had already completed their fifteenth album, 1989's *Hot in the Shade*, when they figured it was time to hit REFRESH. Impressed with the success Larry Mazer was having managing Philadelphia glam-metallurgists Cinderella, who, like KISS, were on Mercury Records, Stanley and Simmons brought him on. But Mazer came with conditions: no more Liza, no more Simmons Records, and the bassist needed to reengage. Mazer believed the main reason the band was struggling was that the real Gene Simmons had been missing from KISS since the hard-edged *Creatures of the Night* in 1982. "Where's he been?" he asked them. "You've got to get him back in the band."

Unfortunately, to Mazer's ears, the record he inherited was a stinker. "A crap album with only three good songs," he says. "I heard 'Hide Your Heart,' 'Rise to It,' and when I heard 'Forever,' I said, 'This could do it.'" And it did. It was easy to imagine the gorgeous, soaring power ballad, written by Stanley and Michael Bolton, as a hit for Heart's Wilson sisters or any number of KISS's hair-farming brethren. But in KISS's own leather-gloved hands, it reached No. 8 on *Billboard*'s Hot 100, becoming the band's biggest single since "Beth."

Mazer briefly quit after a disagreement over finances with Hilsen (who broke with the band in 1992 and became a fugitive from the law two years later). After he rejoined, the band entered the studio with Bob Ezrin for *Revenge*, the first album in more than a decade to sound like classic KISS: sordid, vaguely menacing, and unconcerned with appearances. It was also the first KISS album to feature Eric Singer, who replaced Eric Carr after the drummer died of heart cancer in 1991. The U.S. promo single "Unholy" brought back the Evil Simmons and sold well overseas, and "Domino," a dirty-blues concerned with a big cock and a bitch not old enough to vote, marked the return of Skeevy Simmons. The album's high point: Stanley's "I Just Wanna," an amusingly risqué Eddie Cochran–inspired chant (cowritten by Vinnie Vincent).

While on the road for *Revenge*, Mazer, an inveterate crate-digger, came across *Hard to Believe: A KISS Covers Compilation*, featuring such underground indie bands as Nirvana, the Melvins, All, and Bullet LaVolta—some of the tracks faithfully rendered, others seemingly taking the piss. "My rule in every band, especially KISS, was 'Cool first, money later,'" he says, "which is the opposite of Gene Simmons." He showed the album to the band on the bus.

"I could see the wheels turning in Gene's head," Mazer says. "A week later, I get a call: 'Larry, here's what I want to do. I want you to go to the record company and get two million dollars for *Kiss My Ass: A Tribute to KISS*.' I said, 'That's the dumbest thing I ever heard. What's cool about this is that these bands did it on their own.'" Simmons wouldn't hear no. So Mazer went to Mercury and got the money.

Visiting Simmons at his home in Beverly Hills one day, Mazer spied in his office above the garage a large board. On it was a list of artists paired with KISS songs, such as MADONNA: "I WAS MADE FOR LOVIN' YOU."

"What he'd do is call Slash," Mazer says. "'Slash, we're doing a tribute to KISS. I want Guns N' Roses. Good with you?' And Slash would say, 'Of course! Sounds great!' Ten minutes later, Larry Mazer gets a phone call from Doug Goldstein, manager of Guns N' Roses: 'What the fuck is your client doing calling my client? There's no fucking way I'm putting Guns N' Roses on a KISS tribute record!'"

If Slash was a pipe dream, Simmons almost landed a couple of other Guns N' Roses members—*Use Your Illusion*–era rhythm guitarist Gilby Clarke and drummer Matt Sorum—to do "Calling Dr. Love." When they were considering potential bass players, Clarke mentioned Tom Petersson to Simmons, who told him, "Oh, we have a great relationship with the Cheap Trick guys." But, Clarke laments, "at the last second, Geffen"—Guns N' Roses' label—"pulled us off the record and we couldn't do it." A different supergroup ended up covering that song—Shandi's Addiction, made up of members of Rage Against the Machine, Faith No More, and Tool.

Gary Cherone got the call because his band, Extreme, had had a No. 1 single a few years earlier with "More Than Words" and Simmons wanted them to cover "A World Without Heroes," off of *Music from "The Elder."* "I remember telling him, 'We're a rock band and we're going to be doing the ballad? We love the song, but please let us do 'Calling Dr. Love,'" Cherone says. When Simmons offered "Strutter," Cherone responded, "Sold!"

Kim Thayil remembers being approached for the album and showing interest (Simmons pegged Soundgarden for the portentous "War Machine" from *Creatures of the Night*), but he couldn't convince the other members of the band not named Matt Cameron to do it. He suspects Chris Cornell and Ben Shepherd's dislike of KISS stemmed from their formative years as music fans. "They had big brothers who had extensive record collections and probably wouldn't allow them to listen to things like KISS," Thayil says.

While promoting *KISS My Ass: Classic KISS Regrooved* in June 1994, Simmons announced, "This is the graduating class of the KISS Army—the fans who went on to form their own bands," adding that nearly a hundred different artists wanted to contribute, including Smashing Pumpkins, Cypress Hill, and Sir Mix-a-Lot. Redd Kross, who'd been singing KISS's praises even during the fallow years, had hoped to be considered for the record and were thrilled when Simmons reached out and asked to sing "Deuce" with them at one of their L.A. shows. "But I also thought it was ludicrous," the band's Steven McDonald says. "Curating your own tribute record is like organizing your own surprise birthday. Unfortunately, we didn't quite have the numbers to make the cut." Simmons also claimed, bizarrely, that Kurt Cobain and the Melvins had recorded a version of "Goin' Blind" together. "Ironically, it came in too late," he said, "and another group, Dinosaur Jr., had already recorded the same track."

A punk rock fan from an early age, Dinosaur Jr.'s J Mascis never paid attention to KISS until he picked up the guitar in college and other players that he respected suggested he check out Ace Frehley. When he got the call to participate in the tribute, Mascis was happy to oblige. "It was hilarious," he says of his conversation with Simmons, "because he sounded like a lawyer or businessman, so sleazy on the phone. It was just awesome. He said 'jazzed' a few times and other things that I was impressed by." After submitting his cacophonous yet soulful take on "Goin' Blind," Mascis heard that it was Simmons's favorite.

"But," he says. "I'm not sure he didn't say that to everyone on the album."

## CHAPTER 23

# NOTHIN' TO LOSE

IN 1986, RICHIE RANNO was living in Bergenfield, New Jersey, begrudgingly working for his father's printing business. An unabashed collector, he was also making money on the side by selling rock memorabilia, some of it Starz-related, through ads in magazines.

That November he received in the mail a notification from the IRS, which claimed he owed $74,000 in back taxes. Shocked, he called an accountant friend who discovered that the other four original members of Starz were also going to get the letter. The discrepancies were apparently the result of write-offs by the band's accountants that later had been disallowed. He alerted his ex-bandmates to the unwelcome correspondence.

Michael Lee Smith suspects that once KISS started bringing in enormous sums, Bill Aucoin needed to find deductions to offset his revenues. The singer recalls meeting with an Aucoin accountant who presented him with a blue folder detailing the singer's earnings and expenditures for the year. "This is so typical for that time and place," Smith says. "He's having a Japanese girl give him a manicure while he's talking to me, but he's also on the phone most of the time. I'm looking through it and I see that there are sixty-five thousand dollars in tolls charged against my income. I ask this guy while he's having his nails done, 'What's this sixty-five thousand dollars for tolls?' He tells me in his New York accent, 'You crossed many a bridge, my friend.' That's how he answered my question.

"I think they decided, 'These guys can be our losses,'" Smith adds. "Why else were we put through the crap we were put through?"

By 1986, Brendan Harkin was living down the street from Ranno and they had become the best of friends. The two decided to search for accountants' ledgers, anything that could keep them from getting soaked financially. They snooped around, made some calls, and ended up at two units in a Manhattan storage facility that had belonged to Bill Aucoin before they were locked for nonpayment and controlled by a warehouseman's lien. "We said, 'Look, we just need these file boxes that say STARZ on the outside,'" Ranno recalls. The pair could see that one room also contained a jumble of KISS relics that their former manager had amassed over the years. The bottom line: even if they wanted just the Starz files, they'd have to purchase the entire contents of the units for a $5,000 fee.

After convincing Harkin they'd easily make the money back selling the stuff to collectors, Ranno says each man decided to put up half.

Harkin remembers some details slightly differently. "Richie and I didn't have two nickels to rub together," he says, so they borrowed the money from Harkin's then wife, Caroline Peyton. (A jazz-folkie turned stage performer, Peyton appeared with Michael Lee Smith's brother Rex on Broadway in 1984's *The Human Comedy* and later sang in the Disney animated features *Beauty and the Beast* and *Pocahontas*.) What Harkin and Ranno got for their trouble: hundreds of framed gold and platinum records—presented by Casablanca to Aucoin and Rock Steady to commemorate KISS's sales achievements—as well as tour books, magazines, dolls, equipment that Ranno says did not belong to the band, and "a stray boot or something, but no major costumes."

The framed plaques were the most valuable items, Ranno says, wistful that he may have unloaded them too soon. The market for KISS memorabilia had not yet taken off, so he was asking for the going rate, which during the band's hair-metal days was $50 to $100. "Just a few years after that, that stuff was through the roof," he laments.

"We started just selling stuff," Harkin says. "And that's the first time I ever had any money. I think at one time I had ten thousand dollars.

"We didn't go looking for it—it came to us," he continues. "If you owe the IRS money and you have a corporation, which we did, any of the people individually owe that money. We just wanted to not have to pay the IRS and so we had a happy result. There certainly wasn't anything slimy about it."

Not only did the band members wind up with the necessary documents to settle their debts, but also the haul led Ranno to quit the family business and become a full-time memorabilia dealer. He didn't expect that he'd soon be feeling the wrath of the God of Thunder.

• • • •

RANNO BROUGHT SOME OF his newfound booty to a KISS convention a married couple had been running in Boston. There were only ten dealers in a small hotel conference room, but attendance was good, so he did well. When he invited the pair to expand their reach to New Jersey, they weren't interested. So he and a partner put together their own show, the first New York area KISS convention, at a hotel in Cranford, New Jersey, on June 28, 1987—where they displayed a KISS pinball machine formerly from Aucoin's office, a signed and notarized acknowledgment of the KISS members' blood having been drawn for the Marvel comic, and the band's People's Choice Award from 1977, among other pieces. The couple were not pleased. "They waged war on us, that we stole the idea," Ranno says. "It was the furthest thing from the truth. We begged them to come down and do it."

In late 1988, Ranno received a call from his friend "Nitebob" Czaykowski, who had been mixing live sound for KISS on a European tour. Simmons had heard about his convention and was pissed. "Gene thinks you're making millions of dollars," Ranno remembers Czaykowski saying, "and he's definitely going to get in touch with you." Simmons did phone Ranno not long after and asked him to come to Manhattan. "No, I don't really want to do that," Ranno told him. "You don't want me to run the convention? I won't run the convention anymore. I'm not looking for a fight with you."

"I'm not saying that!" Simmons replied.

"What are you saying?"

"I just want to meet with you."

Ranno relented and went to Simmons's office. Soon after entering, Ranno says, "He starts accusing me of stuff. I said, 'That's it! I'm out of here. Fuck you! Be respectful or I'm leaving.'" As Ranno got up to make good on that threat, Simmons apologized and said plainly, "I want everything that you got from the warehouse."

"Okay, you can pay me for it," Ranno responded. "I paid for it, it's mine. Here's my receipt. It's not yours. It was Bill Aucoin's, then it was the warehouseman's lien, and now it's mine and Brendan's." Simmons began grilling Ranno about his convention. How many people show up? What's he charging for admission? What's the overhead? What's his profit? "He thought we were making a million dollars," Ranno says. "And when he looked at it all, he realized, why argue over pennies? It wasn't a lot of money."

With what he assumed to be Simmons's blessing, Ranno continued organizing his conventions, moving them to East Rutherford's Meadowlands Hilton and then the Rothman Center, a small arena in Hackensack. (Detours into Cleveland and Poughkeepsie, New York, were busts.) Soon, the shows had grown to the point where Ranno was booking a hundred dealers, KISS-associated special guests, panel discussions, and tribute bands.

Skid Row's Sebastian Bach was one of his customers. "Being a big KISS collector, I used to go to the Rainbow Rockatorium," he says, referring to a popular New Jersey memorabilia store. "And somebody tipped me off there that Richie Ranno from Starz could get me a KISS gold record from the '70s. I met him when he came down and I traded a *Skid Row* triple platinum for a *Hotter Than Hell* gold record."

In 1994, Tommy Thayer, who was coordinating projects for Simmons and Stanley, called Ranno to ask if he could send a team to shoot video at his upcoming show. Ranno agreed. "First thing in the morning, their crew was there before anybody, and they're the last ones to leave," he says. "They videotaped every aspect of my convention." Ranno was surprised, then, when he received a cease-and-desist letter from KISS's lawyers, telling him he could no longer use the band logo or the words "KISS Convention" in his marketing materials. "Every time I got a cease and desist, I tore it up," Ranno says, "because back in '88 Gene had said at the meeting it's not a problem.

"One of their lawyers called me up and said, 'Why didn't you respond to this?'" Ranno continues, "'I'm doing this with permission from Gene.' And he said, 'Well, Gene's rescinding that permission.' I said, 'Let's go to court, then. Any court of law and any judge will tell you that if you've been doing something for eight years, it's your thing now.' 'Oh no,' he goes, 'not in this case.' I said, 'I'm not going to stop.'" Soon after the call, Ranno was threatened with a lawsuit. Wanting to avoid any further hassle, he acquiesced and agreed to alter the logo and call his show a "KISS Expo."

On July 17 of that year, Ranno took a dealer's table at the first annual Detroit KISS Convention organized by a collector named Joe Marshall, in nearby Troy, Michigan, where Peter Criss was going to be the star attraction. But even bigger surprise guests would soon undercut that distinction. With lawyers and police in tow and a court order in hand, Simmons and Stanley marched unannounced into the Northfield Hilton convention space. A ruckus erupted on the show floor as the men began to dismantle the KISS museum display owned by a dealer named Al Munson, which featured costumes and props from the band's '70s prime.

When Mark Cicchini, one of the other dealers that day, heard that Simmons and Stanley were on the premises, he immediately thought they were there to scoop up the many bootleg videotapes available for sale. "The biggest moneymaker was always the video," he says. The last thing he expected was for them to confiscate the costumes. Why would they come to Troy for them when Munson lived in New Jersey and had displayed them at Ranno's expos?

Among a sea of shocked and screaming fans, Stanley grabbed a mic on the makeshift stage and announced that he and Simmons had to keep their visit a secret so they could retrieve stuff they claimed was stolen from their warehouse, items he said that were rightfully theirs. "As much as we want you people to see them," he told the crowd, "they really belong to us. So we have to make sure that when you see them, we own them." He and Simmons soon turned the raid into a personal appearance, fielding questions from the freaked-out conventioneers.

The July 19, 1994, edition of the *Detroit News* ran a story about the seizure, which read in part: "According to court papers, the flea market, staged by Ritchie Rannon [sic] of New York [sic], Joseph Marshall of Westland, and a third man identified as John Doe, used the costumes to entice fans to the sale." "I had nothing to do with the convention," Ranno says. "I was just some guy that drove out from Jersey."

In his memoir, Stanley blamed KISS's former manager for the items going public. "Bill Aucoin, who somehow had keys to our warehouse, was secretly selling our stuff out the back door," he wrote. In an interview outtake from the 2004 documentary *KISS Loves You*, Aucoin admitted that since he was no longer working with the band, he did let a warehouse go and claimed that he had offered KISS all of the contents but their business manager wasn't interested. He also suspected that word of the warehouse's fate had never reached the band members and mused that Munson would have been within his rights to fight for the confiscated items.

However, if indeed Simmons and Stanley were not made aware that the goods were going to be sold, they could have been entitled to them through a legal remedy called replevin, an action to recover personal property that was wrongfully or illegally taken. Aucoin himself wasn't above selling KISS-related relics. Cicchini says the former manager would sometimes show up at dealers' hotel rooms before the New Jersey expos with boxes of mementos from his time with the band, such as the key to the city of Cadillac, Michigan, which was given to KISS at a civic breakfast in 1975 after they played a local high school.

Simmons and Stanley held on to the items they repossessed—for a while at least. "Obviously, when something is important to you, whether it is a photo album or something that is near and dear to you from your past, it's rightfully yours," Stanley, perhaps disingenuously, told the *Detroit News*. "To see someone else have it and making money off it is really unfair." Twenty-five years later, Stanley stands by the raid. "Dealing in stolen merchandise that was not owned by those parties is unethical and could have led to charges had we not been dealing with numerous other issues at the time," he says. "No BS rationale would hold up in court. Beyond slimy."

Almost exactly a year after the bust, on Saturday, July 22, 1995, Simmons and Stanley returned to Detroit, this time with Eric Singer and Bruce Kulick, to present their own official KISS Convention at Cobo Hall. No matter that the city's second annual unauthorized show, featuring special guest Ace Frehley, had taken place the previous month. Simmons and Stanley's expo was just one stop of a twenty-six-city tour overseen by Thayer, who had also supervised the making of *KISStory*, a massive coffee-table book published in March by the band themselves. For a $100 admission fee, fans enjoyed, in addition to a surfeit of dealers and authorized displays (of vintage instruments, artwork, and costumes), an acoustic set by the current members, as well as a concert by a tribute band that re-created a '70s gig in full dress. Attributing the idea for the expos to Simmons, Stanley wrote, "I loved the looseness and informality of the format of the conventions."

Even though KISS fan gatherings had been sprouting for years—the band themselves appeared at one in London's Astoria Theatre in May 1992— Richie Ranno suspects that Simmons and Thayer learned how to run their convention by studying the video of his show. "Instead of asking me to help them, and maybe pay me a few bucks, that's how they did it," he says. "That was it for me. I've never really had much contact with them since."

One of Ranno's few run-ins occurred a decade later on April 27, 2002, at an event organized in conjunction with his sixteenth annual expo, at the Rothman Center, to celebrate Frehley's fifty-first birthday. KISS had completed the Australian leg of their Farewell tour a year before, and Frehley's status in the band remained unclear as the group did the occasional promotional and private event with Thayer on lead guitar.

An onstage question-and-answer session with Eddie Trunk quickly devolved into a contentious bitch session, with Frehley accusing Simmons of stealing songwriting credit and saying "all he cares about is making money." Meanwhile, KISS drummer Eric Singer, a guest at the event and the next day's convention, called Ranno to tell him that Simmons was going to show up and present Frehley with the expo's cake. "Eric, he's badmouthing Gene," Ranno told him. "He's threatening him. I don't think Gene should come. Or at least he should know this." Too late. They were in a limo and on their way.

Ranno says he gave Simmons the cake "and he was really rude to me. I said, 'Okay, Gene, you're on your own.'" Surrounded by security, Simmons, in a dark T-shirt and blazer, marched through the crowd to chants of "Gene! Gene! *Gene!*," carrying a rectangular cake emblazoned with the image of a guitar, to where Frehley, wearing a vest with metal shoulder plates over a cut-off T-shirt, was signing autographs. "He would not look up," says Ranno of Frehley. "He wouldn't even acknowledge Gene. He just kept writing and handing things to people while Gene was talking." As Simmons reached over the table to squeeze Frehley's hand, Ranno remembers telling his son, "We should get back because I think Ace is going to throw the cake in Gene's face." Instead, the two musicians exchanged a few words and posed for some snaps, before Simmons beat a quick retreat out the doors and into a waiting car. "I give him credit for coming in," Ranno says. "But he didn't have to be nasty to my son and me." After the event, Frehley called Trunk's radio show to comment on the restraint he showed. "For Gene to fly three thousand miles and bring me a birthday cake," he said, "I didn't think it was right to punch him out."

Ranno supervised the New York–area KISS Expo for six more years, before hotels in the region raised their rents to a degree that made little economic sense to him. Besides, the number of dealers and buyers were dwindling, he says, "because everybody's buying their shit on eBay. Anything the internet can kill it will." Planning and executing his own expo consumed him for three to four months a year, while he'd make his living on weekends, attending conventions across the entire country. It was on one of these trips where he met his second wife. Then, in 1996, after a Chicago convention where he barely made back his expenses, he decided, "I'm not coming here again."

Another of Ranno's few run-ins with Simmons happened on January 21, 2006, the Starz guitarist's fifty-sixth birthday. Ranno was attending the NAMM convention, the premier gathering of music merchants and the tattooed longhairs who love them, in Anaheim, California, with his long-time friend Frank DiMino, the lead singer of Angel. As they strolled down one tight aisle and approached a wide avenue, the two were stopped by security personnel who were clearing a path for a video crew on the crowded floor. Once the group got closer, DiMino—who, with Ranno, covered *Heaven Tonight*'s "On Top of the World" a few years earlier for a Cheap Trick tribute album—recognized a tall, imposing figure in the midst. "It's Gene!" he blurted. It was indeed Simmons along with his son, Nick, who were at NAMM to shoot a segment for their reality TV series, *Gene Simmons Family Jewels*. "Gene was strutting like the cock of the walk," Ranno says. "As he gets close to me and Frank, his head goes to the left and he sees us, and he breaks rhythm for a second. He then goes right back into rhythm and the whole entourage walks by us. The security guy lets us through, we start walking, and I say, 'Hey Frank, he saw us. He didn't say hello. It's unbelievable. Think about how long he knows us!'

"He's such a douche," Ranno continues. "I don't understand what happened to the guy."

In June 2000, six years after the raid in Troy and five years after touring with their own conventions, KISS held a two-day auction at the Paramount Studios Theatre in Hollywood, where they marketed a treasure trove of costumes, instruments, props, and gear, some of the pieces retrieved from the collection of Al Munson. More than 80 percent of the 840 lots were sold, bringing in $1.6 million in bids. The Hard Rock Cafe alone ponied up some $300,000 for 22 lots, and an unidentified buyer paid $189,500 for a full set of costumes from the 1996–1997 reunion tour.

Asked why they decided to let the stuff go, Simmons and Stanley, who had gone to great lengths to get some of it back, responded that they wanted "as many people as possible to have a piece of KISS."

• • • •

WHEN KISS BROUGHT THEIR official convention to Burbank, California, on June 17, 1995, Peter Criss, who was then living in nearby Venice, took his teenage daughter because he wanted her to get a sense of her dad's accomplishments. Once there, he received a hero's welcome from the assembled crowd, and he had been persuaded to perform "Hard Luck Woman" and "Nothin' to Lose" with the group. Soon after, he was sharing the stage with Ace Frehley, when they took their respective solo bands on a North American club tour billed as "the Bad Boys of KISS." Criss was grateful for the opportunity to play with Frehley again, even though at one gig in Oklahoma, they drew ten people.

MTV, excited by the renewed affection the conventions brought to KISS, invited the band to tape a performance for the network's *Unplugged* series. The set would feature the current lineup (with Singer and Kulick) as well as Criss and Frehley guesting on a few songs. For the August 9, 1995, taping, the band called in David Rule to help keep the guitars in tune. Rule, a veteran roadie and sound engineer who'd worked with Starz in 1979 and 1980 and Aerosmith from 1984 to 1988 (and for seven years, beginning in 2001, Cheap Trick), had gone out with KISS five years earlier as Simmons's bass tech on the Hot in the Shade tour. "I remember having conversations with Gene," says Rule, "where he was going, 'I can't believe we did all that stupid crap, carrying that big-ass stage. I'm not doing that crazy shit again. It was too expensive.' Now they only had five or six trucks, and they were making money." Another thing Rule clearly recalls Simmons telling him: "'You'll never again find me in the same building as Peter Criss.' It was like there was no fucking way that was ever going to happen."

But there they all were, in Manhattan's Sony Studios, on a stage decorated with the cover art from *Rock and Roll Over*, playing a career-spanning set acoustically, but amplified electrically, a format that beautifully demonstrated just how exquisite KISS songs—in particular, "Every Time I Look at You," "Hard Luck Woman," "Goin' Blind," and "Comin' Home"—could sound.

On the uncut version of the taping, after KISS ran through a ludicrous chicken-fried "God of Thunder," out ambled Frehley in a Marilyn Monroe tee covered by a polka-dot long-sleeve, followed by Criss in round, rose-colored specs, loose checked shirt, and black vest, looking more like a mop-topped member of the Flamin' Groovies than a hell-raising shock-rock feline. The joy on their faces seemed palpable as the original quartet, playing together for the first time in nearly fifteen years—in their debut group performance without makeup—blasted through the Rolling Stones' "2,000 Man."

Then came the money shot. "The four of them are sitting in a row on barstools doing 'Beth,'" says Rule. "There's that line in the song: 'Me and the boys will be playing all night.' The audience went nuts. I looked at Gene and you could just see the fucking dollar signs in his eyes. He was like, 'Yep. We're doing it.'"

"Despite all the problems, despite all the torture, when we played together it felt like 1974 again," Simmons later wrote. But he also claimed, shockingly, that reforming the original band hadn't ever crossed their minds. For his part,

Stanley thought that a full makeup and costume reunion tour could provide the closure that the band members never really had, and wrote that it was he who had to convince Simmons that it would be financially beneficial to do the shows. And that they had better do them sooner rather than later, before one of those disaster magnets dropped dead.

When Steve West and his band Danger Danger toured with KISS in 1990, a number of the shows were sparsely attended, sometimes drawing 4,000 fans in 10,000-capacity venues. "Paul would make jokes," the drummer says. "'We're expecting a big walk up.' 'I'm probably gonna buy pizza for the crowd tonight.' I used to say to him, 'I don't think you have much to worry about. Anytime you want to call up those other two idiots, you could put the makeup on, and then you don't have to have a worry about empty houses.' He would just smile. I think he always had that in the back of his mind."

Simmons and Stanley never were shy about suggesting that they could imagine sending out a band called KISS on tour without any original members. Simmons even talked about staging a KISS show on Broadway or in Las Vegas, a jukebox musical that would tell the story of "four knuckleheads who come up from the streets of New York and create the band that they never saw onstage." He had a meeting in the early '90s to discuss this very idea with Steve Leber, the former Aerosmith comanager who also launched *Beatlemania*. Leber thought the show could work, but says he suggested to Simmons that the band put the makeup back on instead: "I told Gene, 'There's an audience still out there for you. They still love you. I'll tell you what I'll do. I'll give you ten million dollars—guaranteed you'll make it on the live tour. Instead of being a manager, I'll promote the tour. The only thing is, I need a machine gun, because you're from Israel and I know you guys are going to wind up trying to kill me after I make a hundred million and you make ten.' And then he offered me [to manage] the band for, I think, five or three percent. In my day, we were getting fifteen percent, seventeen percent of AC/DC. So Gene Simmons has me to thank that he didn't do *KISS on Broadway*, because it would have hurt or ended their career."

Rick Nielsen sees the drastic steps KISS took—removing the artifice, only to put it all back on—as an essential element of the band's myth building. "The drama, the hard work, the recording—then for it to do so well, and then it was over," he says. "I know how hard it is to go on the road. With them, it's got to be even worse. To maintain that, and then get rid of their makeup, and then go back to it. Then you think of the alternatives, and what else there is that's like them. There is nothing exactly like them."

• • • •

TIM COLLINS WAS SITTING in his office in Cambridge, Massachusetts, one day in the mid-'90s when he received an unexpected phone call. Gene Simmons was on the line. "I had a little game I used to play with my manager friends," Collins says. "We would call each other under assumed names. I thought somebody like that was calling, saying they were Gene Simmons, because I had never met him—why would he call me? I got on the phone and said, 'What do you want, you fucking piece of shit?' And he started laughing. I said, 'Oh, fuck! Hold on a second, that's just somebody imitating me.'"

"This is your lucky day," Simmons announced. "I'm going to tell you something that's going to change the course of your life. I want to make you the manager of KISS."

Flattered, Collins listened to his spiel. "What Gene wants is nothing about what I do," he says. "I realize he wants Doc McGhee"—the former Mötley Crüe and Bon Jovi manager—"because his hero is P. T. Barnum. My hero is Brian Epstein."

"Gene," Collins told him, "you and I would get along for about twenty minutes and then you'd hate my fucking guts. Doc McGhee is the man for you."

Collins began enumerating McGhee's strengths, until Simmons finally told him, "We're not going to pay anybody twenty percent"—which had been the standard rate at the time. "I don't represent Doc McGhee," Collins responded. "That's between you and him. But he gets twenty percent."

"So," Collins says, "they started talking and Gene said, 'We're only gonna pay five percent.' Doc said, 'I get twenty.' And they went ahead with the deal.

"The last time I spoke to Gene, he goes, 'So we paid him the five percent, but I know that motherfucker stole at least fifteen percent.' And I said, 'No, Doc McGhee is not a thief. He would not steal more than fifteen percent. He told you his deal was twenty percent.' He goes, 'I think you're right!' I said, 'What do you care? You're back on top of the world!'"

CHAPTER 24

# BUSTED

THE RELEASE OF NIRVANA'S *Nevermind* in late 1991 changed everything. Teen spirit had an entirely new smell—and it was dank and musty. The lip-sticked legions of '80s glam saw their popularity wane as their shiny, plastic Sunset Strip inauthenticity got supplanted by a flannel-clad squad from, primarily, Seattle that peddled a grimy, mewling authenticity (which, in some cases, proved to be just as affected).

KISS had jumped on disco's garish bandwagon, flirted with new wave, and shimmied to hair metal, so it came as no surprise when, in 1995, they plunged headlong into grunge. The band members had always tried to keep current and understood that many musicians in some of the scene's biggest acts—Soundgarden, Pearl Jam, Alice in Chains, the Melvins, Mudhoney, Stone Temple Pilots—cited KISS as a major influence. Grunge may have emerged from punk, but its practitioners burrowed deeper to borrow from heavy metal and classic rock.

To oversee their seventeenth album, KISS tapped Alice in Chains producer Toby Wright. Simmons's approach was to transform KISS into a new, more modern band, at one point telling Wright, "I want to be like Billy Corgan!"—the Smashing Pumpkins frontman. Similarly, Bruce Kulick thought KISS needed a harder edge in order to stay relatable. "*Revenge* was barely heavy enough," he says. "But the strength of grunge—it's closer to a heavier, uglier, darker version of *Revenge*." Kulick experimented with dropped-D tuning, a staple of the genre—Soundgarden's "Black Hole Sun" and Nirvana's "All Apologies" used it—which gave his tracks an oppressive, foreboding vibe. "Everything," he says, "just got more metal." By his own admission, Kulick was the one pushing the band to come up with harsher sounds, and his dedication resulted in his earning nine cowrites on the album. "I went to work," he says. "I didn't know they were going to be distracted with the reunion tour. That was in the background, but it had nothing to do with me."

The record, which came to be called *Carnival of Souls: The Final Sessions*, could have been titled *Grungemania*—not the real thing but an incredible simulation. Hardly KISS's worst record—that one came next—its long, lugubrious, dispirited songs didn't suit a band that on their previous album, *Revenge*, recorded their loveliest power ballad ("Every Time I Look at You") and were naughtily singing, "I just wanna *fuh*, I just wanna *fuh*, I just wanna *fuh*-GET you!" All told, *Carnival of Souls*—whose best track, "Childhood's End," written by Simmons with Kulick and his eventual replacement, Tommy Thayer, builds to an eerie kids'-choir crescendo—was an ambitious experiment that nevertheless sucked all the fun out of a band that had previously thrived on it. Stanley himself called it "a big misstep," saying, "I never believed that the world needs a second-rate Soundgarden, Metallica, or Alice in Chains."

His drummer agreed. "I listen to that and go, 'That's not KISS,'" Eric Singer has said. "It's a lot of rock, but no roll."

Mercury shelved the album when Simmons and Stanley set out on a reunion tour with Frehley and Criss, releasing it on October 28, 1997, nearly two years after recording began. Of the delay, Kulick says, "I was tortured by it, because by then some bootlegs got out. Back then it wasn't digital, so everything was in the wrong tempo. It was four generations down." With no tour supporting it, and none of its songs played live, the album became something of a phantom.

To capitalize on the love that grunge bands had been showing them, and in a bid for relevance despite the inherent nostalgia of the tour, KISS tapped Stone Temple Pilots to open the reunion shows. Simmons remembered telling STP frontman Scott Weiland, "Look, you've got to be straight, cut it with all the heroin and the crap, respect the fans, get up onstage, do a great show. It's all yours. We'll support you, but I want you clean onstage."

"Gene, I promise!" Weiland replied.

"It's like what everybody who's a drug addict and alcoholic says," Simmons recalled in 2018. "'I've been clean for a million years and stuff.'" When the band had to bow out because of Weiland's recurring issues, Alice in Chains filled in for the tour's first four gigs.

"Those were fun shows to do," guitarist Jerry Cantrell has said. "KISS were heroes of ours as well." Bassist Mike Inez recalled being starstruck upon meeting one of these heroes. "I was eating food, and . . . KISS is in the hallway all dressed up in their stuff, getting ready to go up," he said. "Gene Simmons—I had not known him at this point—he walks up to me and looks down, 'Hello, Michael. How's the chicken?' So I'm talking to him, and I had to stop him. 'Gene, I can't talk about catering right now, you're the God of Thunder.'" Alice in Chains drummer Sean Kinney said that KISS had wanted to take out his band for a while, but singer Layne Staley resisted. "Me and Jerry especially [wanted to do it]," he said. "I was in the KISS Army and they were bringing back the original lineup. Layne kept saying, 'I don't want to do it.' We gave up on it—we didn't hear about it for a while. They must have asked again, and he said, 'I'll do it.' We rolled out there, and those were the last shows we played in public."

Simmons has said he had the Weiland conversation with Staley right before Alice in Chains went up onstage. "I said, 'Layne, here they are, the fans. They're lined up, it's all yours. Just go out there and do great.' 'Gene, I've straightened up.'" (Staley would die from an overdose of heroin and cocaine on April 5, 2002, exactly eight years after Kurt Cobain killed himself.)

When grunge trailblazers and proud KISS fans the Melvins opened five shows on the tour, the divide between established, legacy act and strange, underground band could not have been more marked. KISS had walked in the Melvins' scuffed-up boots nearly a quarter century earlier, playing on mismatched bills before thousands of nonbelievers. But Simmons was aware of the love the Melvins had for his band; in fact, the covers of the members' three 1992 solo EPs mimicked the artwork on the KISS solo LPs from 1978. He also knew of their sensational version of "Goin' Blind," which he performed with the group at a Melvins show at L.A.'s Palladium in 1993.

"Somehow our name came up to be one of the bands to maybe play some reunion shows," drummer Dale Crover says, "and we were surprised because we thought, 'There's no fucking way we're going to get asked to do that.'" Their first stop: the Superdome in New Orleans. "The band was in a rental car and we had a truck that went ahead of us that had all of our gear. I was pulling up to the gates, trying to get into the Superdome, going, 'Hey, we're the opening band.' 'Yeah, bullshit.' 'No, really, we are.' We had to go get one of KISS's production guys to say, 'Yeah, those guys are good.'"

As they entered the stadium, the Melvins saw KISS warming up. "We just walked right in front of where the seats are on the floor," Crover says. "And they totally acknowledged us when they saw us. It was really funny, Paul Stanley going, 'Hey, Buzz.' And then Gene was trying to hit us with guitar picks." Guitarist Buzz Osborne appreciated being able to attend the band's soundchecks. "They'd be jamming Stones songs," he has said, "so they were good at that kind of thing."

But to the KISS audience, the Melvins barely registered. "They didn't hate us, they didn't like us," Crover says. "It was people our age that were there to see KISS, and they more or less sat patiently through our set. We weren't doing this to sell the band. We were doing this because we got to play with a re-formed KISS. Their being my first concert and band that I loved, I didn't need any more."

Osborne has called the shows "something that was really weird that I would've done for the weirdness factor alone."

The tour, though financially successful, was personally taxing and didn't end well for the reconstituted KISS, leading to yet another breakup. Four years later they would inevitably try again.

• • • •

EPIC RECORDS, DISCOURAGED BY the lackluster sales of 1990's *Busted* (again produced by Richie Zito and featuring a Diane Warren song, but no big hit single), and Cheap Trick, resenting the label's attempts to force them into the middle of the road, finally parted ways. "We weren't trying to get more money or anything," Rick Nielsen said in 1994. "We just wanted them to respect what we were doing.

"We're not sixteen and we're not twenty-one," he added, "but they were trying to make us older than we are."

According to Ken Adamany, "When it came time for the last contract with Epic to expire in 1992, they just weren't that interested." The manager arranged for the band to audition for Warner Bros., whose A&R chief, Roberta Petersen, signed them to a two-album deal. With the new label came a new producer, Petersen's brother Ted Templeman, who had worked with Aerosmith in 1985.

This was supposed to be, as Nielsen said in 1994, the first album of the second half of Cheap Trick's career. "When they came to Warner Bros., they were somewhat in decline," says Bob Merlis, a former publicity executive for the label. "Templeman was thought to be a hitmaker of the highest order, so there was hope for that." It was a typical move for Warner Bros., he says. "They'd sign artists who had a run somewhere and then either bring them back or they'd continue on the path."

Templeman's vision for the record was, in Zander's words, "anti-vision." "It was not to interrupt or influence the band in a bad way," the singer said at the time. But as with Aerosmith, Templeman once again disappointed himself with his efforts, or lack thereof. "I was stumbling around a lot. It was just a mismatch," he says. "I think they needed somebody who was familiar with their work and, probably, a different studio. I don't think Rick was ever happy with his guitar sound, and I didn't really know how to get one for him.

"They played well," he continues, "but I wasn't wild about a lot of the songs. I didn't like 'Woke Up with a Monster' and I told them so. 'Well, *we* like it.'"

"Templeman was in over his head," Carlos says. "He wasn't showing up for half the sessions."

Despite the presence of a few cowrites with friends, on this album the band no longer felt pressured to use outside contributors or to gloss things up with keyboards. However, Carlos claims that by this time the previously prolific band had run out of material, citing as particularly lame one Zander contribution, "Ride the Pony," a leftover from the singer's otherwise splendid 1993 solo album. "On the list of worst Cheap Trick songs ever," Carlos says, "it's usually somewhere near the top."

"I'll be the first to admit that we're the '90s version of Cheap Trick or the Knack, but the last to admit that it hasn't been rewarding," wrote Kurt Cobain in the liner notes for Nirvana's *Incesticide*, ignoring the fact that there already *was* a '90s version of Cheap Trick. If Cheap Trick didn't exactly bend to grunge's mucky sound on *Woke Up with a Monster*, they at least made a few concessions to its look. One was the introduction of a new blotchy logo seemingly inspired by the chicken-scratch work of artist Ralph Steadman. "We all thought we'd try something different," Adamany says of the Warner Bros. art department's attempt to convey a hipper, reinvigorated band. "The original logo was so fantastic, but maybe it was getting a little worn out." (The band ended up waffling, however, by printing the classic logo on the CD itself.) Another was the video for the title track, which featured a sulky, lip-pierced teen dressed in flannel, as well as graphics by grunge poster artist Frank Kozik.

Nielsen was realistic in his initial appraisal of the album. "This isn't the greatest record on earth," he said soon after its completion, "but it's a good Cheap Trick record." The first five songs, particularly the amiable singalong

"You're All I Wanna Do" and the elegantly resigned "Didn't Know I Had It," bear that out. "And we've got to start making good Cheap Trick records again," he added. "Before we know it, we'll get our confidence back up again to make a great Cheap Trick record."

They would eventually do just that with their next album, but it wouldn't be with either Warner Bros. or Adamany. An executive shuffle at the former saw the departure of two of their biggest advocates (Mo Ostin and Lenny Waronker), and a bitter split with the latter (who, at the time, had been battling a serious illness) led the band to retreat and scale back.

They were just about broke when they hired Larry Mazer. The manager, who'd shepherded KISS for a few years in the late '80s and early '90s, had ties to Cheap Trick that went back decades. As a high school senior, he'd helped manage Good God—a jazz fusion band on Atlantic that featured Hank Ransome, who briefly drummed for Cheap Trick when Bun E. Carlos broke his arm—and across the street from his office in downtown Philadelphia was a Victorian house where members of Sick Man of Europe lived. "Then the first Cheap Trick album came out and got a lot of airplay here at [rock station] WMMR," Mazer says. "I lost my mind from the minute it started." He even attended the band's first Philly-area show, on September 6, 1977, at the Other Side in Wilmington, Delaware.

In 1991, when Mazer was managing identical-twin blond rockers Nelson, he took as their opening act House of Lords, a band featuring keyboardist Greg Giuffria, late of Angel, who were signed to Gene Simmons's label and managed by Ken Adamany. House of Lords' tour manager, who had taken a larger role in the Cheap Trick organization after Adamany left, recommended him for the job.

Mazer worked with Cheap Trick on a career-spanning box set and, as he did with KISS, organized a tribute album (featuring Everclear, Joey Ramone, and the Posies) for Grass Records that, owing to label troubles, never got released. "I didn't involve the Cheap Trick members," he says. "They got involved because they were excited about it, but I kept them at arm's length."

Though the band experienced a lovefest on the Rockford date of the 1996 Lollapalooza tour, where they played alongside their fans in Metallica, Soundgarden, Rancid, and the Ramones, out on their own Cheap Trick still couldn't catch a break. Their back-to-basics self-titled independent album, released on Red Ant in 1997, earned them some of the best reviews of their career. But it too fell victim to a label collapse.

While cutting the album in Glen Cove, New York, the band flew out Steve Albini, an engineer known for his work with the gnarled likes of Nirvana, the Jesus Lizard, and Tad, to record two tracks for a one-off single, instigated by Ira Robbins and to be released by Sub Pop, essentially grunge's ground zero. "I think I was trying to impress the band," Robbins says. "I had a sense that Cheap Trick could be cool in a way that they weren't at the time. They were no longer a corporate rock band and they were still great. I thought, 'It'll be really cool if you guys got some indie cred from all these people that dig you.'" Albini had already recorded a caustic version of "He's a Whore" with his own band, Big Black, and Sub Pop chief Jonathan Poneman had played bass in a Seattle-based Cheap Trick cover band called Sick Man of Europe, so it didn't take much persuading. "We liked Steve," Carlos says. "He said all the right things: 'The label told me to remix something and I told them to get fucked.' And we were like, 'That's our kind of guy.'"

They also recorded with Albini a new version of their second album, stripped down to its punchy fundamentals. "He goes, 'You guys are always complaining about it, so let's recut *In Color*,'" Carlos says. "We went and did it in two or three days." Although it was not intended for commercial release—there were hints that songs could appear as B sides or used for films (one track did appear in the *Rock Band 2* video game)—the recording nevertheless leaked online. Some of it's better than the Werman version, Carlos says, before admitting, "Most of it's worse." The band later did some recording at Albini's Electrical Audio in Chicago (a studio that Nielsen's son Miles helped build) for the 2003 album *Special One*, and Albini worked with Carlos on the software program *Bun E. in a Box*, a collection of drum samples from his Cheap Trick oeuvre.

In spring 1997, in a bid to hook the Lollapalooza generation, Cheap Trick agreed to open for Stone Temple Pilots, who were kindred spirits and big fans. *Budokan* was the first album frontman Scott Weiland ever bought, and bassist Robert DeLeo was all in when he heard *Heaven Tonight* at the age of twelve. "I lost my musical virginity up in a tree fort with a Cheap Trick record," he has said. "I *dreamed* of Cheap Trick." The shows may have introduced Cheap Trick to a younger audience, but they did little to boost the band's profile. "Those kids looked at Cheap Trick like they were from Mars," Mazer says.

"The STP fans didn't know who we were," says Carlos. "That was the first time we ran into that." The drummer remembers the difficulties the DeLeo brothers were having trying to keep the notoriously loaded Weiland straight. "They saw him having a glass of wine at dinner one night and almost canceled the entire tour," he says. "And they weren't selling a lot of tickets—between us and them, maybe 5,000 a night in 9,000-seat venues, so half-empty gigs." Making it all the more miserable, Cheap Trick had taken a big pay cut to get out in front of this apathetic crowd. "If they would make, say, ten thousand dollars playing clubs on their own," Mazer says, "they were getting paid three thousand by Stone Temple Pilots."

Dates with ZZ Top fared better, but when they went out with Mötley Crüe that fall, "they weren't selling tickets," Carlos says. "We weren't either. We lost a bunch of money."

Soon, Mazer was out, though he would end up back in the extended KISS family, managing Bruce Kulick's band Union, who, on their 1999 live album, covered Cheap Trick's "Surrender." Why that one? "I find some irony in the words 'got my KISS records out,'" Kulick says with a laugh.

## CHAPTER 25

# SURRENDER

THE SPECIAL GUEST AT the KISS Expo in Zaandam, Holland, on November 11, 2002, did not look well. With his skeletal frame supporting an ample paunch, shaved head accentuating sunken, razor-sharp cheekbones and a bushy goatee, and smoke from an unending chain of cigarettes swirling around him like a malfunctioning fog machine, Sean Delaney, onstage for an interview, looked to be auditioning for *Storytime with Charles Manson*. During the talk he spun many an improbable yarn—claiming the name KISS came from combining an anti-Semitic slur (kike) with the initials of the Nazi army (SS), gossiping about Paul Stanley's alleged sexual timidity, and boasting of kicking the shit out of Casablanca executives—all with the urgency of a motormouth conspiracy theorist.

That's the Delaney who Bryan Kinnaird encountered that same year in a Phoenix diner. A mutual acquaintance had suggested the two meet to potentially collaborate on the musician's memoirs. Delaney had been splitting his time between the Tempe–Phoenix area, where he was born, and Utah, where he had family. Over frequent meals and interview sessions, Delaney told tales of his many lives. Kinnaird, a writer of graphic novels, was both fascinated and exasperated by this gritty raconteur, whose rambling, voluble jabber and grandiose delusions painted a portrait of an ambitious and creative soul eventually beaten down by bitterness and resentment in a body betrayed by years of excess and abuse. "He felt like he nurtured KISS and made them what they were," Kinnaird says. "Then they basically shit all over him and left him out in the cold." Delaney, who in the early '90s performed in a Utah-based Mormon country band called Wasatch, was at the time managing the English country group Smith & Jackson, but, Kinnaird says, "he didn't have any money—not a dime to his name." Kinnaird recalls one particularly odd meeting that epitomized their parleys: "He walks into my apartment and he's critiquing everything. He's asking me if I'm gay. I'm not. He didn't even want to stay inside, he wants to sit on the patio. And this is summertime in Arizona. It's, like, one hundred fifteen degrees.

"He says, 'I've got an in with Paul Shaffer,'" Kinnaird continues. "'We need to get on *David Letterman* as soon as I can get this book done and published.'"

Delaney couldn't keep from blabbing about the book, much to Kinnaird's displeasure. He even called his former partner, Bill Aucoin, to crow that he was going to blow the lid off KISS. "Bill told him, 'Don't do that, Sean. It's a big mistake,'" Kinnaird recalls. When Delaney told his collaborator that he needed to go to Utah for a family function, Kinnaird drove him to the bus station. The writer was attending a Phoenix comic book convention in April 2003 when he received a call from Delaney's niece informing him that her uncle had just died. Kinnaird and a friend drove up to Provo for the funeral service. Delaney, fifty-eight, dead from a stroke, was buried in nearby Orem wearing a KISS shirt. Kinnaird published *Hellbox*, a slim volume based on his conversations with Delaney, the following year.

Richie Fontana recalls Delaney telling him at Lydia Criss's house, "I can't believe I didn't get AIDS. I was no angel." Two other Skatt brothers weren't so fortunate. When the band ended, Pieter Sweval, who was also an accomplished painter, remained in L.A., doing handyman jobs and working the door at the Bunkhouse, a gay country-western bar where his friend Lanny Bass, with whom he collaborated on music, deejayed. "Pieter bounced around, trying to find more work, but times were hard," Bass says. "In the '80s, music was changing and he just couldn't find anybody to work with."

Sweval struggled, at one point sleeping on the streets. "People did not want to rent to people who had AIDS," says his sister, Kristina Sweval Peters. "So he was living very roughly at the end." After he succumbed to complications from the disease on January 23, 1990, at forty-one, his sister and mother stitched a tribute for the AIDS Quilt, which has commemorated the lives of more than 48,000 people. Block number 5536 features a panel with Sweval's six album covers, along with an epitaph written by Peters: "Through the looking glass, we're all brothers under the stars."

David Andez, the force behind "Walk the Night," died, also at forty-one, from AIDS-related illness almost exactly three years later, on January 21, 1993.

· · · ·

**MORE THAN TWENTY YEARS** after *KISS Meets the Phantom of the Park*, the band took another whack at a movie. One idea rejected by Gene Simmons, who'd be producing, might have sounded familiar to anyone who owned a copy of Starz's *Violation*. It was a dystopian tale of "rock and roll being outlawed in the future. In the bowels of the underworld there existed a group of people who listened to and loved the 'forbidden music' of KISS." Instead, the band and the studio, New Line Cinema, settled on KISS's own version of *Rock 'n' Roll High School*. Titled *Detroit Rock City*, the 1999 comedy detailed the exploits of the teen members of Mystery, a Cleveland-based KISS cover band, who journey to the music mecca to catch their heroes in concert. Unlike KISS's previous film, it required no acting by the musicians, whose three-minute concert sequence at the climax includes a delightfully disgusting shot of the audience from the POV of Simmons's prodigious, darting tongue. For the end credits, instead of taking the opportunity to record an original song with the original lineup, Paul Stanley decided to sing a mawkish Diane Warren power ballad, a move that shocked Peter Criss. "There were no drums, no guitars," he exaggerated, adding, "It was Paul and a karaoke machine doing a bad imitation of Steven Tyler." That last point he wasn't overstating.

Like the Ramones movie, *Detroit Rock City* did little business at the box office—becoming something of a cult hit on video—but a few days before it opened, New Line threw quite a party. Before KISS (featuring Frehley and Criss) performed four songs in a parking lot at UCLA, Art Alexakis's band Everclear played a few, including their big hit "Santa Monica," followed by a cover of Thin Lizzy's "The Boys Are Back in Town" from the movie's soundtrack. They ended their set with special guests Rick Nielsen and Robin Zander, whose "Surrender" was also in the film.

"We had done a cover of 'Southern Girls' for a compilation that never came out, but Rick and Robin had heard that record," Alexakis says. "They contacted me, and when they came to Portland in '97, we opened up for them. At the time, we were drawing more than they were, but they were Cheap Trick—I didn't care. So when Rick and Robin want to play 'Surrender'—one of the greatest rock-and-roll songs of all time—with us, I'm like, 'Okay.' My band works it out. At the end of our soundcheck, Robin and Rick come up, we run through it, and then Rick stops: 'Wait a minute, that's the wrong chord.' I go, 'What chord?' 'That one, where you're doing the A—it's this . . .' And he plays some weird three-note chord that I didn't know. I just look at him and say, 'Well, this is the way we play it'—like, *Are you fucking kidding me? Are you telling Rick Nielsen how to play 'Surrender'?* And he sits there with the long beard he had and goes, 'Okay, whatever.' Then we play the song, and after the show, Robin goes, 'That's the way that fucking song should've been played and recorded from the beginning.'"

• • • •

ON APRIL 18, 2003, twenty-nine years after Aerosmith and KISS last shared a stage at the Michigan Palace in Detroit, where Steven Tyler said sayonara to a band he never wanted anything more to do with, pigs finally grew wings, little devils skated figure eights, and monolithic promoter Clear Channel Entertainment announced that the two groups would be embarking on a thirty-two-date coheadlining tour across America, starting August 2 in Hartford, Connecticut.

KISS's manager, Doc McGhee, took credit for the pairing—dubbed, by KISS, the World Domination tour and, by Aerosmith, the Rocksimus Maximus tour—telling *Billboard* that he'd tried to put the bands together two years earlier, but Aerosmith instead went out with Kid Rock. According to Stanley, it was an idea that had been brewing for decades. "We had wanted to tour with them in the '70s," he says. "We wanted to do dates with them, but they wouldn't do them. Finally, somebody made enough sense to them that they realized in this case two and two would equal ten. I know we were all for it. I know Joe was all for it. It made a lot of sense."

Indeed, for Joe Perry the matchup seemed like a natural fit. "We have a lot of fans in common from the '70s," he said. "There's a lot of synergy." He hadn't always been complimentary, however. Not long after the release of the KISS solo albums in 1978, Perry told Ira Robbins, "Not to put them down, because their show is pretty amazing, but they'd like to think they're a rock band. But take the makeup off, put them in a small club with no flames and no costumes, and do you have a rock band as good as an Aerosmith or Cheap Trick?"

As for Tyler . . . well, he mostly kept his mouth shut. "Because he wasn't a KISS fan, he was unhappy about the pairing," Perry later wrote. "He refused to do any press or promotion for the tour." One event he did deign to sit in on was a ninety-minute live radio special that also featured Perry and Hamilton (in Boston) and Simmons and Stanley (in Los Angeles), set up to promote the shows. Lots of clumsy banter, a few listener questions, and some very smooth sales patter from the KISS duo ensued. At one point, Simmons reminded Perry that the Aerosmith guitarist had played on his solo track

"Mongoloid Man" back in the day and promised to bring the demo on the tour so Perry could finally hear it. At another, when asked what their favorite song by the other band was, Simmons replied "Janie's Got a Gun" and Perry offered "Strutter." Producer Jack Douglas, who was in the studio with Aerosmith, cameoed at the beginning of the conversation, attempting to inject a bit of topical humor that instead came off as an unkind non sequitur: "I produced a band called SARS"—referring to the respiratory virus that at the time had been threatening China—"or was it Starz? I can't remember." Later in the interview, after all of the assembled agreed that this would be a great double bill to take to Japan and China, Simmons added, "I know the opening band—this new band that Jack Douglas is producing, the SARS band: Starz." As if to clarify to a baffled radio audience who the hell Starz were, one of the moderators explained they were a Bill Aucoin band, a remark that was followed by guffaws and exaggerated coughing. The musicians also managed to work Cheap Trick into the discussion, specifically a mention of their version of the Move's "California Man."

What they didn't tell the radio audience was that Aerosmith had a few demands that needed to be met before they agreed to the tour. For one, the band insisted KISS go out with at least three original members. Since Frehley decided at the end of their Farewell tour in 2001 that he'd had enough, he declined to participate, preferring instead to focus on his solo career. "I wasn't available emotionally or mentally, and, economically, I didn't need the tour," he has said. "I had gotten to the state of mind of not repeating old things and going on."

As Stanley explained at the time, a year and a half earlier Frehley passive-aggressively had rendered his return impossible. "When you have people in the band who are ambivalent about being there, then they shouldn't be there," he said. "There were certain things that he was requesting that were not to be. Maybe it was his way of putting us in a position where we would reach the end of the relationship." Tommy Thayer, who had been playing the odd show with the band since March 2002, would replace Frehley on the tour, going out in full Spaceman regalia. (Thayer had already gigged with Aerosmith nineteen years before, as a member of Black 'N Blue.)

All of this meant Criss would need to rejoin the band after having refused to take part in the Japan and Australia leg of the Farewell tour over a contract dispute. In his absence, Simmons and Stanley reenlisted Eric Singer to assume the Catman character. Stanley, for one, wasn't looking forward to his old drummer returning, writing in his memoir, "By this point,

Ace had already made it clear he was done. Which left Peter as the third member. *Ugh.*"

Still, in the run-up to the tour with Aerosmith, Stanley and Simmons put a good face on Criss's participation, going so far as to praise the drummer's renewed passion and ability. "There have been nights when the humidity has been up to 85 percent and you might as well be in a steam room," Stanley said. "I can barely hold the guitar some nights, and I think to myself: 'Wow, that guy is out there pounding those drums.'" Simmons hailed what he deemed the drummer's new, refreshing attitude: "I'm the same guy that said Peter was a fuck-up for decades. But Peter has had an epiphany, has been born again. At this late stage in his life, he has matured. We used to joke that his name should be the Ayatollah Criscuola—the moaner. But now Peter is great to be around." That is, until he wasn't.

Criss claimed later that he had been duped into taking part. During initial talks, he wrote, McGhee told Criss's wife Gigi that KISS had been unsuccessful in getting Aerosmith to commit to a joint tour, so the band would be forced to cut back for the next run of shows. The fifty-seven-year-old drummer, assured by his lawyer that he could retire with the money earned from these dates but pissed off that Frehley wouldn't be there at stage left, reluctantly agreed to return. But upon learning KISS would be going out with Aerosmith after all—on a huge tour for which he'd pocket just ten grand a night—he got pissed off all over again.

According to Criss, Joe Perry called him at his New Jersey home. Upset that Frehley had bowed out, Perry asked if the drummer could talk his missing KISS bandmate into reconsidering. "Aerosmith decided that we were going to open every show," Criss wrote. "If Ace wasn't there, Aerosmith didn't feel that they deserved to open for an imitation of KISS."

Nu-metallers Saliva, hard rockers Automatic Black, or Joe Perry discoveries Porch Ghouls would technically start the show, but this tour marked the first time KISS wouldn't be closing since playing with Whitesnake in 1990. Simmons has said that KISS and Aerosmith had long talks concerning who would open: "We took all the ego out of the discussions and just said: 'Who cares? It doesn't matter. We'll do it.' If at this late date in our lives we are still concerned about what people say about Aerosmith going on after us, then we're wearing a hollow crown." Perry intimated in one interview that Aerosmith would close the show because of his band's "more recent presence" before adding, "Uh, I don't even know why." Stanley later admitted that despite the tour's otherwise 50/50 split, it was Tyler who insisted that

Aerosmith play last. "I really don't care," Stanley said in 2012, "because as far as I am concerned, one way or another, you're going to have to come up on the stage, so you can go on before us or after us."

Upon reflection, sixteen years after the tour, Stanley attributes Tyler's antipathy toward his band to KISS's unwavering ambition. Of all the Aerosmith members, Joe Perry and Brad Whitford, thanks to their self-confidence, seemed to have more honest reactions to KISS and appreciated the band for what they were, he says, "as opposed perhaps to Steven, who had to wrestle with his own insecurities."

Joe Perry's friendship with the coheadliner ran so deep that audiences at a tour stop in Oklahoma and later in Los Angeles were treated to the sight of the Aerosmith guitarist lumbering onstage in Paul Stanley's massive boots to join KISS for "Strutter," the first time an outside musician jammed onstage with KISS. (Rick Nielsen would turn up, in a Beatles T-shirt and his own footwear, for "Rock and Roll All Nite" when KISS played Rockford in 2016.) The tour even brought out Bruce Kulick, as a spectator, who admits, "I was more excited to see Aerosmith."

Without Frehley, his erstwhile partner in mischief making, around, Criss wasn't going to miss any opportunity to bust Thayer's balls. "You think you're a rock star. You're a piece of shit," he'd taunt the guitarist like a trick-or-treating Tommy DeVito who's been told to go home and get his shine box. "You used to order my breakfast." In time, Criss grew bored with what he deemed the monotony of the show: The new guitarist's playing was too perfect, he thought, and lacked Frehley's gawky charm. The technical issues that plagued some of the performances—microphone failures and the like—didn't help lighten his mood. He felt neglected by his own team. Aerosmith's crew members, who'd supply him with extra fans to blow pyro smoke out of his face, took far better care of him than his own band did.

Criss wrote that he observed imperious behavior by Thayer as well as static between Simmons and Stanley, adding, "It was so obvious on the tour that Paul was jealous of Tyler." Since KISS weren't allowed to use the ramp that jutted out from the stage and into the audience, Criss saw Stanley's exaggerated stage antics—rapping ad nauseum to the crowd, constantly smacking his own ass, fondling his guitar as if it were a six-string erection—as a form of overcompensation. As far as Stanley was concerned, Criss just lived to bitch, complaining about his accommodations, the length of shows, and his hands hurting. The drummer admitted to perking up during the final performances, though, when he felt he played and sang better than ever. The tour ended at the Save Mart Center in Fresno, California, on December 20, Criss's fifty-eighth birthday.

It was the last concert he'd play as a member of KISS.

. . . .

THE TOUR GROSSED $64 million, after nearly doubling the initial number of dates, and kept relevant two bands that hadn't released studio albums in two years in Aerosmith's case (*Just Push Play* in 2001) and five in KISS's (1998's *Psycho Circus*), but that didn't stop their members from getting on the radio nine years later to air their grievances like a bunch of WWE heels on Festivus Eve. Steven Tyler fired the first potshot during a 2012 interview by stating that seeing KISS on the coheadlining tour was "like watching a different level of concert."

After calling them "a comic-book rock band," he continued: "They've got a couple of hits, but they're more, they're comic book—you see them in their spackled faces. But it *is* different—a KISS lick, a Joe Perry lick—two different worlds, and sometimes depending on the time of day I get offended [by comparisons]."

"It's two different animals," Perry chimed in. "They went the theatrical way and used rock and roll kind of as their soundtrack. And for Aerosmith, the music *is* our show. And from that point of view, it's apples and oranges."

In response, Stanley told the syndicated *Rockline* that Tyler had a chip on his shoulder throughout the tour. "There is some sort of ambivalence or looking down his nose a bit towards KISS," he said. "I have to say that seeing him go on after us and play to an underwhelmed audience, and see people walking out, didn't feel too bad to me."

Despite calling Joey Kramer an asshole and Tyler an even bigger attention hog than Stanley, Criss in his autobiography wrote that he was honored to share the stage with their band. Still, Tyler's comments were disappointing. "It kind of hurt my feelings, 'cause I really like the guys," he said in a New York radio interview. "He didn't give me that impression when we toured together."

Reflecting on the war of words seven years later, Stanley says, "I don't want to insult or attack anybody in the band. They're great guys, for the most part.

"There's no better Aerosmith than Aerosmith," he continues. "As in many bands, there are personalities and flaws in personalities that everyone has to deal with. There's clearly someone in that band who has their own issues that have more to do with them than with us. From the beginning, although we didn't socialize because our schedules kept us apart, I always thought highly of Aerosmith. You don't last fifty years unless you've got something timeless and something that grows parallel to your audience."

In 2004, after enduring a complicated tour with a band for whom they would forever harbor mixed feelings, Aerosmith, to support their fourteenth studio album, *Honkin' on Bobo*, decided to take out a group they absolutely adored.

**· · · ·**

**CHEAP TRICK HAD DONE** a handful of dates with Aerosmith as recently as September 2002, with Run-DMC also on the bill. But the forty-six-date Honkin' on Bobo tour, beginning March 11, 2004, at the United Spirit Arena in Lubbock, Texas, was going to be something special, their first extensive trek with the band. It came as a welcome relief for Cheap Trick, who just six months earlier were slogging away, playing second fiddle to quirky alt-rockers Cake on a club tour. "I wish more of our fans were coming to this," Nielsen said at the time. "The places where we've been playing, we could actually sell out ourselves. But I'm glad we got invited because we're playing to a lot of people that have never heard us."

To help preserve Tyler's vocals, the tour itinerary followed Aerosmith's typical pattern of one day on followed by one day off, which offered something of a respite from Cheap Trick's usual grind. And for Cheap Trick, the money was ridiculously good. "We got headline pay to do forty-five minutes," Carlos says. Epic/Legacy had just issued *The Essential Cheap Trick*, a two-disc compilation of hits and deep cuts, and the band were still flogging *Special One*, which was *their* fourteenth studio album.

While Carlos remembers there being a mutual admiration society between the bands, he did notice some tension within the Aerosmith camp. One afternoon, Tyler came onstage during Cheap Trick's soundcheck and hopped on Carlos's kit, declaring, "Ah, a real drummer. I love these drums. They sound like real drums."

"He was just nailing Joey," Carlos says. "He and Joey weren't getting along."

Despite the pay and the relatively cush schedule, Cheap Trick found that Tyler's throat issues, which led to the cancellation of a half dozen concerts, began to seriously impact their bottom line. "We did the bookwork for the tour," Carlos says, "and we lost money."

The next time the opportunity presented itself, Cheap Trick would be prepared.

Aerosmith again requested that the band join them on the road, for five weeks, beginning in March 2006, on the third leg of their tour supporting the live album *Rockin' the Joint*. Cheap Trick had no new product to push, just the reissues of *Dream Police*, *All Shook Up*, and *Next Position Please*. Considering the bath the band had taken previously, Cheap Trick manager Dave Frey asked the members what they thought. Carlos suggested they look into insuring Aerosmith. When they realized that wasn't an option, they decided to insure themselves.

"We had a five- or six-show deductible," Nielsen says of the policy, issued by Lloyd's of London. The opening date at Hard Rock Live in Hollywood, Florida, seemed to go off without much of a hitch, but it didn't end well for Tyler. "He didn't like the monitors," Carlos says, "and he took the crew into a room and—we found out later—screamed at them for three hours and popped a vessel in his throat."

After the gig, the gear traveled 660 miles to the next venue, in Pensacola. "Three hours before the show, Aerosmith cancel," says Carlos. "Next town, it happens again. Finally, Tom and Robin go, 'Fuck this. We're going home. Call us day of show and let us know if we need to fly out.'"

That frustration extended to the venues, which were not being kept in the loop. The trucks and equipment would show up, but not Aerosmith. There were reports of planes being diverted midair to return to Boston, as the singer's condition changed by the hour. "But they're not calling the show till about five o'clock day of," says Carlos. Ultimately, Aerosmith had to cancel more than a dozen gigs, leading to speculation about Tyler's health, including rumors of throat cancer, which the band's publicist shot down. The singer later underwent surgery to repair damage to his right vocal cord. (Ironically, it was bassist Tom Hamilton who announced the following August that he had completed radiation treatment for throat cancer.)

For Cheap Trick, taking out insurance paid off. "We missed every show because of him," Nielsen says. "Thank God we did that. I'd rather be playing than getting the insurance. If we didn't have insurance, we wouldn't have played or gotten our money." As their policy reimbursed them for all expenses, Carlos says that he and the band "found every scrap of paper, every penny we'd spent, and sent it in and made enough money not to lose our ass that month."

After that, he says, the band swore, "No more opening for Aerosmith, unless it's one hundred percent up front."

. . . .

"I LOVE THEM LIKE brothers," Nielsen says of the guys in Aerosmith. "But I love them like you'd love wives and sisters too. Sometimes they're not in a good mood, or they didn't get a lot of sleep, and they become one- and two-year-olds." Nielsen recalls Jack Douglas being instrumental in hooking up Cheap Trick with Aerosmith. "They heard of us, we heard of them," he says. "They were a big band, and we were just getting going.

"He said good things about us, and that probably pissed them off," Nielsen adds with a laugh. "Bands don't want to talk about anybody else. But I do."

For years Nielsen and Tyler have been especially close. In 1981, the guitarist sent a gift to Mia Tyler, the singer's daughter with Cyrinda Foxe—a custom-made pink sweater with black and white piano keys across the chest and her name stitched underneath in white. Tyler replied with a thank-you note as well as a few Polaroids of the toddler smiling in her new top. In one, she mimics Nielsen by flicking a pick toward the camera.

Unlike many in the Aerosmith camp, Nielsen says he knows just how to approach Tyler. "He's the boss. Nobody ever tells him no. But I do. I'd say, 'Steven, do heroin every *other* day,' and he'd get high every day," he says with a laugh. "Or I'd say, 'Shout on your days off, not right after the show.' He'd ruin his voice for the next day.

"He's funny," Nielsen continues. "He calls me when he doesn't have anybody else to call. And we can talk to each other about anything. If he has a beef with this guy or that guy, I'll talk to him about it. I don't care—they can't throw me out of the band—so we're soul mates like that."

Nielsen didn't see Aerosmith in concert early on—bands rarely watched other bands live unless they were on the same bill—but was intrigued by what he knew of them. "We both had the same roots," he says, "and liked the same bands: the Stones, the Who." But there was one crucial difference between Aerosmith and Cheap Trick. "We never wanted a fifth player, because no one wanted to have the middle seat."

On June 25, 1978, Cheap Trick did a one-off with Aerosmith in Des Moines, Iowa, where after the show the two bands watched from the top floor of the Holiday Inn as a violent storm, with wind gusts of up to seventy-seven miles per hour, devastated the surrounding area. "It was wild," Nielsen said in 2004. "Steven was sitting with me and he was enjoying it. He was going wild—kind of a precursor of things to come with that guy." In spite of the destruction, the incident was a bonding experience. "They were way bigger than we were," Nielsen says, "but they thought we were fun, and we thought they were fun."

Once in 1978, when Cheap Trick were in Boston for a show, Tom Petersson and Joe Perry went for a ride in the guitarist's new car. "Tom comes back and he's like, 'We were doing a hundred twenty and were driving ten minutes and suddenly we were twenty miles out of town,'" Carlos says. "We started hanging out. There was some hanging out when we'd be in New York, like mixing *Budokan* at the Record Plant."

Carlos remembers one time ten years later when his band's jocularity did not go down particularly well with Aerosmith. Live, Joey Kramer sometimes wore clothes covered in electronic drum pads and during his solo he'd rap on himself. "Backstage," Carlos says, "Rick walked up to Steven and went, 'If he hits his nuts, is there a little ding? Does he have a little bell sample down there?' Nobody got the humor."

That humor extended to the band members' off-the-road socializing, such as when Zander and Nielsen, wearing one of his ridiculous sweaters covered with smiling skulls, attended Tyler's second wedding, to Teresa Barrick, in Tulsa, Oklahoma, in May 1988. "We were like sore thumbs," the guitarist says. "It was kind of funny. But you get invited and you are part of the family."

Nielsen also recalls stopping by Aerosmith sessions to yell into their microphones, and sometimes making it onto the finished recording. "I think it was on *Honkin' on Bobo*," he says. "Plus, they've been to my house a number of times. What else are you gonna do in Rockford, Illinois?"

In June 1990, Tim Collins's office faxed Ken Adamany a quote from Tyler that the Cheap Trick manager had solicited to help promote the release of *Busted*, answering the question: What do you think of Cheap Trick? The response was inimitably, nonsensically Tylerian: "Exactly what their name states. It started out copping the Beatles and just when the Beatles broke up we thought they'd kept their legend alive, but noooooo. They took a left turn and became an even greater entity all their own. 'Now that's a cheap trick.'"

• • • •

ON SEPTEMBER 23, 2000, after completing their set at the Hurricane Fest in New Orleans, Cheap Trick took off in Aerosmith's private jet, Aero Force One. Destination: Norwell, Massachusetts, twenty-six miles south of Boston.

They had been invited to perform the following night at a fiftieth birthday party for Joe Perry that the guitarist's wife, Billie, was throwing at Mount Blue, a restaurant partly owned by Perry and Steven Tyler. For Perry, who has called Cheap Trick "one of the best and hardest-working rock and roll bands in the land" and "an inspirational presence," this seemed like the ultimate present. "I'd always wanted to play a full set with them and began woodshedding," Perry wrote. "As a bonus birthday gift, they let me pick out my favorite songs." ("If you don't like our set," Nielsen remembers telling the assembled guests, "blame Joe, not us.")

On this overcast day, Elvis Presley and Marilyn Monroe impersonators mingled on the restaurant's grounds, across from a cemetery, as guests got their fortunes told and palms read. They also enjoyed sampling a smoked whole pig and picked up commemorative JP50 guitar picks, shirts, cigars, and laminated passes (with "Joe Perry" repeated in Cheap Trick logo fashion). Rides and a rock-climbing wall kept the younger partygoers entertained. Waitresses in low-cut black dresses "seemed to almost outnumber the guests," wrote attendee Mach Bell, the last singer in the Joe Perry Project.

At the appointed time, Cheap Trick appeared amid the Aerosmith gear on the eatery's small stage, Zander wearing a red sparkled top and black pants and Nielsen sporting the hideous long braided goatee he had started growing between *Busted* and *Woke Up with a Monster*, replete with dangling price tags that lent him the air of a Mephistophelean Minnie Pearl. They roared through a set that included "On Top of the World," "Come On, Come On," "Clock Strikes Ten," "The Flame," and "That '70s Song," a reworking of Big Star's "In the Street" they recorded as the theme for the sitcom *That '70s Show*. At one point between songs, Nielsen called Perry up to the stage to give him a copy of the book *Guitars of the Stars*, packed with photos of the Cheap Trick guitarist's legendary collection, with the inscription THANKS FOR THE GUITAR LESSONS! After Nielsen announced that the birthday boy was renowned for his love of cheap guitars, Zander presented Perry with a gig bag. Inside was a bronze-colored guitar signed by the band members.

"Dream Police," the set's closer, found Nielsen up to his usual antics. The maniacal rap interlude before his solo, which in concert always resolved in a hysterical geographic shout-out, on this night became "They persecute me right here *at Joe Perry's fiftieth birthday party!*"

After a break, the band returned for a second set, this time with Perry, and opened with "Hello There," on which, Mach Bell observed, he provided harmony to Nielsen's lead lines. "Meanwhile, in the shadows, Steven Tyler lowered himself over the dining room rail and onto a big road case by Joe's amp," Bell wrote. "He was hungry to sing. Joe ignored his colleague and launched into a riff to a song I don't know—but Cheap Trick did!"

Finally, Tyler took to the stage to toast his partner: "Here's to a man that has gone the distance and then some. Here's to a man that has proven that there ain't no substitute for arrogance!" which elicited howls from the crowd. The Beatles' "I'm Down" came next, with Tyler approximating Paul McCartney's approximation of Little Richard's scream-singing, while Nielsen and Zander shared a mic for backup. Tyler continued on with "Day Tripper" before Joey Kramer joined in for "It's All Over Now" and "Train Kept A Rollin'."

For Perry, the evening's true highlight came during his set with Cheap Trick, but it had little to do with the band and everything to do with his less-fortunate days. His guitar tech presented him with Perry's Holy Grail, an ultra-rare Les Paul 1959 tobacco-burst Gibson that the guitarist had sold out of desperation twenty years earlier. It was a gift from Slash, into whose hands it eventually fell and who for a long time had been reluctant to give it up.

In 2016, Cheap Trick were invited to play another fiftieth birthday party, this time for Mike McCready, at Seattle's Neptune Theatre, where the Pearl Jam guitarist, singer Eddie Vedder, and Soundgarden's Matt Cameron helped out on "I Want You to Want Me." "There was something about Cheap Trick that spoke to me," McCready has said of his attraction to the band. "It was the melodies, the songs, what they looked like. All of that made me want this, want to be a rock guitar player."

The same went for Dave Grohl, of Nirvana and Foo Fighters, who has claimed that Cheap Trick were one of the groups that drove him to start a band. "In America's rock-and-roll history," he has said, "how many bands of that era can be considered as heroic as Cheap Trick?"

Nielsen, who has said that he made more money being a songwriter than from playing in the band, appreciates all the flattery, the invitations to do gigs, the special guests who join him onstage for "Surrender." But, he says, "If you really like us, cover some of our songs."

## CHAPTER 26

# GONNA RAISE HELL

GROWING UP IN DETROIT in the '70s, John Varvatos needed music to escape an 850-square-foot existence, in which he and six others shared one bathroom. His headphone cord doubled as a lifeline, linking him with a portable radio and cassette player. After building a successful business designing rock-and-roll clothing, he began featuring musicians in his campaigns. Varvatos had always admired Aerosmith's style, so for fall/winter 2005, Joe Perry (playing pool with his son Tony) became the face of the brand.

In spring/summer 2008, it was Cheap Trick in dark suits, frolicking at the beach on bicycles. The band used an outtake from the Danny Clinch photo session—Nielsen buried up to his chest as the others scoured the sand with metal detectors—for the cover of their 2009 album, *The Latest*. "Rick has told me many times that we helped Cheap Trick get back on track again," Varvatos says. "I'm proud when he says that, but I don't really look at it that way. They're a band I thought it would be fun to have in the campaign."

On November 12, 2008, Varvatos found himself sitting in front of Gene Simmons at an AC/DC concert at Madison Square Garden. "Even he was blown away by AC/DC's show, where the train came busting through," the designer says. "He's pushing down on my shoulders, saying, 'That's fucking unbelievable!'" At one point during the night, the KISS bassist gestured to himself and asked Varvatos, "You don't want to do something with this good-looking face? You put those pussies Cheap Trick in your campaign."

Varvatos never thought to ask KISS because of Gene Simmons's money-hungry reputation. He told Simmons's son, Nick, nearly as much when they happened to meet later on at a Varvatos benefit in Hollywood for Stuart House, a center that treats sexually abused children. Two days later, Simmons phoned him. "Hey, good looking!" he said. "I heard we should be talking." Varvatos explained that in his campaigns all of the artists—which also included Alice Cooper and Iggy Pop—received equal money and equal treatment. "I wouldn't be calling you," Simmons said. "But my son tells me that this is the right thing to do."

In explaining the artists' compensation, Varvatos says, "We paid less than we pay a model, like a ten-thousand-dollar fee. It doesn't matter how many guys are in the band. Yeah, we'll give them some clothes too, but they've got to want to do it." So for the spring/summer 2014 campaign, Clinch shot the elegantly suited KISS, in perfectly greasepainted faces, strolling through lower Manhattan, dressed to kill.

· · · ·

IN FALL 2017, GENE Simmons was a very busy man. Recent activity found him attempting to trademark devil horns (he failed), releasing a movie from his new production company (*Armed Response*, starring Wesley Snipes), publishing a business manual (the power-mad *On Power: My Journey Through the Corridors of Power and How You Can Get More Power*), reviving his S&M comic book (*Dominatrix*), and hawking *The Vault*, a $2,000 eleven-CD box set of demos that he hand-delivered to fans. A reunion with Ace Frehley, with whom he hadn't played live in sixteen years, wasn't likely to be a priority. Yet, there they were, reconciled, on a beautiful late-September evening at a minor-league baseball stadium in St. Paul, Minnesota, for a concert to benefit a charity called The Children Matter.

The lineup also included local favorites the Jayhawks and Flipp, as well as former Eagles guitarist Don Felder and Cheap Trick. Shockingly, for two bands whose fan bases are so inextricably linked, this marked the first time Cheap Trick shared a bill with KISS, or any KISS member, since 1979. Cheap Trick's participation was so crucial to Simmons that, according to Nielsen, he moved the proposed date of the concert to accommodate their schedule.

"Open up your ears, spread your cheeks for the best effin' rock-and-roll band in the universe," Simmons urged the crowd as he introduced Cheap Trick. And for a man given to fits of hyperbole, this was no idle boast. The band proceeded to live up to that description with a crazed thirty-five-minute set that dutifully offered some staples—"Dream Police," "I Want You to Want Me," "Gonna Raise Hell," and "Surrender"—as well as a stunning, strutting "Long Time Coming" off their then-recent studio album, *We're All Alright!*

Last up came Simmons and his crack solo band—featuring members of Nashville's Thee Rock N' Roll Residency—with whom he started playing earlier that year. And, perhaps unsurprisingly, without his Demon getup, the Gene Simmons onstage was the Gene Simmons of reality TV and numerous media appearances: unfiltered, unscripted, and uncouth. When not ranting about how much better records used to sound or misidentifying one of his special guests as "Don Henley," he bantered lasciviously, at one point even ad-libbing "schmeckle," Yiddish for "penis"—likely the first time anyone in the audience ever heard that word uttered at a rock concert, let alone uttered at all.

With three guitarists to compete with, Simmons had his bass turned way up and revealed just how inventive and underrated a player he could be. Three songs in, he introduced a thirteen-year-old drumming prodigy, who pounded out the anal-sex encomium "Nothin' to Lose"—and later, without the kid, he performed the jailbait anthem "Christine Sixteen." Considering the name of the charity, both songs may have seemed like tonally awkward selections, but considering the man of the hour, they came off as perfectly appropriate. After an aggressive "Calling Dr. Love," from the wings emerged a down-to-earth Spaceman, who immediately launched into the ferocious thundering riff of "Parasite" and slayed with the solo. Though the follow-up, "Cold Gin," suffered from a tentative opening, the two former bandmates locked in on the crunchy groove of "Shock Me" and it was as though years of animosity had melted away.

If any one musician can claim to be the embodiment of the nexus connecting KISS to Cheap Trick to Aerosmith to Starz, it's probably Brynn Arens, frontman of Flipp, who revived his group after a long hiatus before appearing at the event. A lunatic showman in a striped Beetlejuice suit, wielding a black Coyote (a geometrically freaky guitar designed by ZZ Top's Billy Gibbons), he led his band through a boisterous set of sugar-sweetened, overcaffeinated arena-ready anthems.

Arens went way back with KISS, having seen them on the Alive! tour in St. Paul, where, in an unusual move, the band performed two shows the same night. "My older brother hid in the bathroom after the first one and caught both," Arens says. "Wish I would have thought of that."

More than a decade later, Simmons showed interest in signing to his label Arens's band Funhouse. Arens's subsequent group, Rattling Bones, were managed by David Krebs in the early '90s and through him they got Jack Douglas to produce some tracks before Krebs lost his label deal with Sony. It was with Flipp, his next band, where Arens displayed his passion for KISS-inspired theatrical rock.

Arens met Rick Nielsen when Flipp played the Minneapolis club First Avenue in the mid-'90s. "Rick got up—when he was not in the best of shape, he was drinking a lot—and jammed with us," Arens says. "We did our version of 'Let It Be,' and when we got done, he came back to the dressing room and said, 'What song did we play together?'"

"Well," Arens told him, "*we* were playing 'Let It Be,' but I think you might have been playing 'Get Back.'"

Flipp's first album was coproduced by Julian Raymond, who had played with Tommy Thayer in the band Movie Star (which evolved into Black 'N Blue) and would later cowrite songs for Cheap Trick and help produce 2006's *Rockford* and other subsequent albums. When they eventually toured with Cheap Trick in the summer of 1997, Flipp had former Aerosmith and KISS crew member "Nitebob" Czaykowski mixing their live sound.

Arens met Richie Ranno, whose band he loved, through Bill Baker, who repaired gear for Ace Frehley and knew the Starz guitarist from the New York–area KISS conventions. By Flipp's second album, 2001's *Blow It Out Your Ass!*, Bill Aucoin was managing them, as their look became more overtly and joyfully ridiculous: Arens, painting his face like a black-and-white cookie; guitarist Chia Karaoke (aka brother Kii Arens, who later designed the cover of Cheap Trick's *Special One*), wearing jumbo specs and eye-popping leisure suits; and bassist Freaky Useless, sporting skintight latex and a foot-high Mohawk. Their drummer wore a fuzzy bucket hat over chartreuse hair and went by the awesome nom de rock Kilo Bale.

Arens credits KISS's former manager with staying out of his way and letting him fly his oversaturated freak flag. When Arens would ask Aucoin, "Bill, what do you think of this?" the answer was always "Fuckin' awesome!" He never heard "I don't know, Brynn. People might be offended" or "You might scare some people with that."

"As a manager, subconsciously or subliminally, he's influencing you," Arens says. "I know Bill's history, so I'm kind of operating off of that." His reverence for Aucoin extended to the manager's logos. *Blow It Out Your Ass!* was originally slated for release through Minneapolis-based Oarfin Records, a name Arens felt did not match his band's Technicolor punk-and-roll image, so he asked Aucoin what ever happened to the Rock Steady logo. "It's yours," he responded. "We can use it on the record." Aucoin, in fact, passed the brand on to Arens.

Flipp's next album, 2002's *Volume*, was coproduced by Everclear's Art Alexakis and released by Artemis Records, founded by former KISS consultant Danny Goldberg. The label soon folded and Flipp split up, with Arens going on to produce the 2010 album by former Joe Perry Project member (and occasional Aerosmith fill-in bassist) David Hull, on which Perry guests. (That same year, Aucoin died of complications from prostate cancer.)

Arens then started the mobster-suited Oddfathers, whose two EPs were produced by Jack Douglas, and who covered "Let Me Go, Rock 'n' Roll" for a 2013 KISS tribute album. While in the studio with the band, Douglas noticed the vintage console radio that Arens had modified into a guitar amp. The producer sent a photo to a friend, who subsequently ordered one, leading Arens to found a company that custom-crafts retro speaker cabinets. That friend was Joe Perry.

## CHAPTER 27

# LET THE MUSIC DO THE TALKING

AS A KID GROWING up in the '70s in the Chicago area and then in Bellingham, Washington, Ken Stringfellow of the Posies, and later a revitalized Big Star, idolized Cheap Trick. "They were really visible to me," he says, "and kids that I knew and looked up to liked their music." He revered their early, classic records and dropped off only when he felt the band did. "The albums without Tom Petersson didn't even make a dent in my small town. They weren't visible. I didn't have MTV." With his Posies partner Jon Auer, he caught the band when they toured *Lap of Luxury* in 1988. "It was great to see them, but they were kind of a nostalgia act," Stringfellow says. "They got their act together over the course of the '90s, so I came back on board." Like so many bands indebted to the Rockford quartet, the Posies played "Surrender" live, and Stringfellow, as a member of the L.A.-based punk collective White Flag (who also covered Starz's "Cherry Baby," and, with Michael Lee Smith, recorded a version of the Runaways' "C'mon"), performed a faithful "He's a Whore" as well as a discordant, Marilyn Manson–inflected "ELO Kiddies."

Early in their career, when the Posies would play in L.A., they'd frequently see Petersson in the front row, singing along. "We got to know him a bit. At that time, in 1990, he was not sober," Stringfellow says. "Really nice, but barely coherent." In 1995, Cheap Trick had a gig in Seattle where the Posies were recording their album *Amazing Disgrace* and requested that they open the show. The Posies, in return, asked if Cheap Trick would be interested in swinging by the studio. "At first it was just going to be Rick playing some guitar noises," says Stringfellow of Nielsen's contribution to the vicious kiss-off "Hate Song."

"They brought like four hundred Heinekens—stacks and stacks of Heinekens," he recalls. "Then Robin said, 'I want to do something.'" Zander proposed adding screams and worked with the engineer to capture his vocals to his exact specifications. "He said, 'Okay, you put a slap delay x amount of milliseconds, blah, blah, blah, and distort *this* much." What impressed Stringfellow even more: before doing his take, Zander cut the filters off two Marlboro Reds and smoked them simultaneously in what seemed like two drags.

When Sean Kelly met Rick Nielsen in June 1997, the Canadian guitarist—who leads the glam band Crash Kelly and has played with some of the country's biggest classic-rock acts, including Coney Hatch, Helix, Honeymoon Suite, and Lee Aaron—was working at Tower Records and got passes to see Cheap Trick open for ZZ Top. He was in a group called 69 Duster at the time and brought a copy of their first CD to present to one of his favorite guitarists. While hanging backstage with Canadian alt-rock royalty Moe Berg of the Pursuit of Happiness and the Rheostatics' Dave Bidini, he approached Nielsen, told him how big a fan he was, and gave him the CD. "He looked at it and went, 'Oh, this will be on the side of a highway pretty soon,'" Kelly says. "He shoved it in his pocket and walked away. He did it in a funny way, but I was like, 'Wow, okay.' He and Zander had a sardonic humor about them. It was quick and fast. They're cutting you up, but you don't mind." Kelly ended the night eating chicken wings with Bun E. Carlos.

• • • •

**THE FIRST TIME SEBASTIAN** Bach met a member of KISS was when Skid Row got signed to Atlantic Records and their manager, Doc McGhee, brought them to Madison Square Garden to see Led Zeppelin play the label's fortieth-anniversary concert. "I met Paul backstage and I just lost my mind," the singer says. He later ran into Ace Frehley at a club in Toronto: "All these girls that I knew—he only let girls into his dressing room—were saying, 'You gotta let this guy Sebastian in because he just loves you.' So he let me in and I was the only dude in there. It was a very crazy night. I ended up offering Ace the chick I was with as a present for him being Ace. Then I drove about three blocks and thought, *What in the fuck am I doing?* I turned around and went back and got her."

A few years later, Stanley and Frehley's group were indirectly responsible for his leaving Skid Row, after Bach's band were offered an opening slot at the 1996 New Year's Eve KISS reunion concert at New Jersey's Continental Airlines Arena. "I was over the moon," he says. "We weren't getting along at the time, but it was a great opportunity. One of the guys said he couldn't do it because he was busy with his side project. I got so mad I called up one of the other guys and left a message on his machine, which was not very nice. People could say it was a 'last straw' kind of thing. That was the last time I was in the band." A Bach-less Skid Row would later support KISS when the four original members reunited again in 2000, and Bach himself would tour with Gene Simmons in 2012 as part of the supergroup Rock 'N' Roll Allstars and perform with Frehley at a pre-party for the KISS Kruise in 2019.

"When we talk about KISS now and you forget about the makeup and the gimmicks, every record is great, the production is great, and every performance is great," says Black Label Society's Zakk Wylde, a former lead guitarist for Ozzy Osbourne. "If somebody said, 'If they didn't have makeup or the flashy show, they'd be nothing,' I'd say, 'No, if they were just a normal rock band in T-shirts and jeans, the songs would still be so great.' It's not just icing and no cake. There's still plenty of cake." When Wylde first joined Osbourne's band at age nineteen, Simmons was close with the singer and his manager-wife Sharon. Wylde remembers once sitting around a table with Simmons. "So, Zakk," the bassist said, "Ozzy says you're playing with him now." With that, Simmons proceeded to offer the young man some advice: "Continue doing what got you here: practice" and "I advise investing in full-body condoms."

Buckcherry were just releasing their 1999 debut album when they went on their first arena tour, opening for KISS (with whom they shared management) in Europe. For singer Josh Todd, it felt like a monthlong traveling School of Rock. "I learned a lot from watching Paul talk to the crowds, especially crowds that didn't speak English," he says. "He was great at commanding an audience and keeping the show going even between songs." Meanwhile, back home, his band's first single, "Lit Up"—with its riff reminiscent of KISS's "Shock Me" (unintentional, Todd insists)—was blowing up on radio and launching their career.

Like so many other skinny boys sporting cuffed white tees, drainpipe jeans, paisley pirate shirts, bullet belts, and weeping-willow coifs, Butch Walker and his band SouthGang prowled L.A.'s Sunset Strip in the late '80s and early '90s, "chasing the last of the hair-metal dragon's tail." Walker, a self-described "young, dumb redneck" from small-town Georgia—whose KISS fandom was rivaled only by his love of Cheap Trick and Aerosmith—learned early on about one dark side of the music business, from a very surprising teacher. Right after SouthGang appeared on the scene, before they even played their first show, Bill Aucoin, no longer working with KISS, appeared to take an interest in the band. But his intentions turned out to be purely prurient. "It's a shock to the system to have some guy call you at three a.m. asking if you want to go party," Walker says. "It's like, 'This is the guy that I've read about my whole life, who pushed KISS into the stratosphere. Should I go do this?' Those thoughts actually go through your head. You're so desperate to be famous, there's a lot of people that would give in and do whatever, with anyone, just to get their break."

He had a better if still somewhat fraught experience working on SouthGang's second album with another KISS associate, Desmond Child, who used tough love and insults to draw quality work out of Walker. "He was like our trainer," Walker says. "I learned so much from him: inner rhyming and phrasing and structures and all that. I still use those techniques in writing songs. They're timeless."

SouthGang was playing at Gazzarri's, a bastion of hair metal on the Sunset Strip, when Walker first met one of the men whose faces had adorned his bedsheets and lunch box. "I just remember walking up to Gene and saying, 'Oh my God. Oh my God'—just spazzing out, having no cool," Walker says. "He gave me that look and a nod like, 'Yeah, thank you. I've heard that a million times.' And that's all I needed."

Years later, a KISS-fanatic friend implored Walker to go with him to an after-party for Simmons at an Atlanta nightclub. "Man, he's not going to let us into his party and he's not going to let us sit at his table," Walker remembers saying. "He's going to be surrounded by twenty paid girls and living out his rock-and-roll fantasy of 'Look what I have and what you don't.'" Nonetheless, Walker relented and, after some exploring, finally found Simmons. "Sure enough," he says, "he's at this big table roped off with twenty girls and no one else. I'm trying my best to get my friend up there to meet him. Gene's just sitting there with this eat-shit smile, waving at us, like, 'Sorry, no, you can't approach us.' That's pretty much what I expected, and that's what I got."

Walker had a slightly more satisfying encounter with Paul Stanley at a party in Malibu. "He was very engaged. And it was sweet to tell him that even though I'm forty-nine years old, you don't lose that being-a-fan thing—at least you shouldn't," he says. "I talked to him for a minute and he also gave me that look and wink and nod like, 'Yeah, I get told that all the fucking time.' But he seemed a bit more sincere about it."

Walker's first meeting with Frehley, in Las Vegas in May 2006, at the VH1 Rock Honors—paying tribute to KISS, Queen, Def Leppard, and Judas Priest—brought up feelings that were much more complicated. Frehley, who was grieving the recent death of his mother, has said that Simmons and Stanley never asked him to perform with KISS that night or even called about the show; Tommy Thayer would be taking on his role. Frehley did, however, agree to join an all-star band featuring Slash, Gilby Clarke, Scott Ian, Tommy Lee, and Rob Zombie, and play "God of Thunder." Backstage, before the show and after Slash offered him a drink, Frehley derailed his sobriety.

Walker was at the event to play bass with his friends the All-American Rejects, who were covering Def Leppard's "Photograph." "I knew everybody there, so I'm hanging out," he says. "Ace walks up, and he's just . . . I don't know." Out of all of the members of KISS, Frehley was Walker's initial fanboy attraction, his inspiration to become a guitar player. So when his clearly hammered hero approached Walker's circle and began throwing around deeply offensive jokes, Walker was appalled. "That was one of the deflating moments for me," he says. "I was like, 'Goddammit, I wish I wouldn't have been here for this.'"

Things took a turn for the absurd when Frehley sat down on the side of the stage next to Walker while KISS, the band he cofounded but hadn't played with in years, performed. "He put his arm around me," Walker says, "and I'm watching Ace look at Tommy being Ace. And he's looking at me, and he's looking out there, and he was just giving me that look like, 'Can you fucking believe this is where it's at?' It was wild—with KISS being my first concert—that my full-circle moment is sitting there with Ace Frehley, watching Ace Frehley, but it's not Ace Frehley."

Frehley has said it was that night in Las Vegas, where he ended up with five women in his room, that eventually put him back on the path to sobriety, writing in his memoir, "I haven't had a drink or any opiates or tranquilizers since September 15, 2006."

• • • •

FOR WALKER, MEETING STEVEN Tyler was another trip entirely. Tyler wanted to connect with him about working on what would become the singer's 2016 solo album and came to one of Walker's gigs in Phoenix. "I was playing this club, and it was sold out on a Friday night," Walker says. "And in the front row, the entire two-hour set, Steven Tyler is just watching me, five feet away. And he never moved. No one bothered him. He never looked away." When Walker left the stage for the encore break, Tyler grabbed him. "Hey, you're Steven Tyler," Walker recalls saying. "He goes, 'You are a badass motherfucker' and just starts hugging me. Then I say, 'Excuse me, I've got to go back out there.' I play two or three more songs and then we go to my bus and sit up until three in the morning. He's playing guitar riffs for me. He can't even hardly play guitar. It was such a cool moment, sitting there and just trying to get in a word with him. The fact that that's as far as it ever got with our relationship makes me happy."

As a teenager in Boston in the mid-'70s, Gary Cherone had his pick of hometown heroes: the J. Geils Band, the Modern Lovers, Boston. He chose Aerosmith. "That was just a badge of honor," he says. "It wasn't, 'I like this band because they fit the zip code.' It was, 'Fuckin' Aerosmith comes from fuckin' Boston, man!'" When he started Extreme in 1985, he wanted to create the biggest band from Boston since Aerosmith. "That," he says, "was our template."

Paul Geary was the drummer and manager of Extreme when they were up-and-coming locals. In 1988, he got a call from Tim Collins. Guns N' Roses, who were scheduled to open for Aerosmith in Maine, had to cancel. "They were looking for who was hot in Boston," Cherone says. "So we go to Maine in our U-Haul, and we're wet behind the ears. We're used to playing clubs, and we see the big stage. I remember seeing cheat sheets with words for some of the songs and Tyler's mic stand with all the scarves. It was just surreal." Six years later Extreme were offered a support slot on a European leg of Aerosmith's Get a Grip tour. The first day, Tyler walked by Cherone to get to the stage. "Before I say hello, I shout out the first line of [*Toys in the Attic*'s] 'No More No More,'" he says. "*Blood stains the ivories of my daddy's baby grand!* Without missing a beat—he's like twenty feet away from me—he turns around and looks at me and says, 'I ain't seen no daylight since we started this band.' I'm looking at my manager and he says, 'That's fuckin' *TYLAHHH!*'"

. . . .

ON A WARM AND CLEAR Tuesday night in January 2018, at the Roxy Theatre on the Sunset Strip, Gary Cherone had a forestage view as rock-and-roll worlds collided. The evening's event, billed as Joe Perry and Friends, was a celebration of *Sweetzerland Manifesto*, the guitarist's sixth solo album, featuring a plethora of guest stars, many of whom were in attendance. The list

THEY JUST SEEM A LITTLE WEIRD

that night read like a who's who of Perry's influences, peers, and progeny—a high-decibel episode of *This Is Your Life*, brought to you by Marshall Amps.

Repping British blues-rock royalty: Terry Reid, whose raspy "Sick & Tired," a blistering Zep-infused rumble, was a highlight of both the album and the concert.

Repping the New York Dolls: David Johansen, who joked to the audience that he had known Perry since they were little. "I remember I was at his house one day," Johansen said, "and he said to his mother—he was about four or maybe five . . . 'Mommy, when I grow up, I'm gonna be a musician.' She said, 'You better make up your mind, Joey, 'cause you can't do both.'"

Repping Cheap Trick: the magnificent Robin Zander.

Repping the glam- and sleaze-rock contingent: Cherone and Slash.

Repping the grungier alternative: Stone Temple Pilots' Robert and Dean DeLeo.

The only thing missing was Starz opening the show.

Perry strode onstage wearing dark aviators and, draped in an assortment of necklaces and scarves that would have been deemed excessive by an ancient fortune teller, launched into a ferocious "Let the Music Do the Talking," with vocals by Cherone, who also ably tackled Aerosmith's "Toys in the Attic" and "Pandora's Box." Perry soon removed his black blazer to expose skinny arms both tanned and tattooed, encircled by multiple bracelets. To perform the single, "Aye, Aye, Aye," Zander appeared in a dark porkpie hat, gripping the mic stand and leaning in to growl, while Perry attacked his custom Gibson B.B. King Lucille adorned with a portrait of his wife, Billie, the song's inspiration (a "smilin' face with those Gibson thighs").

Offstage, familiar figures lurked in the crowd, including Jack Douglas (who helped produce the album), ZZ Top's Billy Gibbons, and Guns N' Roses and Velvet Revolver's Duff McKagan and Matt Sorum. At one VIP table, former Aerosmith tech "Nitebob" Czaykowski sat with former Aerosmith tour mate Gene Simmons, there to support a friend who contributed to his own solo album a half century earlier and, it turns out, to noodge his onetime live sound engineer. "He kept offering me food," Czaykowski says. "'Have a chicken finger. You sure you don't want an onion ring?' I'm like, 'Yeah. I'm definitely sure.'"

After the concert, while Czaykowski was catching up with Perry, the guitarist asked him, "Where'd you watch the show?"

"I sat at a table with Gene Simmons."

As if by reflex, Perry shot back, "Did he make you pick up the check?"

# EPILOGUE

**THE NEW CENTURY ALSO** brought with it a mad burst of inter-band business. Both Rick Nielsen and Joe Perry found themselves contributing licks to the opening theme for *Monday Night Football* in 2006. In 2012, Cheap Trick once again supported Aerosmith on a bunch of North American dates, this time with Daxx Nielsen, Rick's son, and without Bun E. Carlos, who'd acrimoniously fallen out with the band two years earlier. (He still retains a quarter stake in Cheap Trick, despite no longer recording or touring with them.) Robin Zander admitted his competitive streak surfaced when touring with Steven Tyler. "It's like having a big brother, where you're always trying to kick his ass," he said. "I'm pretty confident, but it's fun to watch him." In 2014, Zander went to South Africa with Tyler, this time as part of the all-star supergroup Kings of Chaos (featuring members of Guns N' Roses, ZZ Top, and Extreme). That same year, Cheap Trick played the pre-boarding party for the KISS Kruise (although not with KISS themselves), and Zander performed solo (with his son) on the ship as well as a Beatles set with Tommy Thayer.

Jack Douglas continued to produce sessions for Cheap Trick, including a ripping version of "She Said She Said," replete with a Joe Perry solo, for an all-star tribute to the Beatles, and he worked with Aerosmith on their two most recent studio albums, 2004's *Honkin' on Bobo* and 2012's *Music from Another Dimension!* For a 2020 MusiCares benefit honoring Aerosmith's philanthropic work, Cheap Trick added the band's "Rats in the Cellar" to their repertoire of solid covers. Three years earlier, Cheap Trick paid homage to the group that helped launch them in 1977 by including the KISS logo on the back cover of *We're All Alright!* And in 2019, Ace Frehley announced that Robin Zander would be singing a Humble Pie cover on the guitarist's forthcoming solo album.

NEARLY SIX DECADES INTO their careers, Aerosmith and KISS were busy taking victory laps in their snakeskin shitkickers and dragon-headed platform boots, with the former playing a fiftieth anniversary residency in Las Vegas and the latter embarking on a three-year-long final tour. A rejuvenated Cheap Trick, who parlayed their indie spirit into a twenty-first-century recording spree (six albums and counting), continued to headline clubs and theaters and open for the likes of Def Leppard, Poison, and ZZ Top. "The story of Cheap Trick since the early to mid-'80s has been them getting their confidence back," says Ira Robbins. "You can argue that KISS's story is not that dissimilar. Rock-and-roll bands were never conceived to last forty years. That's fighting against nature."

Starz rejoined that fight by capitalizing on the small but devoted following they had accumulated since their brief five-year run. For years Richie Ranno continued to sell rock memorabilia, teach guitar, and play in various combos at local New Jersey bars and pizza joints. His bandmates, for the most part, took other jobs and had other interests: Michael Lee Smith, an avid builder of plastic model kits, became a process server; Joe X. Dubé, a landscape architect and Ranno's frequent live foil. But they couldn't resist the call of their cult. In the early 2000s, with new bassist George DiAna, they reunited for gigs, and in 2013 headed for the first time to the U.K., where they played with superfans Alex Kane (on guitar) and Ginger Wildheart (on bass). A 2019 club tour with Angel, featuring original members Frank DiMino and Punky Meadows, climaxed in a gig that for one faction of '70s rock fans may have elicited a resounding "so what," but for another caused a collective head explosion. At an amphitheater just outside of St. Louis, both bands—along with Enuff Z'Nuff—opened for old comrade Ace Frehley, then promoting his eighth solo album. Called *Spaceman*, it featured a pair of songs written with his on-again/off-again nemesis, the fire-spewing, blood-spitting, shit-stirring Demon himself, Gene Simmons. Considering the two musicians' history of breaking up and making up—and their achievements always to be linked in admirers' minds—one of their collaborations spoke volumes. Its title: "Without You I'm Nothing."

# ACKNOWLEDGMENTS

**WHEN I FIRST CAME** up with the idea for this book in 2010, I never thought I'd end up writing it in two countries and partly during a global pandemic. But here we are.

To begin, of course, I have to thank all the members of KISS, Cheap Trick, Aerosmith, and Starz, past and present, for creating the art that inspired me to undertake this endeavor. In particular, Bun E. Carlos, Joe X. Dubé, Rick Nielsen, Richie Ranno, Michael Lee Smith, and Paul Stanley all gave generously of their time and endured my Olympic-level follow-up pestering. Former Cheap Trick manager Ken Adamany truly went above and beyond, supplying me with photographs, correspondence, vintage flyers, and other ephemera that illuminated what was, for me, perhaps the most exciting era of modern popular music.

My deepest appreciation goes out to all the other folks I interviewed: Lee Abrams, Barry Ackom, Bob Aird, Art Alexakis, Brynn Arens, Allan Arkush, Sebastian Bach, Sher Bach, Cary Baker, Jay "Hot Sam" Barth, Lanny Bass, Susan Blond, Danny Brant, Bebe Buell, Ken Calvert, Dan Carlisle, Jim Charne, Gary Cherone, Desmond Child, Mark Cicchini, Gilby Clarke, Tim Collins, Lydia Criss, Phil "Magic" Cristian, Dale Crover, Bob "Nitebob" Czaykowski, Jonathan Daniel, Clive Davis, Orville Davis, Chip Dayton, Leon Delaney, Ron Delsener, Dennis DeYoung, Taime Downe, Robert Duncan, Chuck Eddy, Bill Elson, Brad Elvis, Zecca Esquibel, Jim Farber, Michael Fennelly, Marc Ferrari, Richie Fontana, Jackie Fox, Jeff Franklin, Richard Gerstein, Sam Ginsberg, Danny Goldberg, Lynn Goldsmith, Larry Gonsky, Michael Gross, Ian Guenther, Tracii Guns, Donald Handy, Brendan Harkin, Bob Heimall, Tod Howarth, Scott Ian, Neil Jason, Alex Kane, Carol Kaye, Barry Keane, Bob "Kelly" Kelleher, Sean Kelly, Bryan J. Kinnaird, David Krebs, Bruce Kulick,

## ACKNOWLEDGMENTS

Steve Leber, Chris Lendt, Bobby Locke, Elliot Lurie, Jack Malken, J Mascis, Larry Mazer, Steven McDonald, Bob Merlis, Bobby Messano, Jay Messina, Willi Morrison, John "Muzzy" Muzzarelli, Peter "Moose" Oreckinto, Rupert Perry, Kristina Sweval Peters, Binky Philips, Carl Plaster, Fritz Postlethwaite, Mark Radice, Bruce Ravid, Ira Robbins, Rikki Rockett, Gail Rodgers, Carol Ross, Gerald Rothberg, David Rule, John Scher, Allan Schwartzberg, Paul Shaffer, Arnie Silver, Michele Slater, Wesley Strick, Ken Stringfellow, Rick Stuart, Ted Templeman, Kim Thayil, Josh Todd, Dean Tokuno, Eric Troyer, Eddie Trunk, Stephanie Tudor, Ray Tusken, Jaan Uhelszki, John Varvatos, Butch Walker, Mitch Weissman, Bruce Wendell, Tom Werman, Steve West, Richard Whitley, Ginger Wildheart, Zakk Wylde, Richie Zito, and Chip Z'Nuff. Despite my numerous requests, I did not speak to Gene Simmons for this book, but I did draw from an interview I conducted with him for the December 2009 issue of *SPIN* magazine.

Thanks also to those who offered keen insights but whose voices did not make it into the final draft: Bill Baker, Brian Chin, Jim DeTore, Michael "Eppy" Epstein, Michael Freedberg, and Mark Slaughter.

My agent, Roger Freet, took a chance on a first-time author and steered me through uncharted waters (for one thing, forbidding me to call this book "a labor of love") and assuaged my panic attacks with his remarkably soothing phoneside manner. By pulling an ace (or should I say, a Paul?) from his back pocket, he helped make this an infinitely better book.

My editor, Ben Schafer, is a man not only of impeccable taste, but also of enviable patience and boundless enthusiasm. His response to my proposal and manuscript made it all worthwhile. Thanks to copyeditor Susan VanHecke, senior production editor Michael Clark, designers Jeff Williams and Timothy O'Donnell, Carrie Napolitano, Quinn Fariel, Michael Giarratano, and everyone else at Hachette for helping to bring this labor of lo—excuse me—*dream project* to fruition. And a big high five to all the photographers who contributed the images—some previously unseen—that are found within.

Mike Edison, Larry "Ratso" Sloman, and especially David Browne—all of whose own titles are worth seeking out—schooled me in the world of book publishing, offering tips, pointers, even the occasional piece of advice. In my eyes, David's brilliant *Fire and Rain* is the ne plus ultra multistrand, multiartist music biography.

Paul Pollard and Gillian Canavan at Pace Gallery and Tom Prince at *Mosaic* kept me busy with non-music-related assignments that helped buy the proverbial baby new pairs of figurative shoes.

Sean Kelly, whose zeal for all four bands is matched only by my own, read an early draft and offered much-needed perspective, while also supplying important contact info.

Kudos to both JD Doyle, of Queer Music Heritage, and Lee Newton, who shared useful articles and information on the Skatt Bros. and Starz, respectively. Newspapers.com, AmericanRadioHistory.com, Rock's Backpages, Facebook, YouTube, and Temi.com proved to be invaluable online resources.

Anthony DeCurtis, Carla Dragotti, Dave Frey, Ethan Galloway, Dayna Ghiraldi-Travers, Clive Hodson, Adam Holt, Giulian Jones, Bill Meis, Giovanna Melchiorre, John Petkovic, Carrie Thornton, Ken Weinstein, and Jon Wiederhorn all helped me to secure essential interviews.

Much respect to David Hajdu and Jim Meigs, who taught me more about the power of words and the making of magazines than I ever thought I'd learn. Their impact on my career as a writer and editor has been immense and profound.

A guy couldn't ask for better buddies and boosters than Rich Brown, Bob Fingerman, Mitch Friedland, Owen Gleiberman, Mike Haft, Dean Haspiel, Mike Hueston, Jeff Kelson, Glenn Kenny, Ian McCaleb, Jack Rabid, Jason Roth, Eric Saul, Bryan Swirsky, and the late Marc Spitz. Karin Adlhoch, Chris Baldiserra, Ted Bisaillion, Marjorie and Michael Boyle, Fatima Bregman, Ursula Buck, James Evenson, Quirien Muylwyk, Hugh Shewell, Ilene Solomon, and especially Susan Rothfels and Virginia and Finn MacDonald made my family's transition from Brooklyn to Toronto, in the midst of my writing, smoother than it had any right to be. But with family like Shari, Steven, Sydney, Ryan, and Mackenzie Silverman and Brendan, Lily, and Beatrice Boyle, who needs friends? Thanks also to my mom, Helen Brod, who kept wondering when I was going to finish and made sure that I did.

I tip my slightly ragged Starz baseball cap (purchased at a 2010 reunion gig in Teaneck, New Jersey) in the direction of Steve Appleford, Matthew Berlyant, Owen MacDonald, Rebecca Patton, and Scott Schinder for their assistance with transcriptions.

Four gentlemen deserve special mention for all that they brought to this project. When it came to transcripts, Mark Suppanz did some of the heaviest lifting. His precision and efficiency were nothing less than superheroic. My droll and acerbic compadre Rob Kemp cleaned up a ton of interviews, read an early draft, and made crucial suggestions that helped to expand the book's breadth while sharpening its focus. My longtime friend Ira Robbins let me dive into his extraordinary archive and has accompanied me to more

ACKNOWLEDGMENTS

Cheap Trick shows than I can count. (I'm additionally indebted to him and Kristina Juzaitis for their Brooklyn hospitality and first-rate mail-forwarding skills.) Steve Korn—one of my oldest, dearest, and smartest pals—read the manuscript early on, and his encyclopedic brain and bionic, albeit bespectacled, eyes saved me from a lot of grief. I owe him more than I'll ever be able to repay.

Finally, my wife, Rachel, and my daughter, Sasha, the loves of my life, put up with my monthslong, self-imposed subterranean exile, weren't *too* annoyed by how loudly I spoke on the phone, and showered me with constant affection. They made enormous sacrifices to grant me the time and freedom I needed to tell this story, and I am eternally grateful for their support. They are my rocks, as well as the collective beating heart of this book. I could not have written it without them.

# SOURCES AND NOTES

FOR THIS BOOK, I conducted interviews with 136 people—in person, by phone, by email, and via FaceTime and Skype—mostly between October 2017 and April 2020. Some subjects, including Ken Adamany, Bun E. Carlos, Rick Nielsen, Richie Ranno, and Michael Lee Smith, I spoke with on multiple occasions. A number of quotations from Nielsen and Gene Simmons originated in my transcripts of earlier conversations for stories published in *SPIN* magazine. Throughout the book, quotes from interviews I conducted are attributed to their speakers in the present tense.

Others' books, magazine and newspaper articles, interviews, documents, podcasts, video footage, and posts on online forums and social media were vital to the creation of this work and if they are not cited within the text, their efforts are credited in the notes that follow. For YouTube citations, I generally listed the titles provided with the clips on the website, although I have altered a few for the sake of clarity. All chart positions were taken from Billboard.com and back issues of *Billboard* magazine.

## INTRODUCTION

Author interviews with Art Alexakis, Fritz Postlethwaite, Paul Stanley, Stephanie Tudor, Chris Lendt, Carol Ross, Eric Troyer, Gene Simmons, Neil Jason, Allan Schwartzberg, Richard Gerstein, Rick Nielsen, Richie Ranno, Gail Rodgers, Michele Slater, Mitch Weissman, and Butch Walker.

### Notes

1    *an estimated $100 million:* C.K. Lendt, *KISS and Sell: The Making of a Supergroup* (New York: Billboard Books, 1997), 162.

2    *"Nobody in the band"*: Paul Stanley, *Face the Music: A Life Exposed*, paperback ed. (New York: HarperOne, 2016), 229.

2    *"What did we know?"*: Gene Simmons, *KISS and Make-Up* (New York: Crown, 2001), 138.

2    *"We had broads"*: David Leaf and Ken Sharp, *KISS: Behind the Mask* (New York: Warner, 2003), 168.

2    *Doing ninety on Sepulveda*: Peter Criss and Larry "Ratso" Sloman, *Makeup to Breakup: My Life In and Out of KISS* (New York: Scribner, 2012), 169–172.

3    *"People openly laughed"*: Stanley, *Face the Music*, 230.

3    *"The rest of the band"*: Simmons, *KISS and Make-Up*, 138.

3    *"To be honest"*: Ace Frehley, Joe Layden, and John Ostrosky, *No Regrets: A Rock 'n' Roll Memoir* (New York: Gallery/MTV, 2011), 172.

4    *"to reinforce the idea"*: Criss and Sloman, *Makeup to Breakup*, 159.

4    *"We could all pursue"*: Frehley, Layden, and Ostrosky, *No Regrets*, 172.

4    *"These solo packages"*: Wesley Strick, *"Love Gun Is a Real Bazooka,"* *Circus*, August 4, 1977.

5    *"people you respected"*: Leaf and Sharp, *KISS: Behind the Mask*, 308.

5    *"The notion of the record"*: Leaf and Sharp, 309.

5    *"By that point"*: Leaf and Sharp, 307.

5    *"I excitedly played Cher"*: Simmons, *KISS and Make-Up*, 154.

5    *Simmons has claimed*: Simmons, 154.

7    *"We were buddies"*: Eddie Trunk, interview with Joe Perry, https://www.youtube.com /watch?v=QpHGB2k--Xs.

7    *"I was sitting"*: Leaf and Sharp, *KISS: Behind the Mask*, 309.

8    *"The guy sounds like Page"*: Gene Simmons, promotional interviews for KISS solo albums, 1978, https://youtu.be/kF-qcRrV4rI.

9    *"When I listened"*: Leaf and Sharp, *KISS: Behind the Mask*, 310.

9    *"just happened by"*: Simmons, promotional interviews for KISS solo albums.

10   *"to pay back Jiminy Cricket"*: Leaf and Sharp, *KISS: Behind the Mask*, 316.

11   *"I'd give it one star"*: Leaf and Sharp, 307.

## CHAPTER 1

Author interviews with Tom Werman, Paul Stanley, Binky Philips, Bob "Nitebob" Czaykowski, Ira Robbins, and Sher Bach.

## Notes

14   *"servicing the entire band"*: Simmons, *KISS and Make-Up*, 60.

15   *"I'm embarrassed by that album"*: Leaf and Sharp, *KISS: Behind the Mask*, 202.

15   *"a Frankenstein monster"*: Ken Sharp, Paul Stanley, and Gene Simmons, *Nothin' to Lose: The Making of KISS (1972–1975)* (New York: itbooks, 2013), 21.

15   *After his first audition*: Curt Gooch and Jeff Suhs, *KISS Alive Forever* (New York: Billboard Books, 2002), 14.

16   *"someone banging pots"*: Lynn Goldsmith, *KISS: 1977–1980* (New York: Rizzoli, 2017), unpaginated.

17   *"When they started playing"*: Michael Hann, "KISS: Monsters of Rock," *The Guardian*, July 12, 2012, www.theguardian.com/music/2012/jul/12/kiss-monsters-rock.

17   *"I thought their music"*: Leaf and Sharp, *KISS: Behind the Mask*, 180.

18   *"We were rehearsing"*: Hann, "KISS: Monsters of Rock."

19   *"We played and said"*: Sharp, Stanley, and Simmons, *Nothin' to Lose*, 109.

## CHAPTER 2

Author interviews with Clive Davis, Steve Leber, Bob "Kelly" Kelleher, Ron Delsener, David Krebs, Bebe Buell, and Brad Elvis.

## Notes

21   *"Ladies and gentlemen"*: Aerosmith and Stephen Davis, *Walk This Way: The Autobiography of Aerosmith*, paperback ed. (New York: itbooks, 2012), 161.

22   *"We had a big party"*: Sharp, Stanley, and Simmons, *Nothin' to Lose*, 333–334.

23   *"I thought they were the best"*: Ira Robbins, "Perry Meets the Press," *Trouser Press*, November 1978.

24   *For Krebs, the key*: Ed McCormack, "Aerosmith's Wrench Rock," *Rolling Stone*, August 26, 1976.

24   *After the Isleys*: Aerosmith and Davis, *Walk This Way*, 208.

25   *"Todd hated the band"*: Christopher Walsh, "Jack Douglas: Talent, Egos, and Rock's Holy Grail," *East Hampton Star*, October 5, 2017, www.easthamptonstar.com/archive/jack-douglas-talent-egos-and-rocks-holy-grail.

25   *"Todd didn't come in"*: Joe Bosso, "Production Legend Jack Douglas on 18 Career-Defining Records," *Music Radar*, December 19, 2012, www.musicradar.com/news/guitars/production-legend-jack-douglas-on-18-career-defining-records-568681.

25   *"three or four times"*: Joe Perry and David Ritz, *Rocks: My Life In and Out of Aerosmith* (New York: Simon & Schuster, 2014), 131.

26   *"He wasn't like one"*: Aerosmith and Davis, *Walk This Way*, 206.

26   *"KISS at the beginning"*: Aerosmith and Davis, 219.

## CHAPTER 3

Author interviews with Zecca Esquibel, Binky Philips, Carol Kaye, Jay "Hot Sam" Barth, Leon Delaney, Paul Stanley, Bob "Kelly" Kelleher, Peter "Moose" Oreckinto, Ken Calvert, Dan Carlisle, Steve Leber, Michael Fennelly, Donald Handy, Bob "Nitebob" Czaykowski, and Jackie Fox.

### Notes

28   *claimed he worked briefly:* Bryan J. Kinnaird, *Sean Delaney's Hellbox* (Bloomington, IN: Xlibris, 2004), 43.

28   *"Initially we resisted":* Simmons, *KISS and Make-Up*, 84.

29   *"You can hit a guitar string":* Colette Dowling, "An Outrage Called KISS," *New York Times Magazine*, June 19, 1977.

30   *When the next evening's show:* Julian Gill, *KISS on Tour: 1973–1983* (n.p.: KissFAQ .com, 2016), 45.

30   *"People went nuts":* Aerosmith and Davis, *Walk This Way*, 222.

31   *"We're busting our asses":* Perry and Ritz, *Rocks*, 138.

31   *"They'd have their pyro":* Aerosmith and Davis, *Walk This Way*, 222.

31   *"It felt like we were going out":* Sharp, Stanley, and Simmons, *Nothin' to Lose*, 334.

31   *a motorized forklift-like contraption:* Peter Oreckinto, J.R. Smalling, Rick Munroe, and Mick Campise, *Out on the Streets: The True Tales of Life on the Road with the Hottest Band in the Land—KISS* (Burbank, CA: TOKK Publishing, 2014), 109.

31   *"I got into several shoving matches":* Gooch and Suhs, *KISS Alive Forever*, 29–30.

32   *"They had a cutthroat scene":* Aerosmith and Davis, *Walk This Way*, 222.

32   *"they were playing":* Leaf and Sharp, *KISS: Behind the Mask*, 120.

32   *"KISS was in the same":* Sharp, Stanley, and Simmons, *Nothin' to Lose*, 332.

32   *"I remember when we went out":* Mike Calta, interview with Joe Perry and Steven Tyler, "The Mike Calta Show," 102.5 The Bone, October 10, 2012, https://sound cloud.com/themikecaltashow/steven-tyler-and-joe-perry.

32   *One story goes:* Sharp, Stanley, and Simmons, *Nothin' to Lose*, 330.

## CHAPTER 4

Author interviews with Joe X. Dubé, Elliot Lurie, Larry Gonsky, Brendan Harkin, Michael Lee Smith, Bob Heimall, Kristina Sweval Peters, and Clive Davis.

### Notes

41   *"it made us dance":* John S. Wilson, "Music: New Brunswick Group a Hit," *New York Times*, July 9, 1972.

41    *The executive had been implicated:* Ben Fong-Torres, "Clive Davis Ousted; Payola Coverup Charged," *Rolling Stone*, July 5, 1973.

41    *Though he was not charged:* "Clive Davis Guilty in Tax Evasion," *New York Times*, May 25, 1976.

47    *Early in his career:* Fredric Dannen, *Hit Men*, paperback ed. (New York: Vintage, 1991), 68.

## CHAPTER 5

Author interviews with Rick Nielsen, Ken Adamany, Bun E. Carlos, and Cary Baker.

### Notes

48    *the comic actor was arrested:* "Huntz Hall Arrested," *New York Times*, October 30, 1948.

50    *"Not everybody":* Ira Robbins, interview with Rick Nielsen and Tom Petersson, April 1996 (transcript).

50    *In 1968:* Robbins, interview with Rick Nielsen and Tom Petersson.

50    *Two others were:* Dennis Beebe, "Fuse Interview," *It's Psychedelic Baby*, June 30, 2015, www.psychedelicbabymag.com/2015/06/fuse interview.html.

51    *Speaking to:* Ira Robbins, interview with Bun E. Carlos, Rick Nielsen, and Tom Petersson, November 1977 (transcript).

52    *"Our whole thing":* Bill DeYoung, "'The Best Rock Band Around': A Chat with Safety Harbor Resident Robin Zander, of Cheap Trick," *St. Pete Catalyst*, April 4, 2020, https://stpetecatalyst.com/the-best-rock-band-around-a-chat-with-safety -harbor-resident-robin-zander-of-cheap-trick/.

## CHAPTER 6

Author interviews with Scott Ian, Sebastian Bach, and Kim Thayil.

### Notes

54    *One night, Frehley damaged:* Frehley, Layden, and Ostrosky, *No Regrets*, 123–124.

54    *"It was overly compressed":* Leaf and Sharp, *KISS: Behind the Mask*, 223.

55    *He hastily arranged:* "How KISS's *Alive!* Saved Their Record Label—and Changed the Music Industry," *Mental Floss*, July 4, 2018, www.mentalfloss.com/article/62982/101 -masterpieces-kiss-alive.

56    *"Somehow," Simmons observed:* Leaf and Sharp, *KISS: Behind the Mask*, 243.

56    *selling more than nine million:* "How KISS's *Alive!* Saved Their Record Label."

## CHAPTER 7

Author interviews with Brendan Harkin, Binky Philips, Richie Ranno, Rick Stuart, Michael Lee Smith, Larry Gonsky, Rupert Perry, Bruce Ravid, and Carol Ross.

### Notes

63    *It was at a peace vigil:* William Hageman, "Chicago's Backstage Giant," *Chicago Tribune,* January 5, 2003.

67    *"When I first saw them":* David McGee, "Dialogue: The Jack Douglas Theory of Production," *Record World,* December 25, 1976.

68    *"Rather than slog away":* Geoff Barton, "The Brothers," *Sounds,* July 9, 1977.

69    *"It could hurt their chances":* David McGee, "Dialogue: Bill Aucoin on KISS, Rock Steady and the Future," *Record World,* August 14, 1976.

70    *"Brendan could never":* McGee, "Dialogue: The Jack Douglas Theory of Production."

## CHAPTER 8

Author interviews with Jay Messina, Paul Stanley, Butch Walker, Rick Stuart, Sher Bach, and Jackie Fox.

### Notes

71    *he had to get them:* James Campion, *Shout It Out Loud: The Story of KISS's Destroyer and the Making of an American Icon* (New York: Backbeat, 2015), 73.

72    *"It allowed me":* Frehley, Layden, and Ostrosky, *No Regrets,* 143–144.

72    *"We might've done":* McGee, "Dialogue: Bill Aucoin on KISS, Rock Steady and the Future."

72    *"bombast and melodrama":* Robert Christgau, "Christgau's Consumer Guide," *Village Voice,* June 14, 1976.

72    *"best album yet":* John Milward, "Destroyer," *Rolling Stone,* June 3, 1976.

73    *Ezrin "deprived them":* Rick Johnson, "Destroyer," *Creem,* July 1976.

73    *"one of Bob Ezrin's all-time masterpieces":* Lester Bangs, "Rock and Roll Over," *Circus,* February 14, 1977.

73    *"KISS are suffering":* Max Bell, "Destroyer," *New Musical Express,* April 24, 1976.

73    *"KISS retread":* Harry Doherty, "Destroyer," *Melody Maker,* April 17, 1976.

73    *"and that he would never even think":* Campion, *Shout It Out Loud,* 272.

73    *"I said, 'Fuck those guys!'":* Campion, 273.

73    *"I could have done KISS":* Aerosmith and Davis, *Walk This Way,* 292.

74    *"But I don't hold grudges":* Dan Leroy, "He Didn't Write the Songs," *New York Times,* May 8, 2005.

74 *"It wasn't pristine"*: Slash, "The Record That Changed My Life: Slash Discusses Aerosmith's 'Rocks,'" *Guitar World*, August 26, 2013, www.guitarworld.com/gw -archive/record-changed-my-life-slash-discusses-aerosmiths-rocks.

74 *"Brandy" inspired the lyrics*: Stanley, *Face the Music*, 207.

74 *"Give a band a look"*: Stanley, 203.

## CHAPTER 9

Author interviews with Richie Ranno, Ray Tusken, Rupert Perry, Paul Stanley, Joe X. Dubé, Chip Z'Nuff, Chip Dayton, Brendan Harkin, Carol Ross, Rick Stuart, Jeff Franklin, Rick Nielsen, and Michael Lee Smith.

### Notes

76 *"Starz like to take"*: Timothy Green Beckley, "Michael Lee Smith Takes On the Girls," *Super Rock*, February 1978.

77 *"The issue for me"*: Charles M. Young, "Starz Goes Down the Drain," *Rolling Stone*, December 2, 1976.

77 *"The only way I would say"*: Beckley, "Michael Lee Smith Takes On the Girls."

78 *"I might have if I was a KISS fan"*: Barton, "The Brothers."

78 *"Sometimes we'll get people"*: Steve Wosahla, "In the Groove: Starz," *Allentown (N.J.) Messenger-Press*, December 21, 1978.

78 *"Well, I think people just need"*: Hannah G. Spitzer, "Starz: Are They Ready to Nova?," unidentified magazine.

78 *"Bill Aucoin, as far as I know"*: McGee, "The Jack Douglas Theory of Production."

78 *"With KISS and Aerosmith"*: "Starz," *Cash Box*, June 26, 1976.

78 *"you guessed it—Aerosmith meets KISS"*: Max Bell, "Starz," *New Musical Express*, January 15, 1977.

78 *"KISS is a product"*: Lester Bangs, "Starz," *Circus*, January 31, 1977.

79 *"a promising middleweight contender"*: Michael Davis, "Attention Shoppers!," *Creem*, April 1978.

79 *The plan included*: "Starz—ABC Saturday Evening News, 1976," https://youtu.be/juj C2AsBsdk.

80 *At that fiasco*: John Kifner, "3 Shot in Chicago During Rock Riot," *New York Times*, July 28, 1970.

81 *The show went on*: "'Misguided' Blamed for Sox Park Fire," *Chicago Tribune*, July 12, 1976.

81 *The standard line*: "Windy City Show Moved to New Site," *Billboard*, August 14, 1976.

83 *"I think that"*: Martin Popoff, *Cool One: Starz, Violation, Attention Shoppers! & Coliseum Rock* (Toronto: Zunior, 2013), 39.

# CHAPTER 10

Author interviews with Ken Adamany, Bun E. Carlos, Brad Elvis, Tom Werman, Jay Messina, Jim Charne, Rick Nielsen, Susan Blond, Alex Kane, Kim Thayil, Ira Robbins, Bill Elson, Paul Stanley, John "Muzzy" Muzzarelli, Barry Ackom, Fritz Postlethwaite, Lydia Criss, Steven McDonald, Gilby Clarke, Art Alexakis, Jackie Fox, and Tracii Guns.

## Notes

86    *"I was knocked out"*: Bob Lefsetz, "Jack Douglas," *The Bob Lefsetz Podcast*, May 2, 2019, www.iheart.com/podcast/1119-the-bob-lefsetz-podcast-30806836/episode/jack -douglas-30970907/.

87    *Douglas has said that after the show*: Thomas Dew, interview with Jack Douglas, https://youtu.be/-nFi-RTPa5E.

88    *"We were signed with two drummers"*: Andy Greene, "Cheap Trick's Rick Nielsen on Rock and Roll Hall of Fame: 'I'm Verklempt.'" *Rolling Stone*, December 17, 2015. www.rollingstone.com/music/music-news/cheap-tricks-rick-nielsen-on-rock-and -roll-hall-of-fame-im-verklempt-40327/.

90    *"Without missing a beat"*: Tom Barnard, interview with Don Felder, Ace Frehley, Rick Nielsen, and Gene Simmons, KQRS-FM, September 20, 2017, https://youtu.be /r94oLD6FZhc.

90    *"And then I took it"*: Barnard, interview with Don Felder, Ace Frehley, Rick Nielsen, and Gene Simmons.

90    *"Give me my money back"*: Rick Nielsen speech at the Music Academy in Rockford, Illinois, January 18, 2015, https://youtu.be/Ik21Ok5G4W4.

90    *"Literally, I was smitten"*: Barnard, interview with Don Felder, Ace Frehley, Rick Nielsen, and Gene Simmons.

93    *"All those things"*: Ira Robbins, interview with Rick Nielsen, May 2012 (transcript).

93    *"sarcastic, smart, nasty"*: Ira Robbins, "Cheap Trick," *Trouser Press*, April 1977.

93    *"These guys play rock & roll"*: Charles M. Young, "Cheap Trick," *Rolling Stone*, May 5, 1977.

93    *"recalls the Aerosmith of Rocks"*: Robert Christgau, "Cheap Trick," *Village Voice*, www .robertchristgau.com/get_chap.php?k=C&bk=70.

94    *"established no original style"*: Ken Tucker, "Cheap Trick," *Circus*, issue unknown.

94    *The album finally surfaced*: Ira Robbins, interview with Rick Nielsen, September 1980 (transcript).

95    *"They were the lamest"*: Jeff Symonds, "Cheap Trick Threepeats," *E! News*, September 27, 1998, www.eonline.com/news/37062/cheap-trick-threepeats.

95    *"the band that your parents"*: Leaf and Sharp, *KISS: Behind the Mask*, 178.

95 *"You know when you're growing up"*: Gwen Inhat, "Guitar God Rick Nielsen Talks About Cheap Trick's Earliest Hits," *AV Club*, March 10, 2016, https://music.avclub .com/guitar-god-rick-nielsen-talks-about-cheap-trick-s-earli-1798245491.

96 *"We were amazingly flattered"*: Mike Hayes and Ken Sharp, *Reputation Is a Fragile Thing: The Story of Cheap Trick* (Willow Grove, PA: Poptastic!, 1998), 52.

97 *Douglas has said that he chose*: Lefsetz, "Jack Douglas."

99 *"That's not really makeup"*: Cary Baker, "Cheap Trick: Interview," *Big Star Fanzine*, spring 1978.

99 *"We were doing well"*: Steve Harris and Yoichi Shibuya, interview with Rick Nielsen, November 15, 1988, https://youtu.be/PBI-fro18Jw.

100 *"an up-and-thundering hard rock band"*: John Kafentzis, "Not Exactly a 'KISS Good Night' in Spokane," *Spokesman-Review*, August 12, 1977.

101 *"Wait till you go on tour"*: Ira Robbins, interview with Bun E. Carlos, Rick Nielsen, and Tom Petersson, November 1977 (transcript).

101 *"And we're all"*: Robbins, interview with Bun E. Carlos, Rick Nielsen, and Tom Petersson.

101 *"We realized when we were out"*: Tom Kidd, "Cheap Trick: The Long and Winding Road," *Music Connection*, October 17–30, 1988.

102 *"I needed them"*: Warren Huart, interview with Jack Douglas, June 2019, https:// youtu.be/qchBSQZ5QAM.

102 *"It was a parody"*: Interview with Tom Petersson, *From Tokyo to You* DVD, Big Three Entertainment, 2003.

104 *"The label tried to make us"*: Ken Sharp, "Cheap Trick: 'For Us, Budokan Was Like Winning the Lottery,'" *Classic Rock*, November 2008.

104 *"I'll put it to you this way"*: Baker, "Cheap Trick: Interview."

105 *"They put a lot of emphasis"*: Ken Sharp, liner notes to *Cheap Trick Budokan!* box set, Epic/Legacy Recordings, 2008, 6.

105 *"It was inspiration"*: Daisann McLane, "Cheap Trick Find Heaven," *Rolling Stone*, June 14, 1979.

107 *"As a producer in Japan"*: Interview with Norio Nonaka, *Cheap Trick Budokan!* box set DVD, Epic/Legacy Recordings, 2008.

108 *"I had offered Aerosmith"*: Matt Hurwitz, "Classic Tracks: *Cheap Trick at Budokan*," *Mix*, August 9, 2017, www.mixonline.com/recording/classic-tracks-cheap-trick -budokan-430181.

109 *"I think it's a pretty shitty record"*: Steve Harris, interview with Robin Zander (Cheap Trick, part 7), 1990, https://youtu.be/d5laLOlyDoQ.

109 *"Budokan came out"*: Steve Harris, interview with Tom Petersson (Cheap Trick, part 10), 1990, https://youtu.be/7cLxy4l1dUU.

## CHAPTER 11

Author interviews with Bob "Nitebob" Czaykowski, Bebe Buell, Robert Duncan, Jaan Uhelszki, Lynn Goldsmith, Ira Robbins, Michael Gross, Gerald Rothberg, Wesley Strick, Jonathan Daniel, Art Alexakis, Gilby Clarke, Gary Cherone, Kim Thayil, and Danny Goldberg.

### Notes

118   *He claimed that ad pages:* Larry Harris, Curt Gooch, and Jeff Suhs, *And Party Every Day: The Inside Story of Casablanca Records* (New York: Backbeat, 2009), 108.

118   *"gave Circus the incentive":* Leaf and Sharp, *KISS: Behind the Mask,* 155.

119   *"The best thing about being so successful":* Strick, "Love Gun Is a Real Bazooka."

119   *"Japanese women":* Strick.

119   *"Starz sweats sex":* Wesley Strick, "Upstarts: Starz Sweatz Noise," *Circus,* September 28, 1976.

119   *" 'Cherry Baby' . . . sounds":* Wesley Strick, "Starz Story," *Circus,* April 28, 1977.

119   *"a band without":* Wesley Strick, "Attention Shoppers!," *Circus,* issue unknown.

## CHAPTER 12

Author interviews with Bill Elson, John Scher, Jeff Franklin, Ron Delsener, Dennis DeYoung, Sam Ginsberg, and Art Alexakis.

### Notes

122   *He treated the music:* Jim Farber, "The Legendary Promoters of Rock: Inside an Eye-Opening New Documentary," *The Guardian,* November 14, 2018, www.theguardian .com/film/2018/nov/14/the-shows-the-thing-documentary-frank-barsalona-rock -promoters.

122   *By 1979, he was representing:* "Billboard International Talent Directory 1979–80," *Billboard,* September 15, 1979.

123   *These promoters encouraged:* Farber, "The Legendary Promoters of Rock."

126   *"the beginning of the end":* Perry and Ritz, *Rocks,* 170.

126   *Jack Douglas admitted:* Aerosmith and Davis, *Walk This Way,* 292.

126   *"A lot of the time":* Aerosmith and Davis, 296.

## CHAPTER 13

Author interviews with Richie Ranno, Joe X. Dubé, Michael Lee Smith, Brendan Harkin, Arnie Silver, Jackie Fox, Steve West, Rikki Rockett, Gail Rodgers, Jonathan Daniel, Jack Malken, Ray Tusken, Orville Davis, Bobby Messano, Bruce Ravid, and Marc Ferrari.

## Notes

130 *"an English knock-off"*: Aerosmith and Davis, *Walk This Way*, 271.

131 *"Yeah, 1976 had Aerosmith"*: Nikki Sixx, "The Artist as Critic," *Details*, July 1991.

131 *"Such a cool song"*: Nikki Sixx (@NikkiSixx), Twitter, October 21, 2019, https://twitter.com/nikkisixx/status/1186450518568161282.

135 *"Nobody will ever know"*: Brendan Harkin, The Other Board forum, March 22, 2009, www.tapatalk.com/groups/starzfanzcentral/attention-shoppers-t2773-s10.html.

136 *"Fleetwood Mac doesn't have an image"*: Richard Hogan, "Starz Erase Their Punk Image," *Circus*, March 2, 1978.

137 *"All of those gimmicks"*: Zach Dunkin, "Starz and Foghat Pack Center," *Indianapolis News*, February 20, 1978.

138 *"went around Toronto"*: Popoff, *Cool One*, 47.

142 *"We put about a half million dollars"*: Michael Butler, "Episode 273: An Interview with Bill Aucoin," *Rock and Roll Geek Show*, podcast, November 2007, http://rockandrollgeek.libsyn.com/rock-and-roll-geek-show-273-an-interview-with-bill-aucoin.

## CHAPTER 14

Author interviews with Allan Arkush, Bun E. Carlos, Richard Whitley, Ken Adamany, Mark Cicchini, and Sebastian Bach.

## Notes

145 *Nielsen has said:* Hayes and Sharp, *Reputation Is a Fragile Thing*, 71.

145 *Nielsen also had another project:* Robbins, interview with Rick Nielsen and Tom Petersson.

## CHAPTER 15

Author interviews with Paul Shaffer, Neil Jason, Willi Morrison, Richie Fontana, Gail Rodgers, Ian Guenther, Barry Keane, Bobby Locke, Dean Tokuno, Jim Farber, Chuck Eddy, Bob Aird, and Danny Brant.

## Notes

147 *Casablanca put some sixty-nine albums:* Harris, Gooch, and Suhs, *And Party Every Day*, 280–289.

147 *"force-fed millions of albums"*: Dannen, *Hit Men*, 5.

147 *"rash of cheap signings"*: Harris, Gooch, and Suhs, *And Party Every Day*, 245.

147 *Casablanca designated his debut:* Harris, Gooch, and Suhs, 282–283.

149 *In its capsule review:* "Highway," *Cash Box*, January 20, 1979.

153  *"There's a lot of influence"*: Dwight Russ, "Three Are Gay, Three Just Play, and Skatt Ain't No Family Name!," *In Touch for Men*, September/October 1980.

154  *"For those of our kind"*: "Skatt Bros.," *The Advocate*, May 1, 1980.

154  *"a gale-force rock band"*: Russ, "Three Are Gay, Three Just Play."

154  *"a strong debut"*: "Strange Spirits," *Record World*, December 1, 1979.

154  *"Here comes some"*: Greg Beebe, "Quick Discs," *Santa Cruz (CA) Sentinel*, February 8, 1980.

155  *As if to remove all doubt*: Gayle Rubin, "Music from a Bygone Era," *Cuir Underground*, May 1997, www.black-rose.com/cuiru/archive/3-4/musichist.html.

155  *And in an unofficial YouTube video*: Fan-made Skatt Bros. "Walk the Night" music video, https://youtu.be/7ogydMMtHZA.

155  *Jake Shears*: Peter Robinson, "Jake Shears Interview," *Popjustice*, August 26, 2009, https://www.popjustice.com/articles/jake-shears-interview-2/.

157  *the song hit No. 13*: "Hits of the World," *Billboard*, November 1, 1980.

## CHAPTER 16

Author interviews with Desmond Child, Ira Robbins, Chuck Eddy, Jay Messina, and Gene Simmons.

### Notes

161  *"The girls"*: Stanley, *Face the Music*, 235.

162  *"That evening was a declaration"*: Dave Hoekstra, "The Night Disco Died," *Chicago*, July 2016.

163  *"Pretty crappy"*: Leaf and Sharp, *KISS: Behind the Mask*, 331.

163  *"Vini's input"*: Leaf and Sharp, 334.

164  *"Maybe they thought"*: Criss and Sloman, *Makeup to Breakup*, 198.

164  *"I wanted to give him"*: Frehley, Layden, and Ostrosky, *No Regrets*, 211.

165  *During all this turmoil*: Stanley, *Face the Music*, 244–245.

165  *They had to have been*: "KISS Intro Eric Carr—Kids Are People Too '80," https://youtu.be/wWNJ8Ndh6kI.

166  *"in a blur of drinking"*: Frehley, Layden, and Ostrosky, *No Regrets*, 218.

166  *freebase-addicted*: Stanley, *Face the Music*, 269.

166  *and who initially took 25 percent*: Geraldine Fabrikant, "Talking Money with KISS: The Bad Boys Start Watching Their Pockets," *New York Times*, February 23, 1997.

166  *Simmons and Stanley let him go*: Stanley, *Face the Music*, 271.

166  *"He was effective"*: Fabrikant, "Talking Money with KISS."

## CHAPTER 17

Author interviews with Ken Adamany, Bun E. Carlos, Carol Kaye, and Marc Ferrari.

### Notes

168    *recorded with members of:* Julian Gill, *Gene Simmons: The Vault Supplement* (n.p.: KissFAQ.com, 2018), 82.

169    *But for the band:* Joe Daly, "The Wild and Deadly Story Behind the 1979 World Series of Rock," *Louder*, October 17, 2019, www.loudersound.com/features/the -wild-and-deadly-story-behind-the-1979-world-series-of-rock.

169    *"Being in Aerosmith":* Aerosmith and Davis, *Walk This Way*, 348.

169    *"I swore that night":* Aerosmith and Davis, 347.

169    *"We were pretty burned out":* Steve Appleford, "Aerosmith's Joe Perry Talks Stripped-Down New Solo Album, Fiery Release Show," *Rolling Stone*, January 18, 2018, www .rollingstone.com/music/music-features/aerosmiths-joe-perry-talks-stripped-down -new-solo-album-fiery-release-show-204218/.

169    *"a friend of Jack's":* Aerosmith and Davis, *Walk This Way*, 376.

## CHAPTER 18

Author interviews with Bun E. Carlos, Tom Werman, Rick Nielsen, Carl Plaster, Tim Collins, Steven McDonald, Bob "Nitebob" Czaykowski, Ira Robbins, Ken Adamany, Phil "Magic" Cristian, and Arnie Silver.

### Notes

171    *Petersson had fallen ill:* Ira Robbins, interview with Tom Petersson, fall 1980 (transcript).

171    *"He left for medical reasons":* Kidd, "Cheap Trick: The Long and Winding Road."

174    *Martin worked hard:* George Martin letter to Ken Adamany, March 31, 1980.

174    *"After a while":* Moira McCormick, "Tom Peterson Hoping for Life After Cheap Trick," *Billboard*, September 15, 1984.

174    *"We should never have gotten":* Robbins, interview with Rick Nielsen and Tom Petersson.

174    *Comita has said:* B.J. Kramp and Ken Mills, "#40: Pete Comita," *Cheap Talk*, podcast, March 20, 2017, http://cheaptalktrickchat.blogspot.com.

175    *Zander taking his KISS record out:* Robert Lawson, *Still Competition: The Listener's Guide to Cheap Trick* (Victoria, BC: Friesen, 2017), 76.

175    *"There's no fire":* Sharp, *Cheap Trick Budokan!*, 19.

176    *"I went berserk":* Aerosmith and Davis, *Walk This Way*, 391.

177   CBS Records sued Cheap Trick: "CBS Sues Cheap Trick Over Contract Dispute," Cash Box, August 15, 1981.

177   the band countersued: "Cheap Trick Files Pact Suit," Billboard, August 22, 1981.

178   "Pete got in the studio": Robbins, interview with Rick Nielsen and Tom Petersson.

179   The previous night: Aerosmith and Davis, Walk This Way, 419.

179   Soon after Mercury Records: Freddie Tieken, "The Beat Goes On," http://fred dietieken.com/1960s-1970s/.

181   "Seemingly, from the minute we arrived": Eric Carmen, EricCarmen.com community, March 5, 2011, http://ericcarmen.com/forums/index.php?/topic/22702-rock-super -session/&page=2.

181   "It turned into another": B.J. Kramp and Ken Mills, "#41: Thom Mooney," Cheap Talk, podcast, May 19, 2017, http://cheaptalktrickchat.blogspot.com.

182   "That's a piece of shit": Steve Harris, interview with Rick Nielsen (Cheap Trick, part 8), 1990, https://youtu.be/k61q_JEkrRU.

182   While living in L.A.: Steve Harris, interview with Tom Petersson (Cheap Trick, part 10), 1990, https://youtu.be/7cLxy4l1dUU.

182   playing what Petersson described: Steve Harris, interview with Tom Petersson (Cheap Trick, part 9), 1990, https://youtu.be/FT2EVZbuG9g.

182   "He just took off": Steve Harris, interview with Robin Zander (Cheap Trick, part 6), 1990, https://youtu.be/Tz_NbtcnAOQ.

## CHAPTER 19

Author interviews with Jaan Uhelszki, Steven McDonald, Scott Ian, Dale Crover, Butch Walker, Eddie Trunk, Alex Kane, and Ginger Wildheart.

## CHAPTER 20

Author interviews with Richie Ranno, Lee Abrams, Eddie Trunk, Ray Tusken, and Bruce Wendell.

### Notes

190   increased its share: Marc Fisher, Something in the Air: Radio, Rock, and the Revolution That Shaped a Generation (New York: Random House, 2007), 195–196.

192   "Superstars hasn't limited": "Capitol's Tusken Applauds Superstars Special Projects," Cash Box, April 29, 1978.

## CHAPTER 21

Author interviews with Mark Radice, Bun E. Carlos, Rick Nielsen, Ira Robbins, Ken Adamany, Brad Elvis, Tod Howarth, Bruce Kulick, Tracii Guns, Chip Z'Nuff, Taime Downe, Eddie Trunk, and Desmond Child.

### Notes

196   *But John Lennon's murder:* Tom Matthews, "(Just Like) Starting Over," *Milwaukee*, December 2014.

197   *"The mix took a little longer":* Nina Blackwood, interview with Rick Nielsen and Robin Zander, MTV, 1985, https://youtu.be/8ch0AuOFUR8.

199   *a gig that Rick Nielsen:* Hayes and Sharp, *Reputation Is a Fragile Thing*, 122.

## CHAPTER 22

Author interviews with Desmond Child, Paul Stanley, Scott Ian, Tim Collins, Ted Templeman, Bun E. Carlos, Richie Zito, Tracii Guns, Bruce Kulick, Larry Mazer, Gilby Clarke, Gary Cherone, Kim Thayil, Steven McDonald, and J Mascis.

### Notes

206   *"But it turned into":* Aerosmith and Davis, *Walk This Way*, 431.

206   *"without the finishing touches":* Aerosmith and Davis, 431.

207   *"control addict":* Joey Kramer, William Patrick, and Keith Garde, *Hit Hard: A Story of Hitting Rock Bottom at the Top*, paperback ed. (New York: HarperOne, 2010), 196.

208   *"I told [Kalodner]":* Aerosmith and Davis, *Walk This Way*, 443.

209   *"Tyler says I ruined his career":* Aerosmith and Davis, 443.

210   *"I loved writing":* Steven Tyler and David Dalton, *Does the Noise in My Head Bother You?: A Rock 'n' Roll Memoir* (New York: Ecco, 2011), 244.

211   *"One of the main reasons":* Harris and Shibuya, interview with Rick Nielsen.

212   *"I knew it could be":* Ira Robbins, interview with Robin Zander, April 1996 (transcript).

212   *"We can take a crappy song":* Robbins, interview with Rick Nielsen and Tom Petersson.

212   *"They sounded stupid":* Steve Harris, interview with Tom Petersson (Cheap Trick, part 11), 1990, https://youtu.be/_CjftSs4E6A.

212   *"We didn't want":* Robbins, interview with Rick Nielsen and Tom Petersson.

213   *"It gave us a pretty good feeling":* Steve Baltin, "Cheap Trick Set to Resume Aerosmith Tour," *Rolling Stone*, September 19, 2012, www.rollingstone.com/music /music-news/cheap-trick-set-to-resume-aerosmith-tour-204688/.

214    *the arena tour fizzled:* Gooch and Suhs, *KISS Alive Forever*, 165.

214    *Faced with a multimillion-dollar tax debt:* Stanley, *Face the Music*, 312–313.

214    *hired Paul Stanley's psychotherapist:* Stanley, 325.

216    *Simmons pegged:* Tentative artist listing for *KISS My Ass* tribute album, *KISS the Auction* catalog, Butterfields/Greg Manning Auctions, 2000, 151.

216    *"This is the graduating class":* J.D. Considine, "KISS Is Still KISS, as Sung by Diverse Devotees," *Baltimore Sun*, July 19, 1994, www.baltimoresun.com/news/bs-xpm -1994-06-19-1994170172-story.html.

216    *"Ironically, it came in too late":* Considine, "KISS Is Still KISS."

# CHAPTER 23

Author interviews with Richie Ranno, Brendan Harkin, Sebastian Bach, Mark Cicchini, David Rule, Steve West, Steve Leber, Rick Nielsen, and Tim Collins.

## Notes

222    *"As much as we want you":* "Gene & Paul KISS Convention Raid, 1994," https://you tu.be/4BBEO-3_dgw.

222    *"According to court papers":* James A. McClear, "Rockers Roll into Troy to Get Stolen Loot," *Detroit News*, July 19, 1994.

222    *"Bill Aucoin, who somehow had keys":* Stanley, *Face the Music*, 311.

222    *In an interview outtake:* "Bill Aucoin Interview—KISS Manager—Costume Confiscation Controversy (*KISS Loves You* Outtake)," https://youtu.be/I8vSY4fEpmk.

223    *"Obviously, when something":* McClear, "Rockers Roll into Troy to Get Stolen Loot."

223    *"I loved the looseness":* Stanley, *Face the Music*, 346.

224    *"For Gene to fly":* "Ace Frehley Birthday Bash: 4/27/02," https://youtu.be/9n4Eej G1w8Q.

225    *"as many people as possible":* "Fans Bring in $1.6 Million in Bids from KISS Auction," *Chicago Tribune*, June 26, 2000, www.chicagotribune.com/news/ct-xpm-2000-06-26 -0006270042-story.html.

225    *When KISS brought:* Criss and Sloman, *Makeup to Breakup*, 267.

225    *Criss was grateful:* Criss and Sloman, 270.

226    *"Despite all the problems":* Simmons, *KISS and Makeup*, 231–232.

226    *For his part, Stanley thought:* Stanley, *Face the Music*, 349.

227    *"four knuckleheads":* Darren Paltrowitz, "Gene Simmons on the New 'Gene Simmons Vault,' the Beatles, Van Halen, His New Magazine, and Doing Good Deeds," *Inquisitr*, September 25, 2017, www.inquisitr.com/4512178/gene-simmons-on-the -new-gene-simmons-vault-the-beatles-van-halen-his-new-magazine-and-doing -good-deeds/.

## CHAPTER 24

Author interviews with Bruce Kulick, Dale Crover, Ken Adamany, Bun E. Carlos, Bob Merlis, Larry Mazer, and Ira Robbins.

### Notes

229   *"I want to be like Billy Corgan!"*: Leaf and Sharp, *KISS: Behind the Mask*, 402.

230   *"a big misstep"*: Leaf and Sharp, 401.

230   *"I listen to that"*: Leaf and Sharp, 403.

230   *Simmons remembered*: Meltdown, interview with Gene Simmons, 101 WRIF, January 19, 2018, https://wrif.com/episodes/radio-chatter-gene-simmons-2/.

231   *"Those were fun shows"*: Brett Buchanan, "Alice in Chains Reveal Weird Moment with KISS on 1996 Tour," AlternativeNation.net, March 17, 2017, www.alternative nation.net/alice-in-chains-reveal-weird-moment-kiss-1996-tour/.

231   *"I was eating food"*: Buchanan, "Alice in Chains Reveal Weird Moment."

231   *"Me and Jerry"*: Greg Prato, *Grunge Is Dead: The Oral History of Seattle Rock Music* (Toronto: ECW Press, 2009), 412.

231   *"I said, 'Layne, here they are'"*: Meltdown, interview with Gene Simmons.

232   *"They'd be jamming"*: "Melvins Lesson: King Buzzo on Covering KISS," https://youtu.be/GPmgpvZKwys.

232   *"something that was really weird"*: Gary Suarez, "Buzz Osbourne: The MetalSucks Interview (Part Two)," MetalSucks.net, May 10, 2010, www.metalsucks.net/2010 /05/10/buzz-osborne-the-metalsucks-interview-part-two/.

232   *"We weren't trying"*: Steve Harris and Yoichi Shibuya, interview with Rick Nielsen and Robin Zander, April 1994, https://youtu.be/jIJyLAmWzVU.

233   *"It was not to interrupt"*: Harris and Shibuya, interview with Rick Nielsen and Robin Zander.

233   *"This isn't the greatest"*: Harris and Shibuya, interview with Rick Nielsen and Robin Zander.

235   *"I lost my musical virginity"*: Chris Epting, "Stone Temple Pilots' Robert DeLeo Shares His '70s Childhood Memories, Photos (Exclusive)," *Noisecreep*, September 5, 2012, https://noisecreep.com/stone-temple-pilots-robert-deleo/.

## CHAPTER 25

Author interviews with Bryan J. Kinnaird, Richie Fontana, Lanny Bass, Kristina Sweval Peters, Art Alexakis, Paul Stanley, Bruce Kulick, Rick Nielsen, Bun E. Carlos, and Ken Adamany.

## Notes

237   *The special guest:* "KISS Expo Zaandam 2002 Sean Delaney–Eric Singer," https://youtu.be/SnNcilTi098.

239   *"rock and roll being outlawed":* Gene Simmons, *Sex Money KISS* (Beverly Hills: Simmons Books/New Millennium Press, 2003), 208.

239   *"There were no drums":* Criss and Sloman, *Makeup to Breakup*, 313.

240   *KISS's manager, Doc McGhee:* Ray Waddell, "KISS, Aerosmith Unite for Co-Headlining Tour," *Billboard*, August 9, 2003.

240   *"We have a lot of fans in common":* John Soeder, "Walk This Way All Nite," *Cleveland Plain Dealer*, August 29, 2003.

240   *"Not to put them down":* Robbins, "Joe Perry Meets the Press."

240   *"Because he wasn't a KISS fan":* Perry and Ritz, *Rocks*, 327.

241   *"I wasn't available":* "Exclusive: Frehley's Fine Without KISS," *Billboard*, August 1, 2003, www.billboard.com/articles/news/69715/exclusive-frehleys-fine-without-kiss.

241   *"When you have people":* Chris Ingham, "KISS: On the Road Again," *Louder*, October 22, 2003, www.loudersound.com/features/kiss-on-the-road-again.

241   *"By this point":* Stanley, *Face the Music*, 419.

242   *"There have been nights":* Ingham, "KISS: On the Road Again."

242   *"I'm the same guy":* Ingham.

242   *"Aerosmith decided":* Criss and Sloman, *Makeup to Breakup*, 329.

242   *"We took all the ego":* Ingham, "KISS: On the Road Again."

242   *"more recent presence":* Soeder, "Walk This Way All Nite."

243   *"I really don't care":* Randall Roberts, "Rock Beef: Paul Stanley Responds to Aerosmith's KISS Dis," *Los Angeles Times*, October 17, 2012, www.latimes.com/entertainment/music/la-xpm-2012-oct-17-la-et-ms-paul-stanley-kiss-steven-tyler-aerosmith-20121016-story.html.

243   *Without Frehley:* Criss and Sloman, *Makeup to Breakup*, 329–330.

243   *"It was so obvious":* Criss and Sloman, 332–333.

243   *As far as Stanley was concerned:* Stanley, *Face the Music*, 420.

244   *"like watching a different level":* Calta, interview with Joe Perry and Steven Tyler.

244   *"There is some sort of ambivalence":* Roberts, "Rock Beef."

244   *Despite calling Joey Kramer:* Criss and Sloman, *Makeup to Breakup*, 331–332.

244   *"It kind of hurt my feelings":* "Original KISS Drummer Says His Feelings Were Hurt by Steven Tyler's 'Comic-Book' Comments," Blabblermouth.net, October 23, 2012, www.blabbermouth.net/news/original-kiss-drummer-says-his-feelings-were-hurt-by-steven-tyler-s-comic-book-comments/.

246   *rumors of throat cancer:* Jon Wiederhorn, "Aerosmith Cancel Tour; Singer to Undergo Throat Surgery," MTV News, March 22, 2006, www.mtv.com/news/1526788/aerosmith-cancel-tour-singer-to-undergo-throat-surgery/.

247 *"It was wild"*: Sarah Kloewer, "Cheap Trick Returns to Play Again with Aerosmith," *Iowa State Daily*, May 3, 2004, www.iowastatedaily.com/cheap-trick-returns-to-play-again-with-aerosmith/article_edf43698-f3cf-5997-8829-1fbca55e2e97.html.

249 *"one of the best"*: Perry and Ritz, *Rocks*, 138.

249 *"an inspirational presence"*: Perry and Ritz, 331.

249 *"I'd always wanted"*: Perry and Ritz, 311.

249 *Waitresses in low-cut black dresses*: Many of this chapter's details and quotes regarding Joe Perry's fiftieth birthday party originated in reports by former Joe Perry Project singer Mach Bell and Cheap Trick tour manager Carla Dragotti, archived at Rock This Way, www.rockthisway.net/news/news_september00.htm.

250 *It was a gift from Slash*: Perry and Ritz, *Rocks*, 313.

250 *"There was something"*: "Mike McCready on Cheap Trick," https://youtu.be/teed45jGSWg.

250 *"In America's rock-and-roll history"*: "Dave Grohl on Cheap Trick," https://youtu.be/qzsbkBGDaW4.

250 *Nielsen, who has said*: Harris and Shibuya, interview with Rick Nielsen and Robin Zander.

## CHAPTER 26

Author interviews with John Varvatos and Brynn Arens. A portion of this chapter was adapted from the author's review of the Children Matter benefit concert, which appeared in the December 2017 issue of *Classic Rock*.

## CHAPTER 27

Author interviews with Sebastian Bach, Ken Stringfellow, Sean Kelly, Zakk Wylde, Josh Todd, Butch Walker, Gary Cherone, and Bob "Nitebob" Czaykowski.

### Notes

260 *Backstage, before the show*: Frehley, Layden, and Ostrosky, *No Regrets*, 288.

260 *Frehley has said*: Eddie Trunk, interview with Ace Frehley, November 21, 2019, https://youtu.be/pAJmWyIV7fw.

260 *"I haven't had a drink"*: Frehley, Layden, and Ostrosky, *No Regrets*, 289.

## EPILOGUE

Author interview with Ira Robbins.

### Note

263 *"It's like having a big brother"*: Baltin, "Cheap Trick Set to Resume Aerosmith Tour."

# INDEX